DearS

VOL. 3

by
PEACH-PIT

HAMBURG // LONDON // LOS ANGELES // TOKYO

DearS Vol. 3
Created by Peach-Pit

Translation - Christine Schilling
English Adaptation - Anna Wenger
Associate Editor - Peter Ahlstrom
Retouch and Lettering - Benchcomix
Production Artist - Eric Pineda
Cover Design - Raymond Makowski

Editor - Luis Reyes
Digital Imaging Manager - Chris Buford
Pre-Press Manager - Antonio DePietro
Production Managers - Jennifer Miller and Mutsumi Miyazaki
Art Director - Matt Alford
Managing Editor - Jill Freshney
VP of Production - Ron Klamert
Editor-in-Chief - Mike Kiley
President and C.O.O. - John Parker
Publisher and C.E.O. - Stuart Levy

A  Manga

TOKYOPOP Inc.
5900 Wilshire Blvd. Suite 2000
Los Angeles, CA 90036

E-mail: info@TOKYOPOP.com
Come visit us online at www.TOKYOPOP.com

ISBN: 1-59532-310-4
First TOKYOPOP printing: July 2005
10 9 8 7 6 5 4 3
Printed in the USA

DearS

ディアーズ

03

ピーチピット

PEACH-PIT

presents

CONTENTS

CHARACTER & STORY

Neneko Izumi
和泉寧々子
TAKEYA'S CHILDHOOD FRIEND, CLASSMATE AND THE DAUGHTER OF HIS LANDLORD. SHE'S REALLY GOOD AT KEEPING TAKEYA OUT OF TROUBLE AND REN OFF TAKEYA.

Miu
ミゥ
THE OFFICIAL DEARS EXCHANGE STUDENT AT KOHARU HIGH NOW. SHE AND REN BOTH ATTEND THE SCHOOL.

Takeya Ikuhara
幾原武哉
A HIGH-SCHOOL STUDENT LIVING ALONE ON AN ALLOTMENT FROM HIS ABSENT PARENTS. THROUGH A SEEMINGLY RANDOM SEQUENCE OF EVENTS, HE HAS BECOME

Ren
レン
A FEMALE DEARS THAT FATE HAS LAID IN THE HANDS OF ONE TAKEYA IKUHARA. SHE SLEEPS IN HIS CLOSET.

A man of DearS
ディアーズの男
A YOUNG MAN WHOSE TASK IS TO GUARANTEE THE SECURITY OF THE DEARS COMMUNITY. HE ATTEMPTED TO BRING REN BACK, BUT TAKEYA STOPPED HIM.

Hikoro Oikawa
及川彦郎
NICKNAME: OIHIKO. TAKEYA'S CLASSMATE AND A MANIACAL FAN OF THE DEARS.

Teacher-Mitsuka
蜜香先生
TAKEYA'S HOMEROOM TEACHER AND SPANISH INSTRUCTOR. SHE'S AN ENTHUSIASTIC TEACHER AND AN ECSTATIC EXHIBITIONIST.

Khi
キィ
A MEDIATOR FOR THE DEARS COMMUNITY. HE IS ALSO PARTICIPATING IN THE HOMESTAY PROGRAM, LIVING IN AN AVERAGE JAPANESE HOUSEHOLD.

OUTLINE

ONE DAY, TAKEYA, A HIGH-SCHOOL STUDENT LIVING ON HIS OWN IN A SMALL APARTMENT, ENCOUNTERS A GIRL OF THE DEARS RACE—AN ALIEN PEOPLE WHO ONE YEAR AGO MADE AN EMERGENCY LANDING IN TOKYO BAY. ALL THE DEARS BECAME CITIZENS OF JAPAN, STUDYING ITS LANGUAGE AND CUSTOMS IN THE HOPES OF INTEGRATING THE RACE. HOWEVER, THIS GIRL TAKEYA RUNS ACROSS CAN HARDLY SPEAK THE LANGUAGE AT ALL. WHEN THE GIRL COLLAPSES FROM HUNGER, TAKEYA HAS NO CHOICE BUT TO BRING HER HOME. UNABLE TO PRONOUNCE HER REAL NAME, HE NAMES HER REN. REN LEARNS THE LANGUAGE QUICKLY AND SOON TAKES TO CALLING TAKEYA HER "MASTER," TRYING TO HELP OUT HIS LIFE AS BEST SHE CAN BUT INEVITABLY EATING HIM OUT OF HEARTH AND HOME. WHEN SHE FOLLOWS TAKEYA TO SCHOOL ONE DAY, THE STUDENTS AND FACULTY MISTAKE HER FOR THE DEARS EXCHANGE STUDENT THEY WERE EXPECTING AND ENROLL HER. WHEN MIU—THE REAL EXCHANGE STUDENT—ARRIVES, SHE CHALLENGES REN. THEY BOTH END UP STAYING, BUT SOON LEARN THAT THE DEARS COMMUNITY HAD ORDERED REN'S IMMEDIATE RETURN, CLAIMING THAT SHE IS A DEFECTIVE UNIT. THEY SEND BOTH KHI, A DIPLOMATIC MEDIATOR, AND A MYSTERIOUS MAN WHO IS MORE ABOUT USING FORCE TO GET REN BACK. TAKEYA, HOWEVER, EXERCISES HIS RIGHT AS REN'S OWNER AND DEMANDS THAT REN BE ABLE TO STAY WITH HIM AS HIS SLAVE. BUT WHAT NOW?

13th Contact

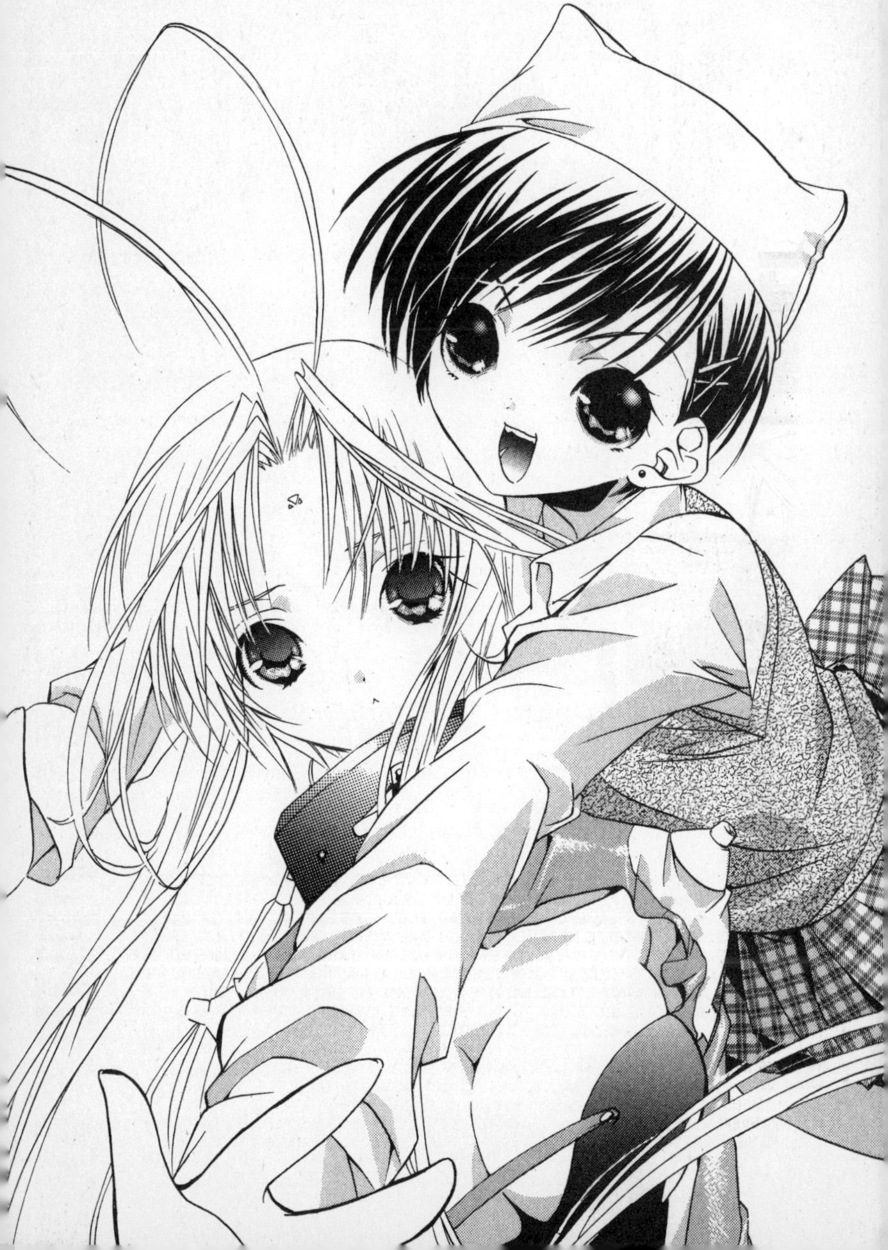

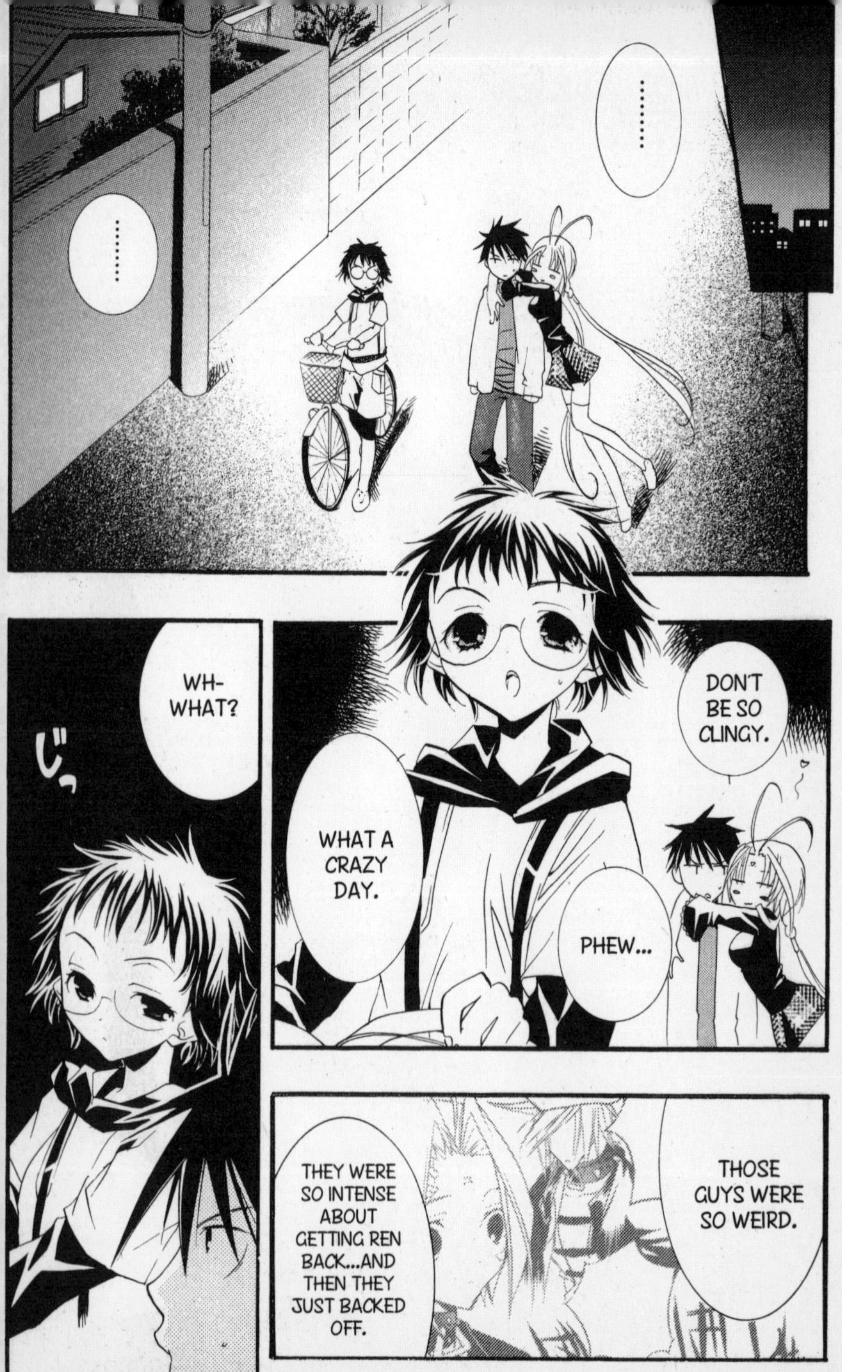
……
……
DON'T BE SO CLINGY.
PHEW...
WHAT A CRAZY DAY.
THOSE GUYS WERE SO WEIRD.
THEY WERE SO INTENSE ABOUT GETTING REN BACK...AND THEN THEY JUST BACKED OFF.
WH-WHAT?
じっ

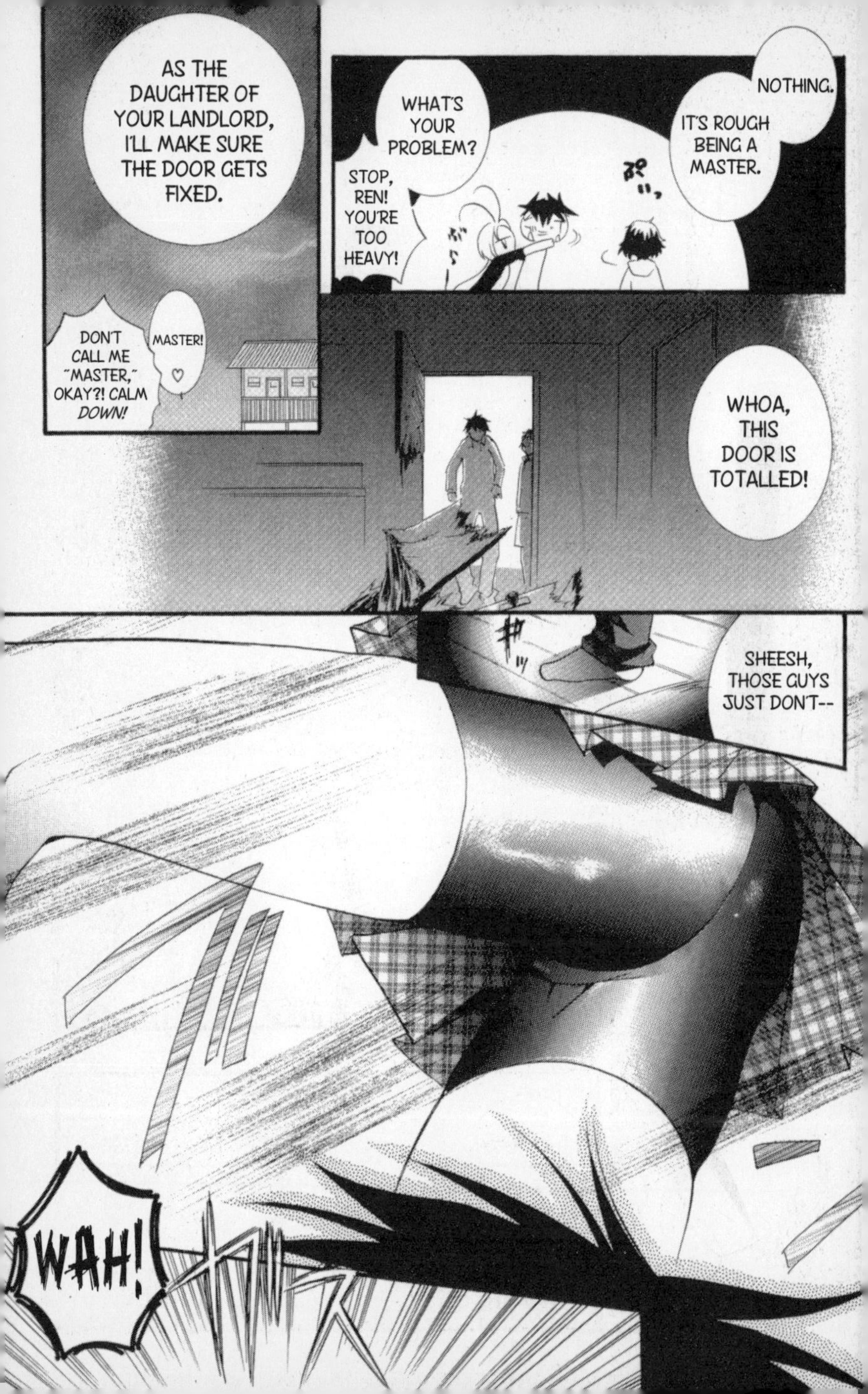
NOTHING.
IT'S ROUGH BEING A MASTER.
WHAT'S YOUR PROBLEM?
STOP, REN! YOU'RE TOO HEAVY!
WHOA, THIS DOOR IS TOTALLED!
AS THE DAUGHTER OF YOUR LANDLORD, I'LL MAKE SURE THE DOOR GETS FIXED.
MASTER! ♡
DON'T CALL ME "MASTER," OKAY?! CALM *DOWN!*
SHEESH, THOSE GUYS JUST DON'T--
WAH!

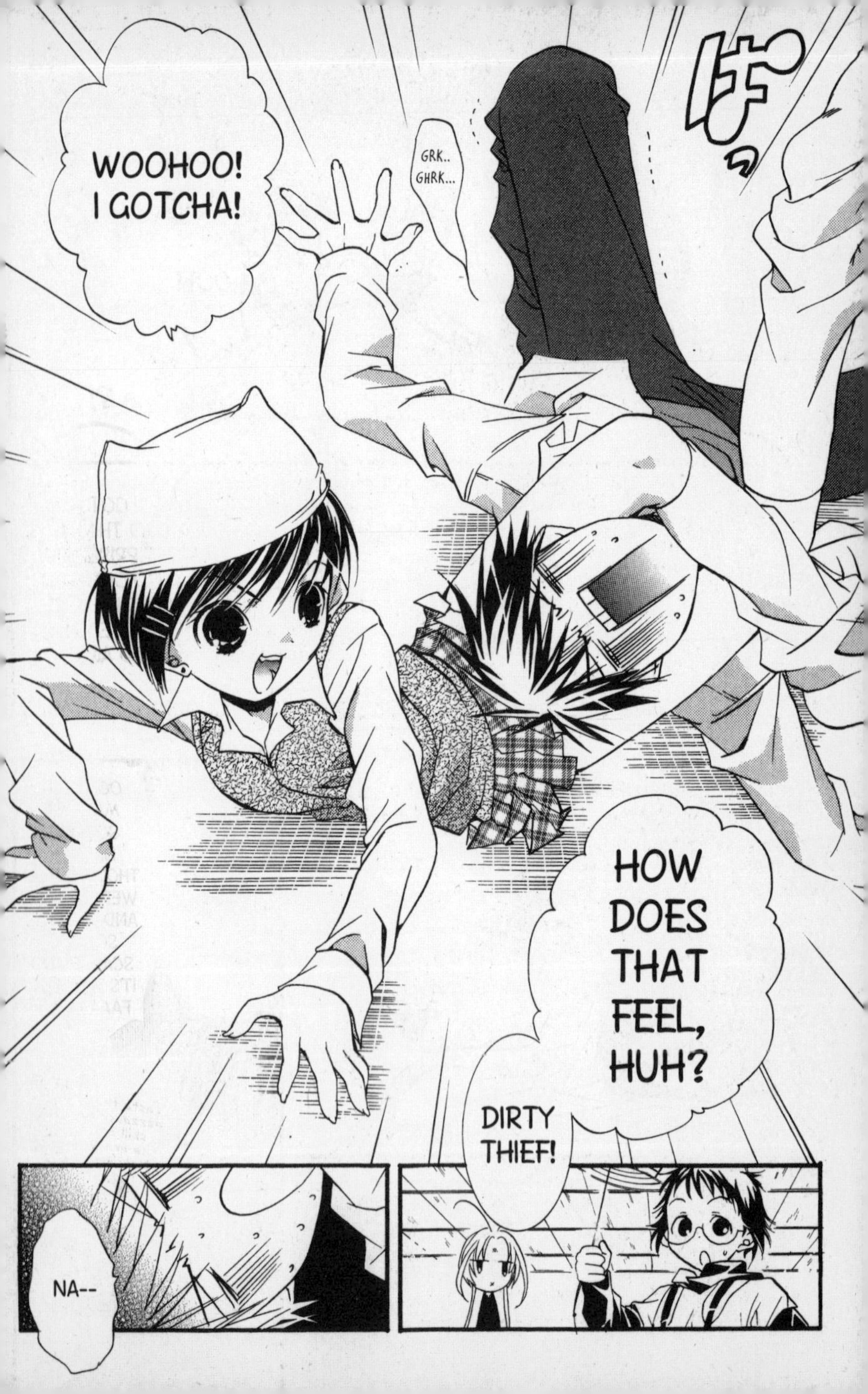
ぼっ
GRK.. GHRK...
WOOHOO! I GOTCHA!
HOW DOES THAT FEEL, HUH?
DIRTY THIEF!
NA--

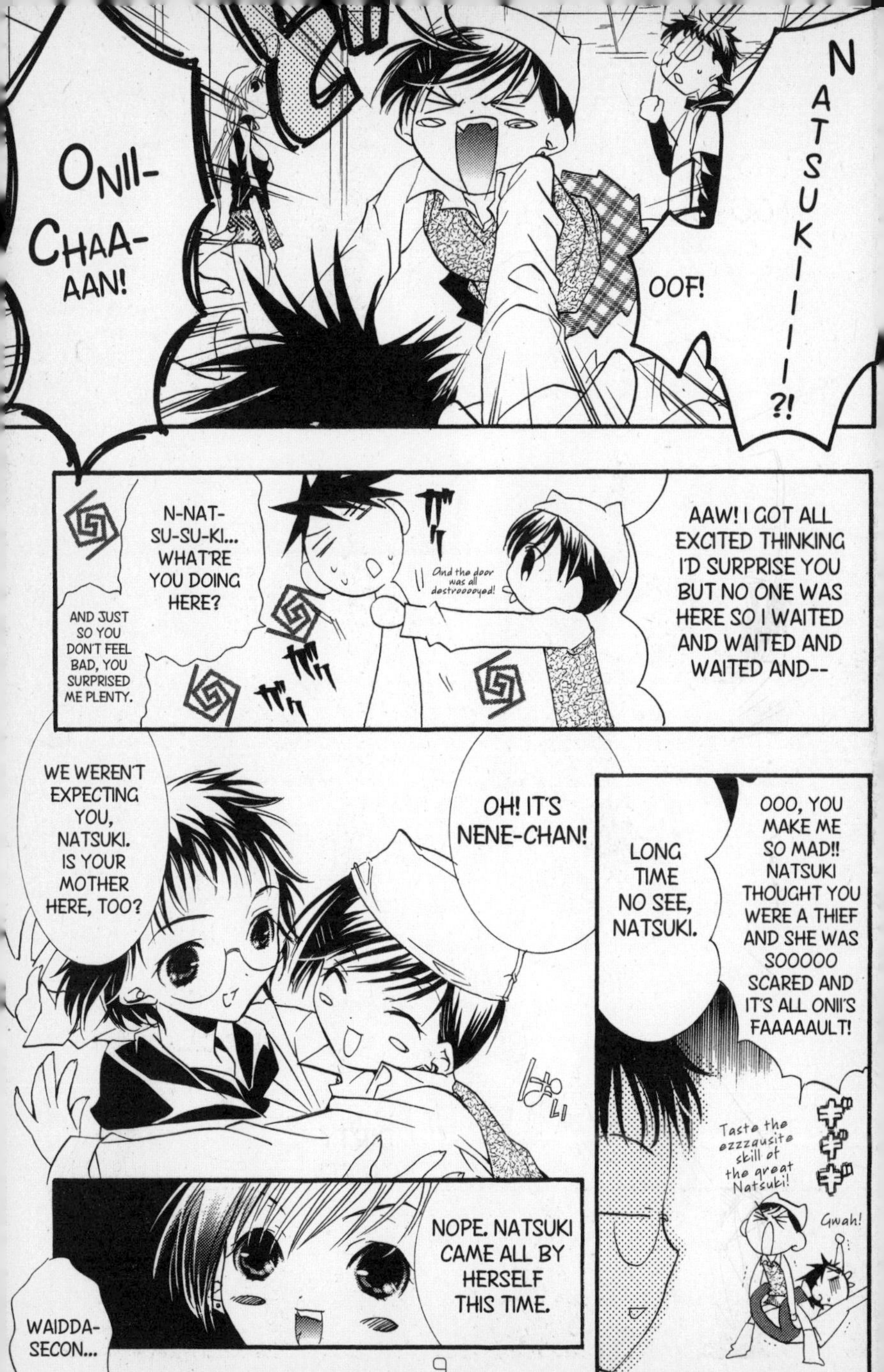
NATSUKI------?!
OOF!
ONII-CHAAAAN!
AAW! I GOT ALL EXCITED THINKING I'D SURPRISE YOU BUT NO ONE WAS HERE SO I WAITED AND WAITED AND WAITED AND--
And the door was all destroooooyed!
N-NAT-SU-SU-KI... WHAT'RE YOU DOING HERE?
AND JUST SO YOU DON'T FEEL BAD, YOU SURPRISED ME PLENTY.
OOO, YOU MAKE ME SO MAD!! NATSUKI THOUGHT YOU WERE A THIEF AND SHE WAS SOOOOO SCARED AND IT'S ALL ONII'S FAAAAAULT!
LONG TIME NO SEE, NATSUKI.
Taste the ezzzqusite skill of the great Natsuki!
Gwah!
OH! IT'S NENE-CHAN!
WE WEREN'T EXPECTING YOU, NATSUKI. IS YOUR MOTHER HERE, TOO?
NOPE. NATSUKI CAME ALL BY HERSELF THIS TIME.
WAIDDA-SECON...

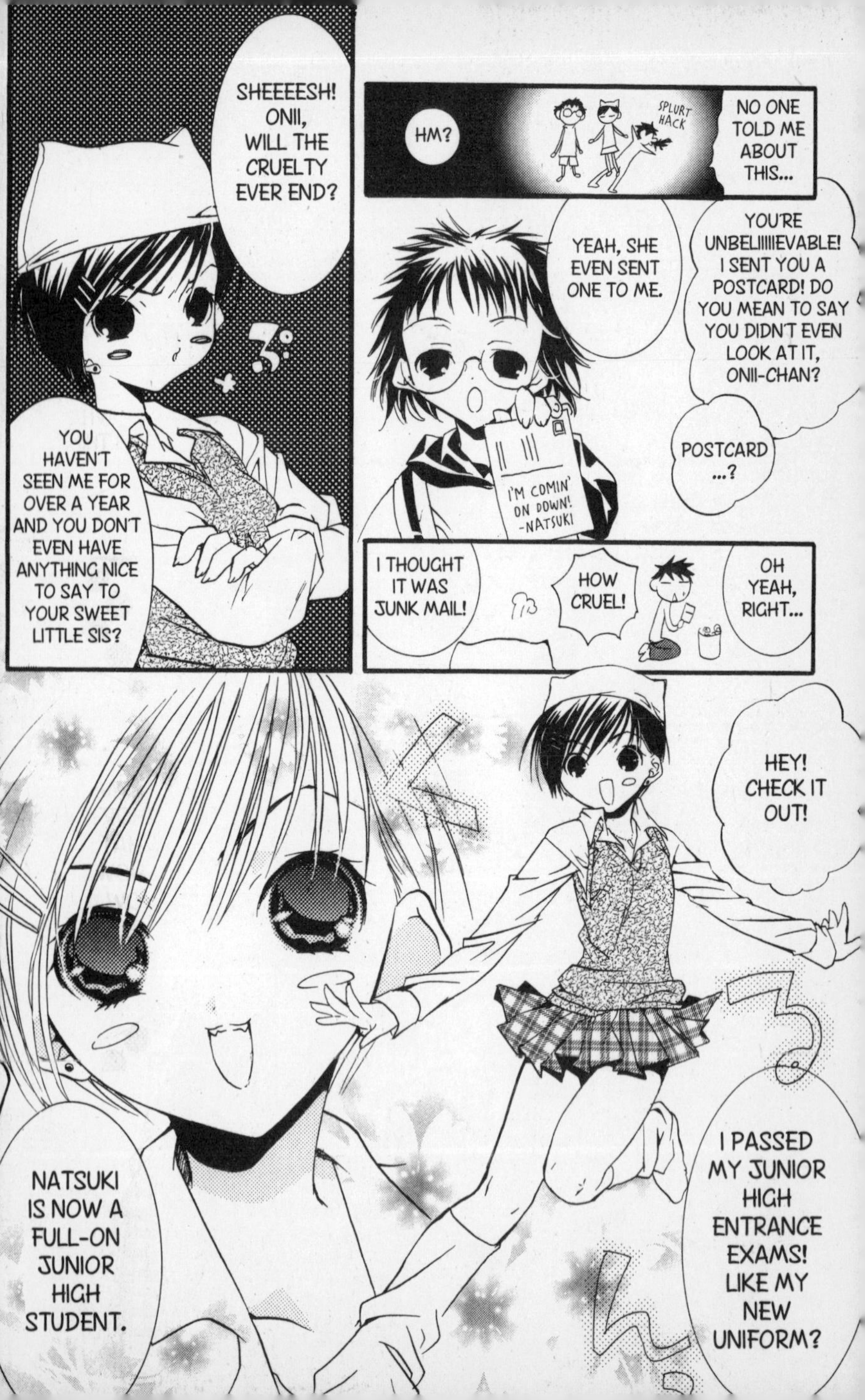
NO ONE TOLD ME ABOUT THIS...
SPLURT HACK
HM?
YOU'RE UNBELIIIIIEVABLE! I SENT YOU A POSTCARD! DO YOU MEAN TO SAY YOU DIDN'T EVEN LOOK AT IT, ONII-CHAN?
POSTCARD ...?
YEAH, SHE EVEN SENT ONE TO ME.
I'M COMIN' ON DOWN! -NATSUKI
OH YEAH, RIGHT...
HOW CRUEL!
I THOUGHT IT WAS JUNK MAIL!
SHEEEESH! ONII, WILL THE CRUELTY EVER END?
YOU HAVEN'T SEEN ME FOR OVER A YEAR AND YOU DON'T EVEN HAVE ANYTHING NICE TO SAY TO YOUR SWEET LITTLE SIS?
HEY! CHECK IT OUT!
I PASSED MY JUNIOR HIGH ENTRANCE EXAMS! LIKE MY NEW UNIFORM?
NATSUKI IS NOW A FULL-ON JUNIOR HIGH STUDENT.

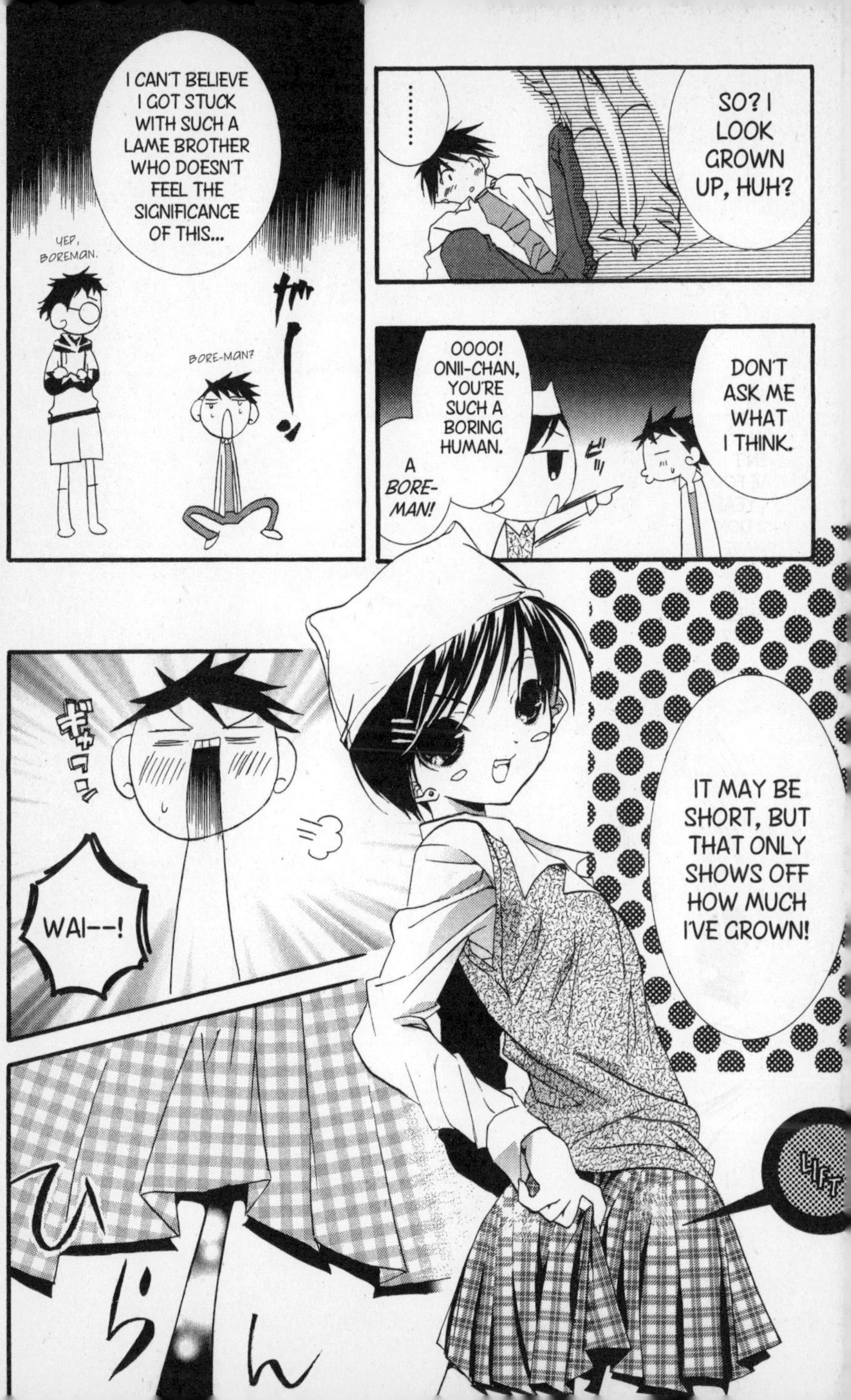
SO? I LOOK GROWN UP, HUH?
......
DON'T ASK ME WHAT I THINK.
OOOO! ONII-CHAN, YOU'RE SUCH A BORING HUMAN.
A BORE-MAN!
I CAN'T BELIEVE I GOT STUCK WITH SUCH A LAME BROTHER WHO DOESN'T FEEL THE SIGNIFICANCE OF THIS...
YEP, BOREMAN.
BORE-MAN?
IT MAY BE SHORT, BUT THAT ONLY SHOWS OFF HOW MUCH I'VE GROWN!
LIFT
WAI--!

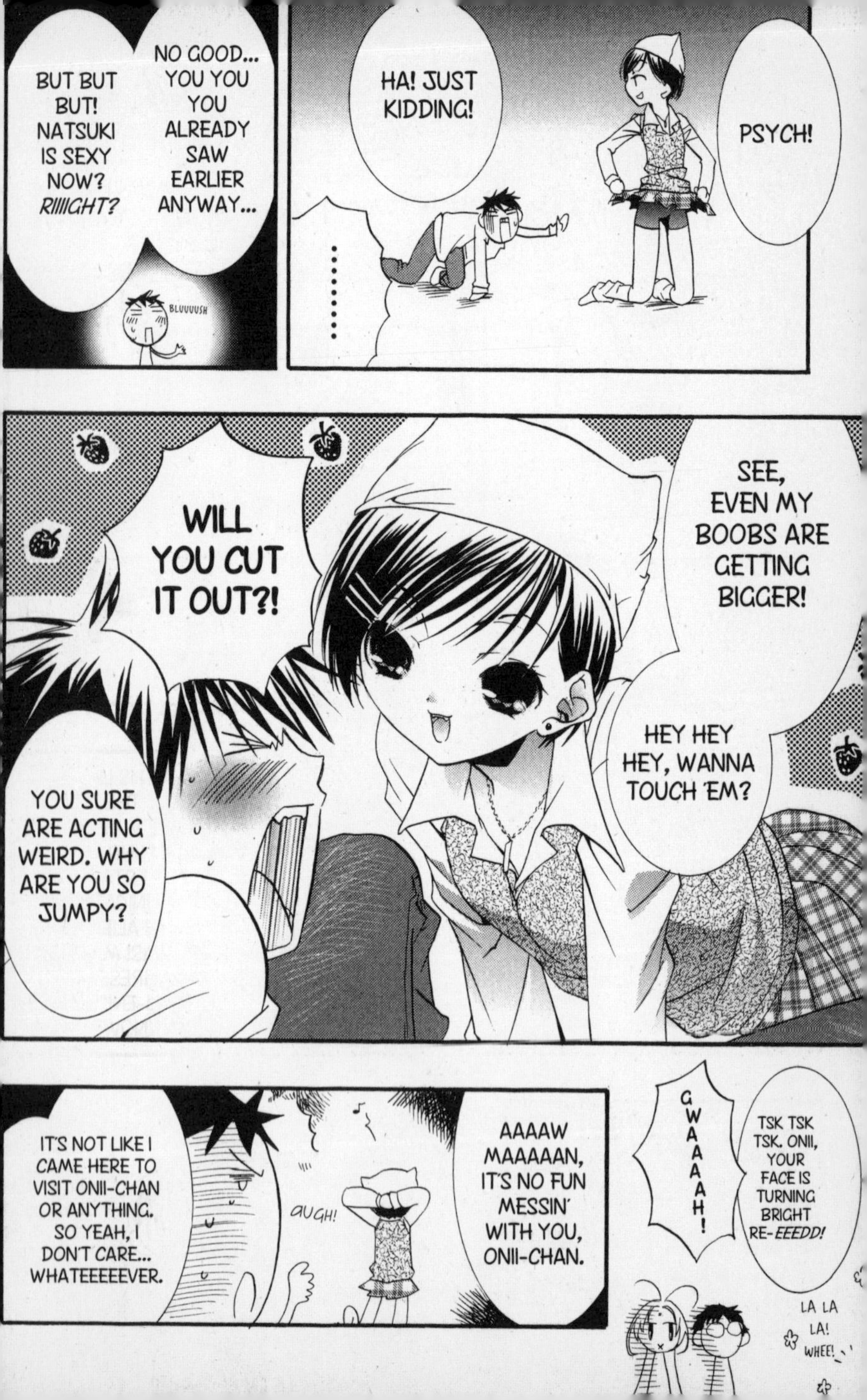
PSYCH!
HA! JUST KIDDING!
NO GOOD... YOU YOU YOU ALREADY SAW EARLIER ANYWAY...
BUT BUT BUT! NATSUKI IS SEXY NOW? *RIIIGHT?*
BLUUUUSH
SEE, EVEN MY BOOBS ARE GETTING BIGGER!
HEY HEY HEY, WANNA TOUCH 'EM?
WILL YOU CUT IT OUT?!
YOU SURE ARE ACTING WEIRD. WHY ARE YOU SO JUMPY?
TSK TSK TSK. ONII, YOUR FACE IS TURNING BRIGHT RE-*EEEDD!*
GWAAAAAH!
LA LA LA! WHEE!
AAAAW MAAAAAN, IT'S NO FUN MESSIN' WITH YOU, ONII-CHAN.
AUGH!
IT'S NOT LIKE I CAME HERE TO VISIT ONII-CHAN OR ANYTHING. SO YEAH, I DON'T CARE... WHATEEEEEVER.

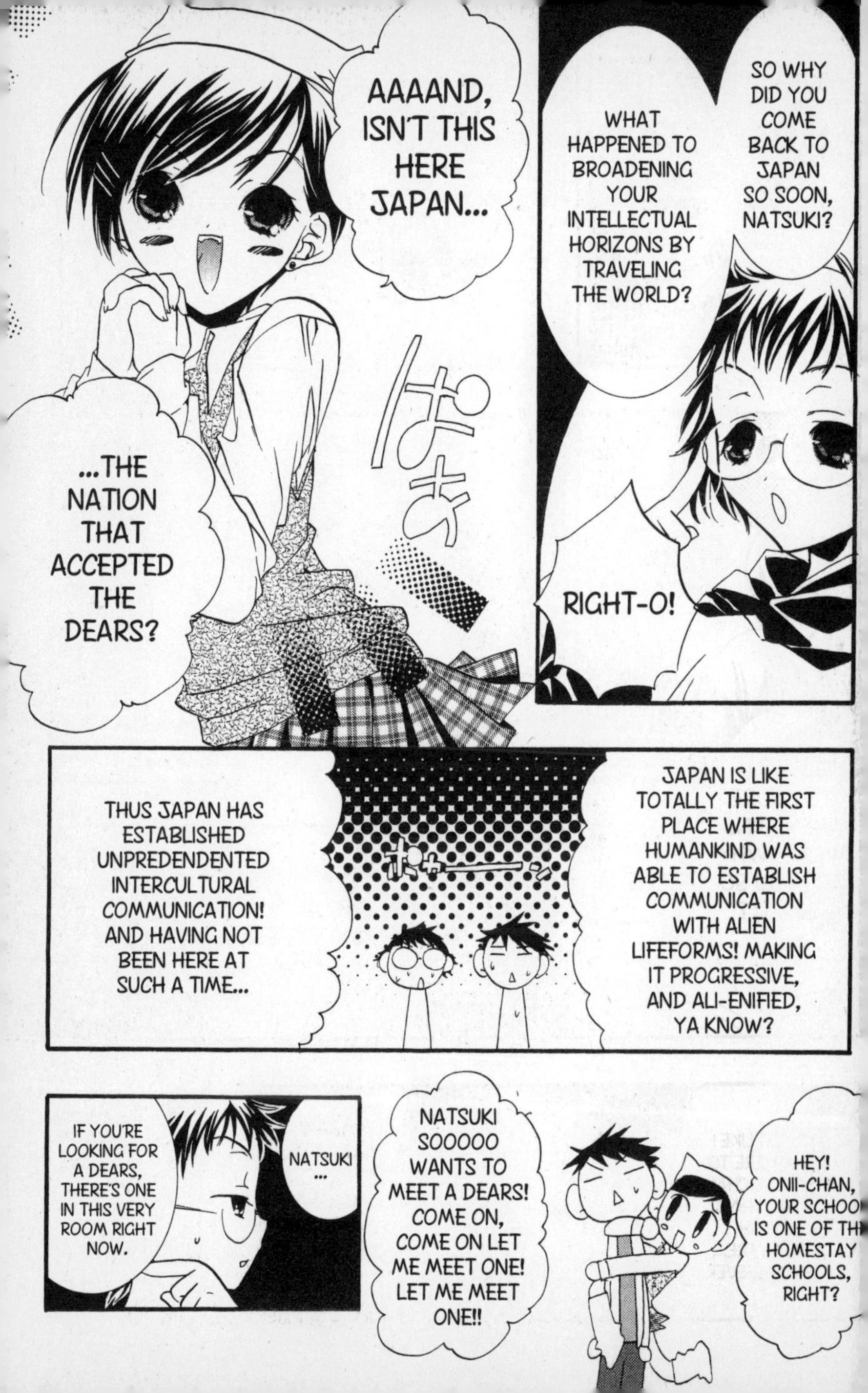

SO WHY DID YOU COME BACK TO JAPAN SO SOON, NATSUKI?
WHAT HAPPENED TO BROADENING YOUR INTELLECTUAL HORIZONS BY TRAVELING THE WORLD?
RIGHT-O!
AAAAND, ISN'T THIS HERE JAPAN...
...THE NATION THAT ACCEPTED THE DEARS?
ぱあ
JAPAN IS LIKE TOTALLY THE FIRST PLACE WHERE HUMANKIND WAS ABLE TO ESTABLISH COMMUNICATION WITH ALIEN LIFEFORMS! MAKING IT PROGRESSIVE, AND ALI-ENIFIED, YA KNOW?
THUS JAPAN HAS ESTABLISHED UNPREDENDENTED INTERCULTURAL COMMUNICATION! AND HAVING NOT BEEN HERE AT SUCH A TIME...
HEY! ONII-CHAN, YOUR SCHOO IS ONE OF TH HOMESTAY SCHOOLS, RIGHT?
NATSUKI SOOOOO WANTS TO MEET A DEARS! COME ON, COME ON LET ME MEET ONE! LET ME MEET ONE!!
NATSUKI ...
IF YOU'RE LOOKING FOR A DEARS, THERE'S ONE IN THIS VERY ROOM RIGHT NOW.

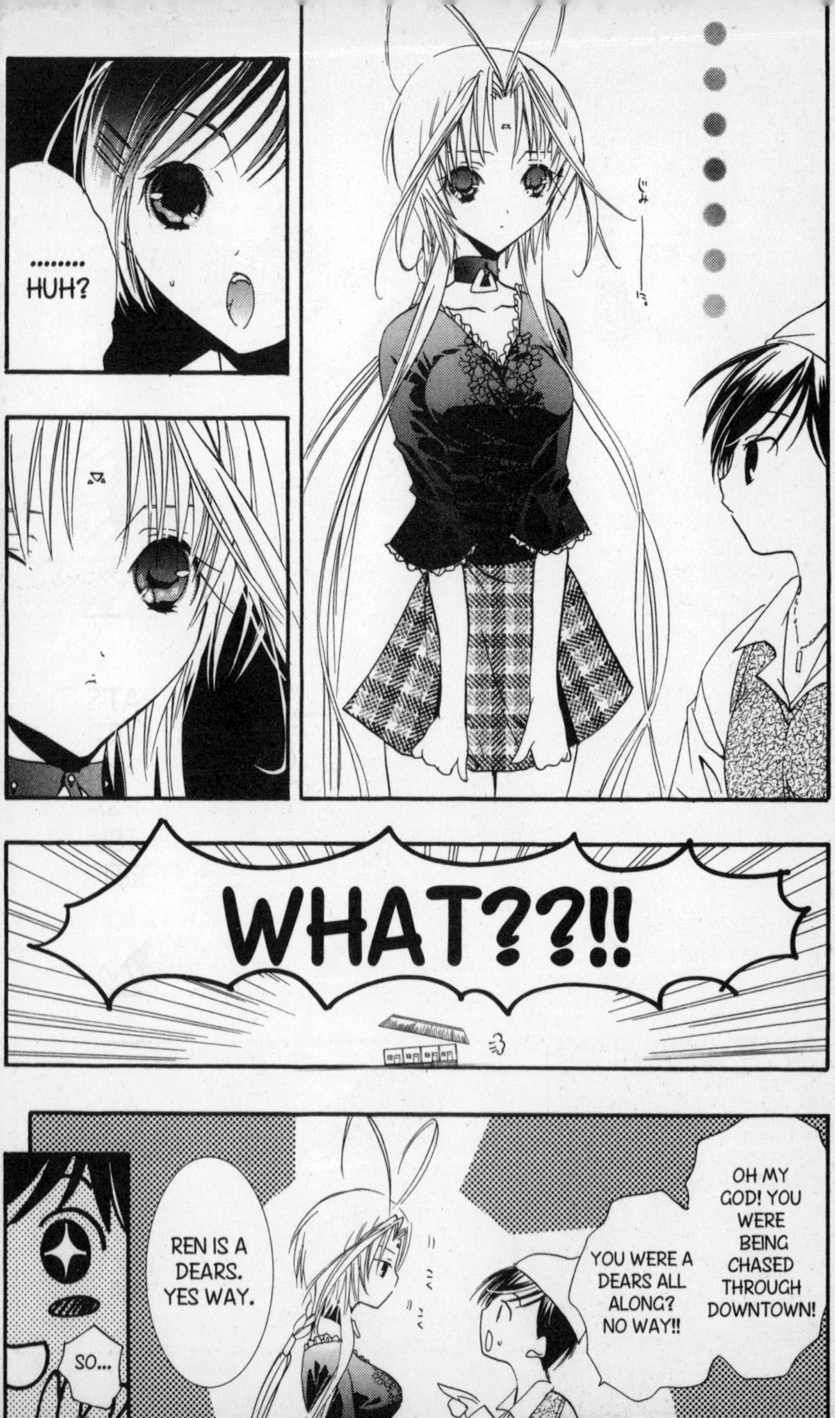

....
HUH?
WHAT??!!
OH MY GOD! YOU WERE BEING CHASED THROUGH DOWNTOWN!
YOU WERE A DEARS ALL ALONG? NO WAY!!
REN IS A DEARS. YES WAY.
SO...

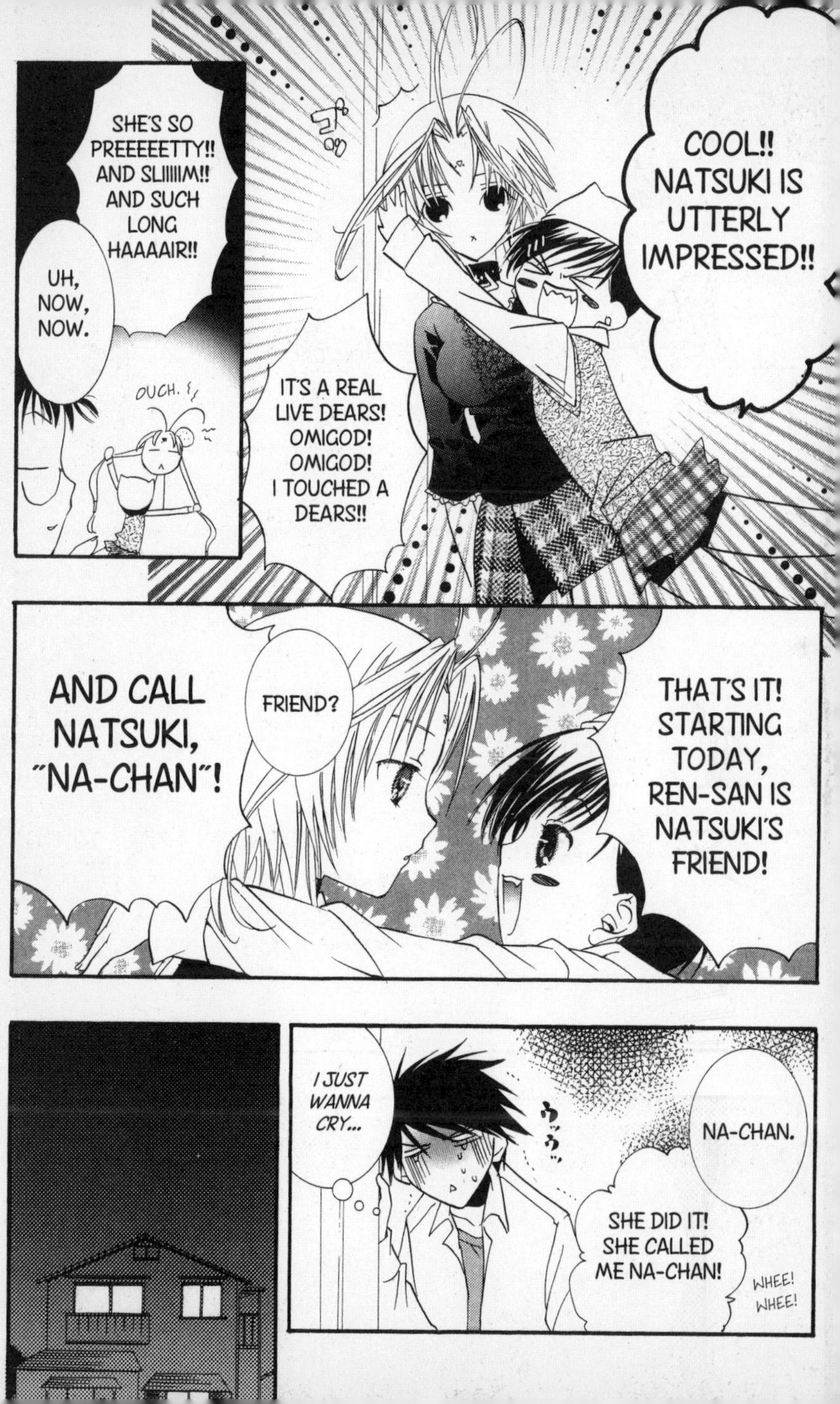
COOL!! NATSUKI IS UTTERLY IMPRESSED!!
IT'S A REAL LIVE DEARS! OMIGOD! OMIGOD! I TOUCHED A DEARS!!
SHE'S SO PREEEEETTY!! AND SLIIIIIM!! AND SUCH LONG HAAAAIR!!
UH, NOW, NOW.
OUCH.
THAT'S IT! STARTING TODAY, REN-SAN IS NATSUKI'S FRIEND!
FRIEND?
AND CALL NATSUKI, "NA-CHAN"!
NA-CHAN.
SHE DID IT! SHE CALLED ME NA-CHAN!
WHEE! WHEE!
I JUST WANNA CRY...

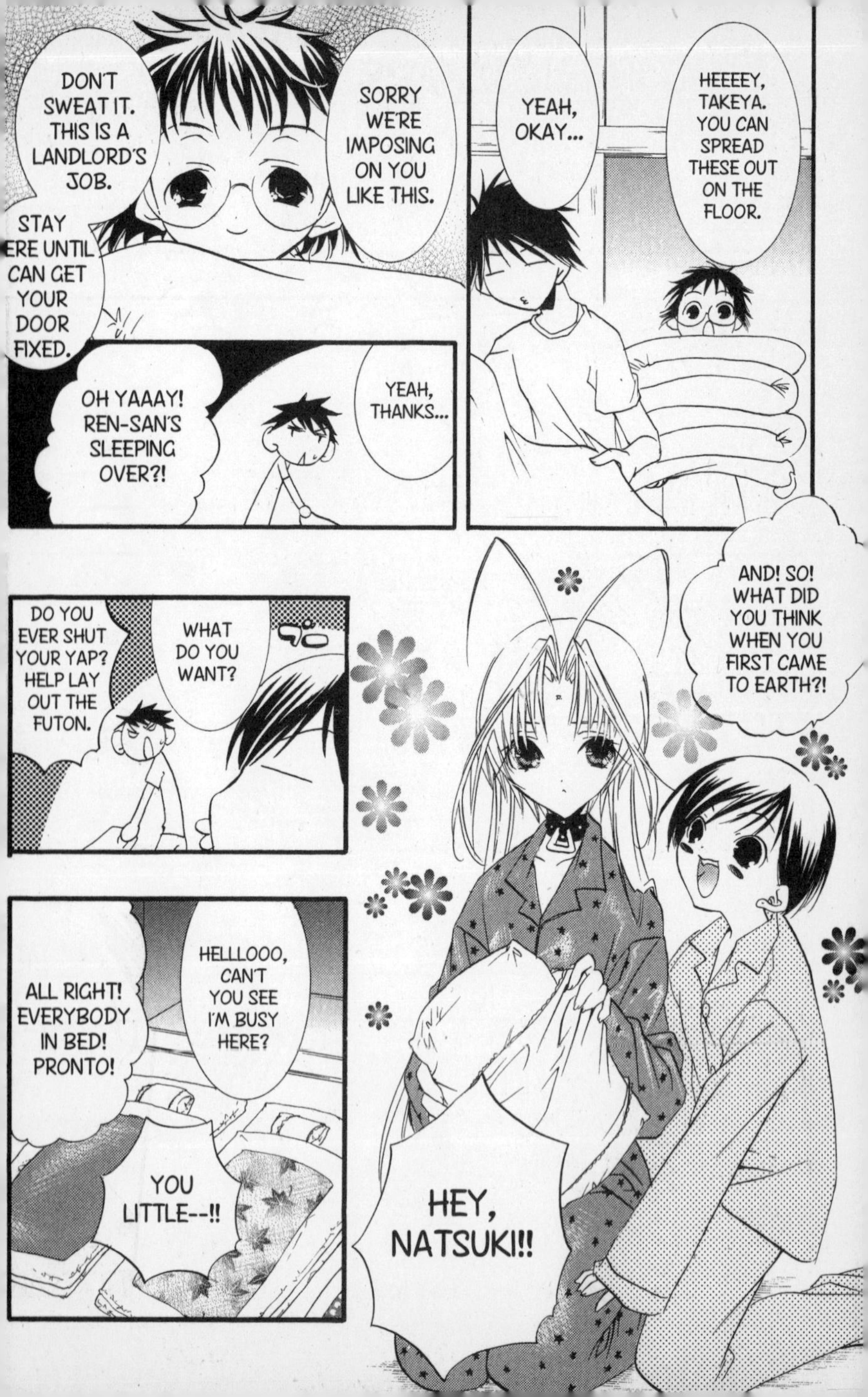
HEEEEY, TAKEYA. YOU CAN SPREAD THESE OUT ON THE FLOOR.
YEAH, OKAY...
SORRY WE'RE IMPOSING ON YOU LIKE THIS.
DON'T SWEAT IT. THIS IS A LANDLORD'S JOB.
STAY ERE UNTIL CAN GET YOUR DOOR FIXED.
YEAH, THANKS...
OH YAAAY! REN-SAN'S SLEEPING OVER?!
AND! SO! WHAT DID YOU THINK WHEN YOU FIRST CAME TO EARTH?!
HEY, NATSUKI!!
WHAT DO YOU WANT?
DO YOU EVER SHUT YOUR YAP? HELP LAY OUT THE FUTON.
HELLLOOO, CAN'T YOU SEE I'M BUSY HERE?
ALL RIGHT! EVERYBODY IN BED! PRONTO!
YOU LITTLE--!!

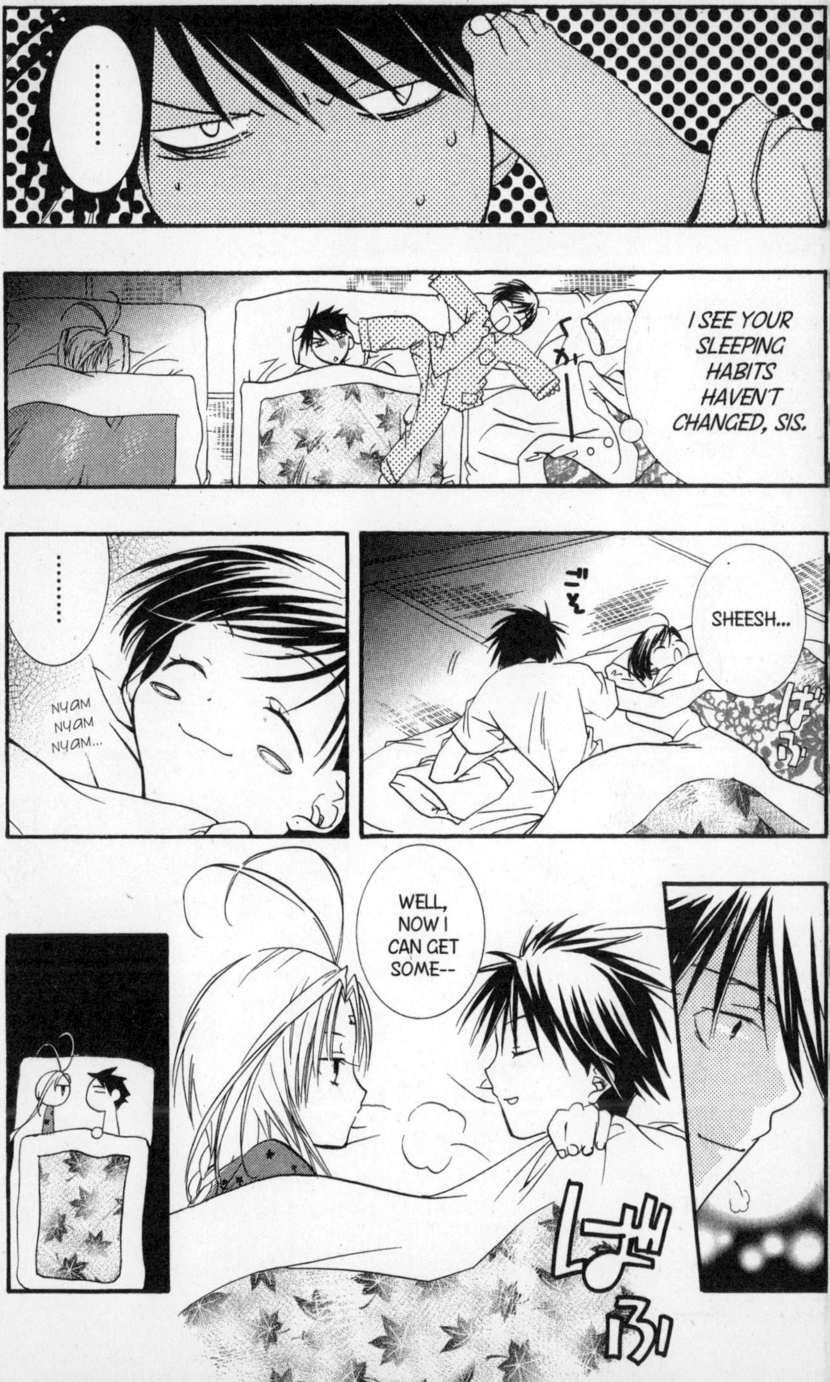
……
I SEE YOUR SLEEPING HABITS HAVEN'T CHANGED, SIS.
SHEESH...
……
NYAM NYAM NYAM...
WELL, NOW I CAN GET SOME--

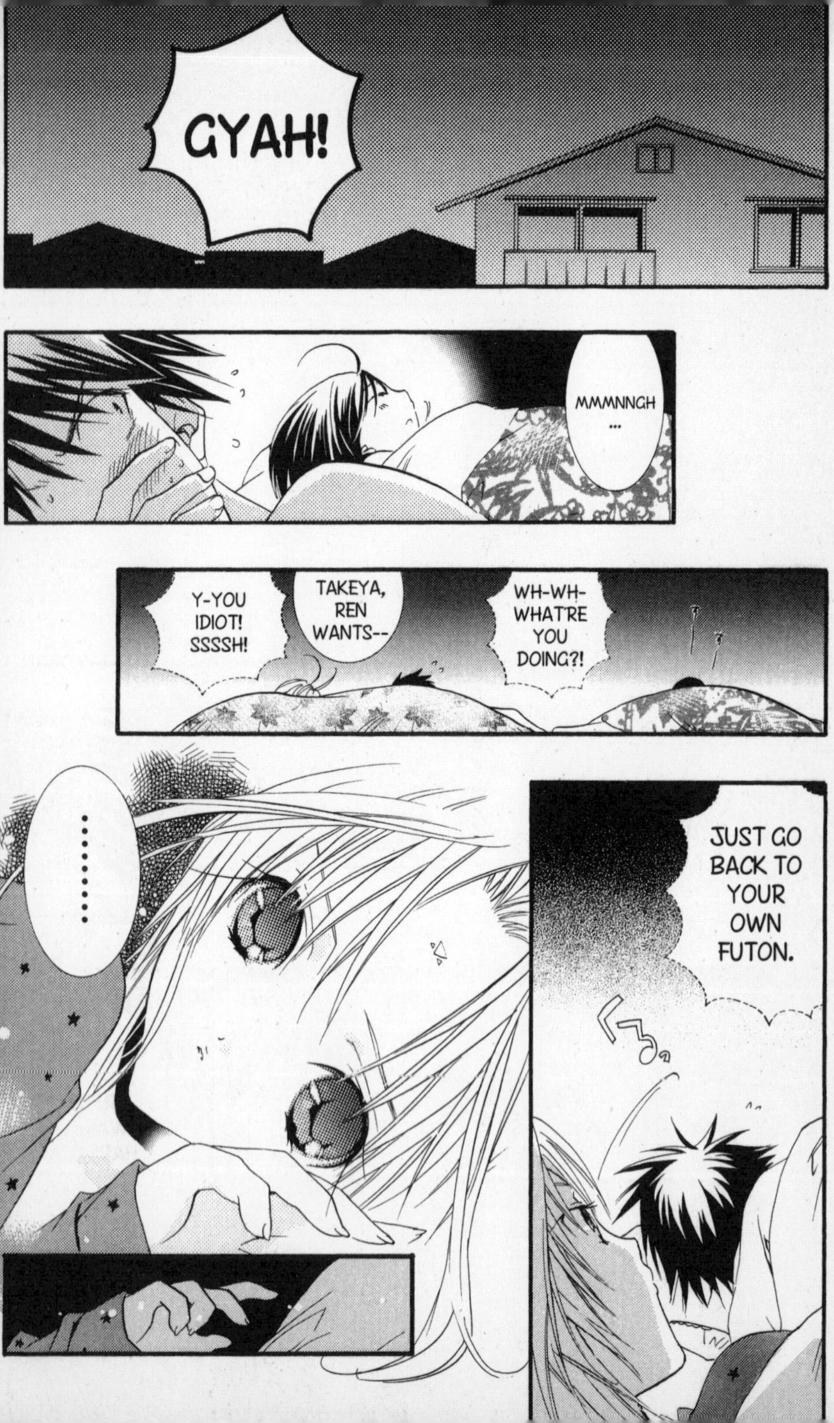
GYAH!
MMMNNGH ...
WH-WH-WHAT'RE YOU DOING?!
TAKEYA, REN WANTS--
Y-YOU IDIOT! SSSSH!
JUST GO BACK TO YOUR OWN FUTON.
....

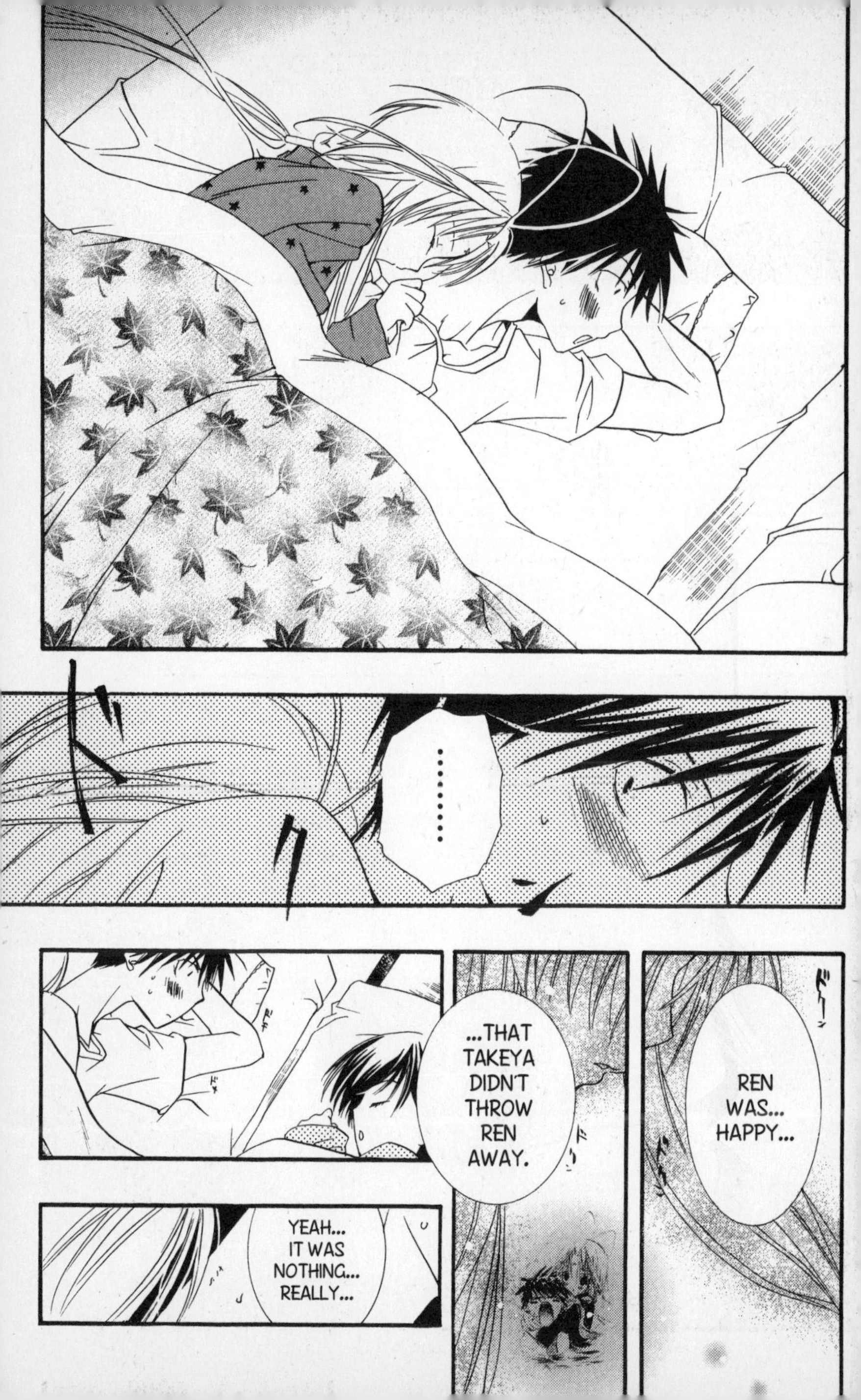

......
REN WAS... HAPPY...
...THAT TAKEYA DIDN'T THROW REN AWAY.
YEAH... IT WAS NOTHING... REALLY...

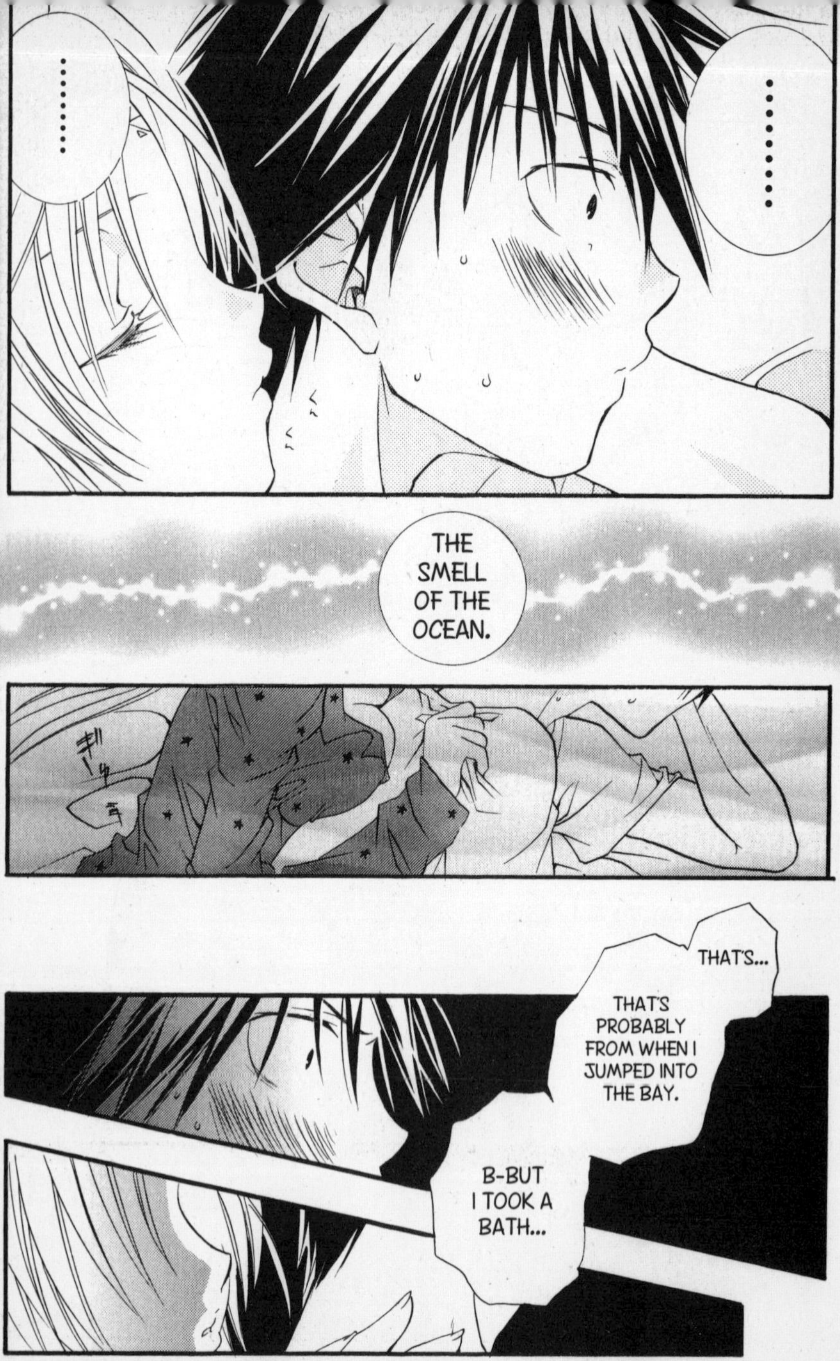
......
......
THE SMELL OF THE OCEAN.
THAT'S...
THAT'S PROBABLY FROM WHEN I JUMPED INTO THE BAY.
B-BUT I TOOK A BATH...

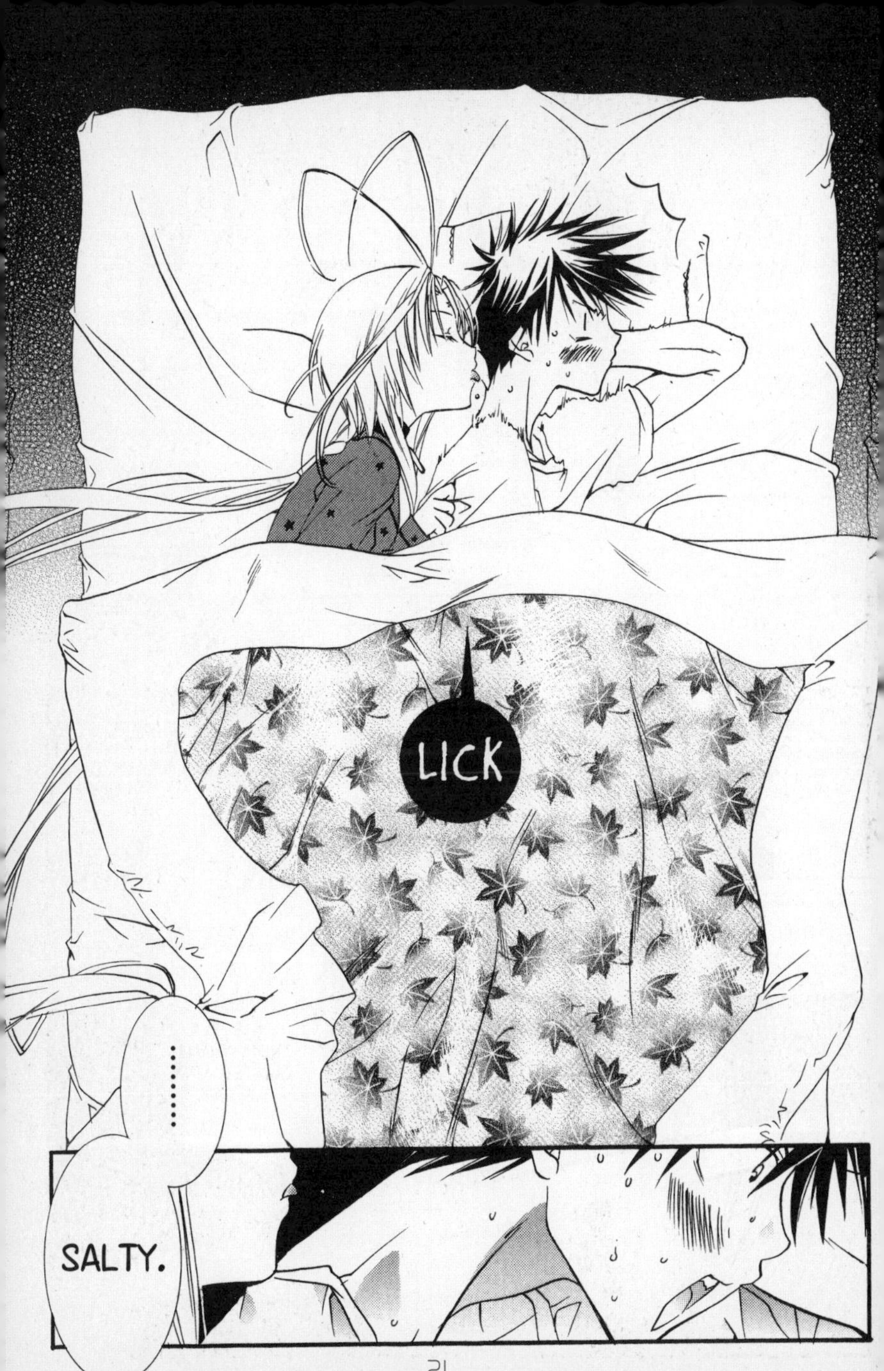
LICK
......
SALTY.

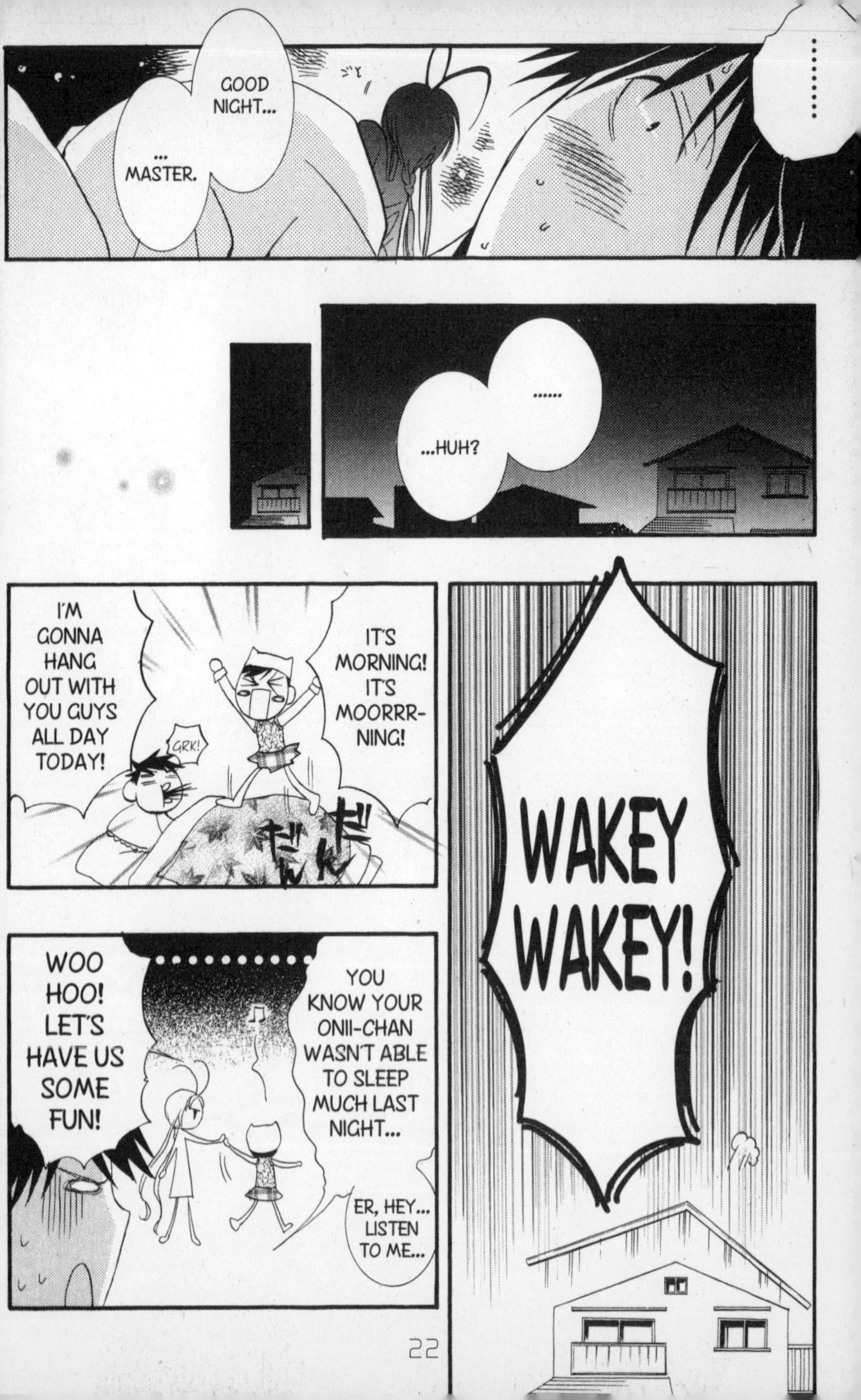
....
GOOD NIGHT...
... MASTER.
......
...HUH?
WAKEY WAKEY!
IT'S MORNING! IT'S MOORRR-NING!
GRK!
I'M GONNA HANG OUT WITH YOU GUYS ALL DAY TODAY!
....
YOU KNOW YOUR ONII-CHAN WASN'T ABLE TO SLEEP MUCH LAST NIGHT...
WOO HOO! LET'S HAVE US SOME FUN!
ER, HEY... LISTEN TO ME...

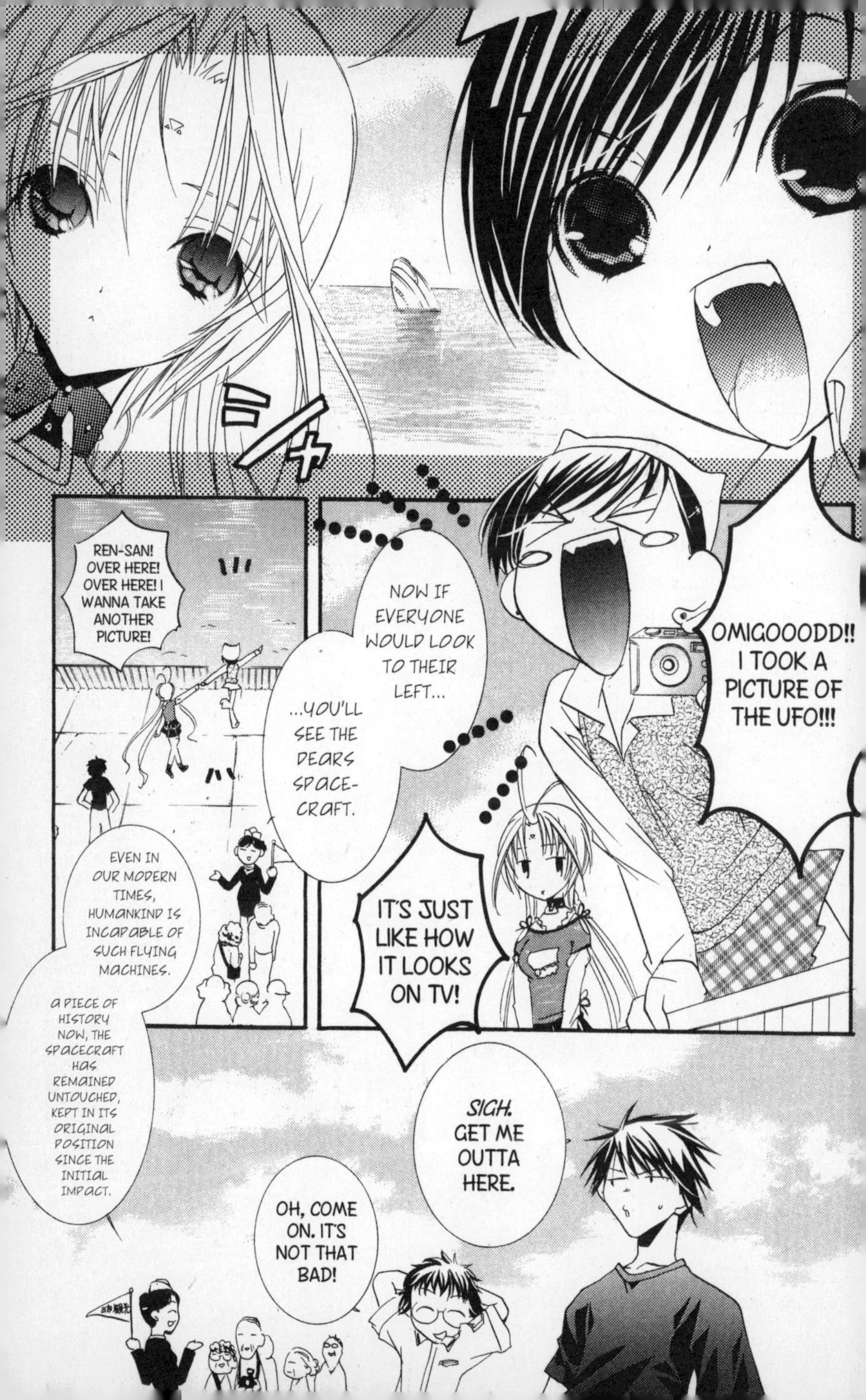
OMIGOOOODD!! I TOOK A PICTURE OF THE UFO!!!
IT'S JUST LIKE HOW IT LOOKS ON TV!
NOW IF EVERYONE WOULD LOOK TO THEIR LEFT...
...YOU'LL SEE THE DEARS SPACE-CRAFT.
REN-SAN! OVER HERE! OVER HERE! I WANNA TAKE ANOTHER PICTURE!
EVEN IN OUR MODERN TIMES, HUMANKIND IS INCAPABLE OF SUCH FLYING MACHINES.
SIGH. GET ME OUTTA HERE.
OH, COME ON. IT'S NOT THAT BAD!
A PIECE OF HISTORY NOW, THE SPACECRAFT HAS REMAINED UNTOUCHED, KEPT IN ITS ORIGINAL POSITION SINCE THE INITIAL IMPACT.

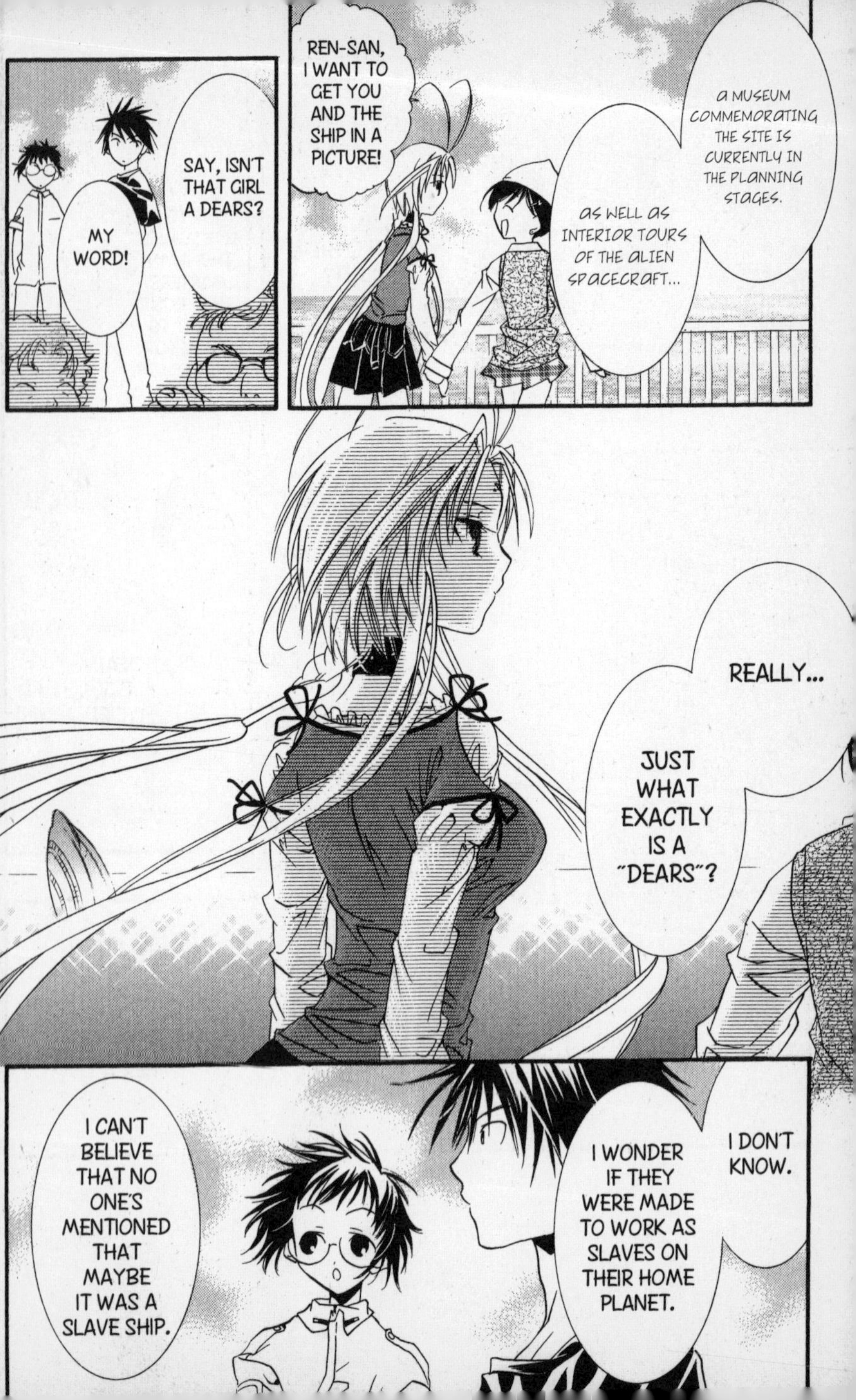
A MUSEUM COMMEMORATING THE SITE IS CURRENTLY IN THE PLANNING STAGES.
AS WELL AS INTERIOR TOURS OF THE ALIEN SPACECRAFT...
REN-SAN, I WANT TO GET YOU AND THE SHIP IN A PICTURE!
SAY, ISN'T THAT GIRL A DEARS?
MY WORD!
REALLY...
JUST WHAT EXACTLY IS A "DEARS"?
I DON'T KNOW.
I WONDER IF THEY WERE MADE TO WORK AS SLAVES ON THEIR HOME PLANET.
I CAN'T BELIEVE THAT NO ONE'S MENTIONED THAT MAYBE IT WAS A SLAVE SHIP.

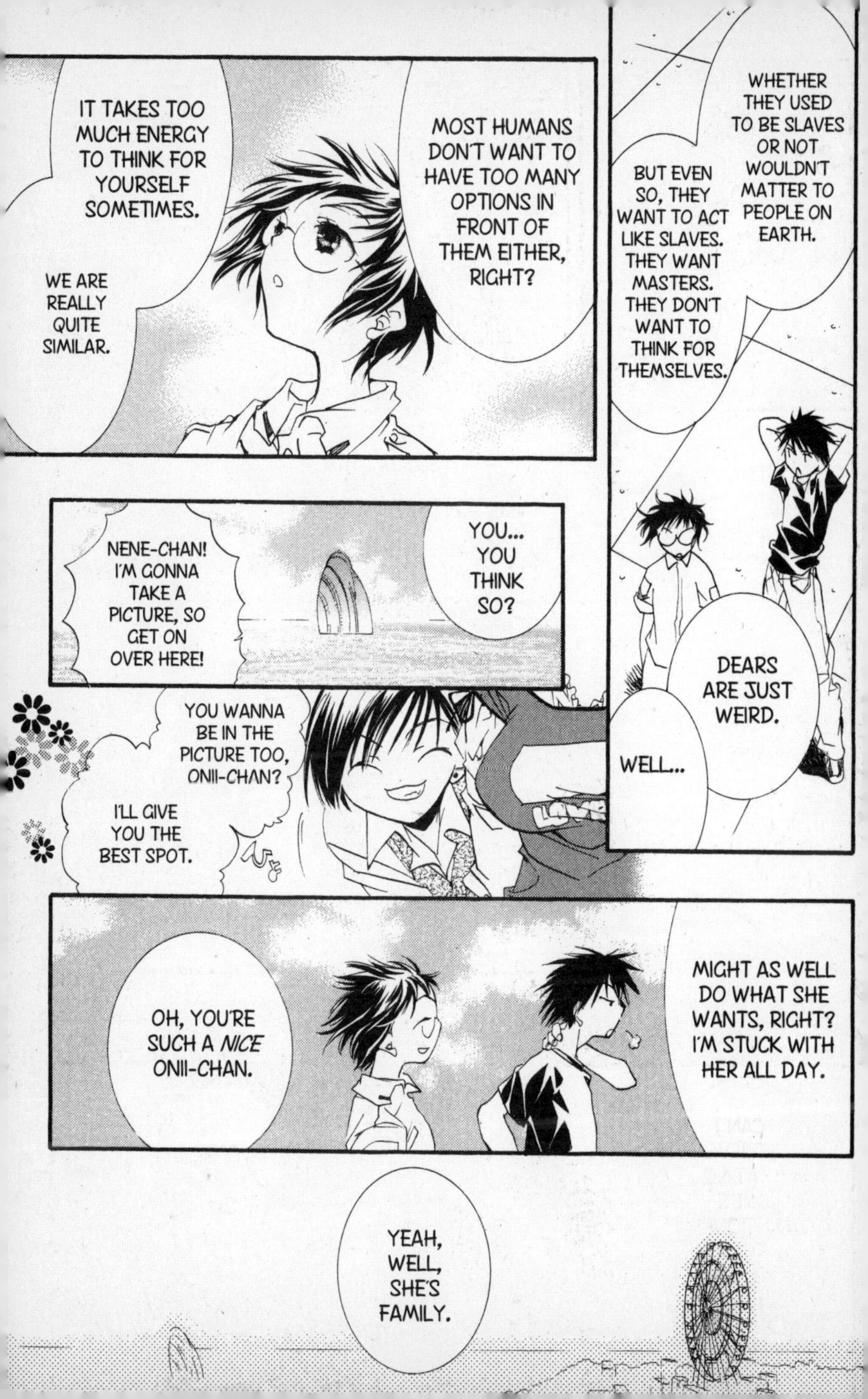
WHETHER THEY USED TO BE SLAVES OR NOT WOULDN'T MATTER TO PEOPLE ON EARTH.
BUT EVEN SO, THEY WANT TO ACT LIKE SLAVES. THEY WANT MASTERS. THEY DON'T WANT TO THINK FOR THEMSELVES.
DEARS ARE JUST WEIRD.
WELL...
MOST HUMANS DON'T WANT TO HAVE TOO MANY OPTIONS IN FRONT OF THEM EITHER, RIGHT?
IT TAKES TOO MUCH ENERGY TO THINK FOR YOURSELF SOMETIMES.
WE ARE REALLY QUITE SIMILAR.
YOU... YOU THINK SO?
NENE-CHAN! I'M GONNA TAKE A PICTURE, SO GET ON OVER HERE!
YOU WANNA BE IN THE PICTURE TOO, ONII-CHAN?
I'LL GIVE YOU THE BEST SPOT.
MIGHT AS WELL DO WHAT SHE WANTS, RIGHT? I'M STUCK WITH HER ALL DAY.
OH, YOU'RE SUCH A *NICE* ONII-CHAN.
YEAH, WELL, SHE'S FAMILY.

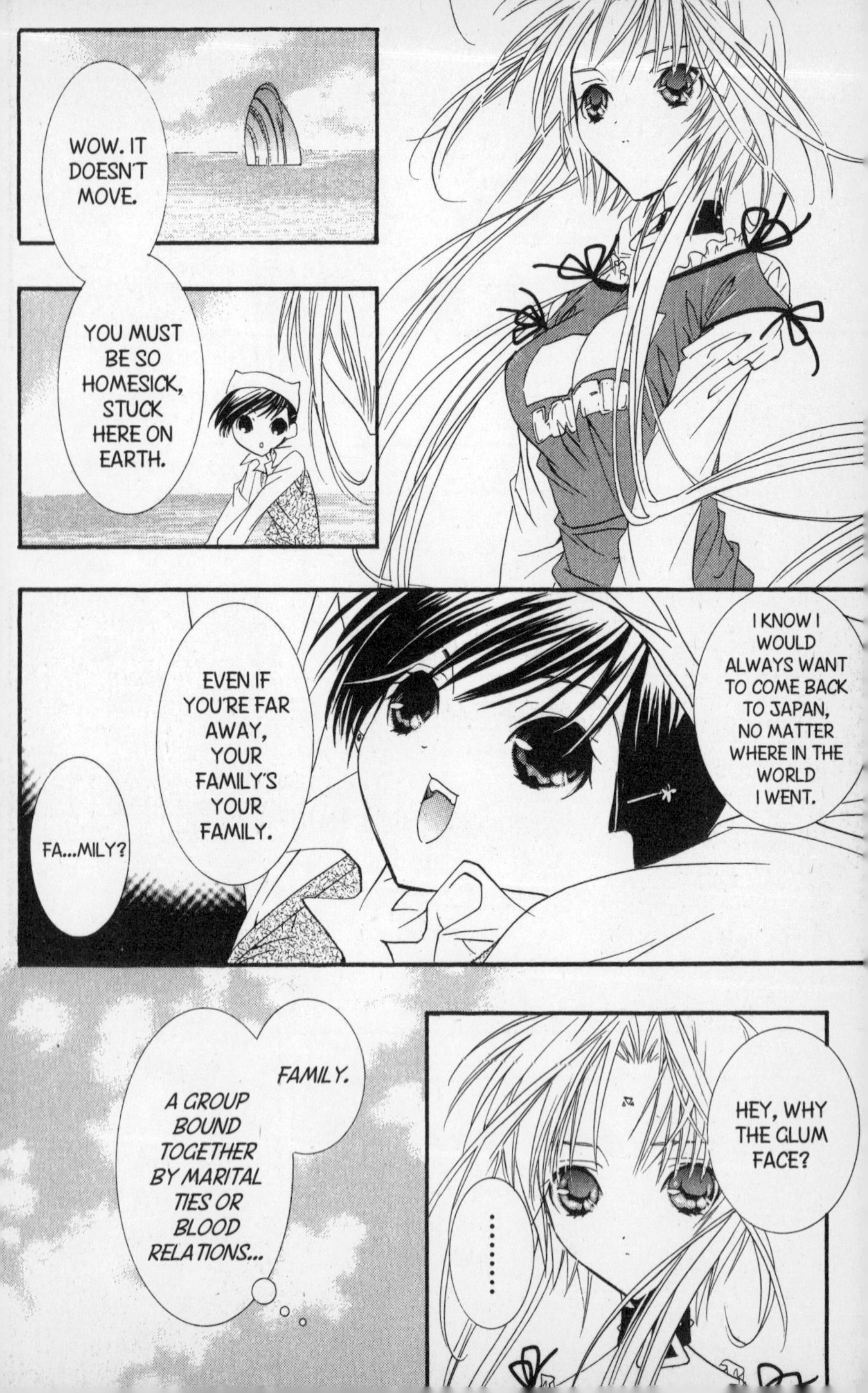
WOW. IT DOESN'T MOVE.
YOU MUST BE SO HOMESICK, STUCK HERE ON EARTH.
I KNOW I WOULD ALWAYS WANT TO COME BACK TO JAPAN, NO MATTER WHERE IN THE WORLD I WENT.
EVEN IF YOU'RE FAR AWAY, YOUR FAMILY'S YOUR FAMILY.
FA...MILY?
HEY, WHY THE GLUM FACE?
....
FAMILY.
A GROUP BOUND TOGETHER BY MARITAL TIES OR BLOOD RELATIONS...

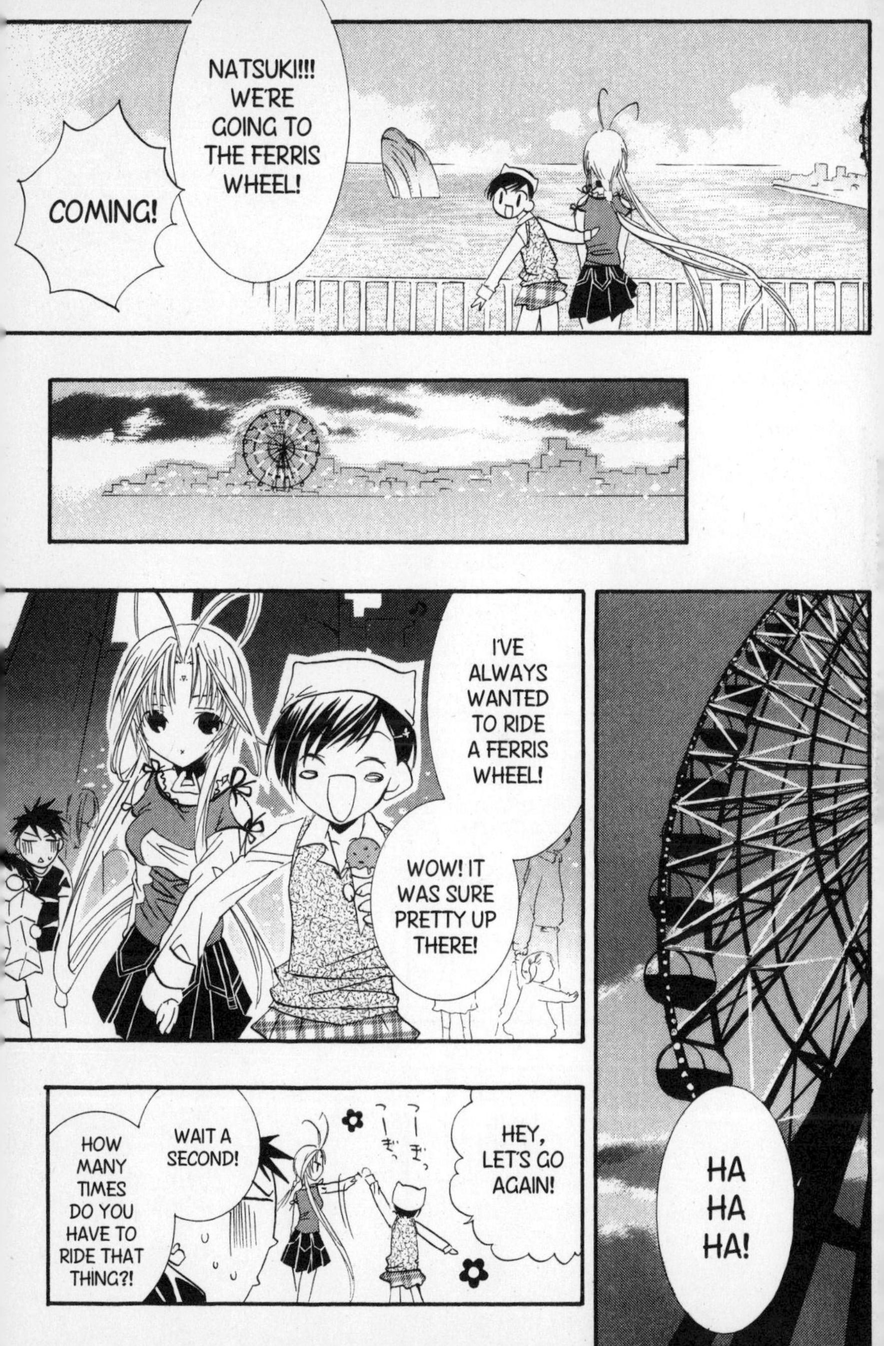
NATSUKI!!! WE'RE GOING TO THE FERRIS WHEEL!
COMING!
HA HA HA!
I'VE ALWAYS WANTED TO RIDE A FERRIS WHEEL!
WOW! IT WAS SURE PRETTY UP THERE!
HEY, LET'S GO AGAIN!
WAIT A SECOND!
HOW MANY TIMES DO YOU HAVE TO RIDE THAT THING?!

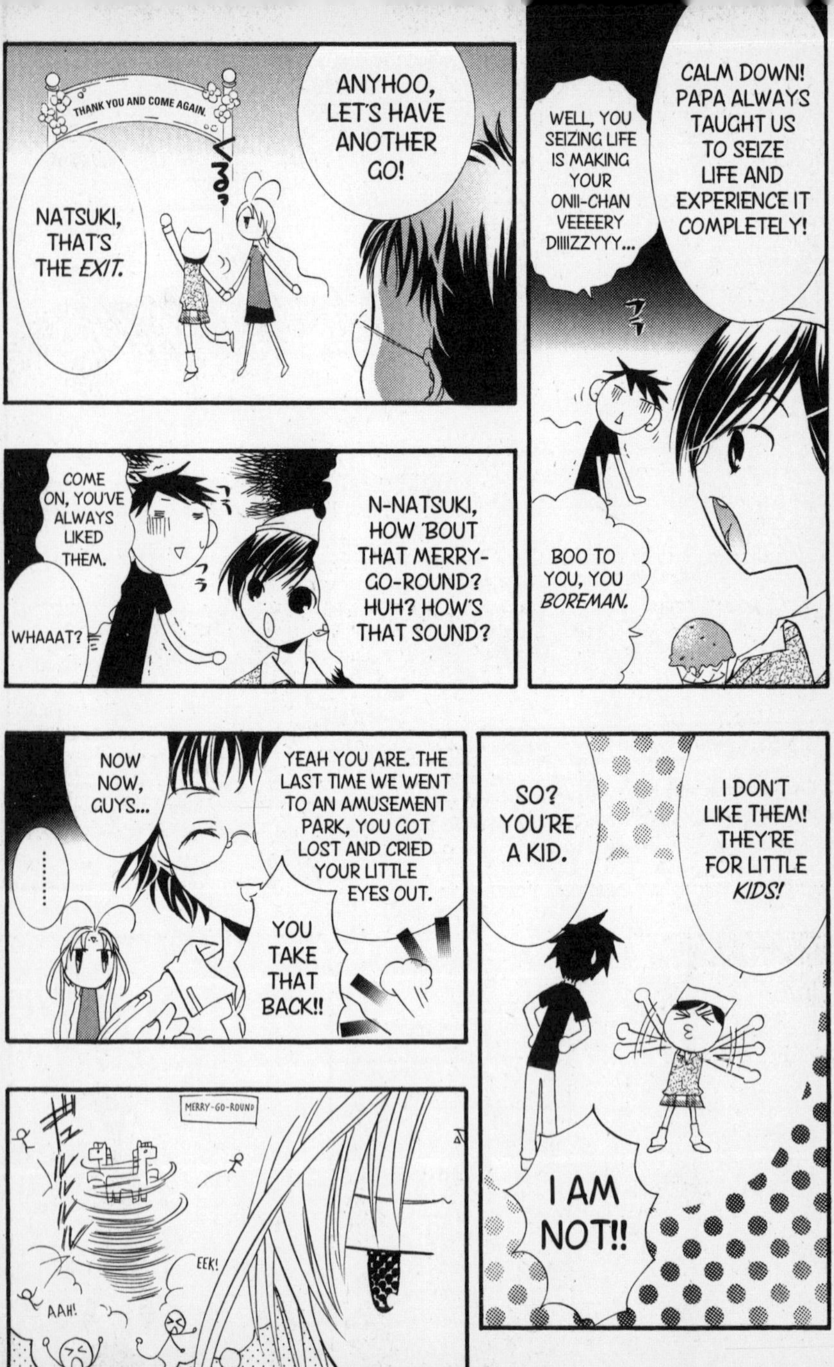
CALM DOWN! PAPA ALWAYS TAUGHT US TO SEIZE LIFE AND EXPERIENCE IT COMPLETELY!
WELL, YOU SEIZING LIFE IS MAKING YOUR ONII-CHAN VEEEERY DIIIIZZYYY...
BOO TO YOU, YOU *BOREMAN.*
ANYHOO, LET'S HAVE ANOTHER GO!
THANK YOU AND COME AGAIN.
NATSUKI, THAT'S THE *EXIT.*
N-NATSUKI, HOW 'BOUT THAT MERRY-GO-ROUND? HUH? HOW'S THAT SOUND?
COME ON, YOU'VE ALWAYS LIKED THEM.
WHAAAT?
I DON'T LIKE THEM! THEY'RE FOR LITTLE *KIDS!*
SO? YOU'RE A KID.
I AM NOT!!
YEAH YOU ARE. THE LAST TIME WE WENT TO AN AMUSEMENT PARK, YOU GOT LOST AND CRIED YOUR LITTLE EYES OUT.
YOU TAKE THAT BACK!!
NOW NOW, GUYS...
....
MERRY-GO-ROUND
EEK!
AAH!
INSIDE REN'S HEAD

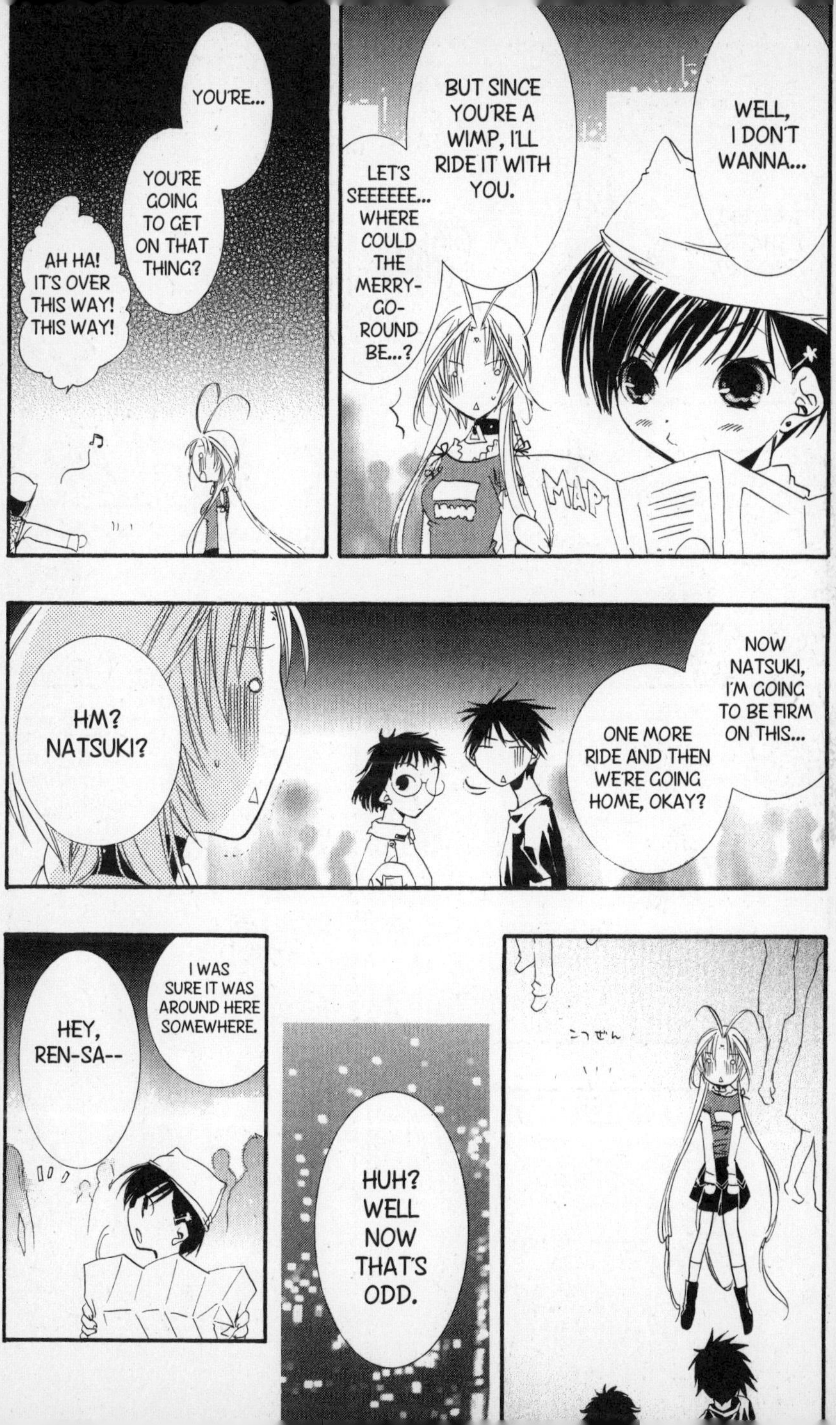
WELL, I DON'T WANNA...
BUT SINCE YOU'RE A WIMP, I'LL RIDE IT WITH YOU.
LET'S SEEEEEE... WHERE COULD THE MERRY-GO-ROUND BE...?
MAP
YOU'RE...
YOU'RE GOING TO GET ON THAT THING?
AH HA! IT'S OVER THIS WAY! THIS WAY!
NOW NATSUKI, I'M GOING TO BE FIRM ON THIS...
ONE MORE RIDE AND THEN WE'RE GOING HOME, OKAY?
HM? NATSUKI?
こつぜん
I WAS SURE IT WAS AROUND HERE SOMEWHERE.
HEY, REN-SA--
HUH? WELL NOW THAT'S ODD.

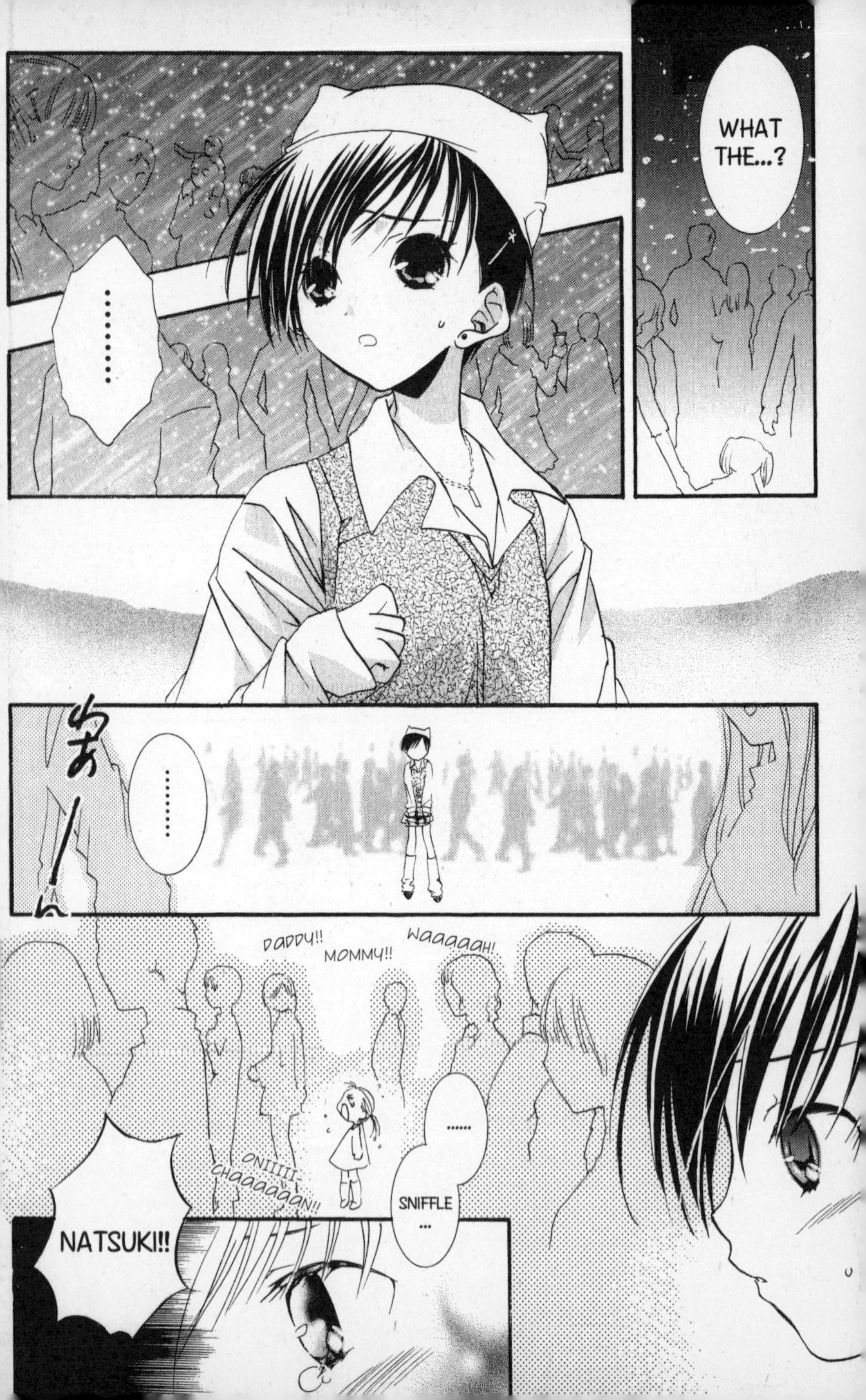
WHAT THE...?
....
....
わあーん
Waaaaah!
MOMMY!!
DADDY!!
......
SNIFFLE ...
ONIIIII-CHAAAAAAN!!
NATSUKI!!

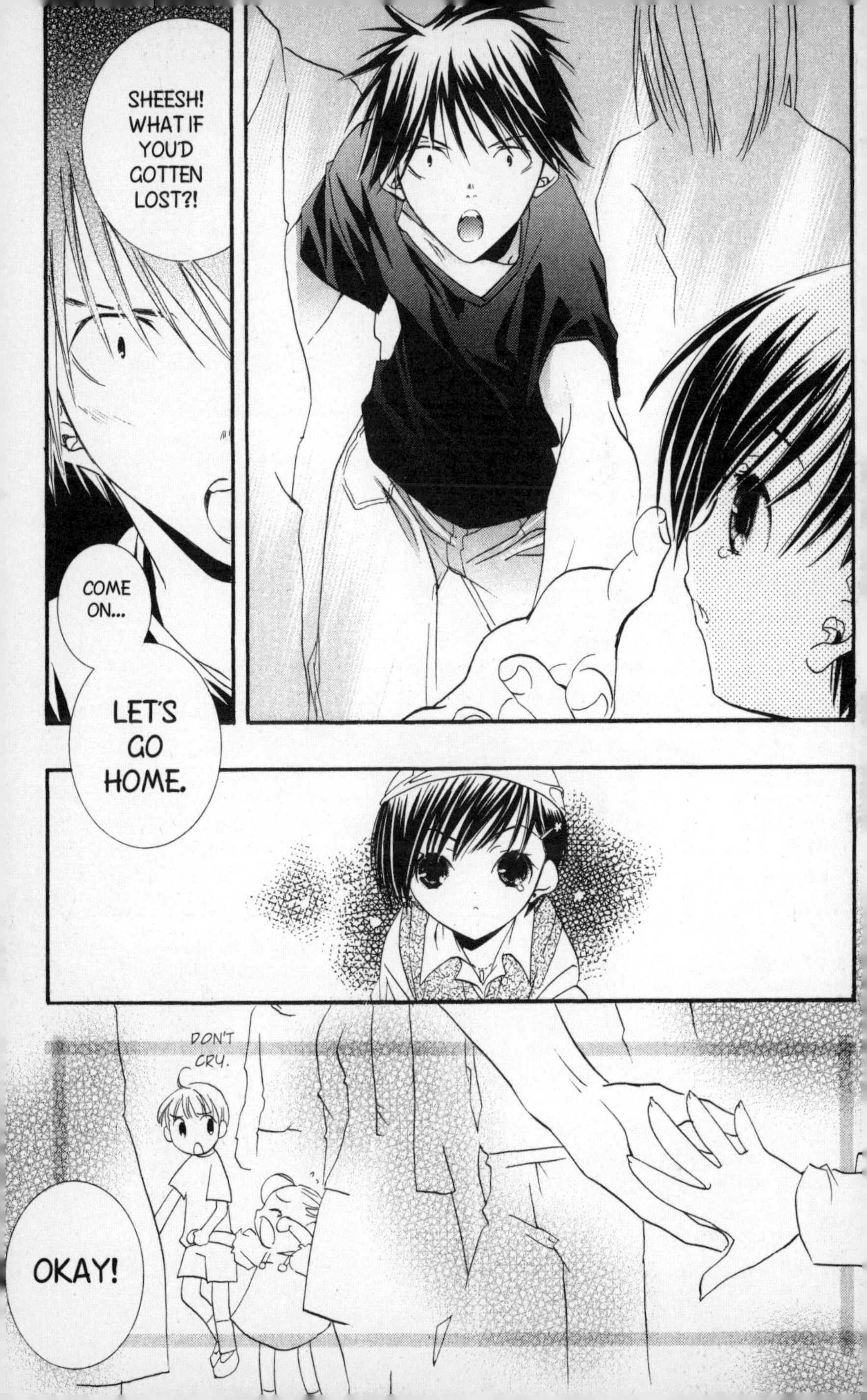
SHEESH! WHAT IF YOU'D GOTTEN LOST?!
COME ON...
LET'S GO HOME.
DON'T CRY.
OKAY!

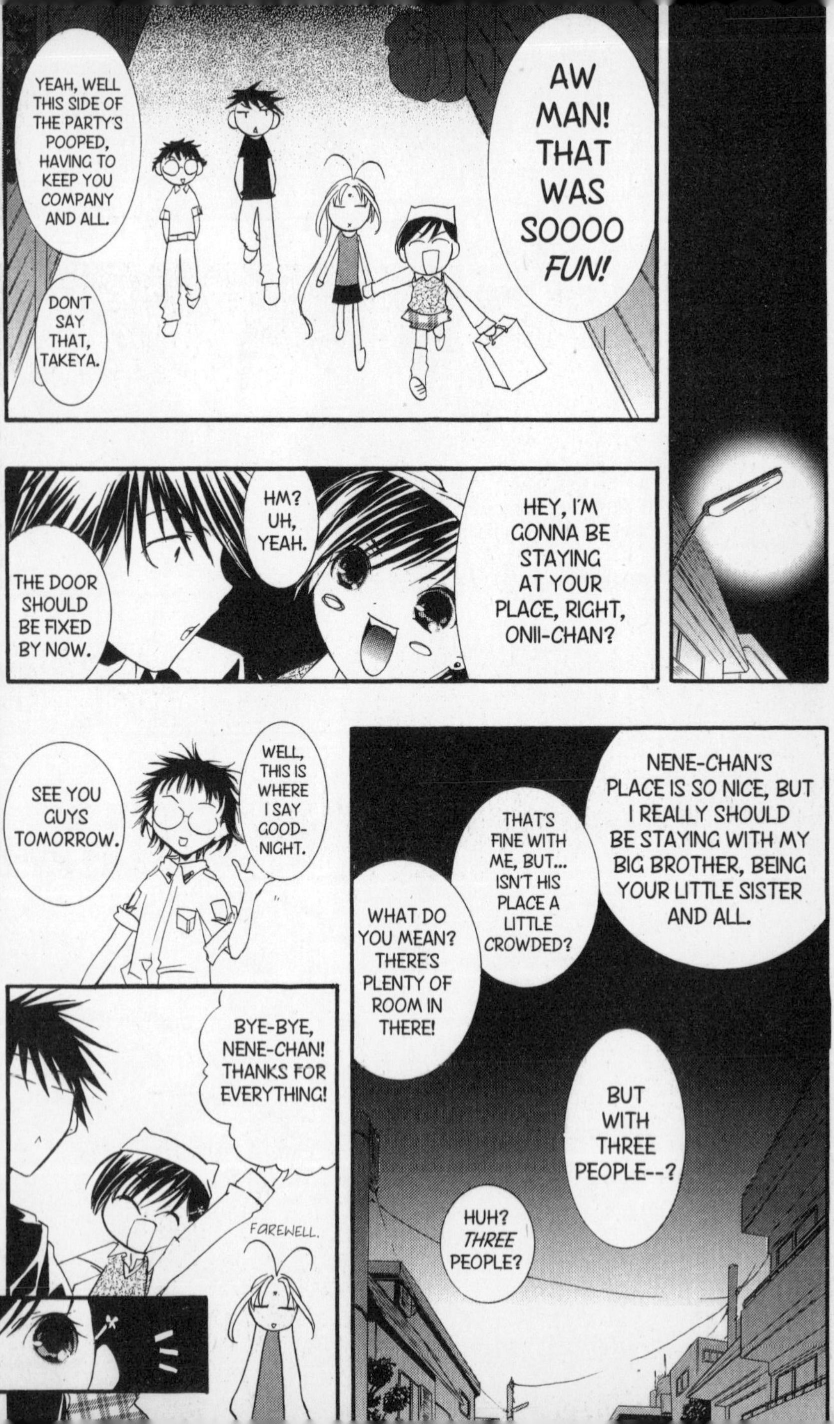
AW MAN! THAT WAS SOOOO *FUN!*
YEAH, WELL THIS SIDE OF THE PARTY'S POOPED, HAVING TO KEEP YOU COMPANY AND ALL.
DON'T SAY THAT, TAKEYA.
HEY, I'M GONNA BE STAYING AT YOUR PLACE, RIGHT, ONII-CHAN?
HM? UH, YEAH.
THE DOOR SHOULD BE FIXED BY NOW.
NENE-CHAN'S PLACE IS SO NICE, BUT I REALLY SHOULD BE STAYING WITH MY BIG BROTHER, BEING YOUR LITTLE SISTER AND ALL.
THAT'S FINE WITH ME, BUT... ISN'T HIS PLACE A LITTLE CROWDED?
WHAT DO YOU MEAN? THERE'S PLENTY OF ROOM IN THERE!
BUT WITH THREE PEOPLE--?
HUH? *THREE* PEOPLE?
WELL, THIS IS WHERE I SAY GOOD-NIGHT.
SEE YOU GUYS TOMORROW.
BYE-BYE, NENE-CHAN! THANKS FOR EVERYTHING!
FAREWELL.

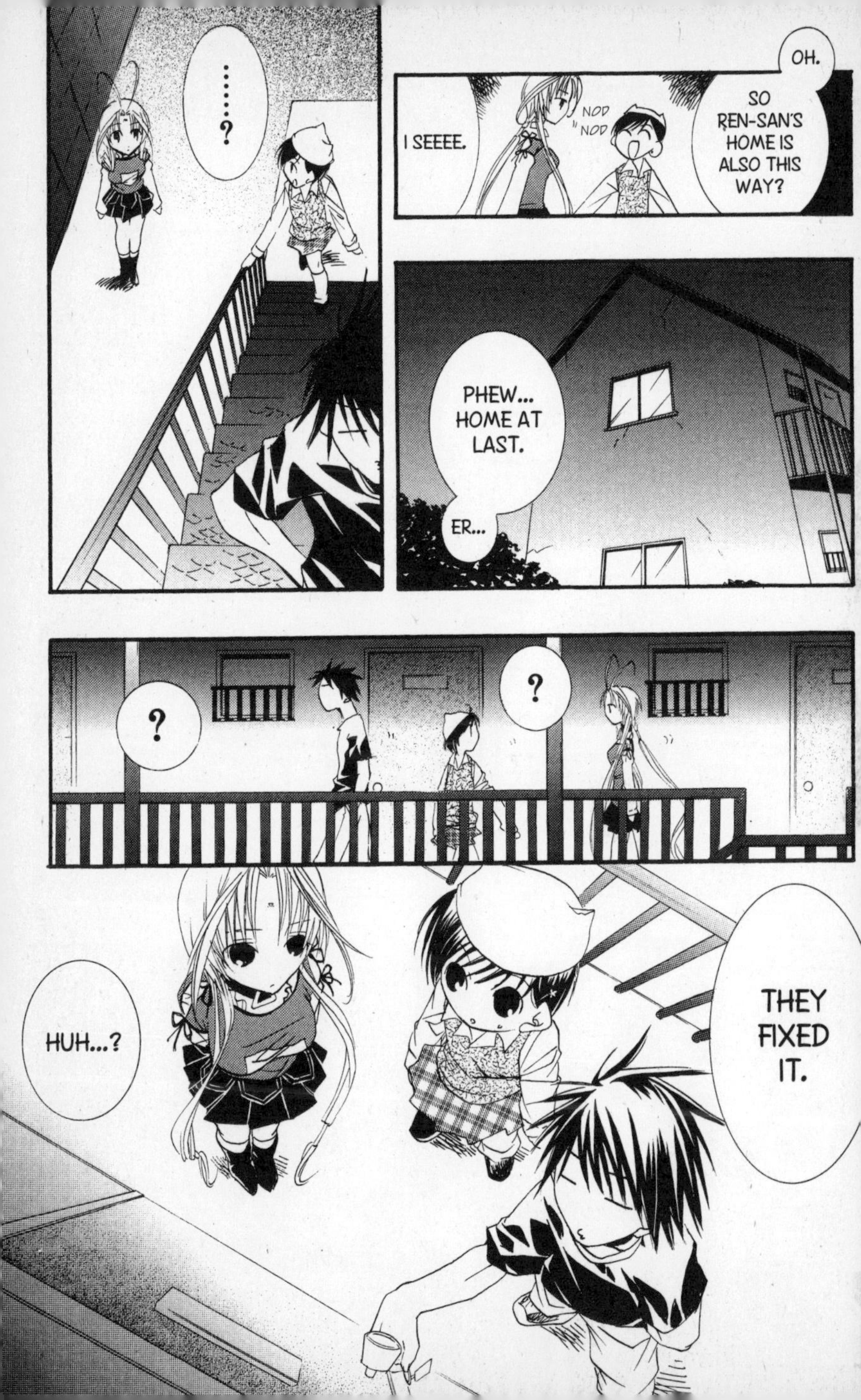
OH.
SO REN-SAN'S HOME IS ALSO THIS WAY?
NOD NOD
I SEEEE.
PHEW... HOME AT LAST.
ER...
......?
?
?
THEY FIXED IT.
HUH...?

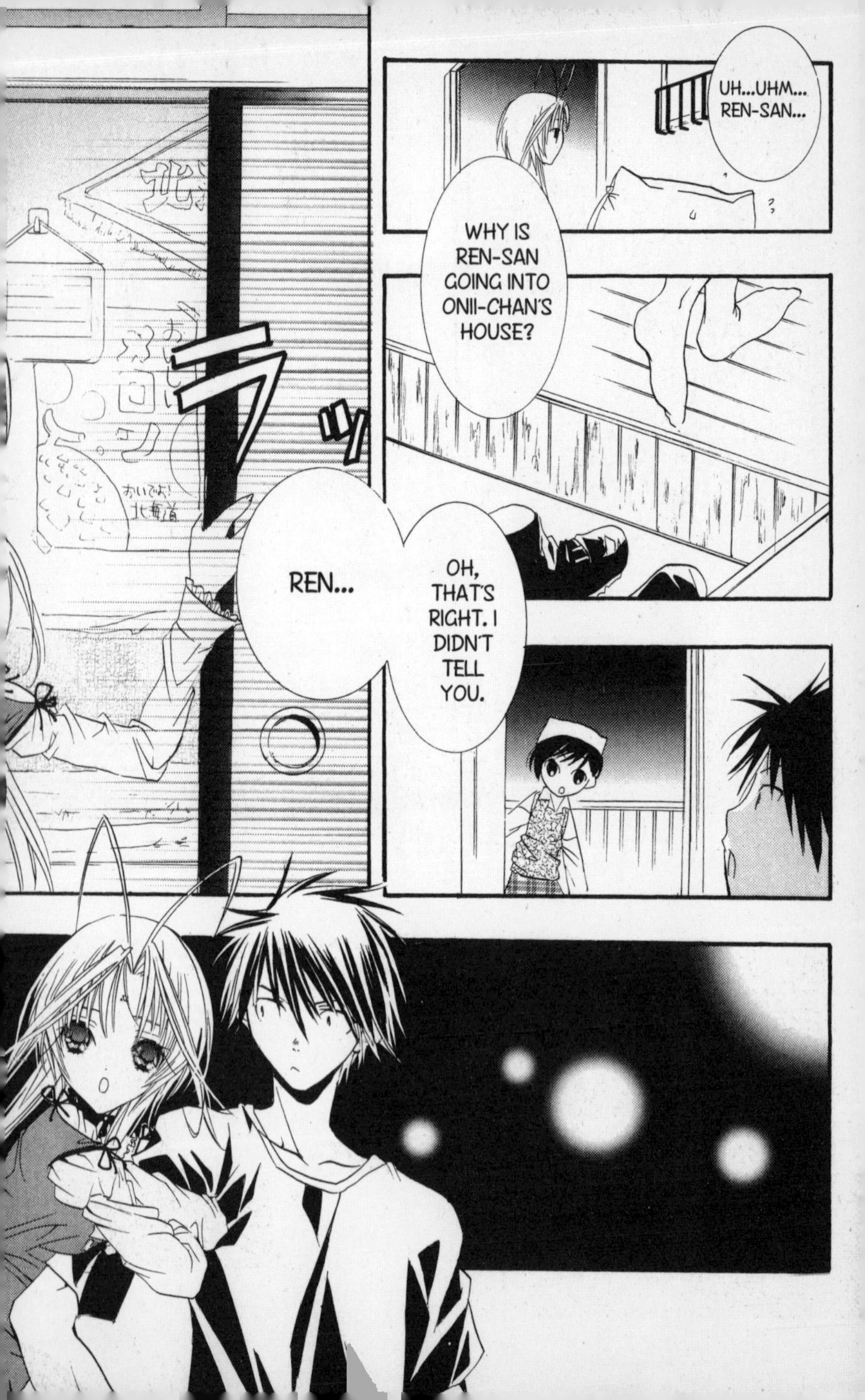
UH...UHM... REN-SAN...
WHY IS REN-SAN GOING INTO ONII-CHAN'S HOUSE?
OH, THAT'S RIGHT. I DIDN'T TELL YOU.
REN...

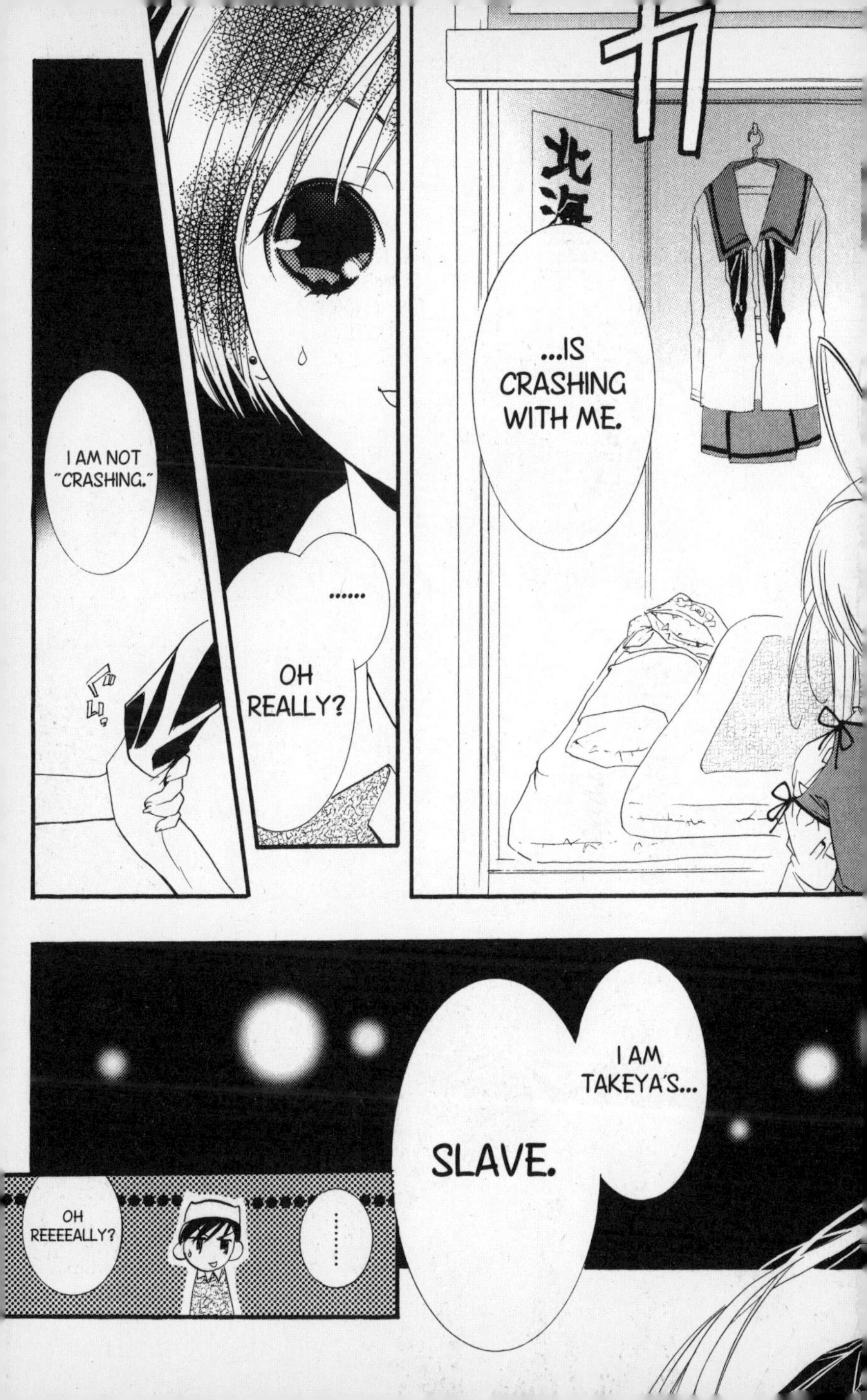
...IS CRASHING WITH ME.
I AM NOT "CRASHING."
...... OH REALLY?
I AM TAKEYA'S... SLAVE.
......
OH REEEEALLY?

14th Contact

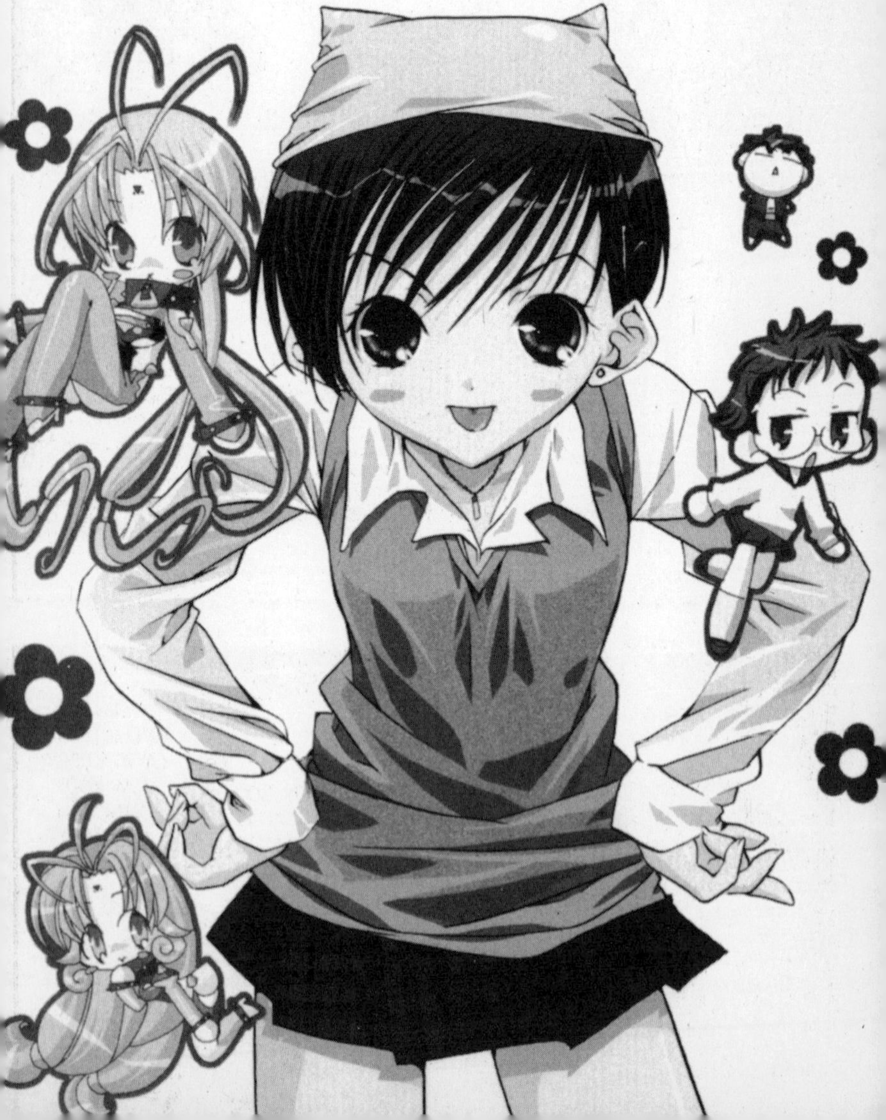

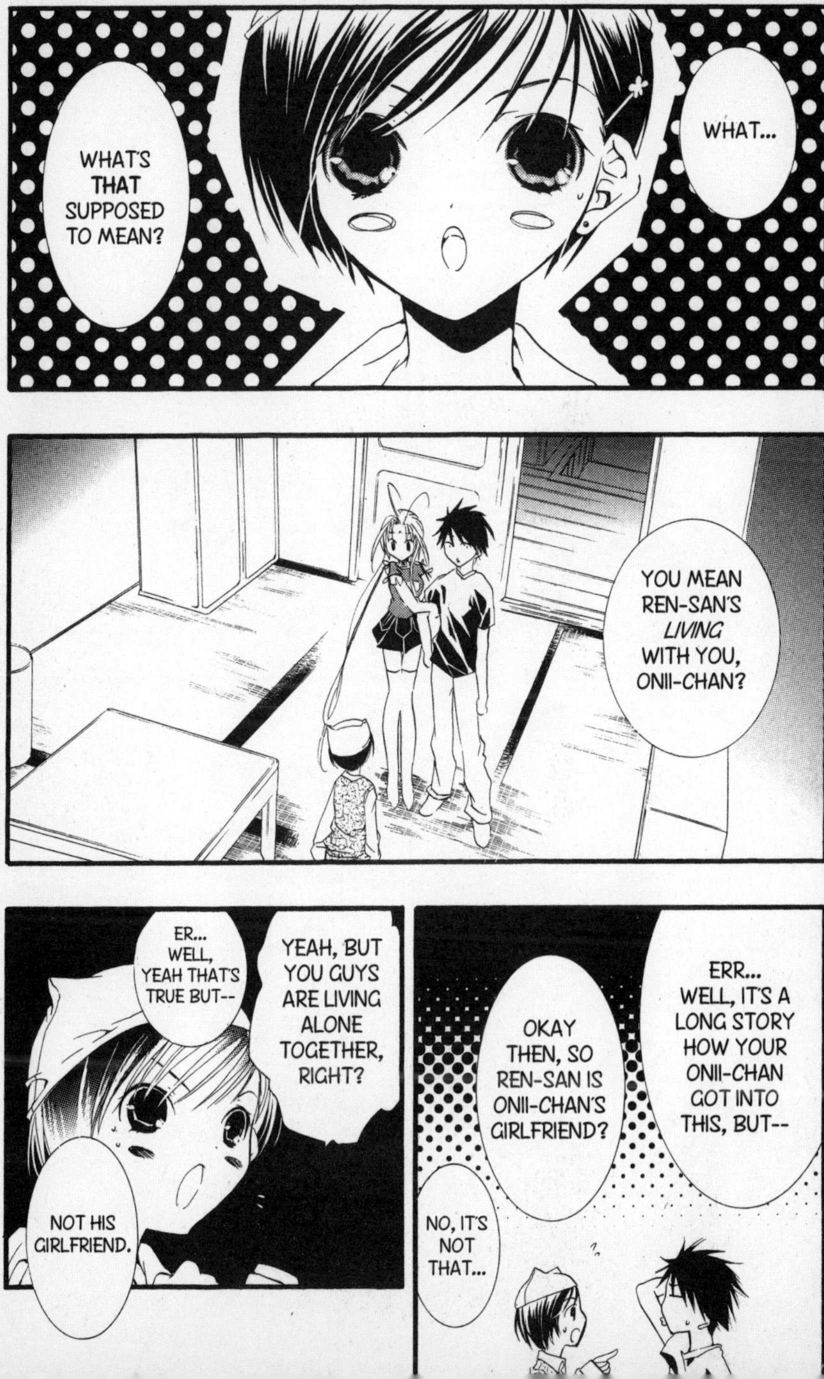
WHAT...
WHAT'S THAT SUPPOSED TO MEAN?
YOU MEAN REN-SAN'S *LIVING* WITH YOU, ONII-CHAN?
ERR... WELL, IT'S A LONG STORY HOW YOUR ONII-CHAN GOT INTO THIS, BUT--
OKAY THEN, SO REN-SAN IS ONII-CHAN'S GIRLFRIEND?
NO, IT'S NOT THAT...
YEAH, BUT YOU GUYS ARE LIVING ALONE TOGETHER, RIGHT?
ER... WELL, YEAH THAT'S TRUE BUT--
NOT HIS GIRLFRIEND.

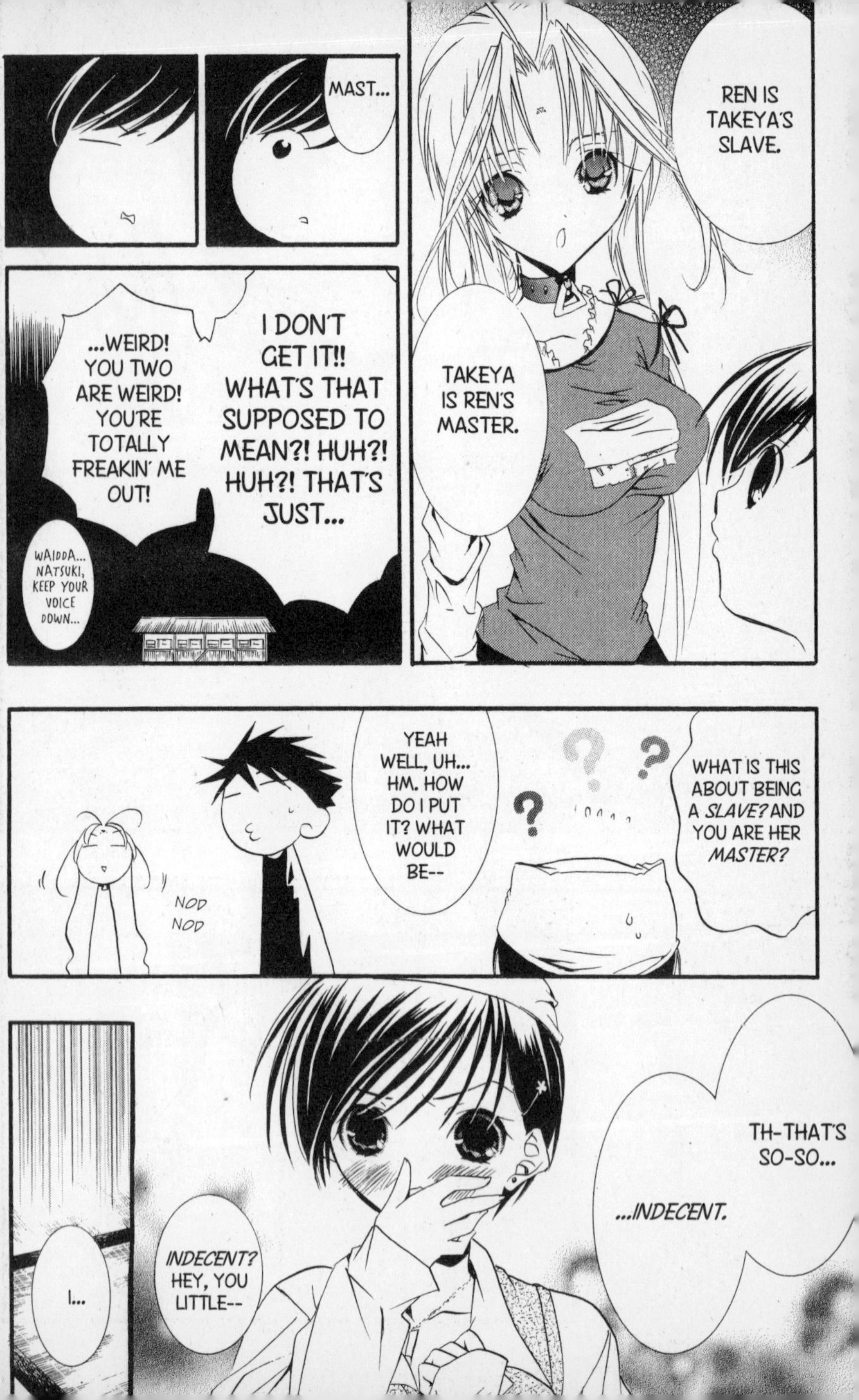
REN IS TAKEYA'S SLAVE.
TAKEYA IS REN'S MASTER.
MAST...
I DON'T GET IT!! WHAT'S THAT SUPPOSED TO MEAN?! HUH?! HUH?! THAT'S JUST...
...WEIRD! YOU TWO ARE WEIRD! YOU'RE TOTALLY FREAKIN' ME OUT!
WAIDDA... NATSUKI, KEEP YOUR VOICE DOWN...
WHAT IS THIS ABOUT BEING A *SLAVE?* AND YOU ARE HER *MASTER?*
YEAH WELL, UH... HM. HOW DO I PUT IT? WHAT WOULD BE--
NOD NOD
TH-THAT'S SO-SO...
...INDECENT.
INDECENT? HEY, YOU LITTLE--
I...

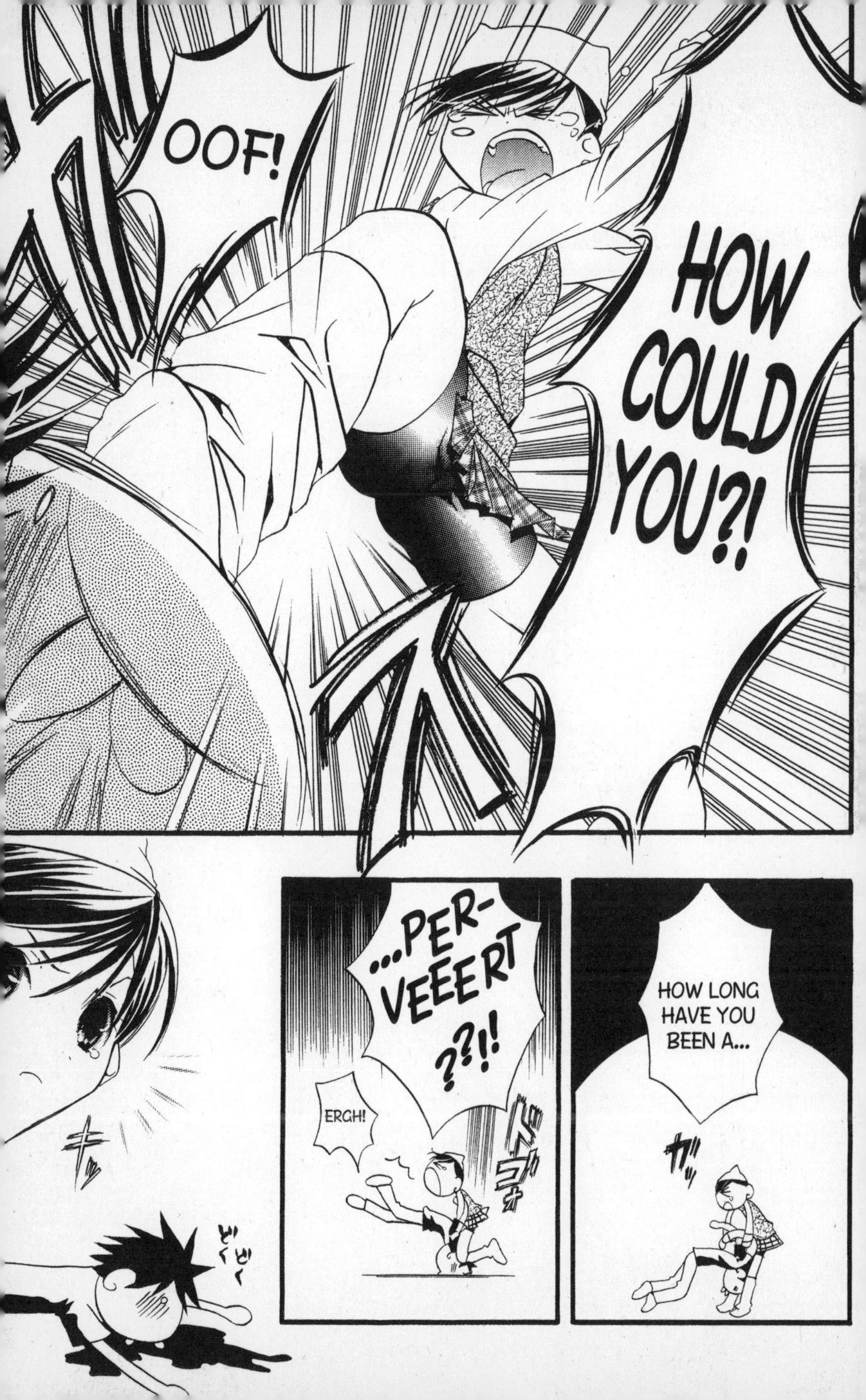
HOW COULD YOU?!
OOF!
HOW LONG HAVE YOU BEEN A...
ガッ
...PER-VEEERT??!!
ERGH!
キッ
ビクビク

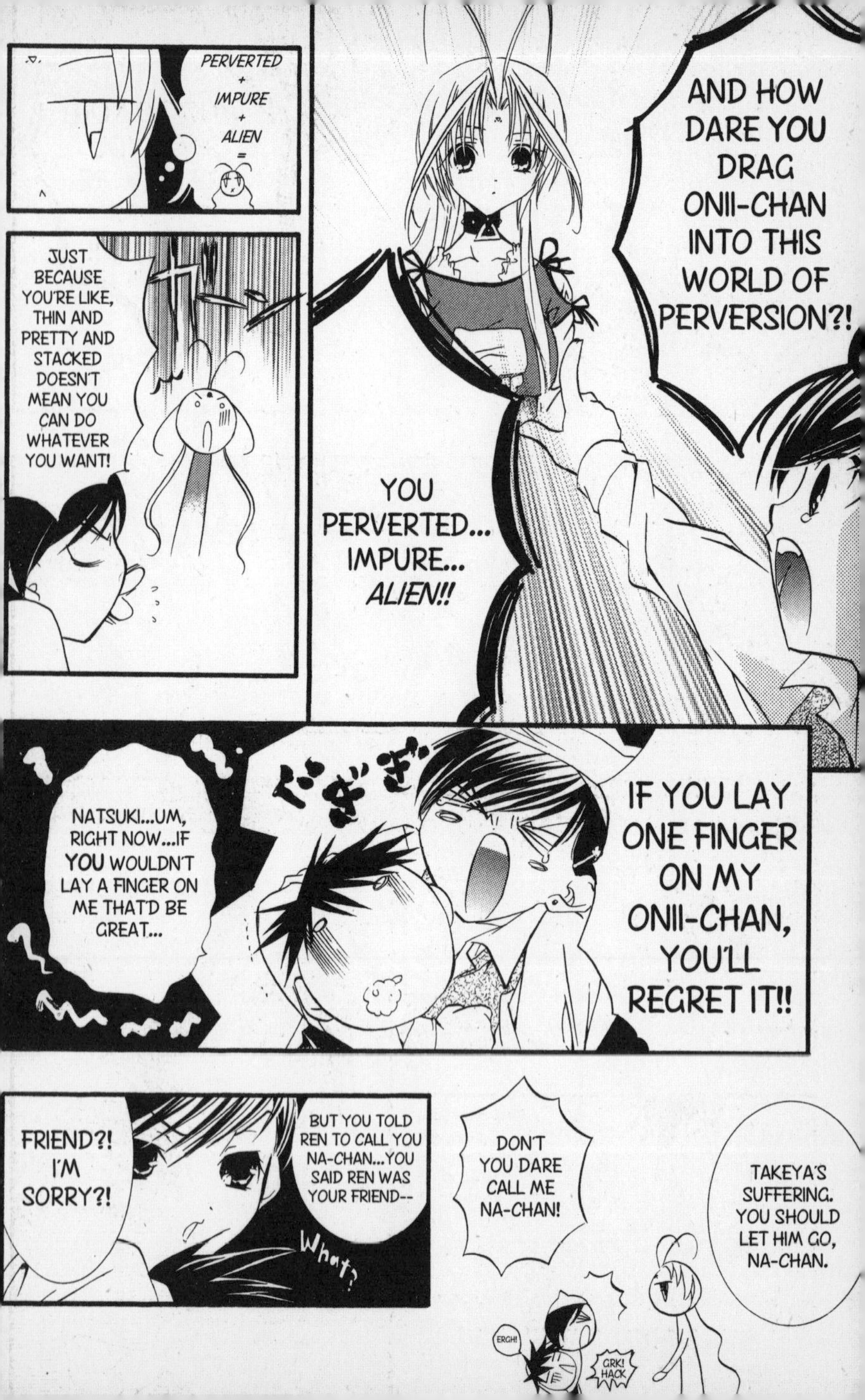
AND HOW DARE YOU DRAG ONII-CHAN INTO THIS WORLD OF PERVERSION?!
YOU PERVERTED... IMPURE... *ALIEN!!*
PERVERTED + IMPURE + ALIEN =
JUST BECAUSE YOU'RE LIKE, THIN AND PRETTY AND STACKED DOESN'T MEAN YOU CAN DO WHATEVER YOU WANT!
IF YOU LAY ONE FINGER ON MY ONII-CHAN, YOU'LL REGRET IT!!
ぐぎぎ
NATSUKI...UM, RIGHT NOW...IF **YOU** WOULDN'T LAY A FINGER ON ME THAT'D BE GREAT...
TAKEYA'S SUFFERING. YOU SHOULD LET HIM GO, NA-CHAN.
DON'T YOU DARE CALL ME NA-CHAN!
ERGH!
GRK! HACK
BUT YOU TOLD REN TO CALL YOU NA-CHAN...YOU SAID REN WAS YOUR FRIEND--
FRIEND?! I'M SORRY?!
What?

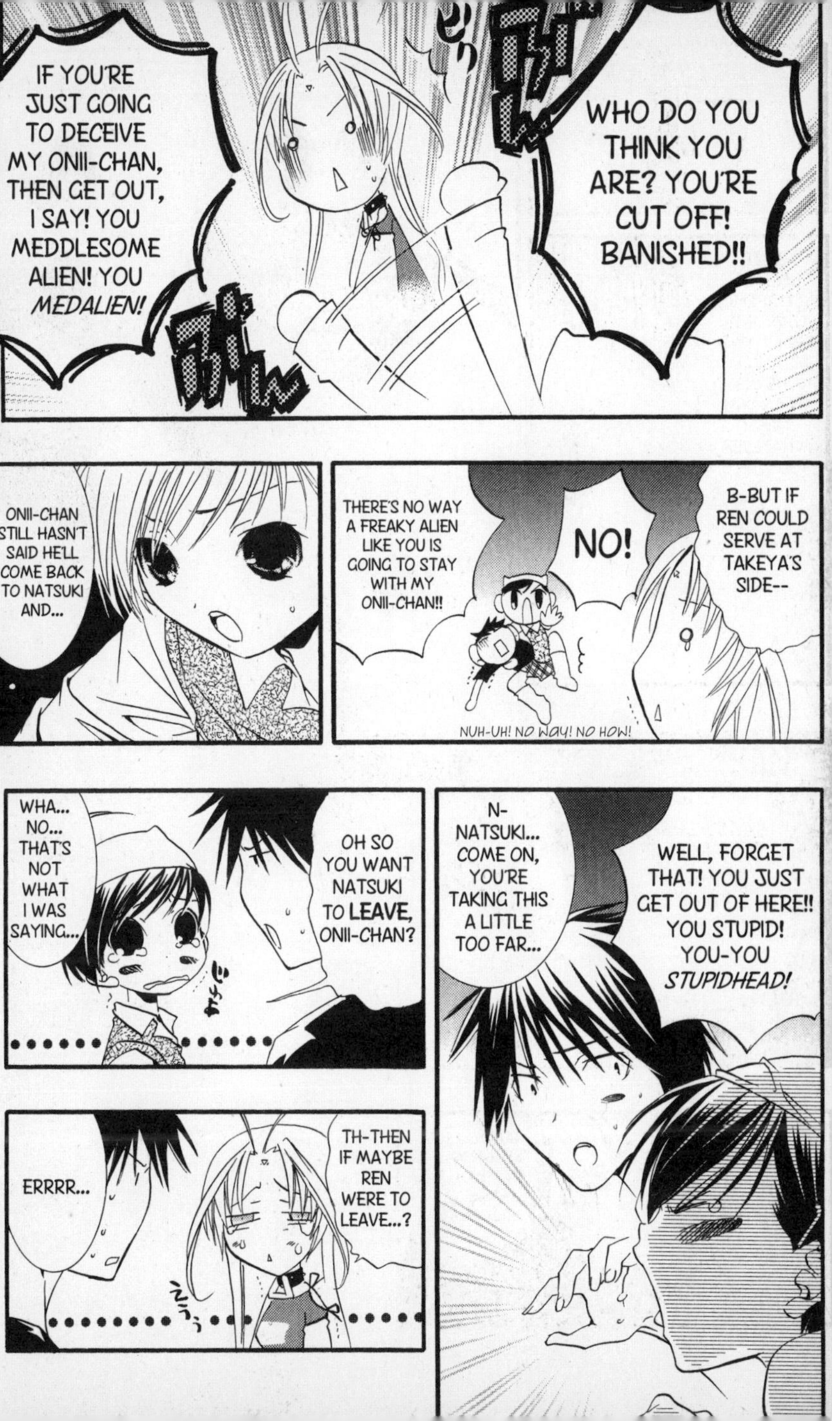
WHO DO YOU THINK YOU ARE? YOU'RE CUT OFF! BANISHED!!
IF YOU'RE JUST GOING TO DECEIVE MY ONII-CHAN, THEN GET OUT, I SAY! YOU MEDDLESOME ALIEN! YOU *MEDALIEN!*
B-BUT IF REN COULD SERVE AT TAKEYA'S SIDE--
NO!
THERE'S NO WAY A FREAKY ALIEN LIKE YOU IS GOING TO STAY WITH MY ONII-CHAN!!
NUH-UH! NO WAY! NO HOW!
ONII-CHAN STILL HASN'T SAID HE'LL COME BACK TO NATSUKI AND...
WELL, FORGET THAT! YOU JUST GET OUT OF HERE!! YOU STUPID! YOU-YOU *STUPIDHEAD!*
N-NATSUKI... COME ON, YOU'RE TAKING THIS A LITTLE TOO FAR...
OH SO YOU WANT NATSUKI TO **LEAVE**, ONII-CHAN?
WHA... NO... THAT'S NOT WHAT I WAS SAYING...
••••••••
TH-THEN IF MAYBE REN WERE TO LEAVE...?
ERRRR...
••••••••

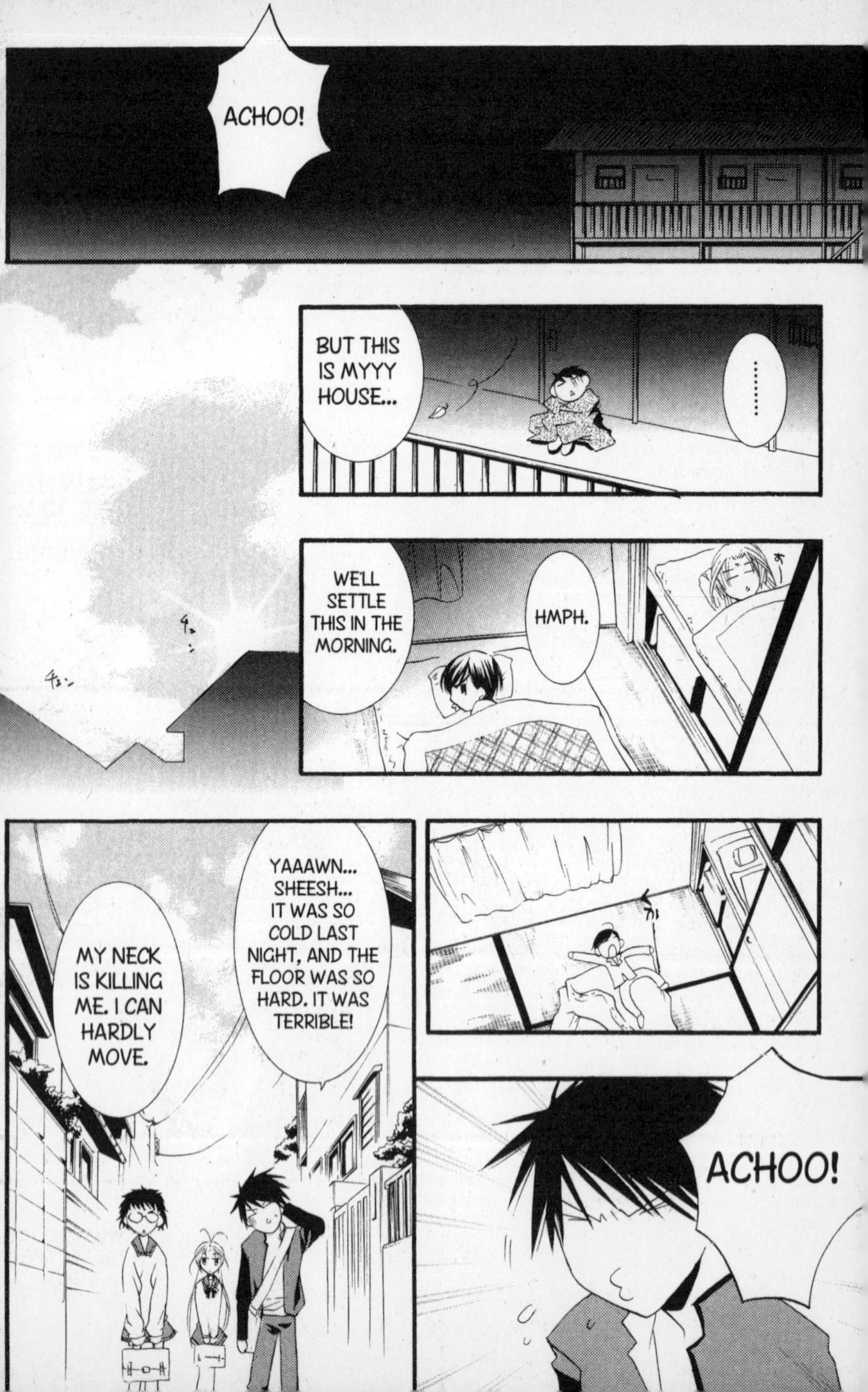
ACHOO!
....
BUT THIS IS MYYY HOUSE...
HMPH.
WE'LL SETTLE THIS IN THE MORNING.
ACHOO!
YAAAWN... SHEESH... IT WAS SO COLD LAST NIGHT, AND THE FLOOR WAS SO HARD. IT WAS TERRIBLE!
MY NECK IS KILLING ME. I CAN HARDLY MOVE.

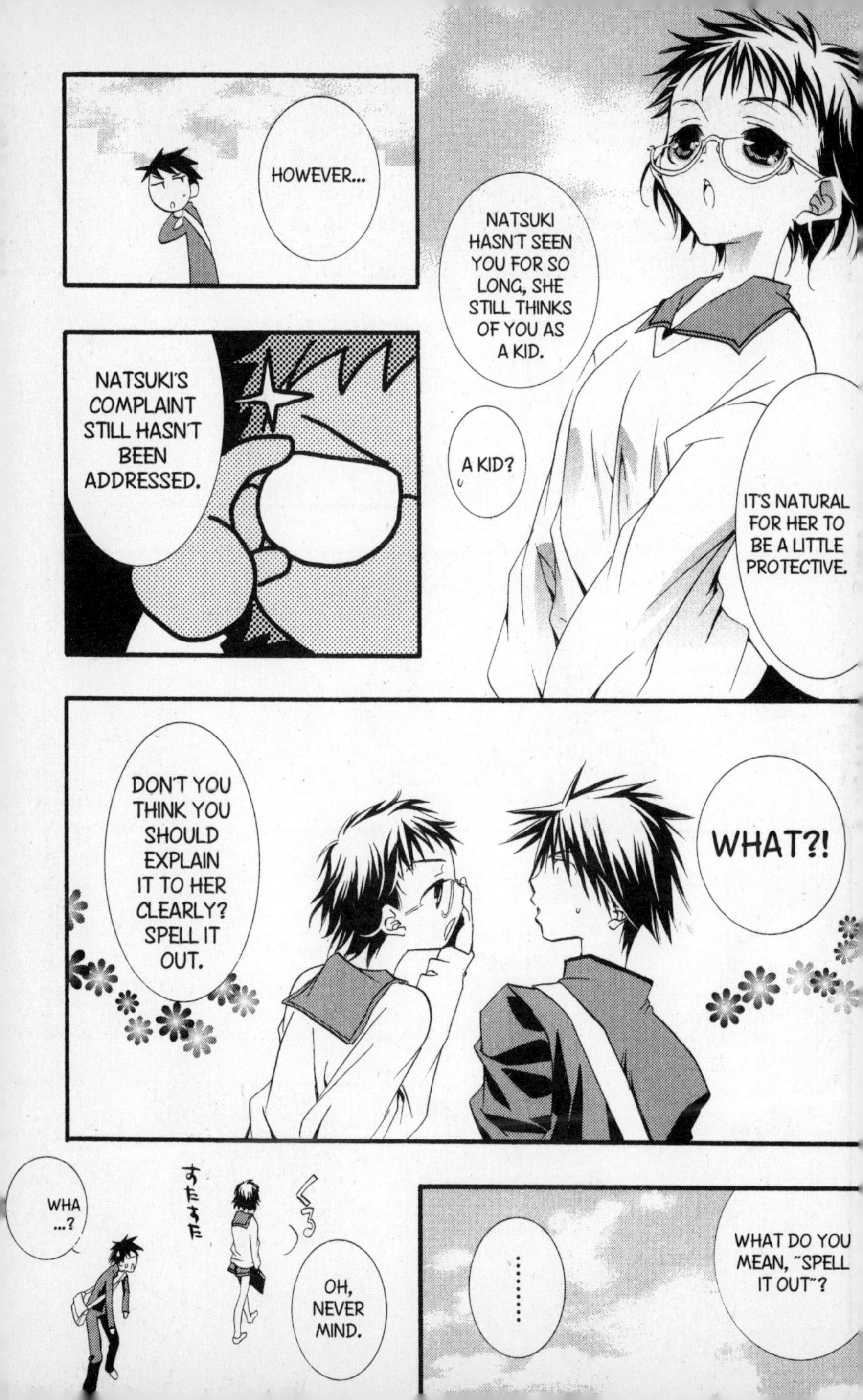
NATSUKI HASN'T SEEN YOU FOR SO LONG, SHE STILL THINKS OF YOU AS A KID.
A KID?
IT'S NATURAL FOR HER TO BE A LITTLE PROTECTIVE.
HOWEVER...
NATSUKI'S COMPLAINT STILL HASN'T BEEN ADDRESSED.
DON'T YOU THINK YOU SHOULD EXPLAIN IT TO HER CLEARLY? SPELL IT OUT.
WHAT?!
WHAT DO YOU MEAN, "SPELL IT OUT"?
......
OH, NEVER MIND.
くる
すたすた
WHA ...?

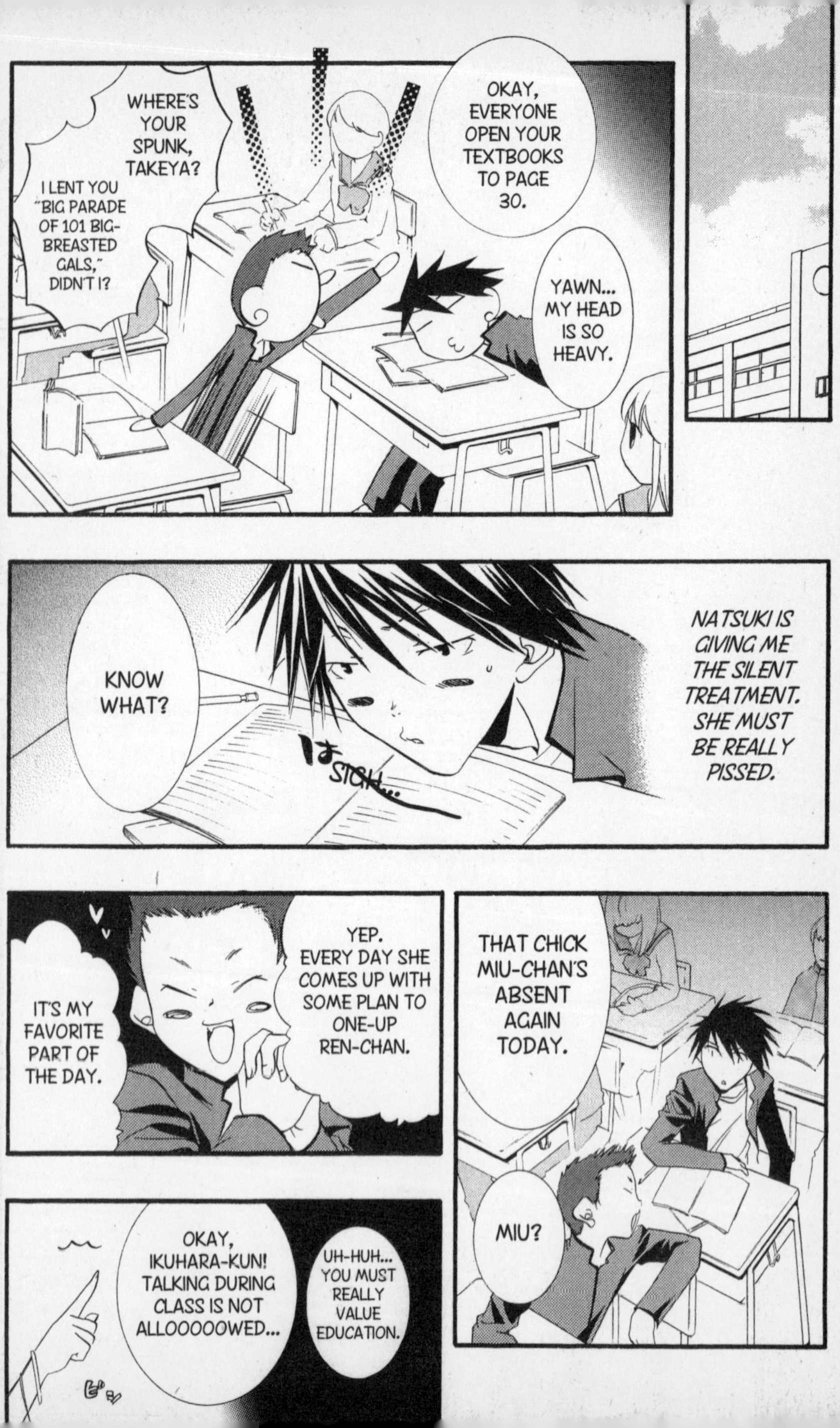
OKAY, EVERYONE OPEN YOUR TEXTBOOKS TO PAGE 30.
YAWN... MY HEAD IS SO HEAVY.
WHERE'S YOUR SPUNK, TAKEYA?
I LENT YOU "BIG PARADE OF 101 BIG-BREASTED GALS," DIDN'T I?
NATSUKI IS GIVING ME THE SILENT TREATMENT. SHE MUST BE REALLY PISSED.
は SIGH...
KNOW WHAT?
THAT CHICK MIU-CHAN'S ABSENT AGAIN TODAY.
MIU?
YEP. EVERY DAY SHE COMES UP WITH SOME PLAN TO ONE-UP REN-CHAN.
IT'S MY FAVORITE PART OF THE DAY.
UH-HUH... YOU MUST REALLY VALUE EDUCATION.
OKAY, IKUHARA-KUN! TALKING DURING CLASS IS NOT ALLOOOOOWED...

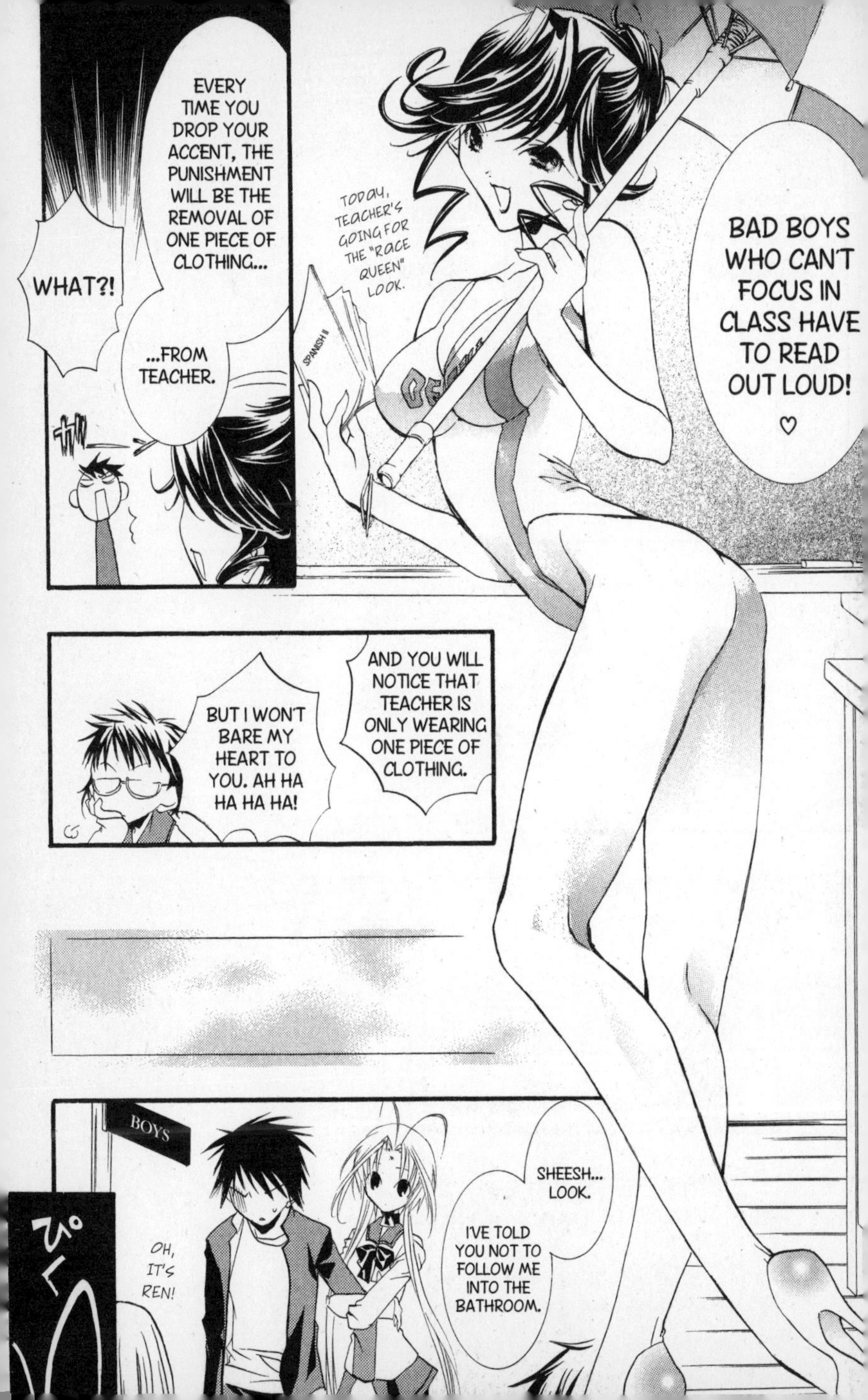
BAD BOYS WHO CAN'T FOCUS IN CLASS HAVE TO READ OUT LOUD! ♡
TODAY, TEACHER'S GOING FOR THE "RACE QUEEN" LOOK.
SPANISH II
EVERY TIME YOU DROP YOUR ACCENT, THE PUNISHMENT WILL BE THE REMOVAL OF ONE PIECE OF CLOTHING...
WHAT?!
...FROM TEACHER.
AND YOU WILL NOTICE THAT TEACHER IS ONLY WEARING ONE PIECE OF CLOTHING.
BUT I WON'T BARE MY HEART TO YOU. AH HA HA HA HA!
BOYS
SHEESH... LOOK.
I'VE TOLD YOU NOT TO FOLLOW ME INTO THE BATHROOM.
OH, IT'S REN!

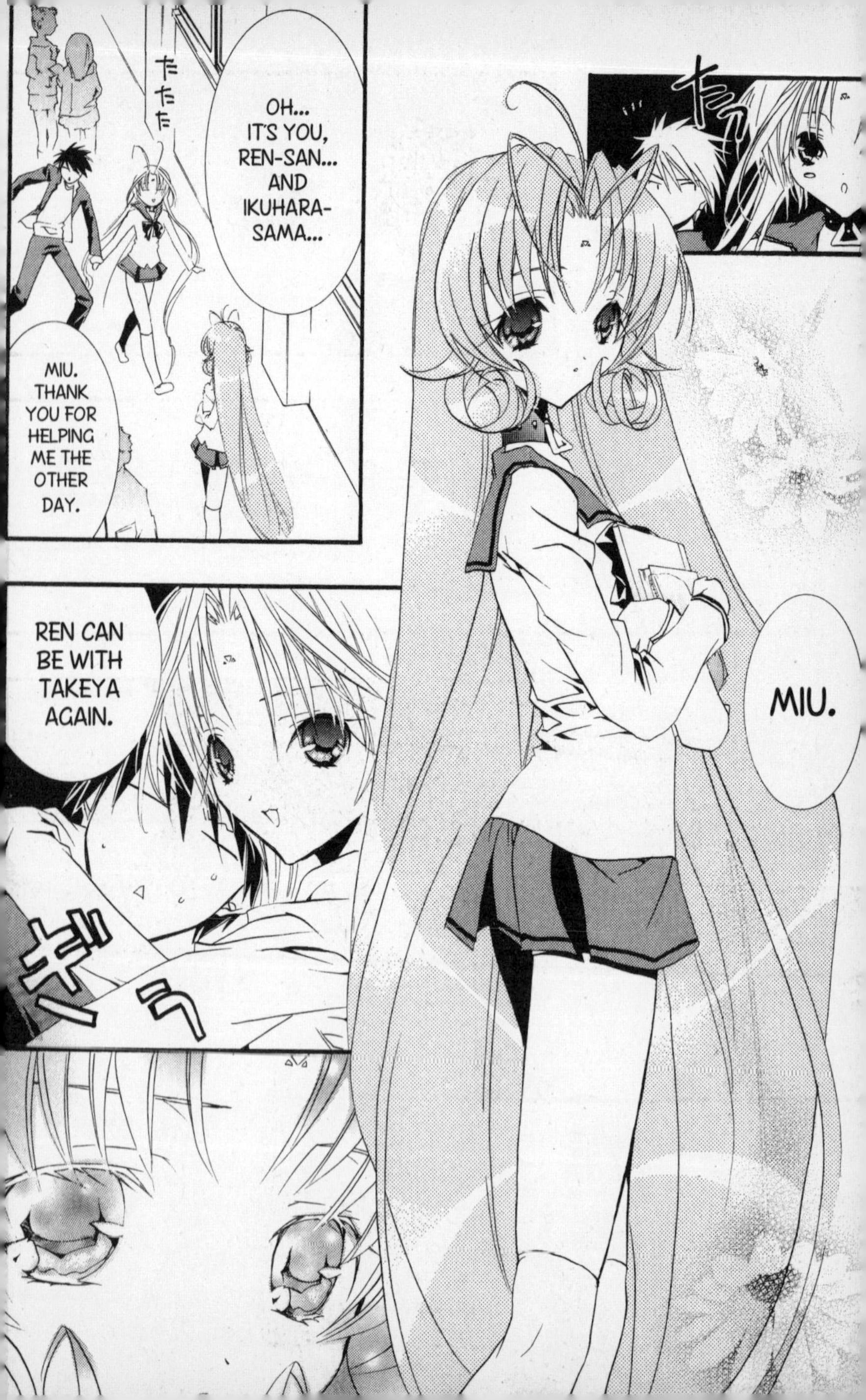
MIU.
OH... IT'S YOU, REN-SAN... AND IKUHARA-SAMA...
たたた
MIU. THANK YOU FOR HELPING ME THE OTHER DAY.
REN CAN BE WITH TAKEYA AGAIN.

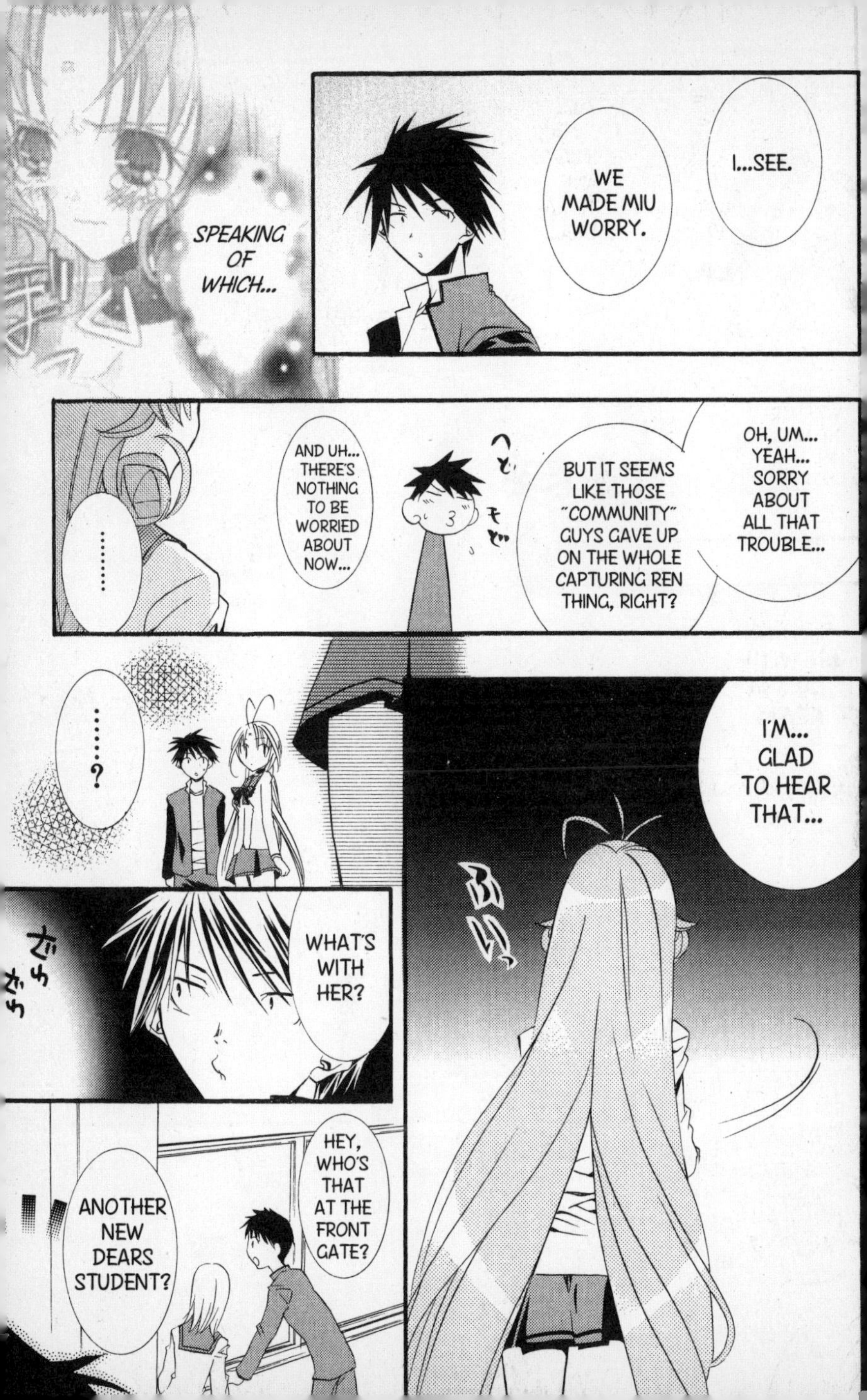
I...SEE.
WE MADE MIU WORRY.
SPEAKING OF WHICH...
OH, UM... YEAH... SORRY ABOUT ALL THAT TROUBLE...
BUT IT SEEMS LIKE THOSE "COMMUNITY" GUYS GAVE UP ON THE WHOLE CAPTURING REN THING, RIGHT?
AND UH... THERE'S NOTHING TO BE WORRIED ABOUT NOW...
......
I'M... GLAD TO HEAR THAT...
......?
WHAT'S WITH HER?
HEY, WHO'S THAT AT THE FRONT GATE?
ANOTHER NEW DEARS STUDENT?

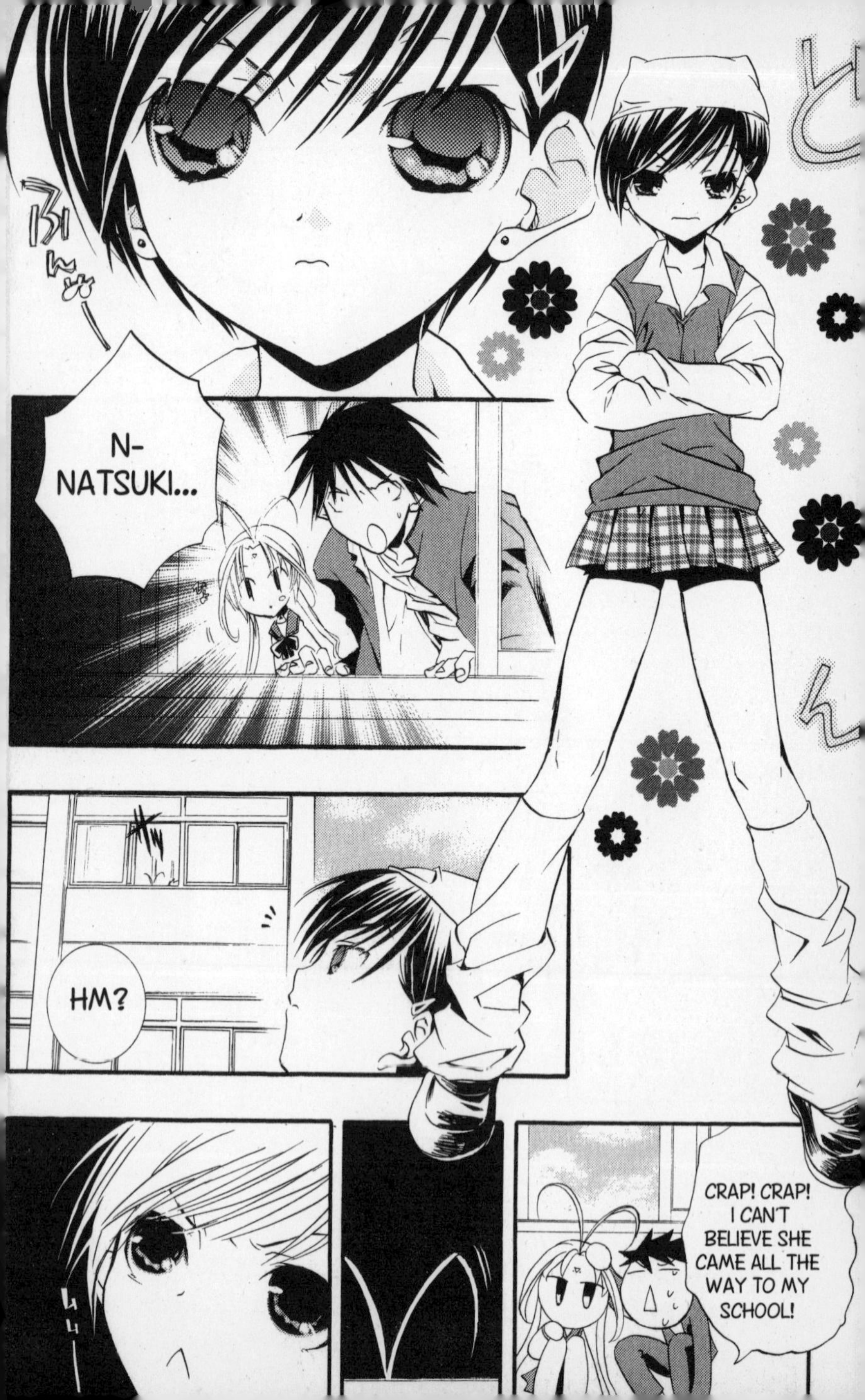
N-NATSUKI...
HM?
CRAP! CRAP! I CAN'T BELIEVE SHE CAME ALL THE WAY TO MY SCHOOL!

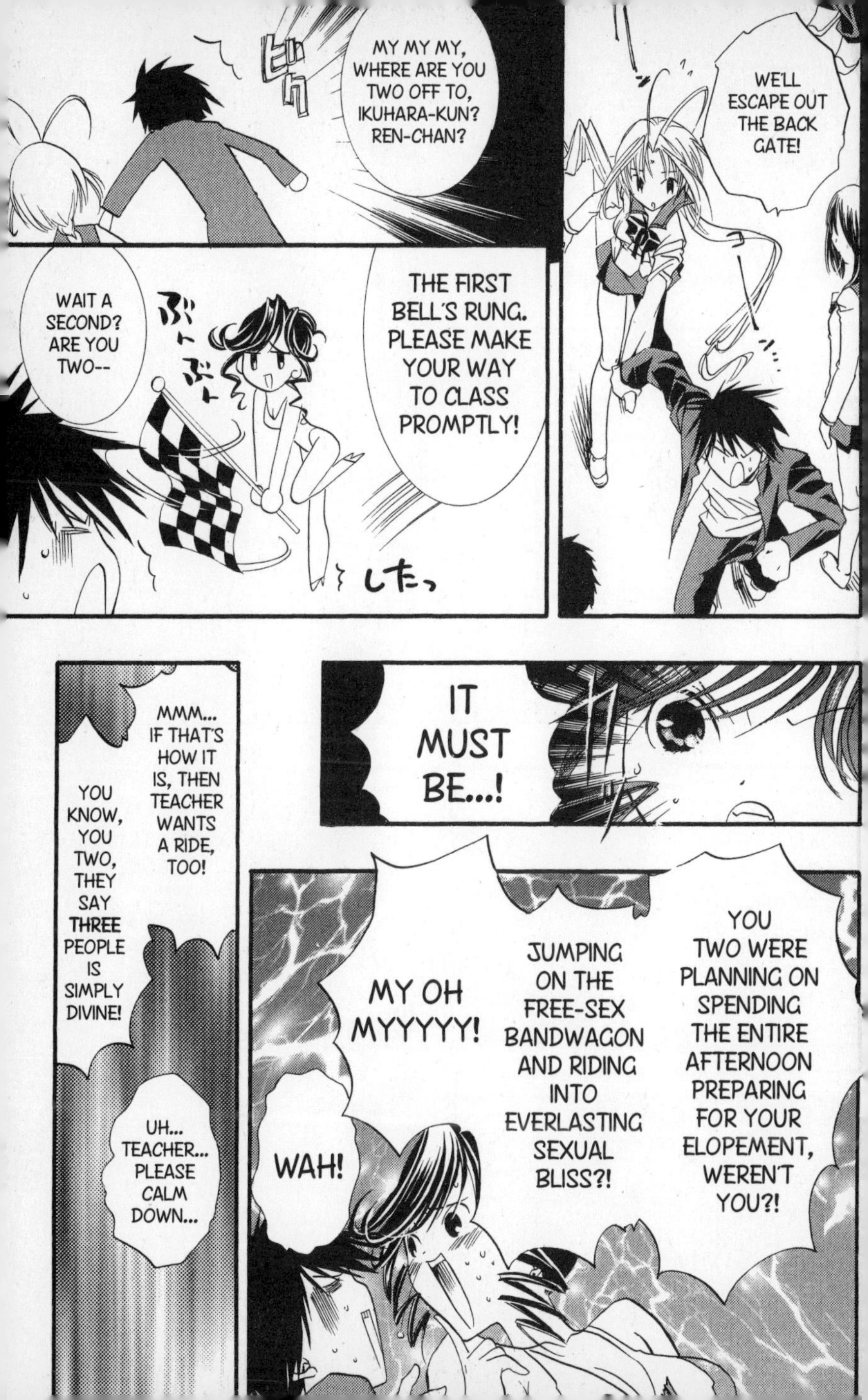
WE'LL ESCAPE OUT THE BACK GATE!
MY MY MY, WHERE ARE YOU TWO OFF TO, IKUHARA-KUN? REN-CHAN?
THE FIRST BELL'S RUNG. PLEASE MAKE YOUR WAY TO CLASS PROMPTLY!
WAIT A SECOND? ARE YOU TWO--
したっ
IT MUST BE...!
YOU TWO WERE PLANNING ON SPENDING THE ENTIRE AFTERNOON PREPARING FOR YOUR ELOPEMENT, WEREN'T YOU?!
JUMPING ON THE FREE-SEX BANDWAGON AND RIDING INTO EVERLASTING SEXUAL BLISS?!
MY OH MYYYYY!
WAH!
MMM... IF THAT'S HOW IT IS, THEN TEACHER WANTS A RIDE, TOO!
YOU KNOW, YOU TWO, THEY SAY THREE PEOPLE IS SIMPLY DIVINE!
UH... TEACHER... PLEASE CALM DOWN...

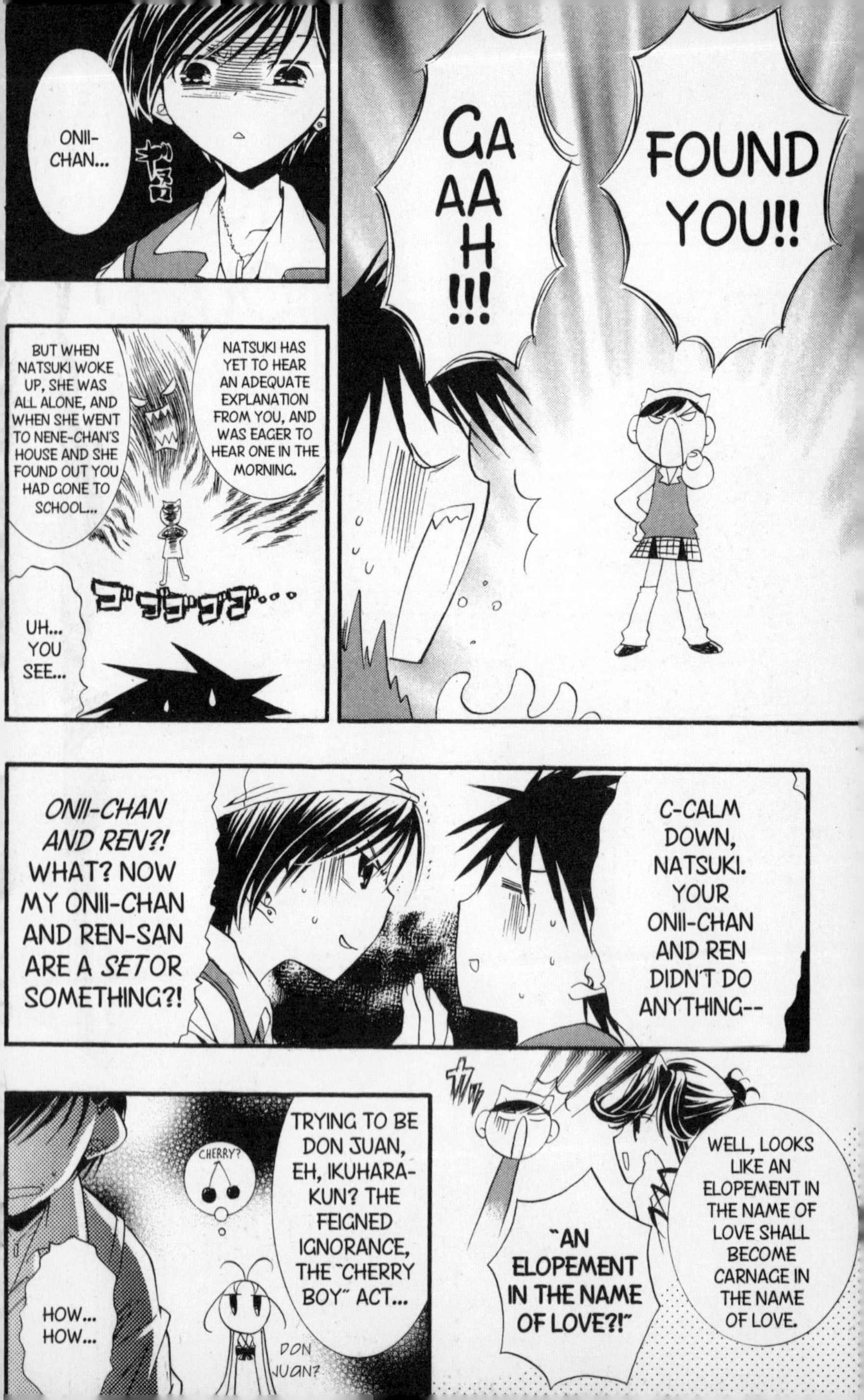
FOUND YOU!!
GAAAH!!!
ONII-CHAN...
NATSUKI HAS YET TO HEAR AN ADEQUATE EXPLANATION FROM YOU, AND WAS EAGER TO HEAR ONE IN THE MORNING.
BUT WHEN NATSUKI WOKE UP, SHE WAS ALL ALONE, AND WHEN SHE WENT TO NENE-CHAN'S HOUSE AND SHE FOUND OUT YOU HAD GONE TO SCHOOL...
UH... YOU SEE...
C-CALM DOWN, NATSUKI. YOUR ONII-CHAN AND REN DIDN'T DO ANYTHING--
ONII-CHAN AND REN?! WHAT? NOW MY ONII-CHAN AND REN-SAN ARE A SET OR SOMETHING?!
WELL, LOOKS LIKE AN ELOPEMENT IN THE NAME OF LOVE SHALL BECOME CARNAGE IN THE NAME OF LOVE.
"AN ELOPEMENT IN THE NAME OF LOVE?!"
TRYING TO BE DON JUAN, EH, IKUHARA-KUN? THE FEIGNED IGNORANCE, THE "CHERRY BOY" ACT...
CHERRY?
DON JUAN?
HOW... HOW...

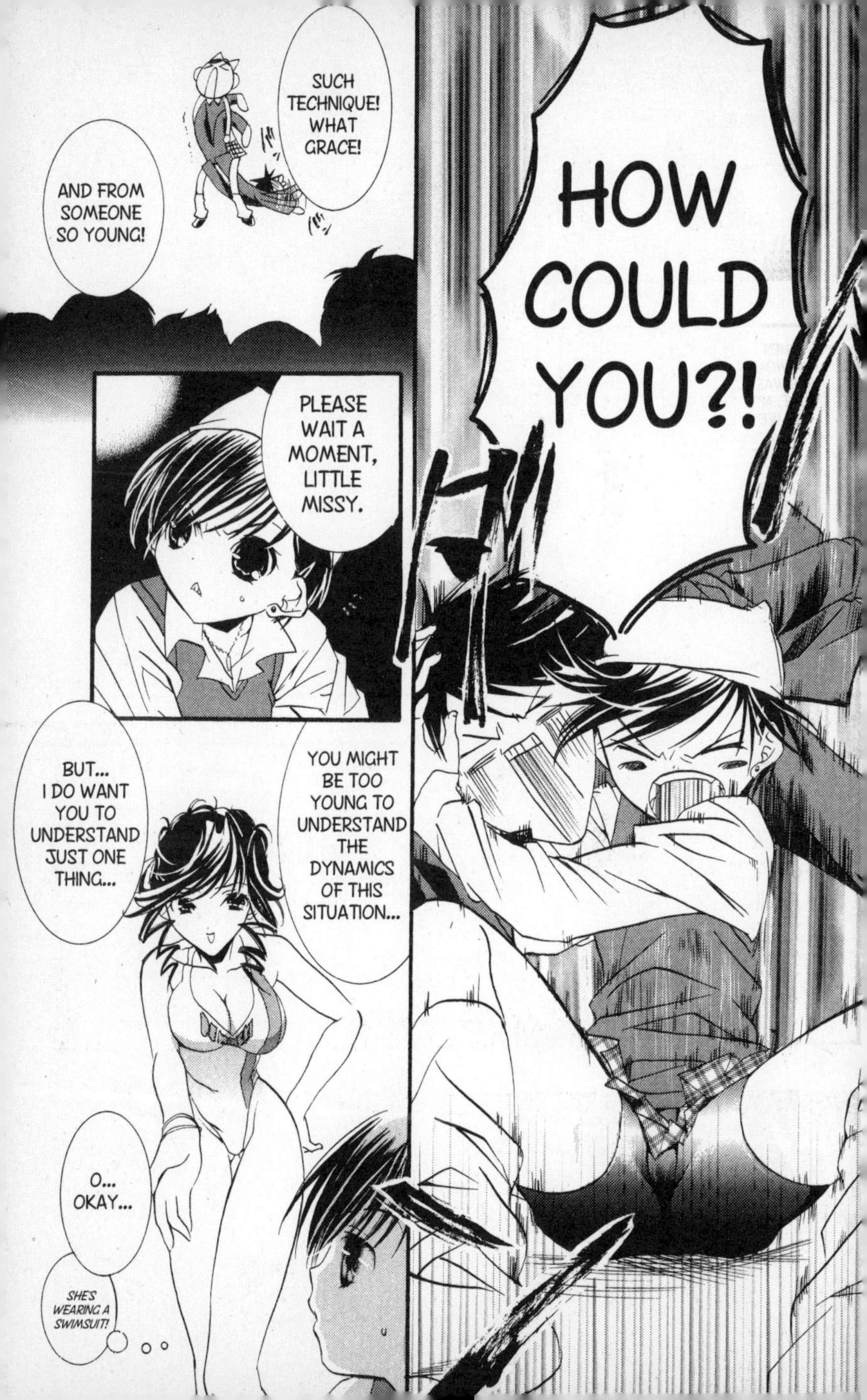
HOW COULD YOU?!
SUCH TECHNIQUE! WHAT GRACE!
AND FROM SOMEONE SO YOUNG!
PLEASE WAIT A MOMENT, LITTLE MISSY.
YOU MIGHT BE TOO YOUNG TO UNDERSTAND THE DYNAMICS OF THIS SITUATION...
BUT... I DO WANT YOU TO UNDERSTAND JUST ONE THING...
O... OKAY...
SHE'S WEARING A SWIMSUIT!

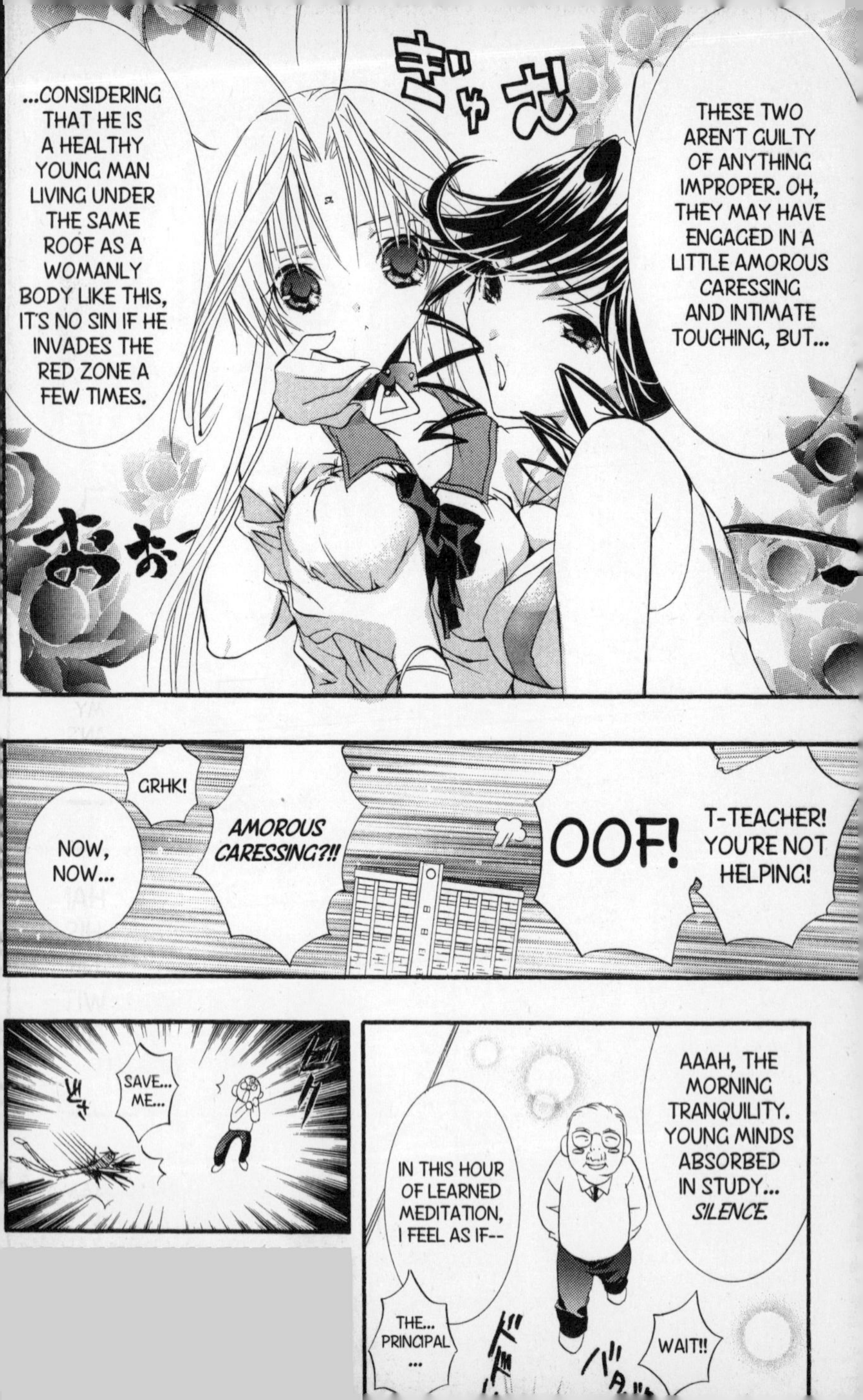
THESE TWO AREN'T GUILTY OF ANYTHING IMPROPER. OH, THEY MAY HAVE ENGAGED IN A LITTLE AMOROUS CARESSING AND INTIMATE TOUCHING, BUT...
ぎゅむ
...CONSIDERING THAT HE IS A HEALTHY YOUNG MAN LIVING UNDER THE SAME ROOF AS A WOMANLY BODY LIKE THIS, IT'S NO SIN IF HE INVADES THE RED ZONE A FEW TIMES.
T-TEACHER! YOU'RE NOT HELPING!
OOF!
AMOROUS CARESSING?!!
GRHK!
NOW, NOW...
AAAH, THE MORNING TRANQUILITY. YOUNG MINDS ABSORBED IN STUDY... SILENCE.
IN THIS HOUR OF LEARNED MEDITATION, I FEEL AS IF--
WAIT!!
THE... PRINCIPAL ...
SAVE... ME...

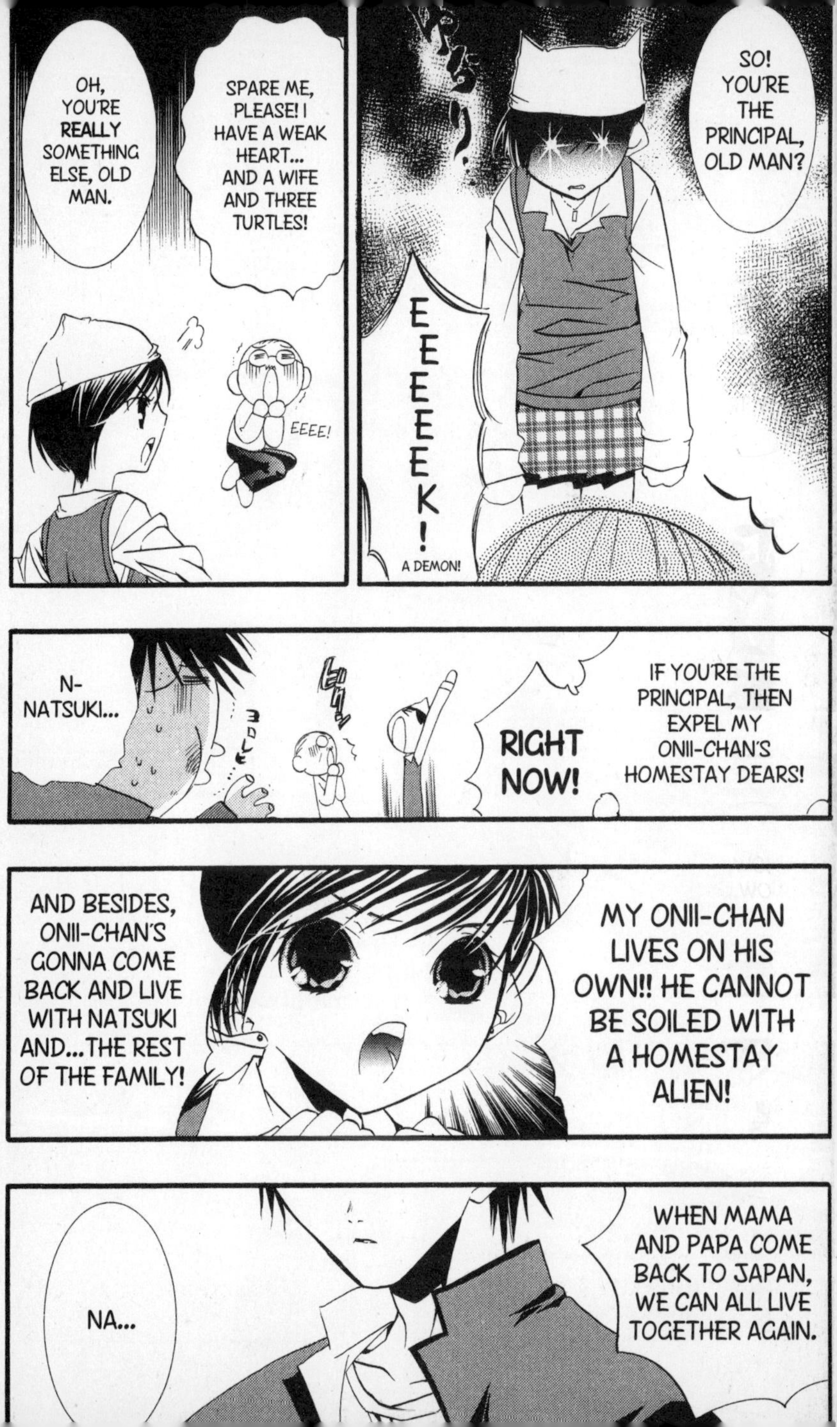
SO! YOU'RE THE PRINCIPAL, OLD MAN?
EEEEEK!
A DEMON!
SPARE ME, PLEASE! I HAVE A WEAK HEART... AND A WIFE AND THREE TURTLES!
OH, YOU'RE REALLY SOMETHING ELSE, OLD MAN.
EEEE!
IF YOU'RE THE PRINCIPAL, THEN EXPEL MY ONII-CHAN'S HOMESTAY DEARS!
RIGHT NOW!
N-NATSUKI...
MY ONII-CHAN LIVES ON HIS OWN!! HE CANNOT BE SOILED WITH A HOMESTAY ALIEN!
AND BESIDES, ONII-CHAN'S GONNA COME BACK AND LIVE WITH NATSUKI AND...THE REST OF THE FAMILY!
WHEN MAMA AND PAPA COME BACK TO JAPAN, WE CAN ALL LIVE TOGETHER AGAIN.
NA...

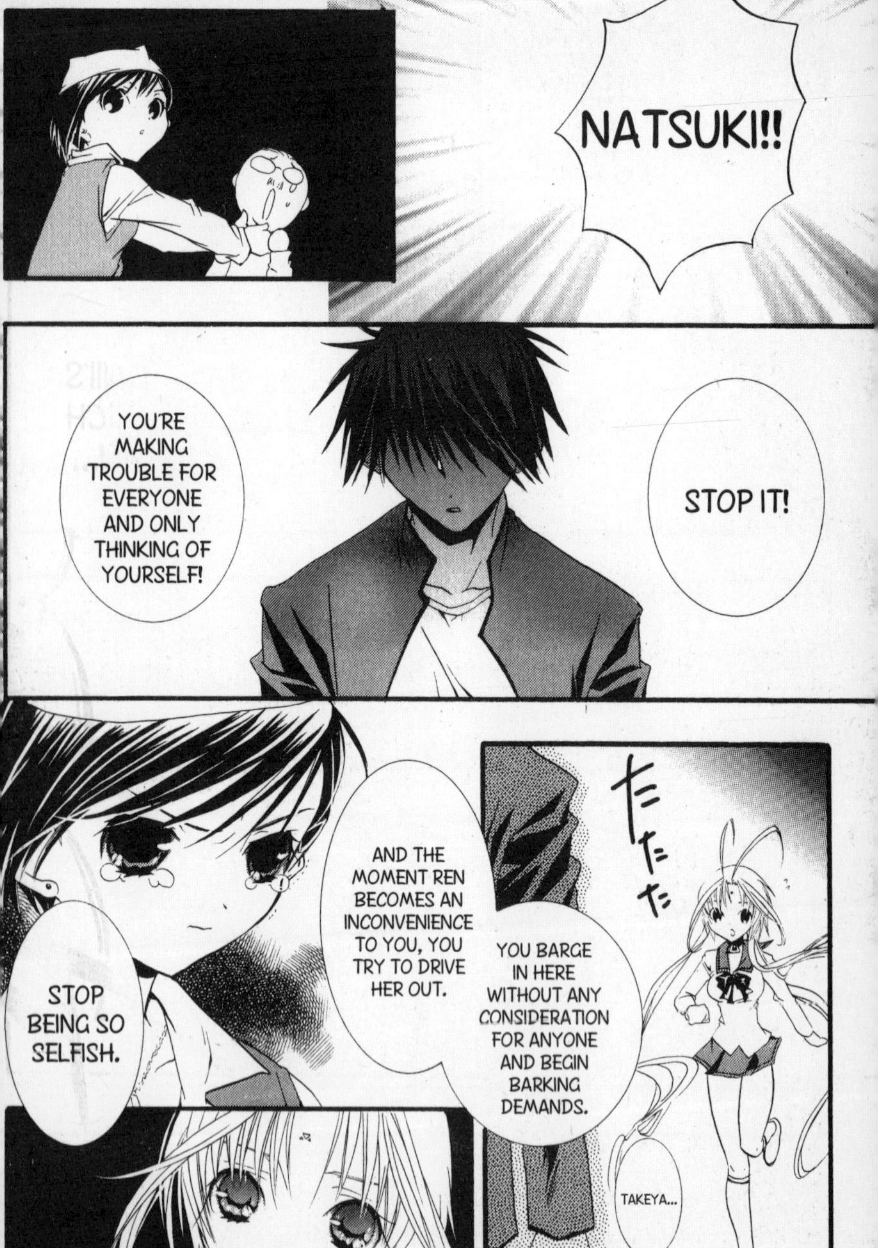
NATSUKI!!
STOP IT!
YOU'RE MAKING TROUBLE FOR EVERYONE AND ONLY THINKING OF YOURSELF!
たたた
TAKEYA...
YOU BARGE IN HERE WITHOUT ANY CONSIDERATION FOR ANYONE AND BEGIN BARKING DEMANDS.
AND THE MOMENT REN BECOMES AN INCONVENIENCE TO YOU, YOU TRY TO DRIVE HER OUT.
STOP BEING SO SELFISH.

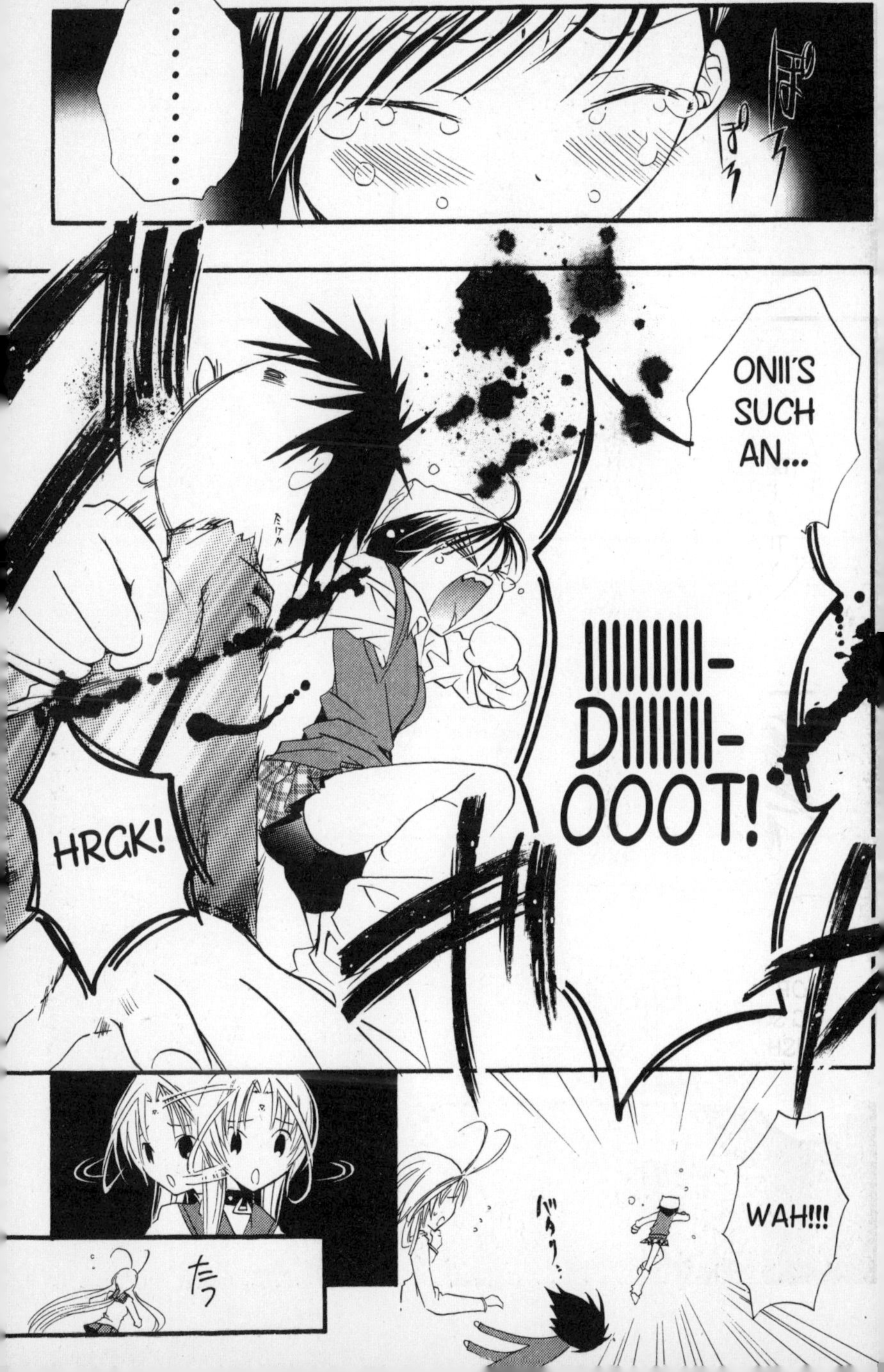
......
ONII'S SUCH AN...
IIIIIIIIII-DIIIIIII-OOOT!
HRGK!
WAH!!!
たっ

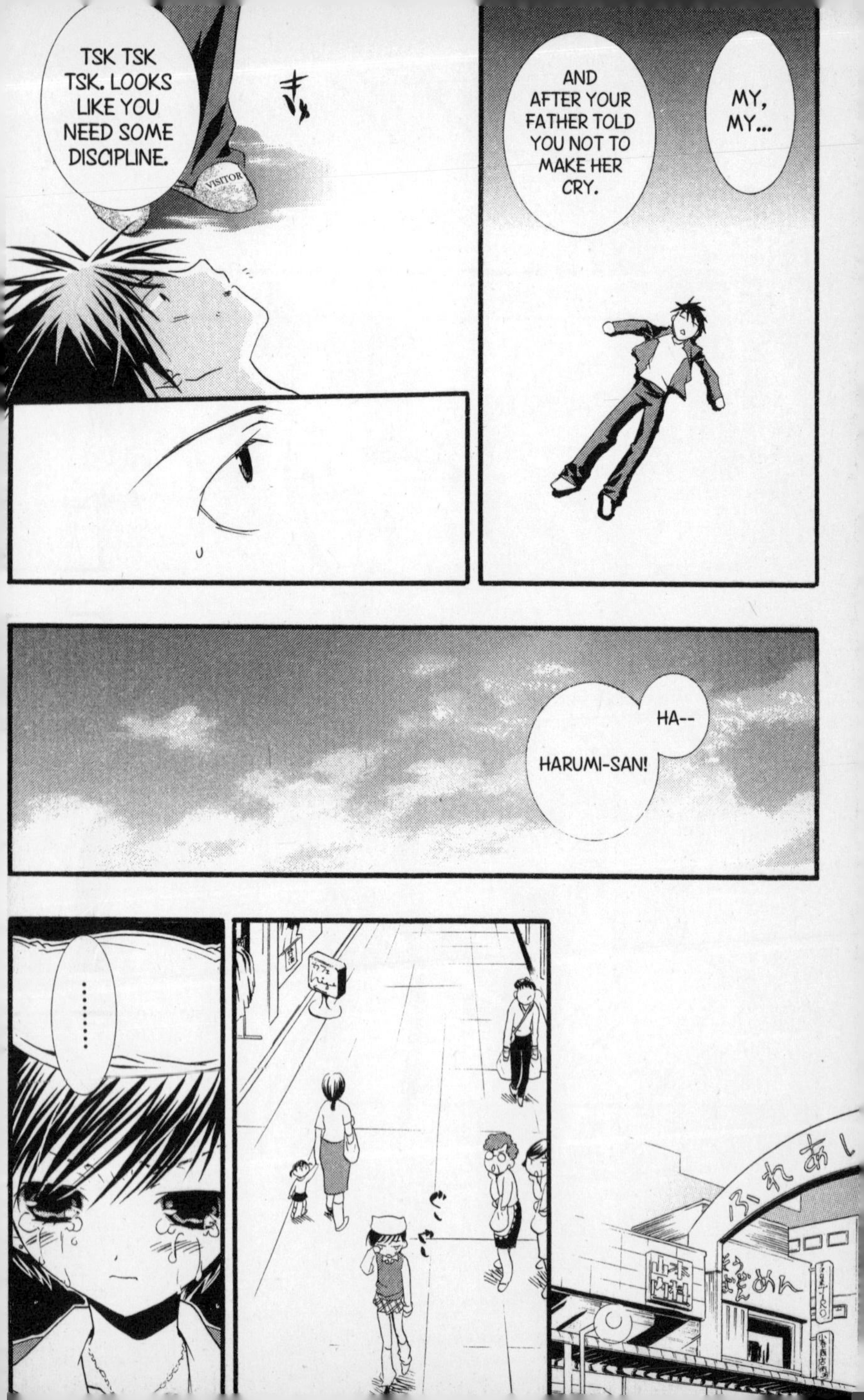
MY, MY...
AND AFTER YOUR FATHER TOLD YOU NOT TO MAKE HER CRY.
TSK TSK TSK. LOOKS LIKE YOU NEED SOME DISCIPLINE.
VISITOR
HA--
HARUMI-SAN!
......

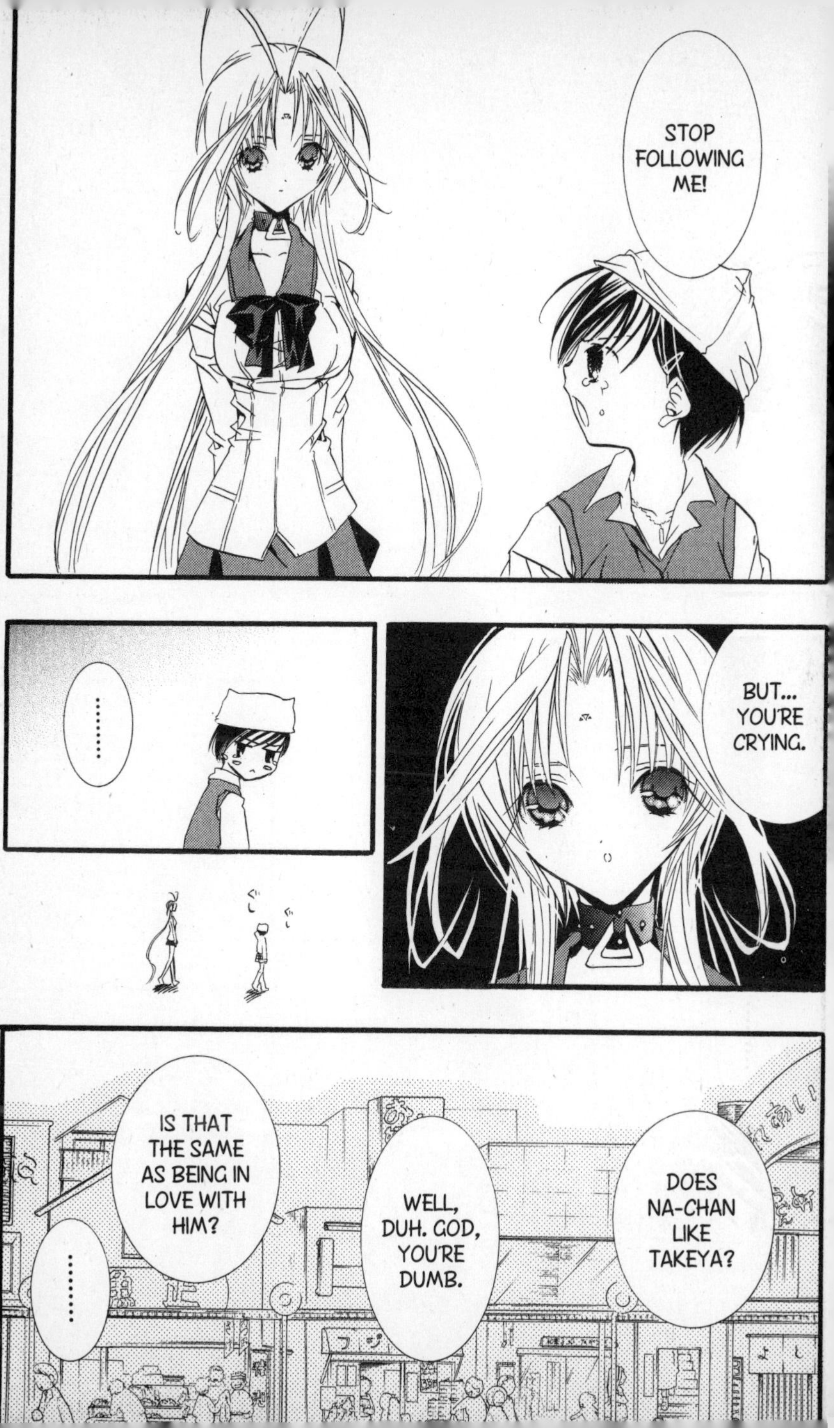
STOP FOLLOWING ME!
BUT... YOU'RE CRYING.
......
DOES NA-CHAN LIKE TAKEYA?
WELL, DUH. GOD, YOU'RE DUMB.
IS THAT THE SAME AS BEING IN LOVE WITH HIM?
......

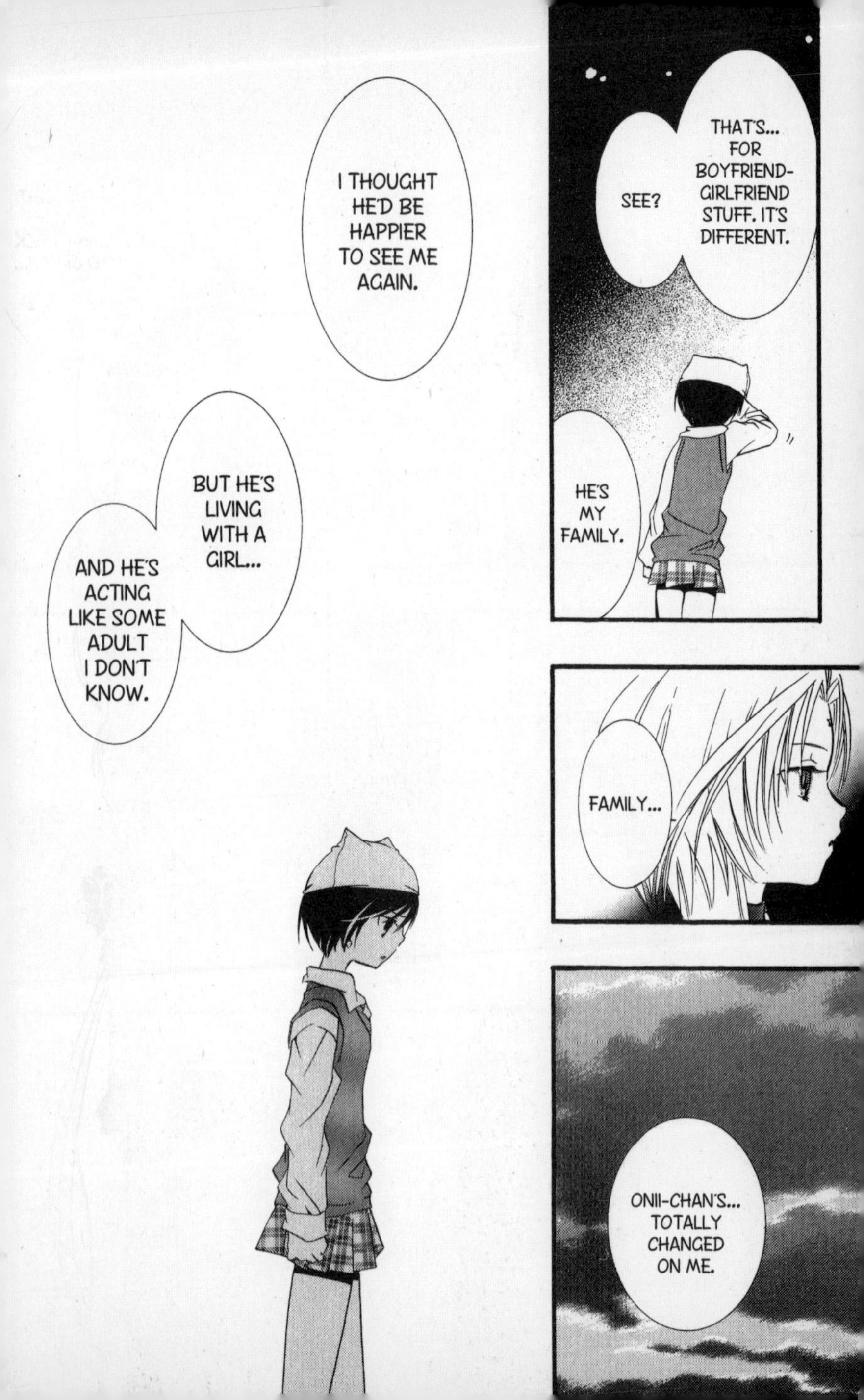
THAT'S... FOR BOYFRIEND-GIRLFRIEND STUFF. IT'S DIFFERENT.
SEE?
HE'S MY FAMILY.
FAMILY...
ONII-CHAN'S... TOTALLY CHANGED ON ME.
I THOUGHT HE'D BE HAPPIER TO SEE ME AGAIN.
BUT HE'S LIVING WITH A GIRL...
AND HE'S ACTING LIKE SOME ADULT I DON'T KNOW.

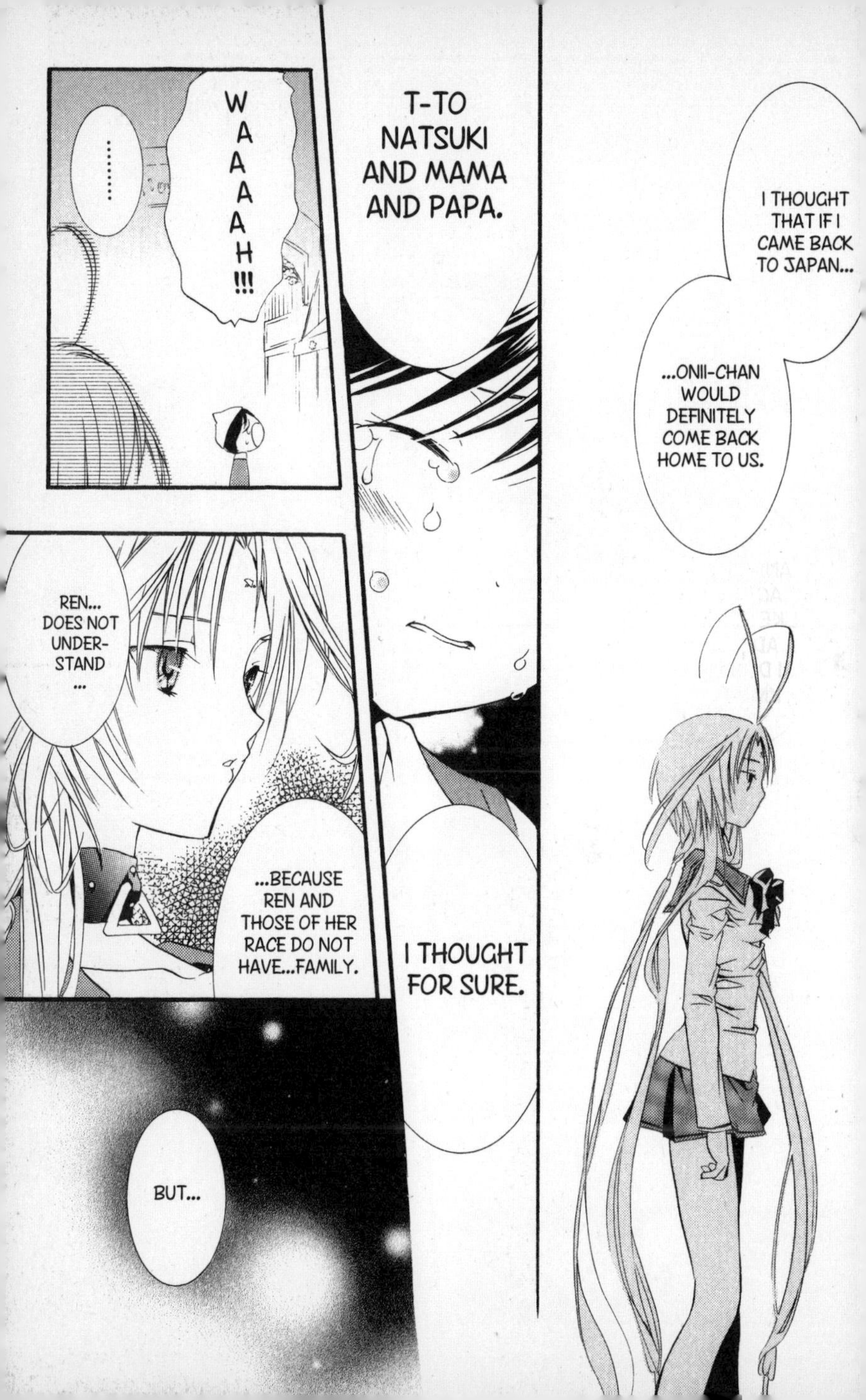
I THOUGHT THAT IF I CAME BACK TO JAPAN...
...ONII-CHAN WOULD DEFINITELY COME BACK HOME TO US.
T-TO NATSUKI AND MAMA AND PAPA.
I THOUGHT FOR SURE.
WAAAAH!!!
......
REN... DOES NOT UNDER-STAND...
...BECAUSE REN AND THOSE OF HER RACE DO NOT HAVE...FAMILY.
BUT...

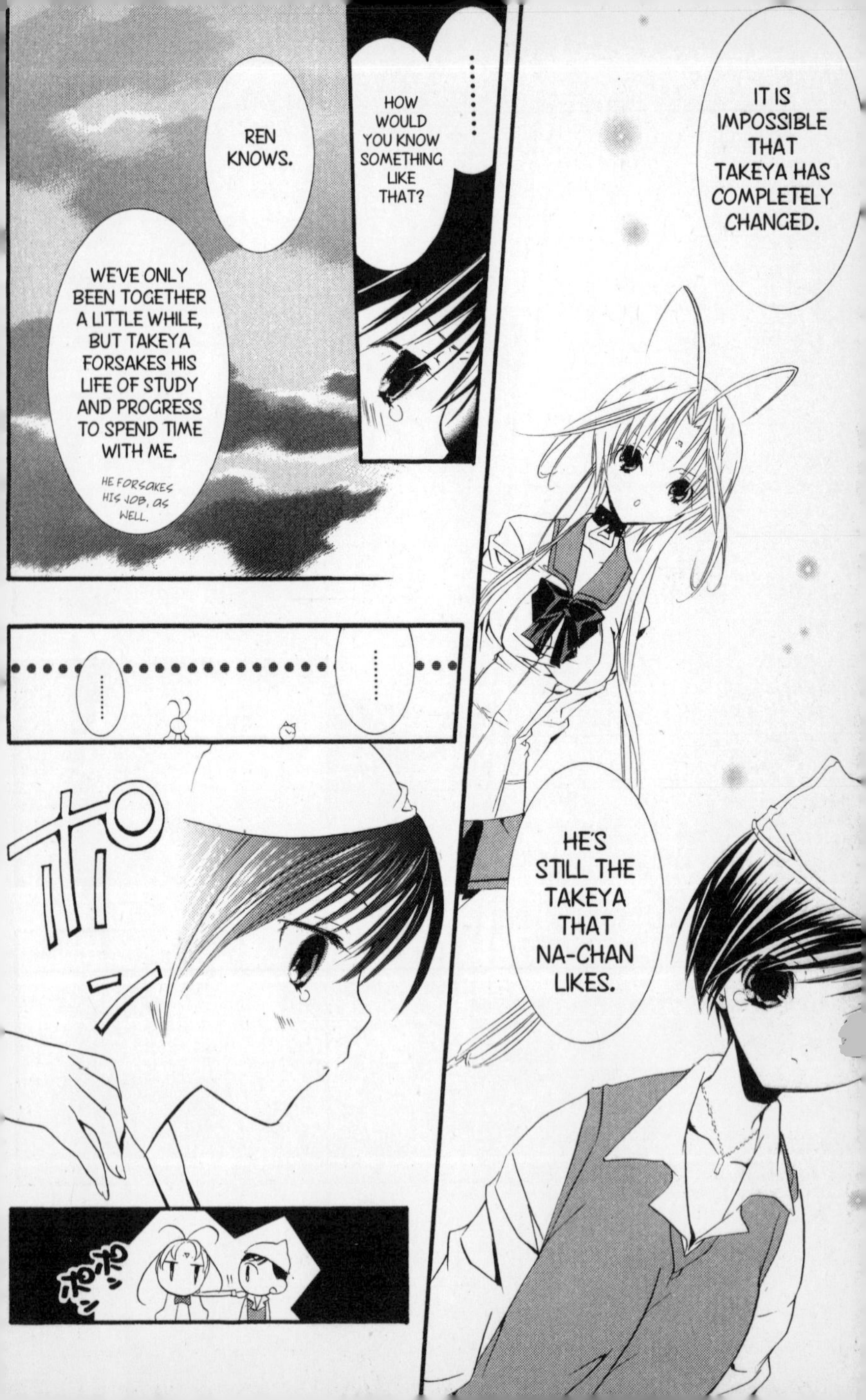
IT IS IMPOSSIBLE THAT TAKEYA HAS COMPLETELY CHANGED.
HE'S STILL THE TAKEYA THAT NA-CHAN LIKES.
......
HOW WOULD YOU KNOW SOMETHING LIKE THAT?
REN KNOWS.
WE'VE ONLY BEEN TOGETHER A LITTLE WHILE, BUT TAKEYA FORSAKES HIS LIFE OF STUDY AND PROGRESS TO SPEND TIME WITH ME.
HE FORSAKES HIS JOB, AS WELL.
......
......
ポン
ポンポン

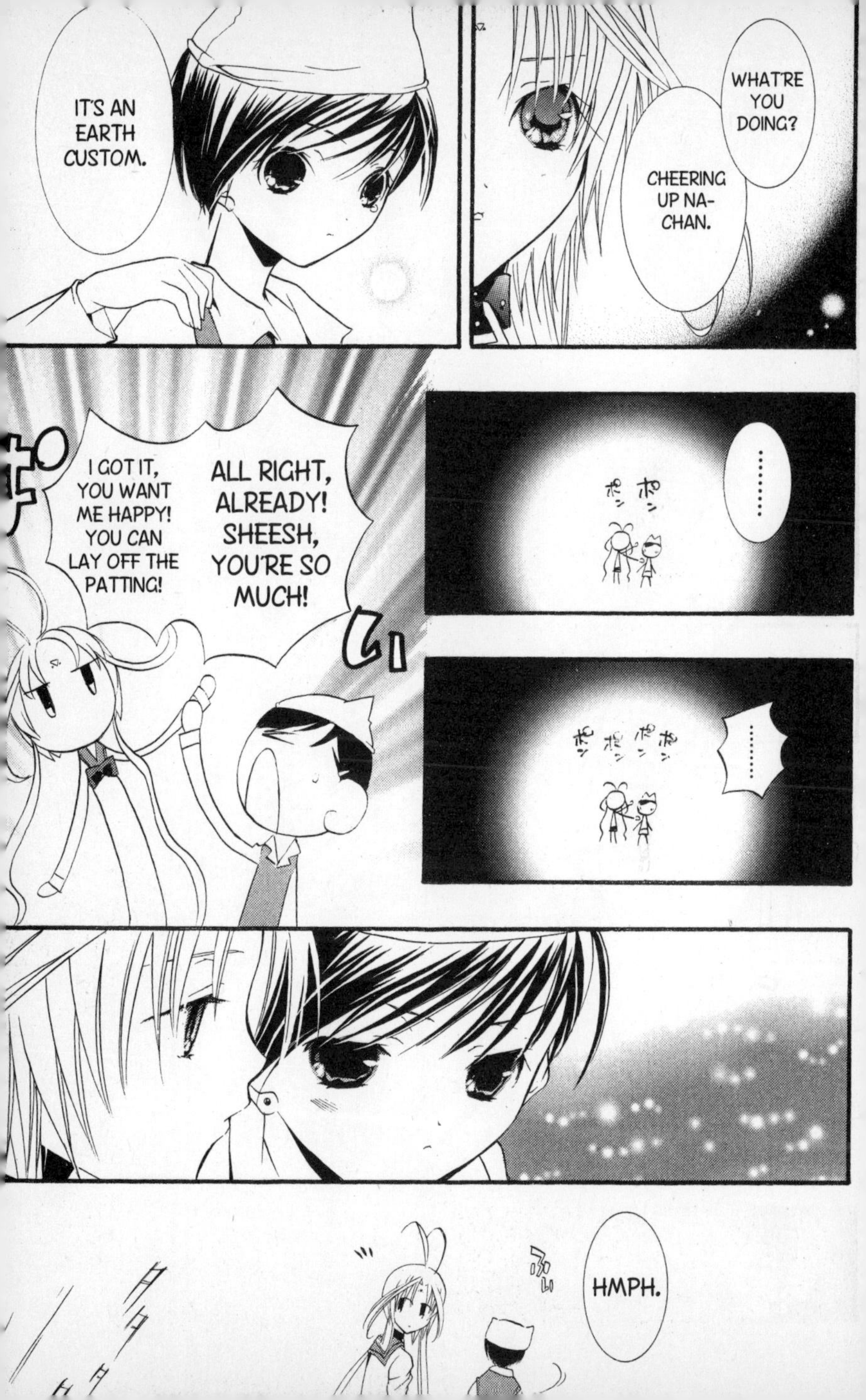
WHAT'RE YOU DOING?
CHEERING UP NA-CHAN.
IT'S AN EARTH CUSTOM.
......
ポン ポン
......
ポン ポン ポン ポン
ALL RIGHT, ALREADY! SHEESH, YOU'RE SO MUCH!
I GOT IT, YOU WANT ME HAPPY! YOU CAN LAY OFF THE PATTING!
HMPH.

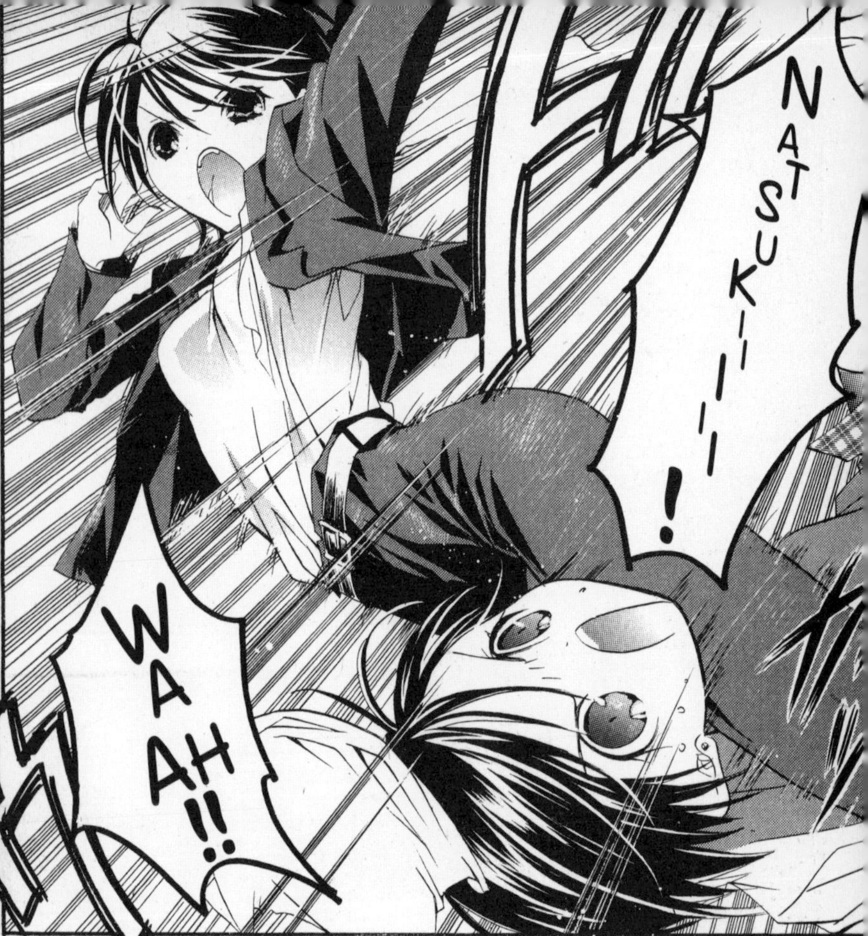
NATSUKIIII!
WAAAH!!

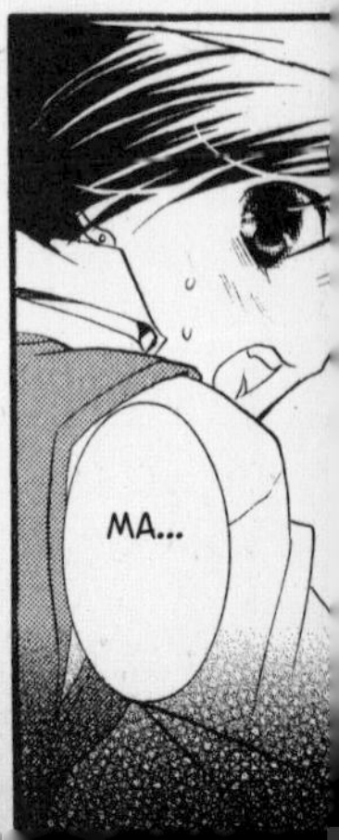
MA...

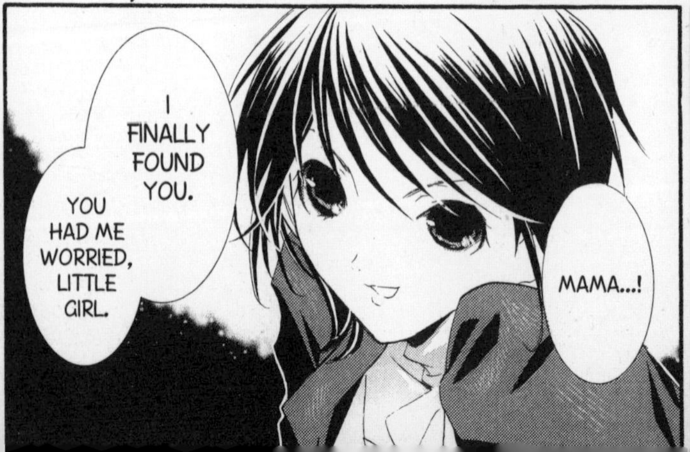
MAMA...!
I FINALLY FOUND YOU.
YOU HAD ME WORRIED, LITTLE GIRL.

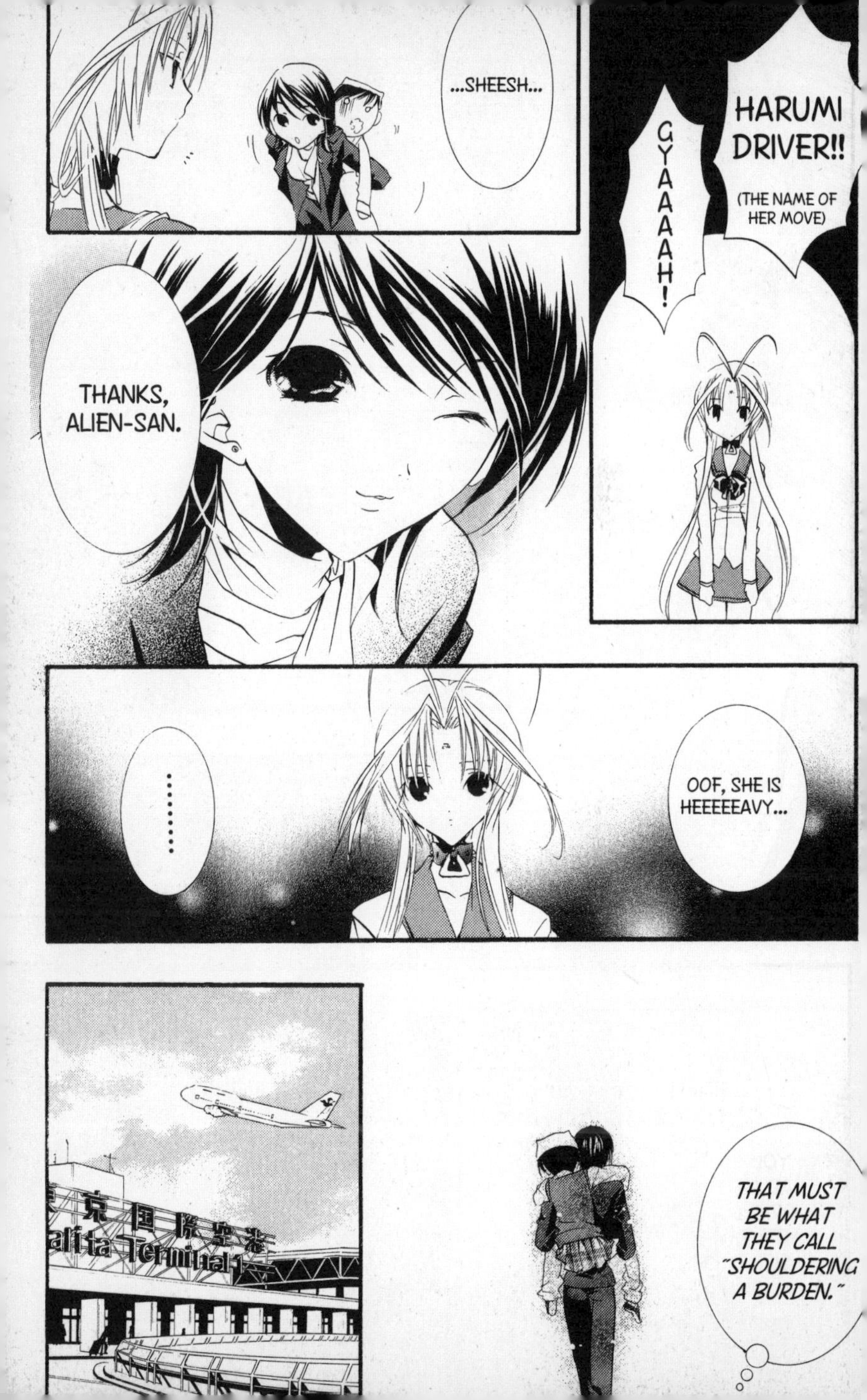
HARUMI DRIVER!!
(THE NAME OF HER MOVE)
GYAAAAAH!
...SHEESH...
THANKS, ALIEN-SAN.
OOF, SHE IS HEEEEEAVY...
....
THAT MUST BE WHAT THEY CALL "SHOULDERING A BURDEN."

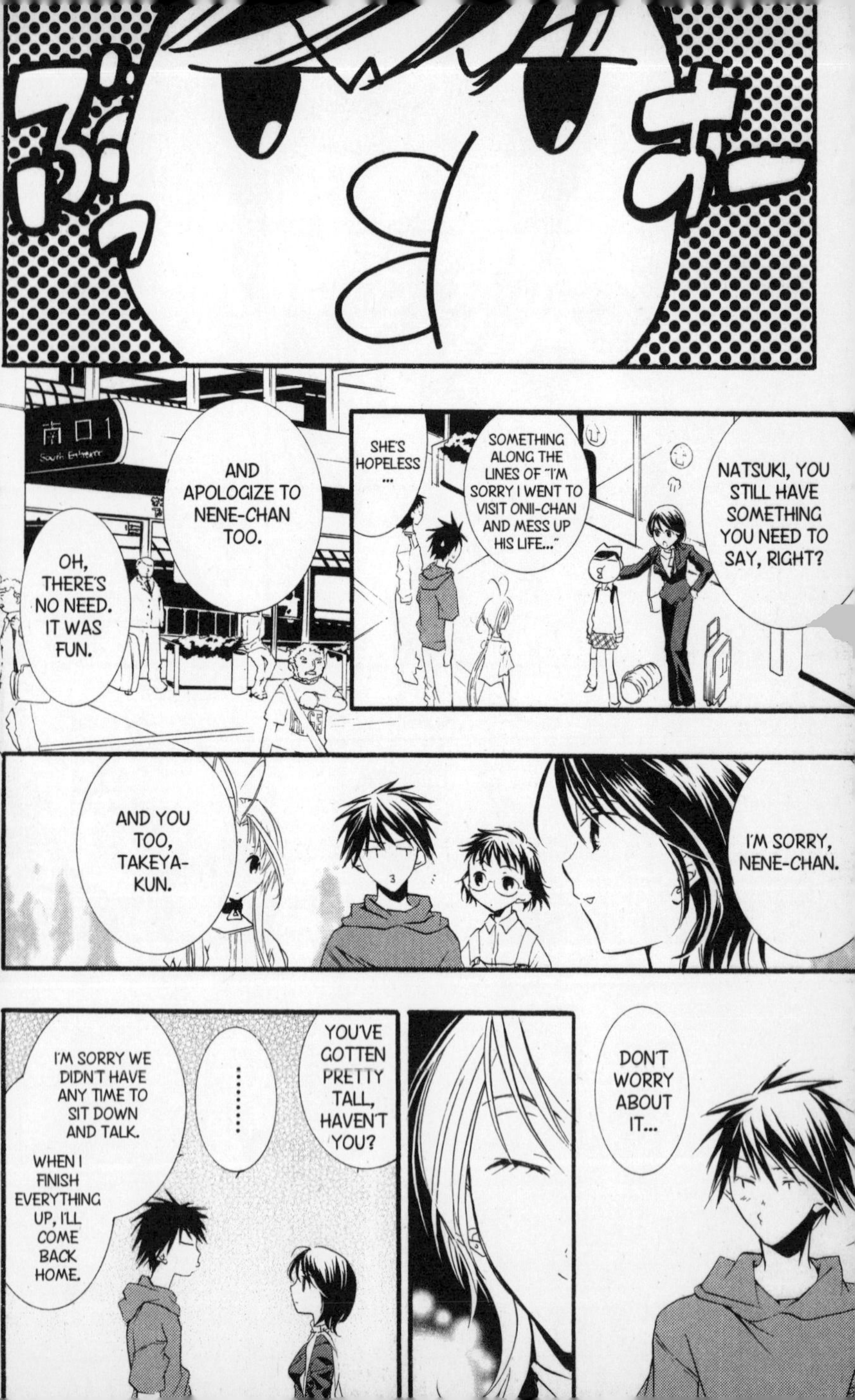
ぷっ
NATSUKI, YOU STILL HAVE SOMETHING YOU NEED TO SAY, RIGHT?
SOMETHING ALONG THE LINES OF "I'M SORRY I WENT TO VISIT ONII-CHAN AND MESS UP HIS LIFE..."
SHE'S HOPELESS ...
南口1
AND APOLOGIZE TO NENE-CHAN TOO.
OH, THERE'S NO NEED. IT WAS FUN.
I'M SORRY, NENE-CHAN.
AND YOU TOO, TAKEYA-KUN.
DON'T WORRY ABOUT IT...
YOU'VE GOTTEN PRETTY TALL, HAVEN'T YOU?
......
I'M SORRY WE DIDN'T HAVE ANY TIME TO SIT DOWN AND TALK.
WHEN I FINISH EVERYTHING UP, I'LL COME BACK HOME.

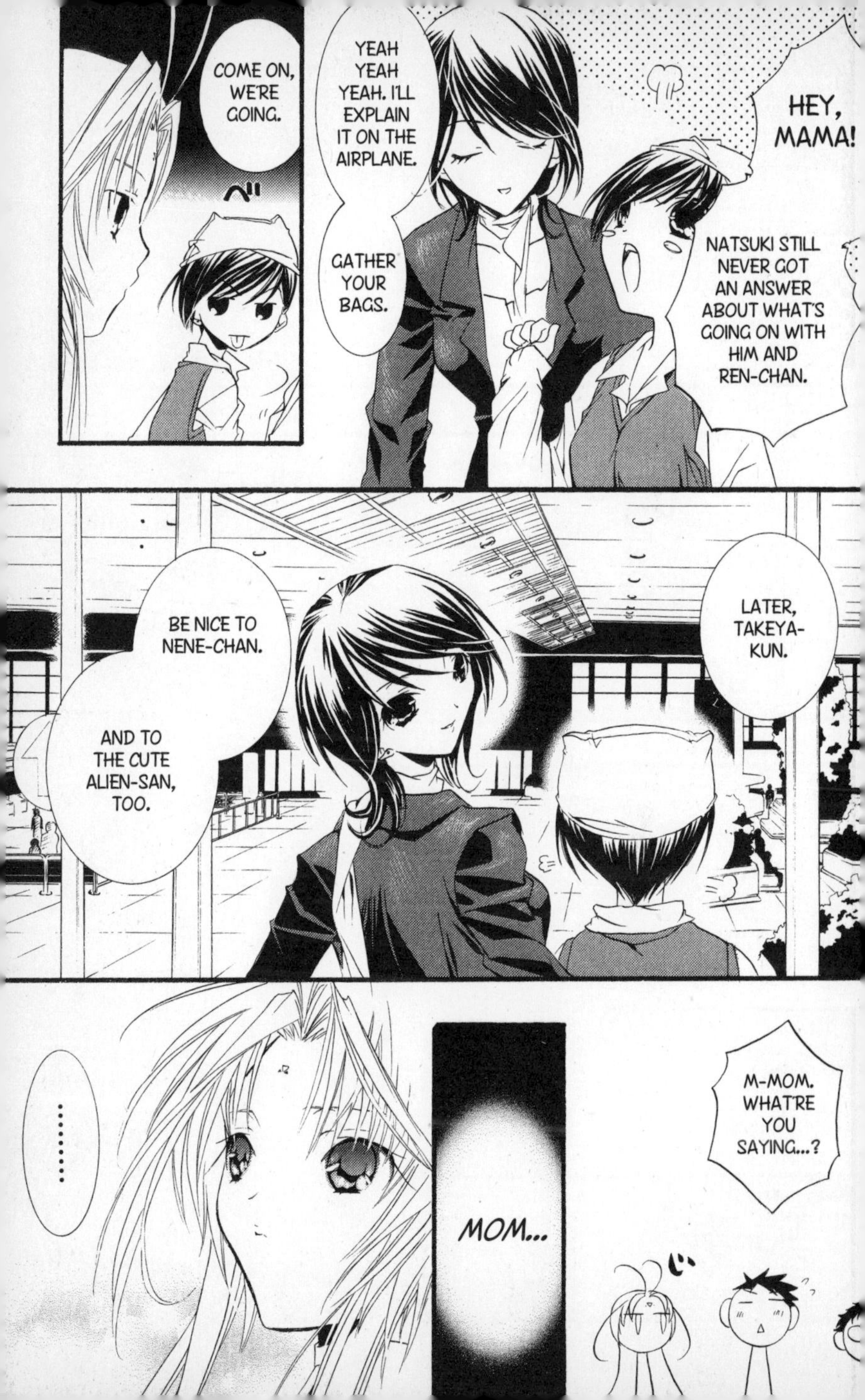
HEY, MAMA!
NATSUKI STILL NEVER GOT AN ANSWER ABOUT WHAT'S GOING ON WITH HIM AND REN-CHAN.
YEAH YEAH YEAH. I'LL EXPLAIN IT ON THE AIRPLANE.
GATHER YOUR BAGS.
COME ON, WE'RE GOING.
べ
LATER, TAKEYA-KUN.
BE NICE TO NENE-CHAN.
AND TO THE CUTE ALIEN-SAN, TOO.
M-MOM. WHAT'RE YOU SAYING...?
じ
MOM...
......

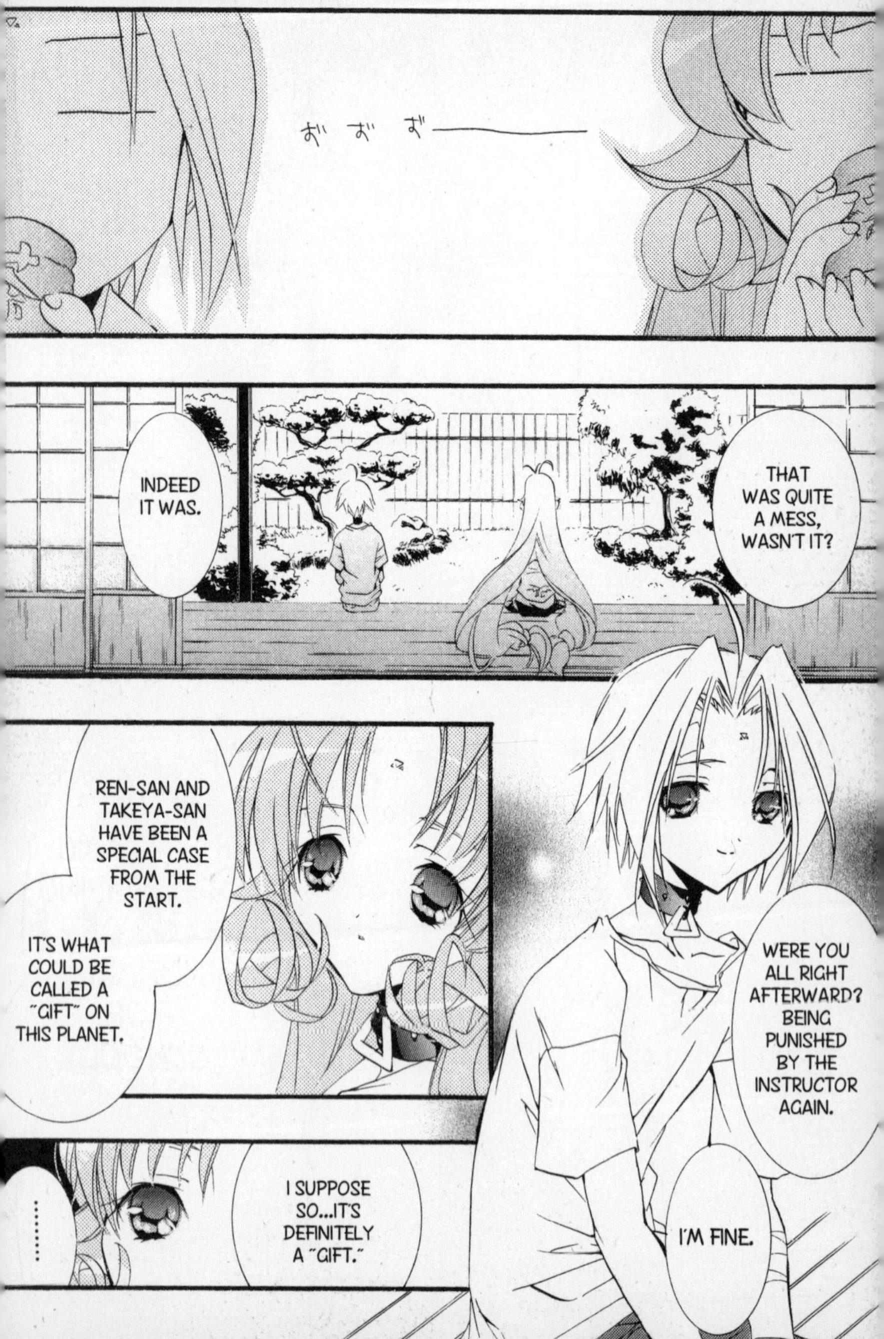
おおず——
THAT WAS QUITE A MESS, WASN'T IT?
INDEED IT WAS.
WERE YOU ALL RIGHT AFTERWARD? BEING PUNISHED BY THE INSTRUCTOR AGAIN.
I'M FINE.
REN-SAN AND TAKEYA-SAN HAVE BEEN A SPECIAL CASE FROM THE START.
IT'S WHAT COULD BE CALLED A "GIFT" ON THIS PLANET.
I SUPPOSE SO...IT'S DEFINITELY A "GIFT."
....

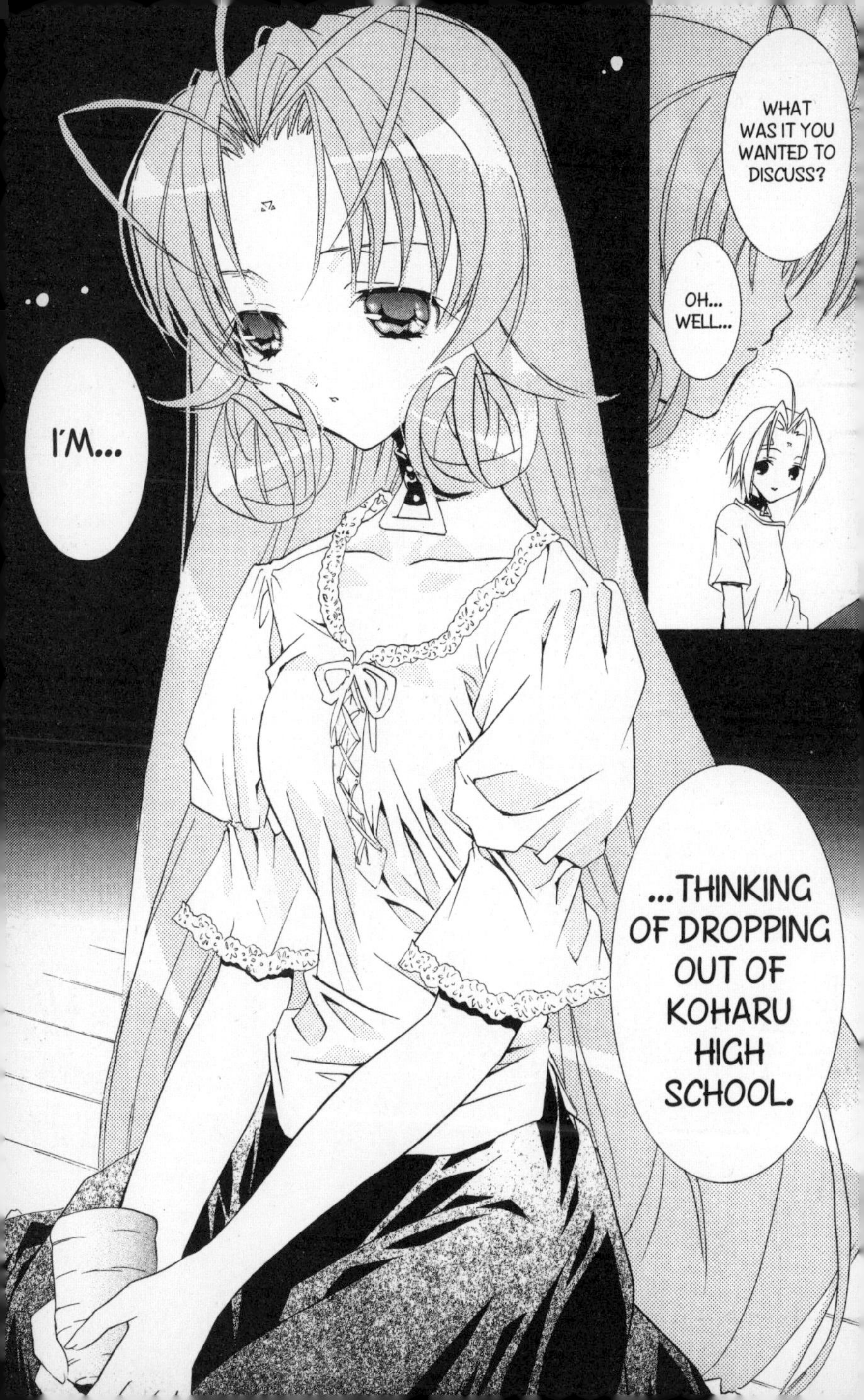
WHAT WAS IT YOU WANTED TO DISCUSS?
OH... WELL...
I'M...
...THINKING OF DROPPING OUT OF KOHARU HIGH SCHOOL.

15th Contact

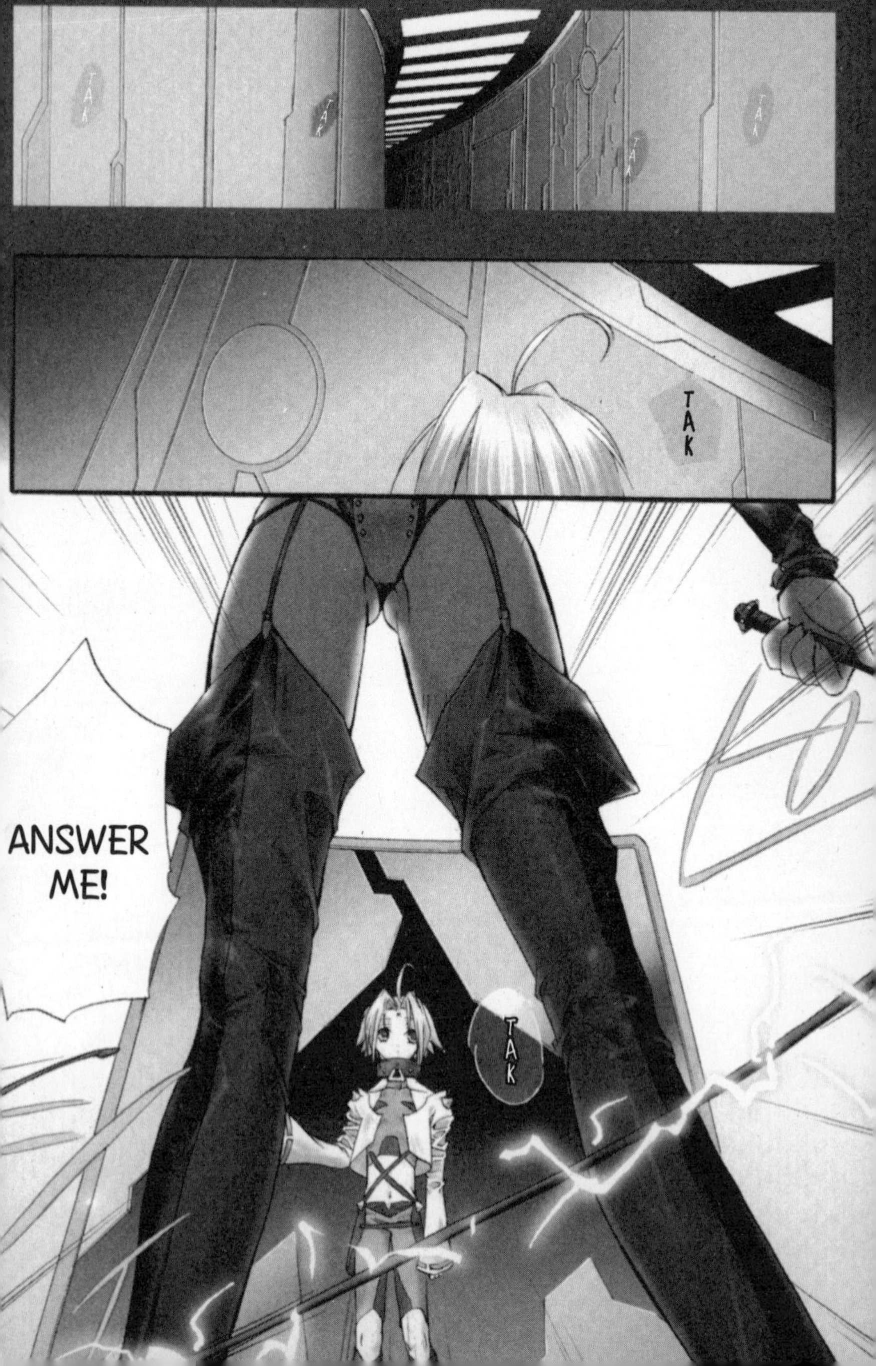
TAK
TAK
TAK
TAK
TAK
ANSWER ME!
TAK

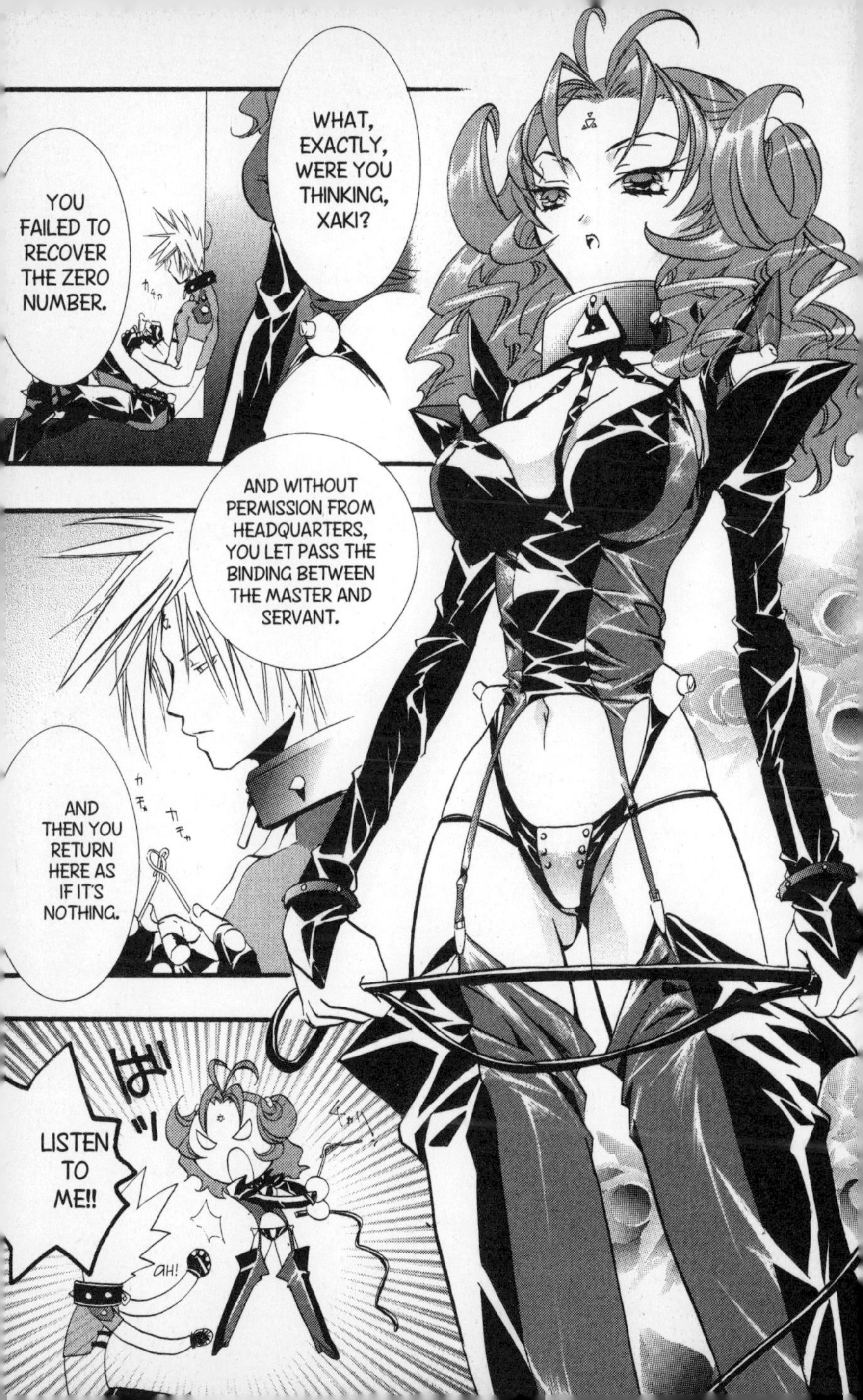
WHAT, EXACTLY, WERE YOU THINKING, XAKI?
YOU FAILED TO RECOVER THE ZERO NUMBER.
AND WITHOUT PERMISSION FROM HEADQUARTERS, YOU LET PASS THE BINDING BETWEEN THE MASTER AND SERVANT.
AND THEN YOU RETURN HERE AS IF IT'S NOTHING.
LISTEN TO ME!!
AH!

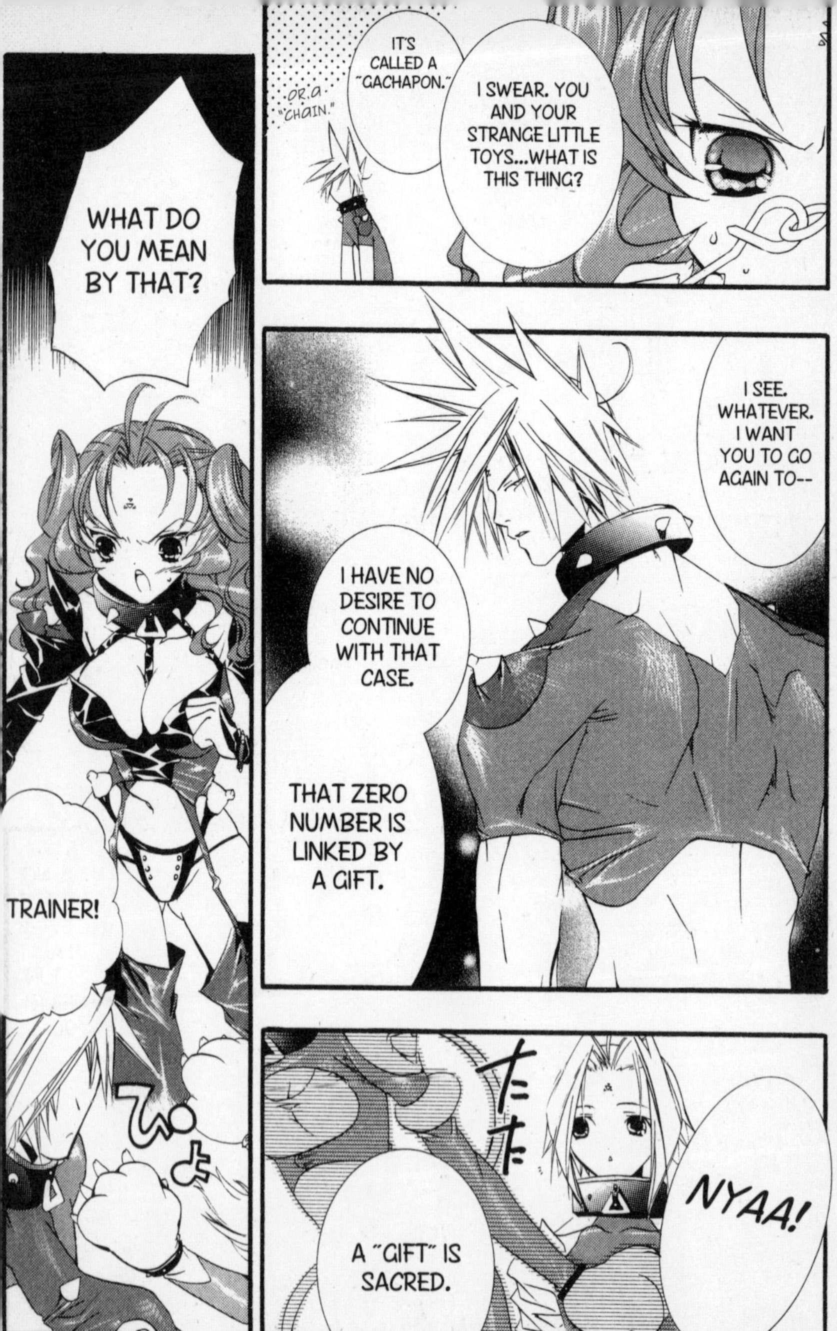
I SWEAR. YOU AND YOUR STRANGE LITTLE TOYS...WHAT IS THIS THING?
IT'S CALLED A "GACHAPON."
OR A "CHAIN."
I SEE. WHATEVER. I WANT YOU TO GO AGAIN TO--
I HAVE NO DESIRE TO CONTINUE WITH THAT CASE.
THAT ZERO NUMBER IS LINKED BY A GIFT.
NYAA!
A "GIFT" IS SACRED.
WHAT DO YOU MEAN BY THAT?
TRAINER!

TRANSLATOR'S NOTE: NYAA IS THE JAPANESE WORD FOR THE SOUND A CAT MAKES.

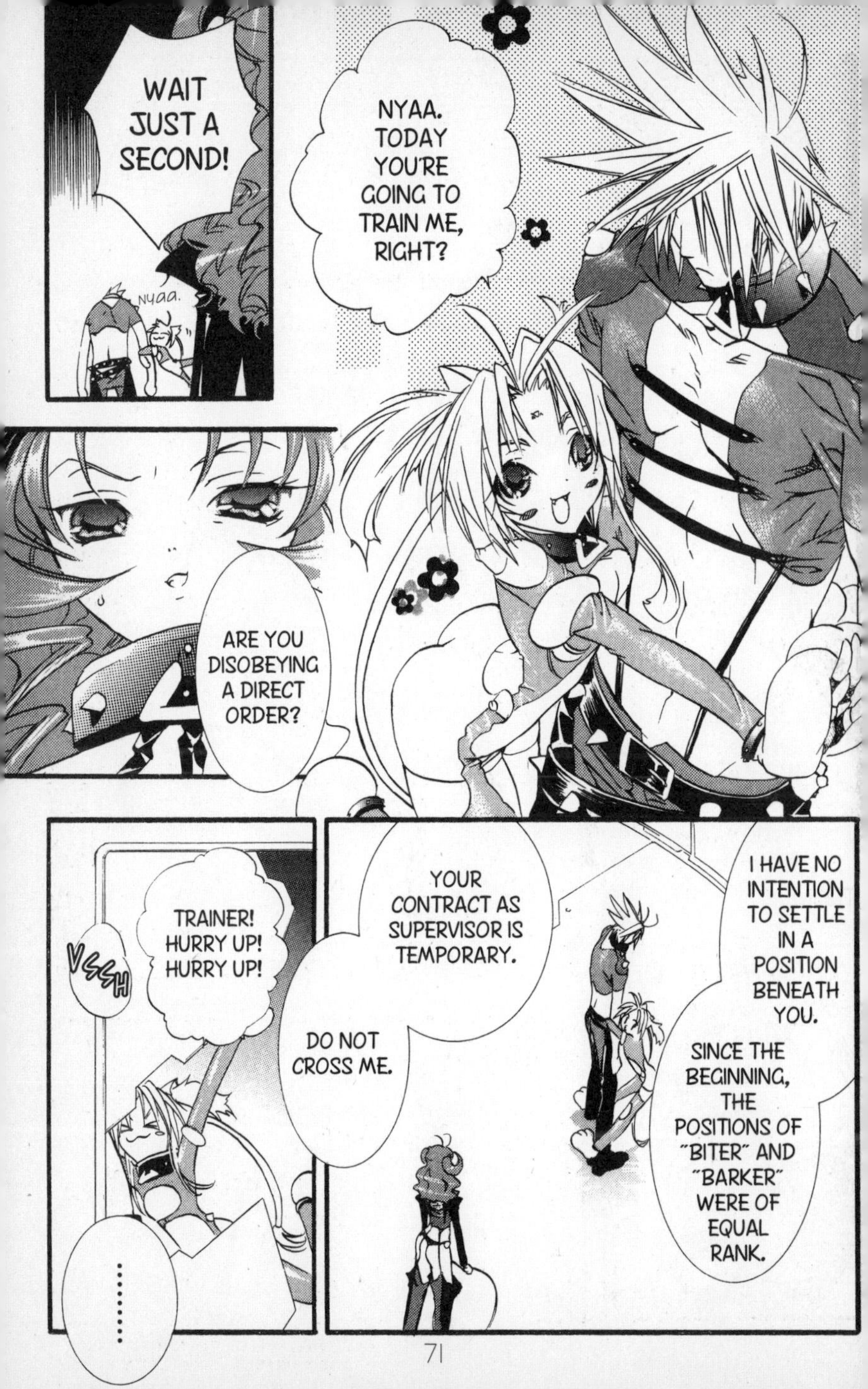
NYAA. TODAY YOU'RE GOING TO TRAIN ME, RIGHT?
WAIT JUST A SECOND!
NYAA.
ARE YOU DISOBEYING A DIRECT ORDER?
I HAVE NO INTENTION TO SETTLE IN A POSITION BENEATH YOU.
SINCE THE BEGINNING, THE POSITIONS OF "BITER" AND "BARKER" WERE OF EQUAL RANK.
YOUR CONTRACT AS SUPERVISOR IS TEMPORARY.
DO NOT CROSS ME.
TRAINER! HURRY UP! HURRY UP!
VSSH
......

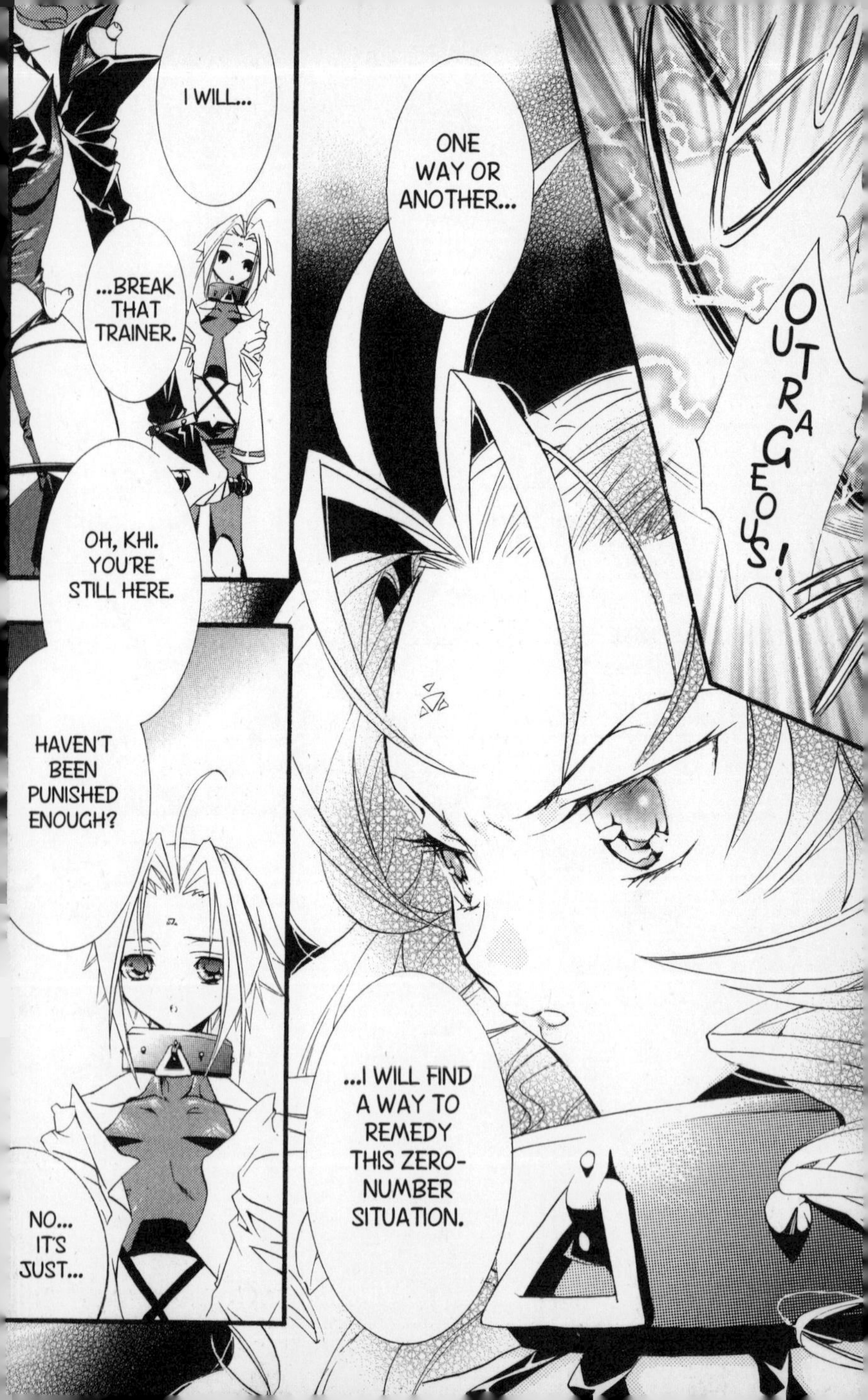
OUTRAGEOUS!
ONE WAY OR ANOTHER...
...I WILL FIND A WAY TO REMEDY THIS ZERO-NUMBER SITUATION.
I WILL...
...BREAK THAT TRAINER.
OH, KHI. YOU'RE STILL HERE.
HAVEN'T BEEN PUNISHED ENOUGH?
NO... IT'S JUST...

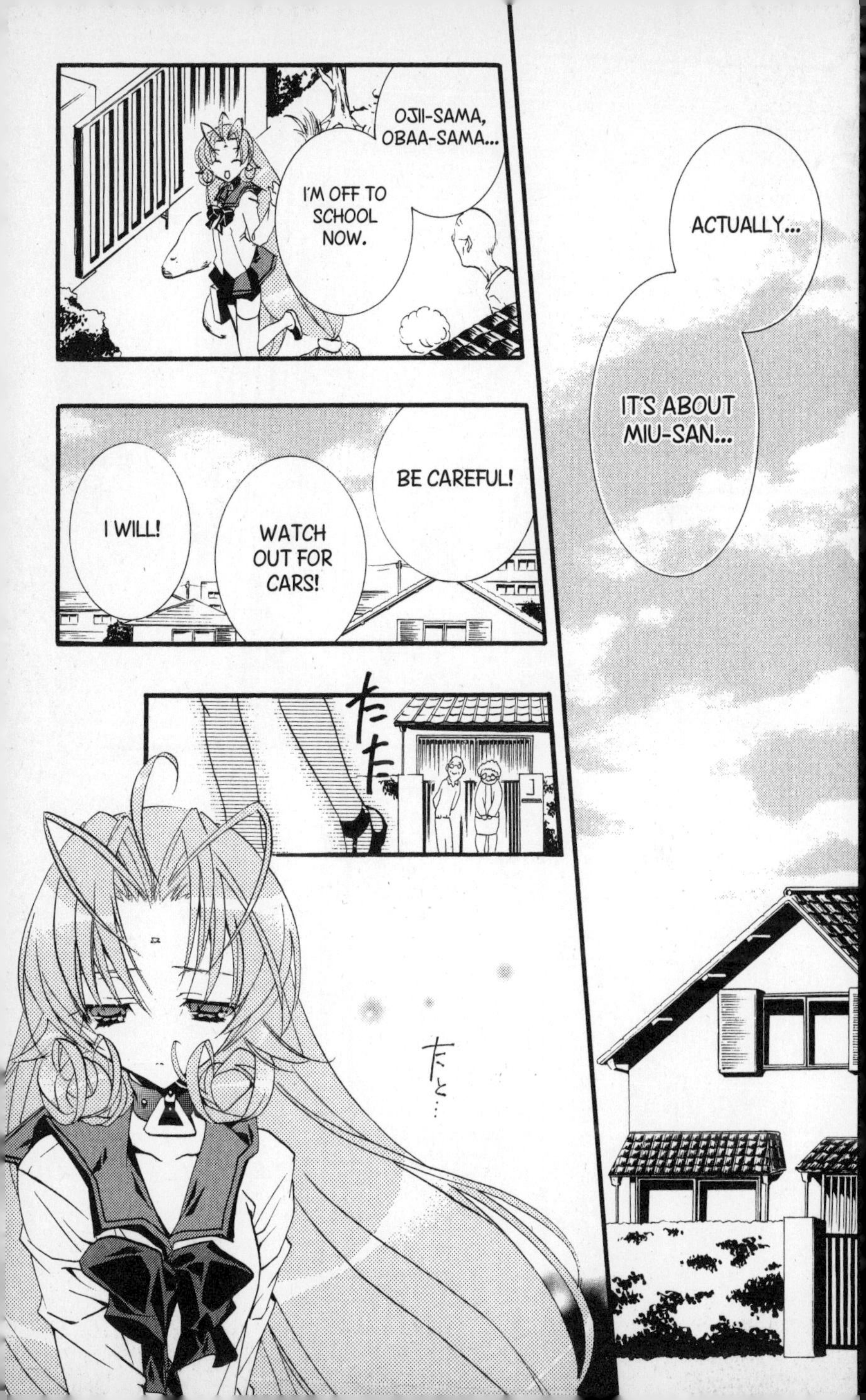
ACTUALLY...
IT'S ABOUT MIU-SAN...
OJII-SAMA, OBAA-SAMA...
I'M OFF TO SCHOOL NOW.
BE CAREFUL!
WATCH OUT FOR CARS!
I WILL!
たた
たと…

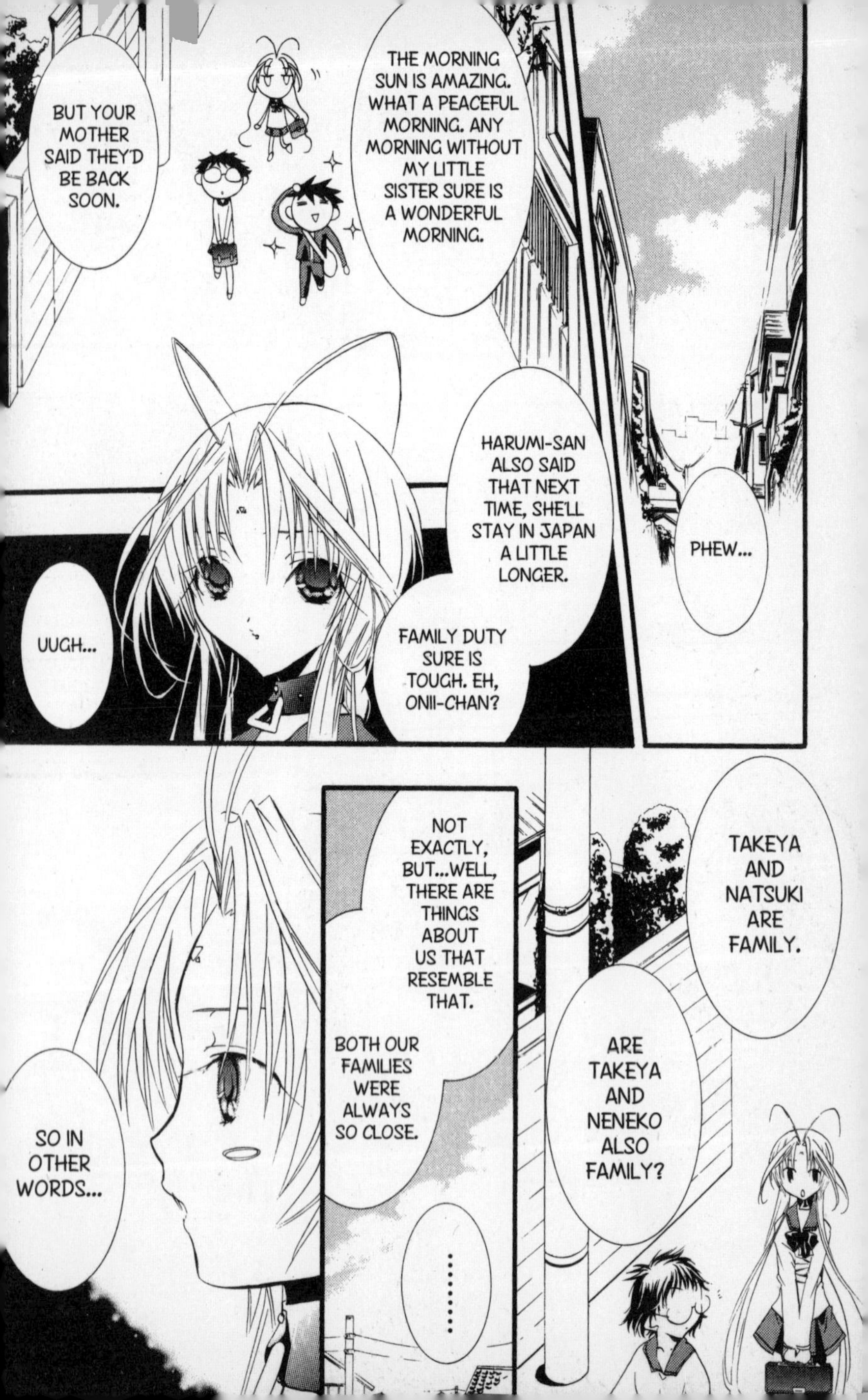
THE MORNING SUN IS AMAZING. WHAT A PEACEFUL MORNING. ANY MORNING WITHOUT MY LITTLE SISTER SURE IS A WONDERFUL MORNING.
BUT YOUR MOTHER SAID THEY'D BE BACK SOON.
HARUMI-SAN ALSO SAID THAT NEXT TIME, SHE'LL STAY IN JAPAN A LITTLE LONGER.
PHEW...
FAMILY DUTY SURE IS TOUGH. EH, ONII-CHAN?
UUGH...
TAKEYA AND NATSUKI ARE FAMILY.
ARE TAKEYA AND NENEKO ALSO FAMILY?
NOT EXACTLY, BUT...WELL, THERE ARE THINGS ABOUT US THAT RESEMBLE THAT.
BOTH OUR FAMILIES WERE ALWAYS SO CLOSE.
....
SO IN OTHER WORDS...

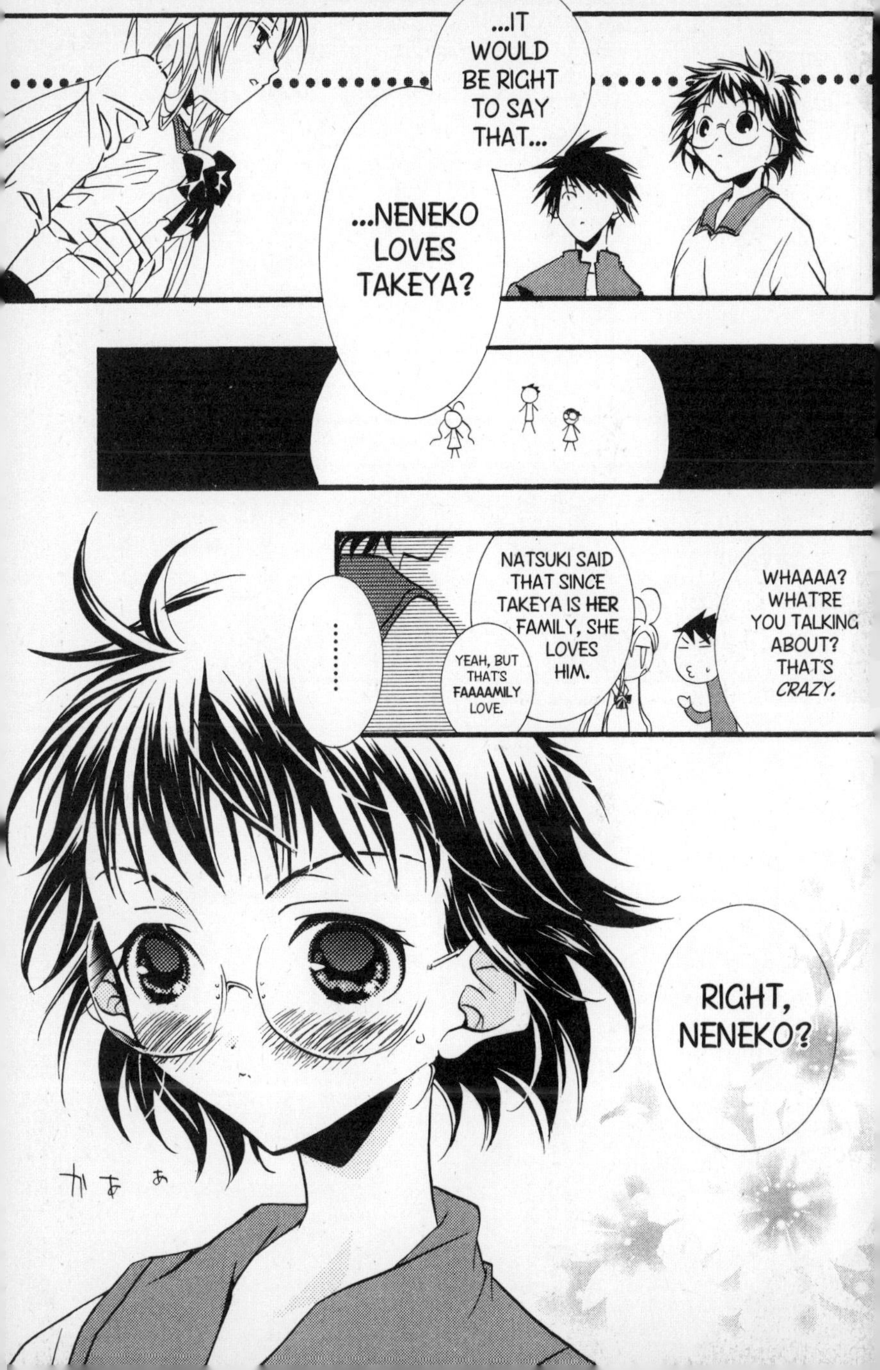
...IT WOULD BE RIGHT TO SAY THAT...
...NENEKO LOVES TAKEYA?
WHAAAA? WHAT'RE YOU TALKING ABOUT? THAT'S *CRAZY.*
NATSUKI SAID THAT SINCE TAKEYA IS HER FAMILY, SHE LOVES HIM.
YEAH, BUT THAT'S FAAAAMILY LOVE.
....
RIGHT, NENEKO?
かあ あ

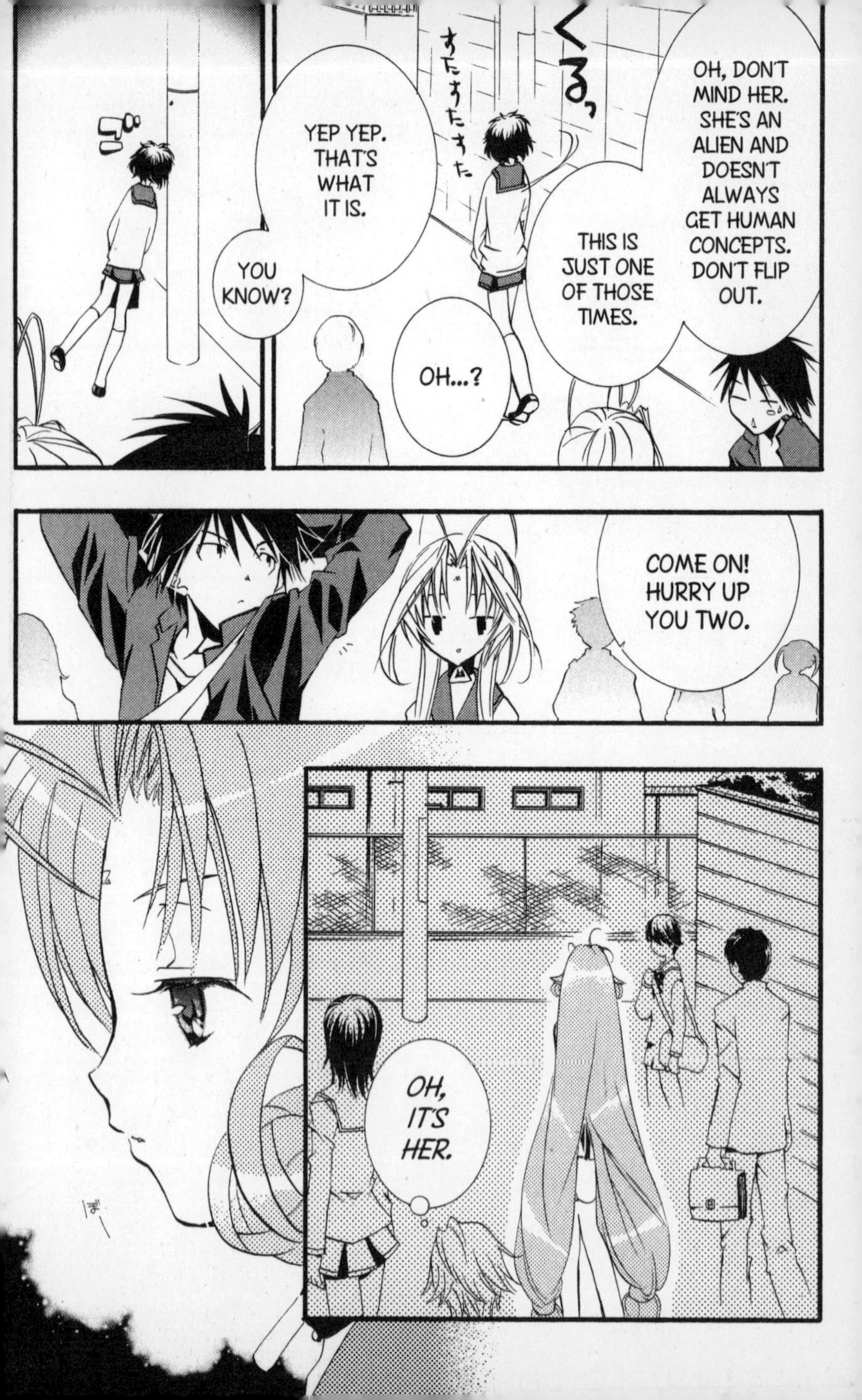
OH, DON'T MIND HER. SHE'S AN ALIEN AND DOESN'T ALWAYS GET HUMAN CONCEPTS. DON'T FLIP OUT.
THIS IS JUST ONE OF THOSE TIMES.
くるっ
すたすたすた
YEP YEP. THAT'S WHAT IT IS.
OH...?
YOU KNOW?
COME ON! HURRY UP YOU TWO.
OH, IT'S HER.

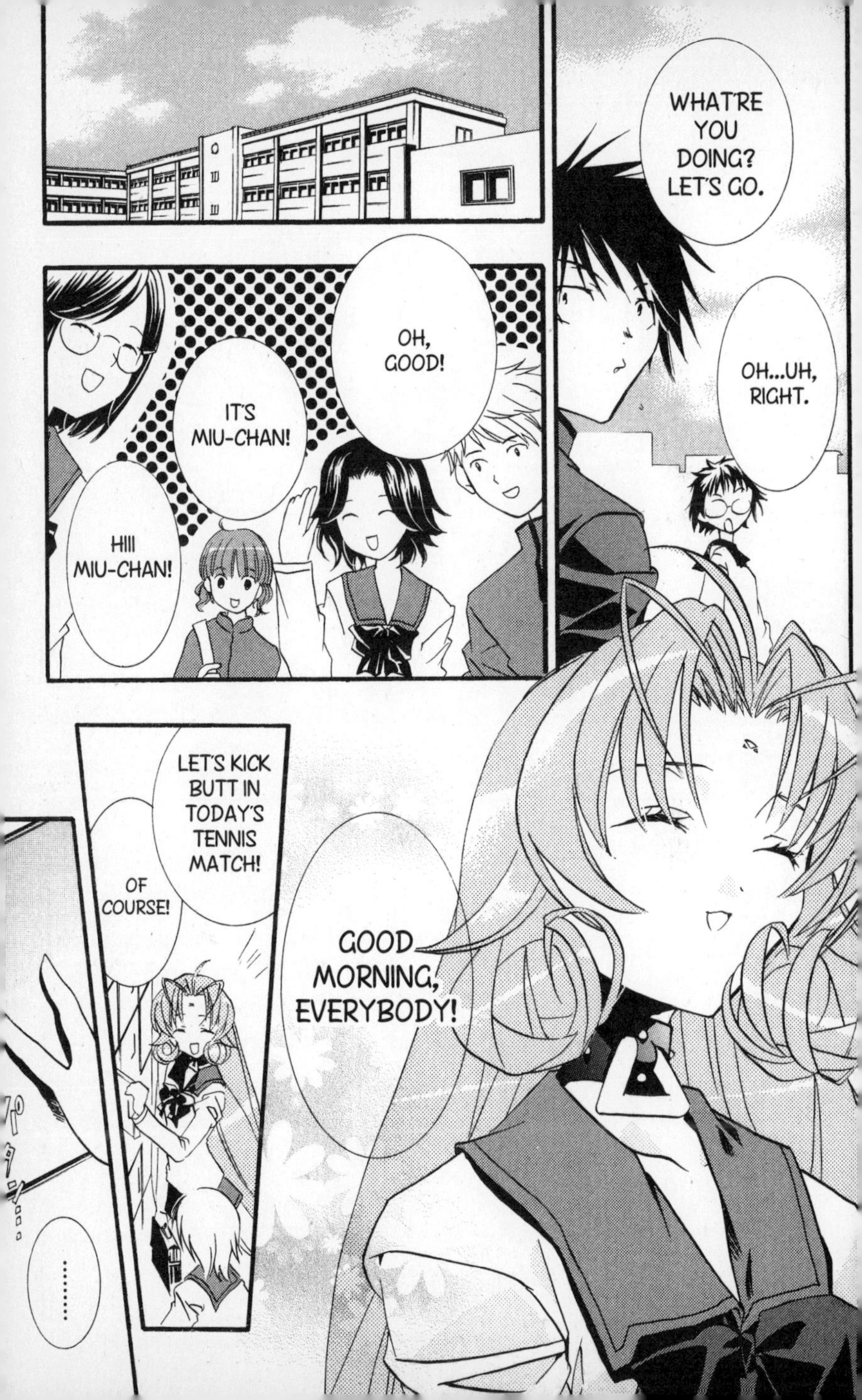
WHAT'RE YOU DOING? LET'S GO.
OH...UH, RIGHT.
OH, GOOD!
IT'S MIU-CHAN!
HIII MIU-CHAN!
GOOD MORNING, EVERYBODY!
LET'S KICK BUTT IN TODAY'S TENNIS MATCH!
OF COURSE!
....

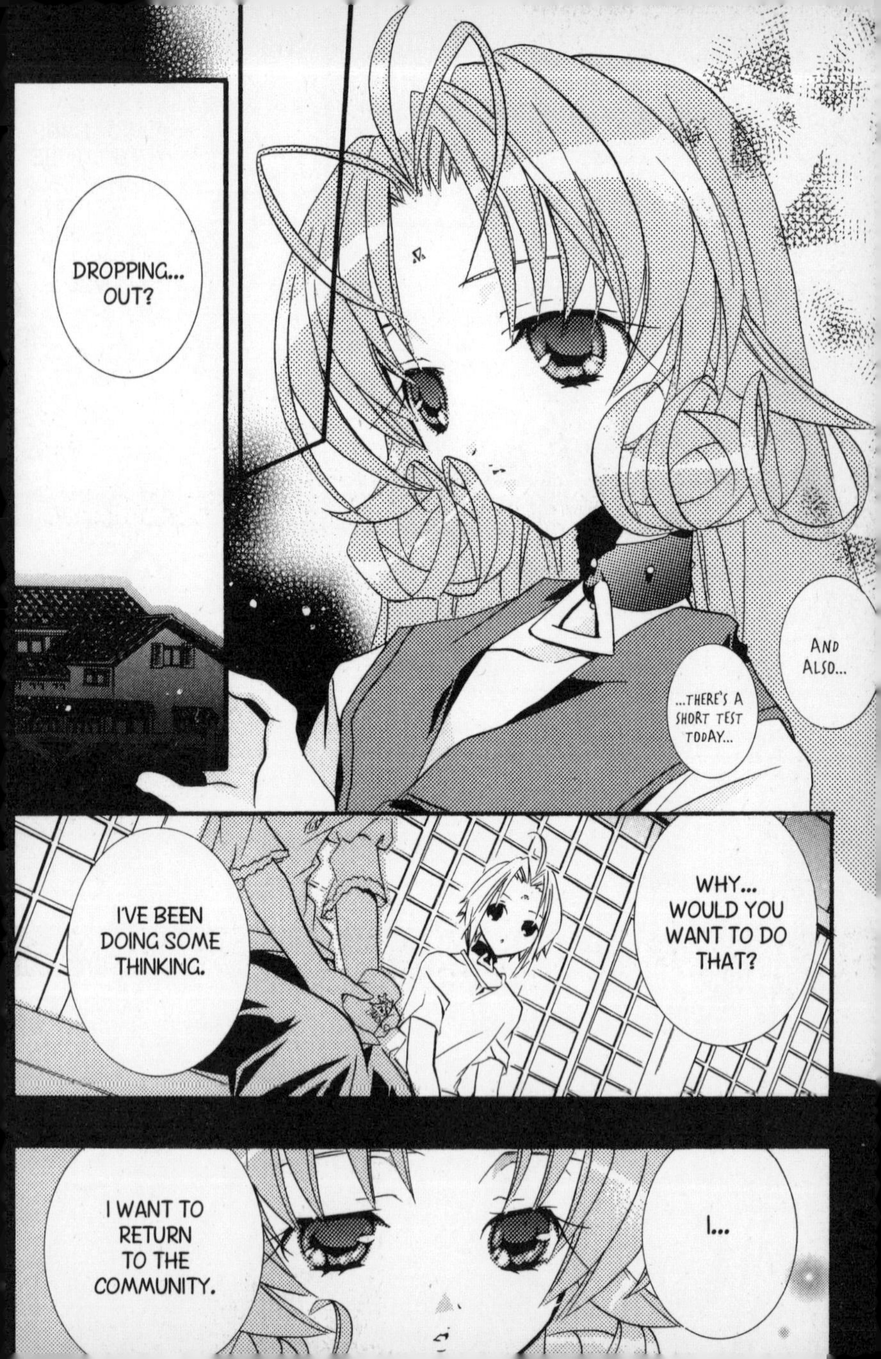

AND ALSO...
...THERE'S A SHORT TEST TODAY...
DROPPING... OUT?
WHY... WOULD YOU WANT TO DO THAT?
I'VE BEEN DOING SOME THINKING.
I...
I WANT TO RETURN TO THE COMMUNITY.

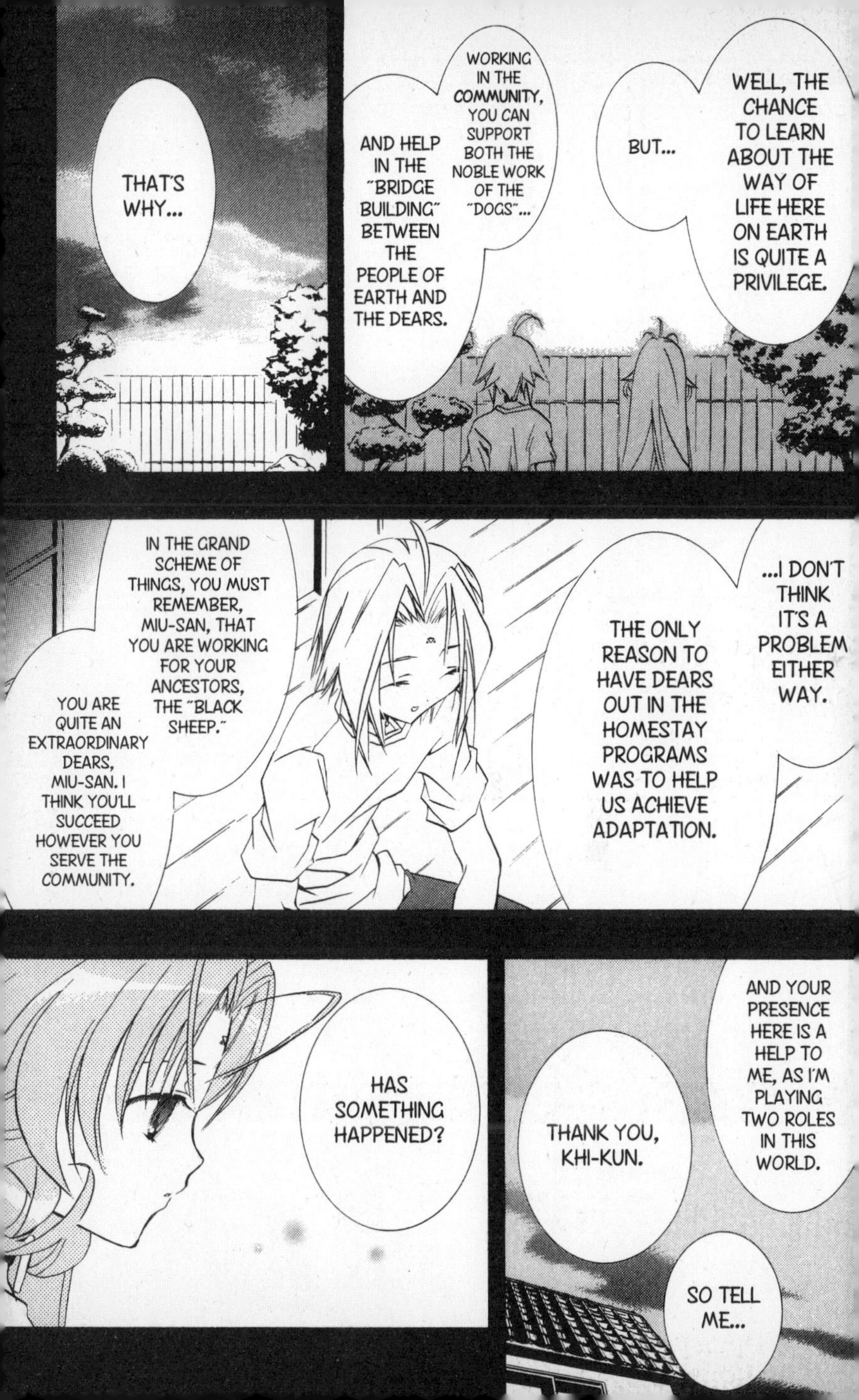
WELL, THE CHANCE TO LEARN ABOUT THE WAY OF LIFE HERE ON EARTH IS QUITE A PRIVILEGE.
BUT...
WORKING IN THE COMMUNITY, YOU CAN SUPPORT BOTH THE NOBLE WORK OF THE "DOGS"...
AND HELP IN THE "BRIDGE BUILDING" BETWEEN THE PEOPLE OF EARTH AND THE DEARS.
THAT'S WHY...
...I DON'T THINK IT'S A PROBLEM EITHER WAY.
THE ONLY REASON TO HAVE DEARS OUT IN THE HOMESTAY PROGRAMS WAS TO HELP US ACHIEVE ADAPTATION.
IN THE GRAND SCHEME OF THINGS, YOU MUST REMEMBER, MIU-SAN, THAT YOU ARE WORKING FOR YOUR ANCESTORS, THE "BLACK SHEEP."
YOU ARE QUITE AN EXTRAORDINARY DEARS, MIU-SAN. I THINK YOU'LL SUCCEED HOWEVER YOU SERVE THE COMMUNITY.
AND YOUR PRESENCE HERE IS A HELP TO ME, AS I'M PLAYING TWO ROLES IN THIS WORLD.
THANK YOU, KHI-KUN.
SO TELL ME...
HAS SOMETHING HAPPENED?

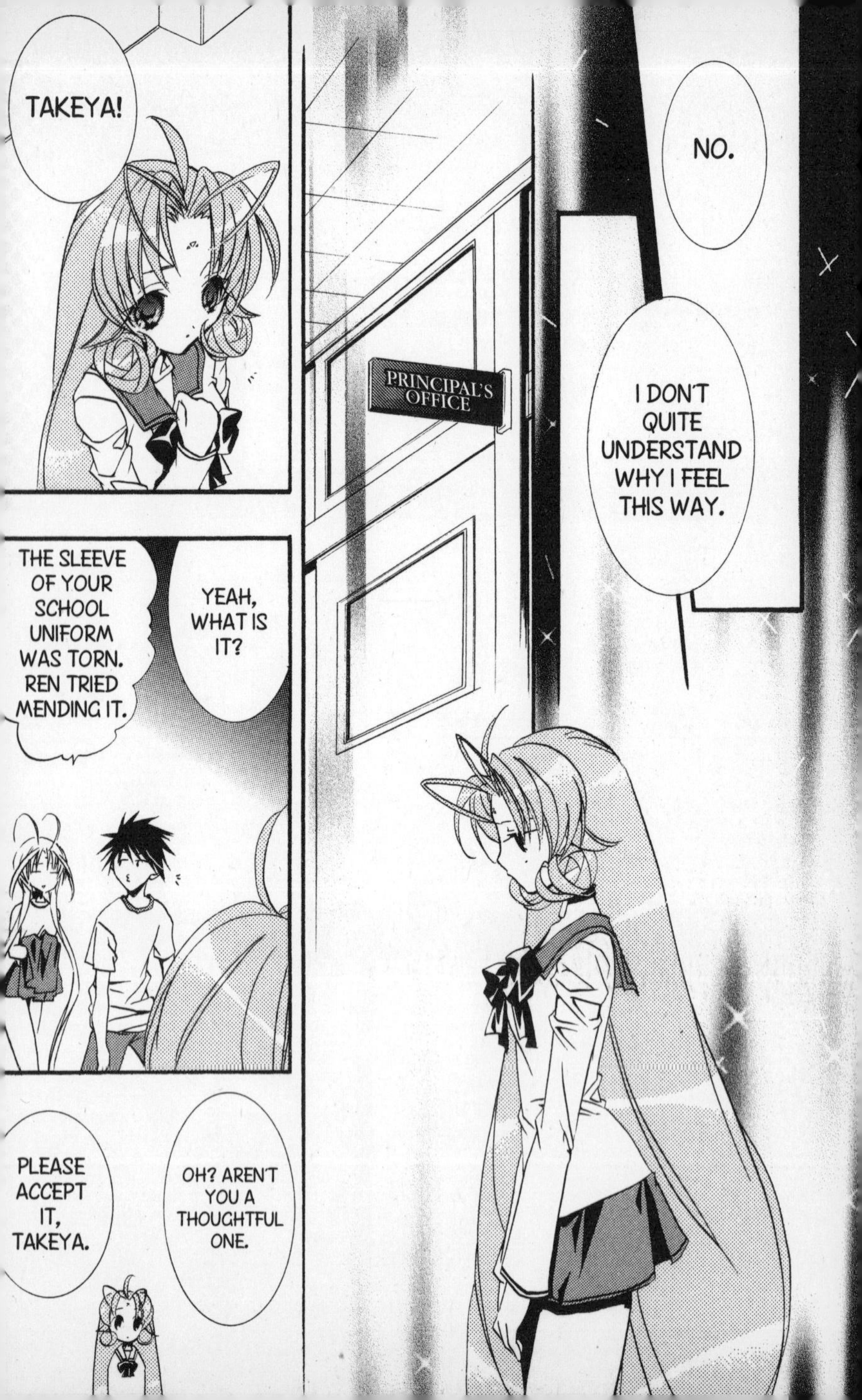
NO.
I DON'T QUITE UNDERSTAND WHY I FEEL THIS WAY.
PRINCIPAL'S OFFICE
TAKEYA!
YEAH, WHAT IS IT?
THE SLEEVE OF YOUR SCHOOL UNIFORM WAS TORN. REN TRIED MENDING IT.
OH? AREN'T YOU A THOUGHTFUL ONE.
PLEASE ACCEPT IT, TAKEYA.

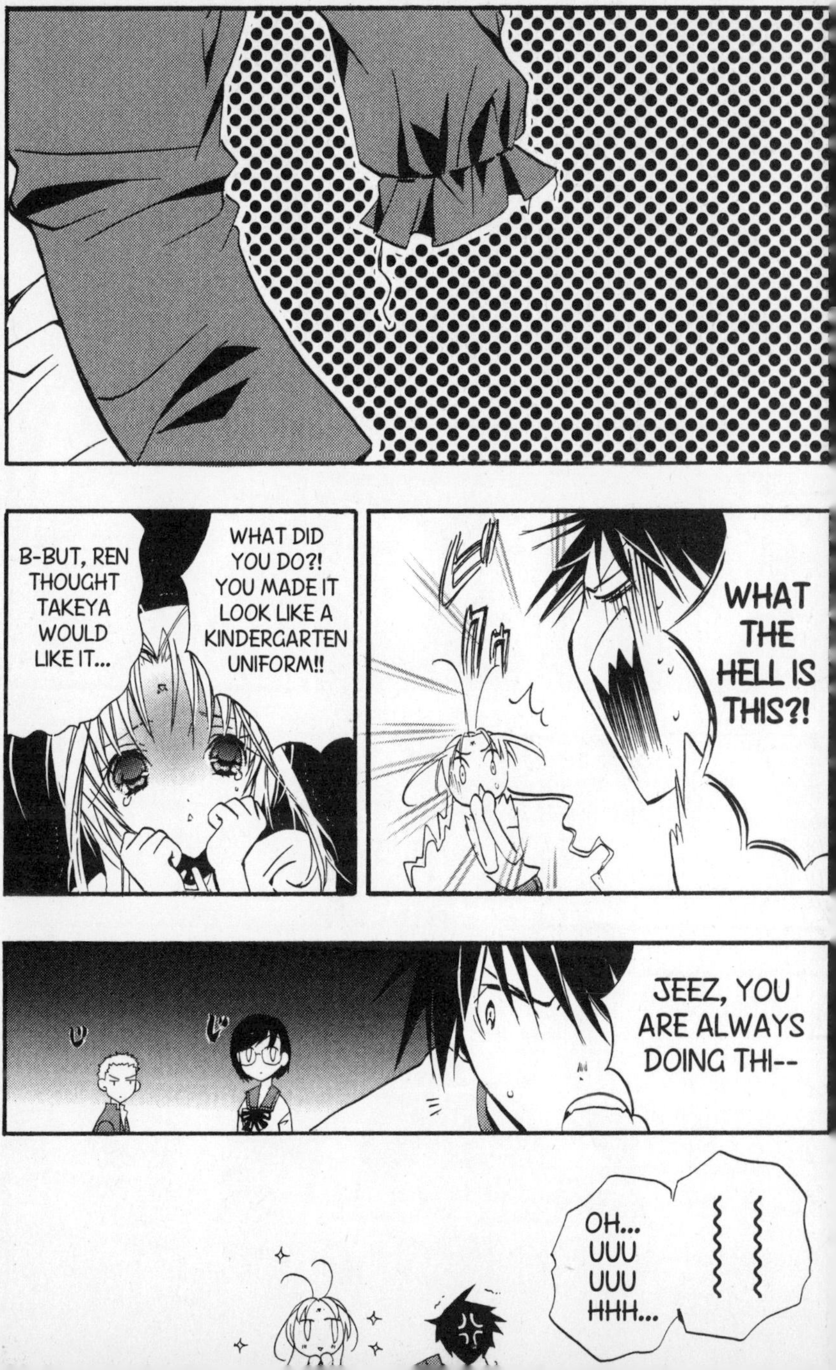
WHAT THE HELL IS THIS?!
WHAT DID YOU DO?! YOU MADE IT LOOK LIKE A KINDERGARTEN UNIFORM!!
B-BUT, REN THOUGHT TAKEYA WOULD LIKE IT...
JEEZ, YOU ARE ALWAYS DOING THI--
OH... UUU UUU HHH...

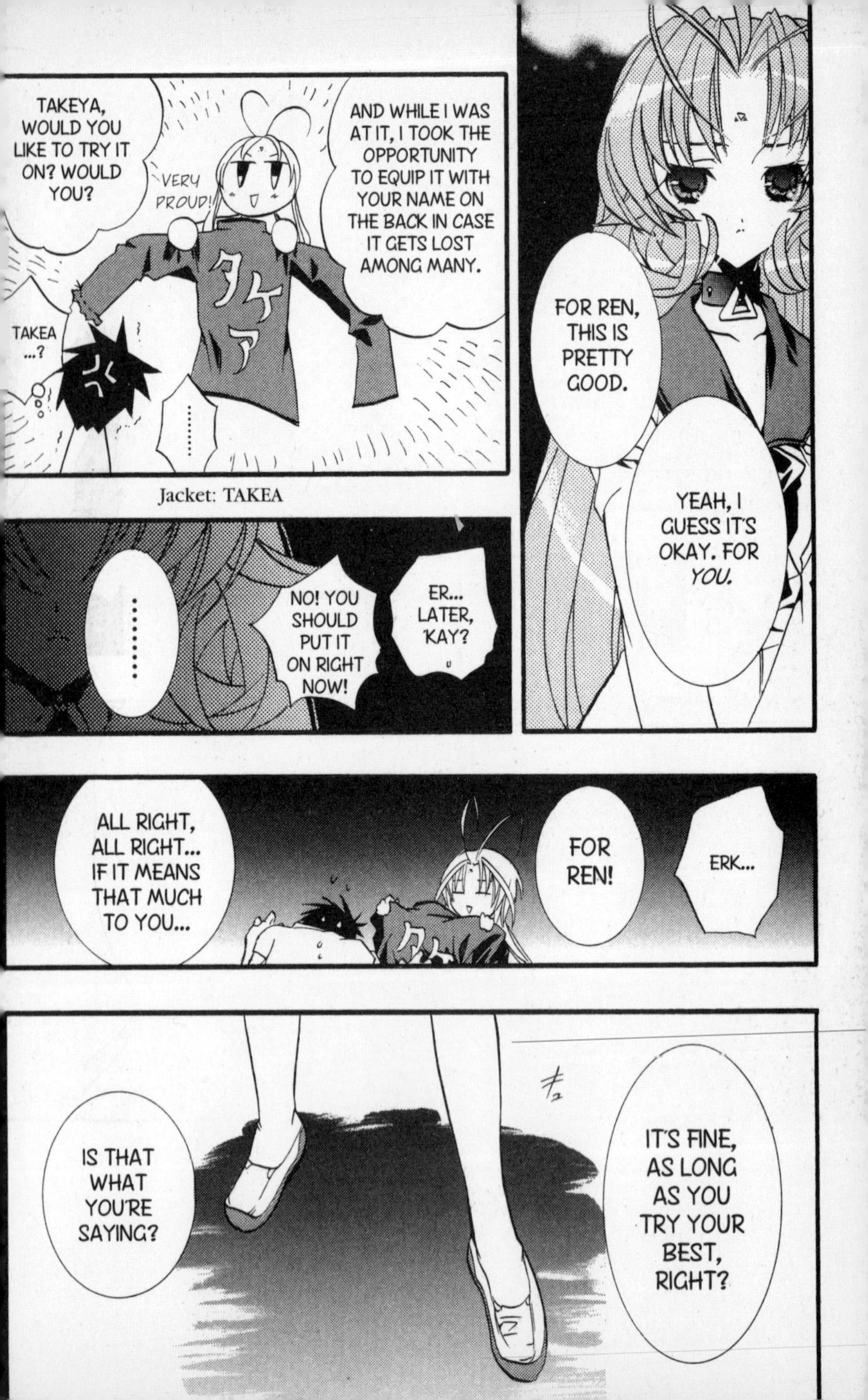
FOR REN, THIS IS PRETTY GOOD.
YEAH, I GUESS IT'S OKAY. FOR *YOU.*
AND WHILE I WAS AT IT, I TOOK THE OPPORTUNITY TO EQUIP IT WITH YOUR NAME ON THE BACK IN CASE IT GETS LOST AMONG MANY.
VERY PROUD!
TAKEYA, WOULD YOU LIKE TO TRY IT ON? WOULD YOU?
TAKEA ...?
......
Jacket: TAKEA
ER... LATER, 'KAY?
NO! YOU SHOULD PUT IT ON RIGHT NOW!
....
ERK...
FOR REN!
ALL RIGHT, ALL RIGHT... IF IT MEANS THAT MUCH TO YOU...
IT'S FINE, AS LONG AS YOU TRY YOUR BEST, RIGHT?
IS THAT WHAT YOU'RE SAYING?

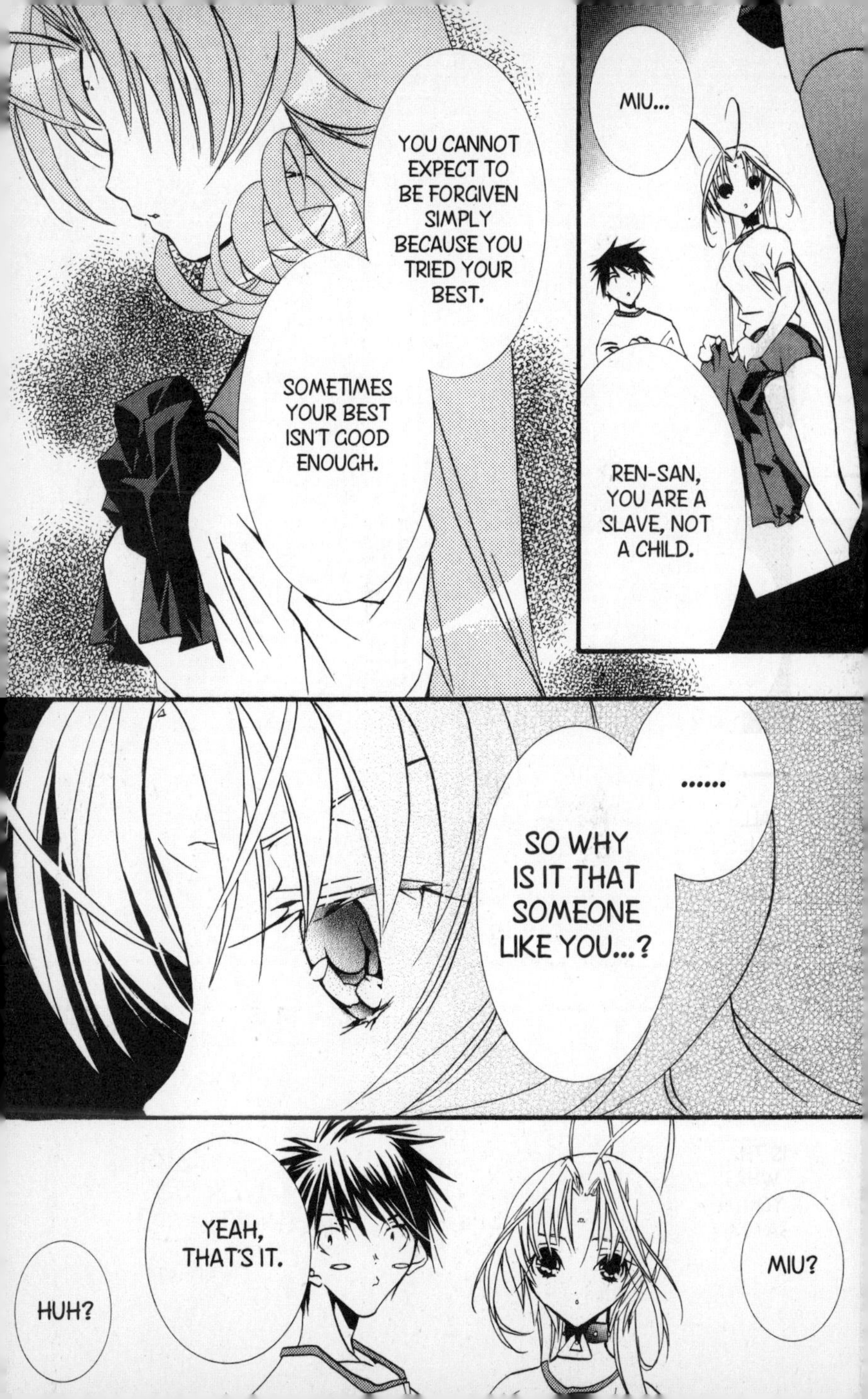
MIU...
REN-SAN, YOU ARE A SLAVE, NOT A CHILD.
YOU CANNOT EXPECT TO BE FORGIVEN SIMPLY BECAUSE YOU TRIED YOUR BEST.
SOMETIMES YOUR BEST ISN'T GOOD ENOUGH.
......
SO WHY IS IT THAT SOMEONE LIKE YOU...?
MIU?
YEAH, THAT'S IT.
HUH?

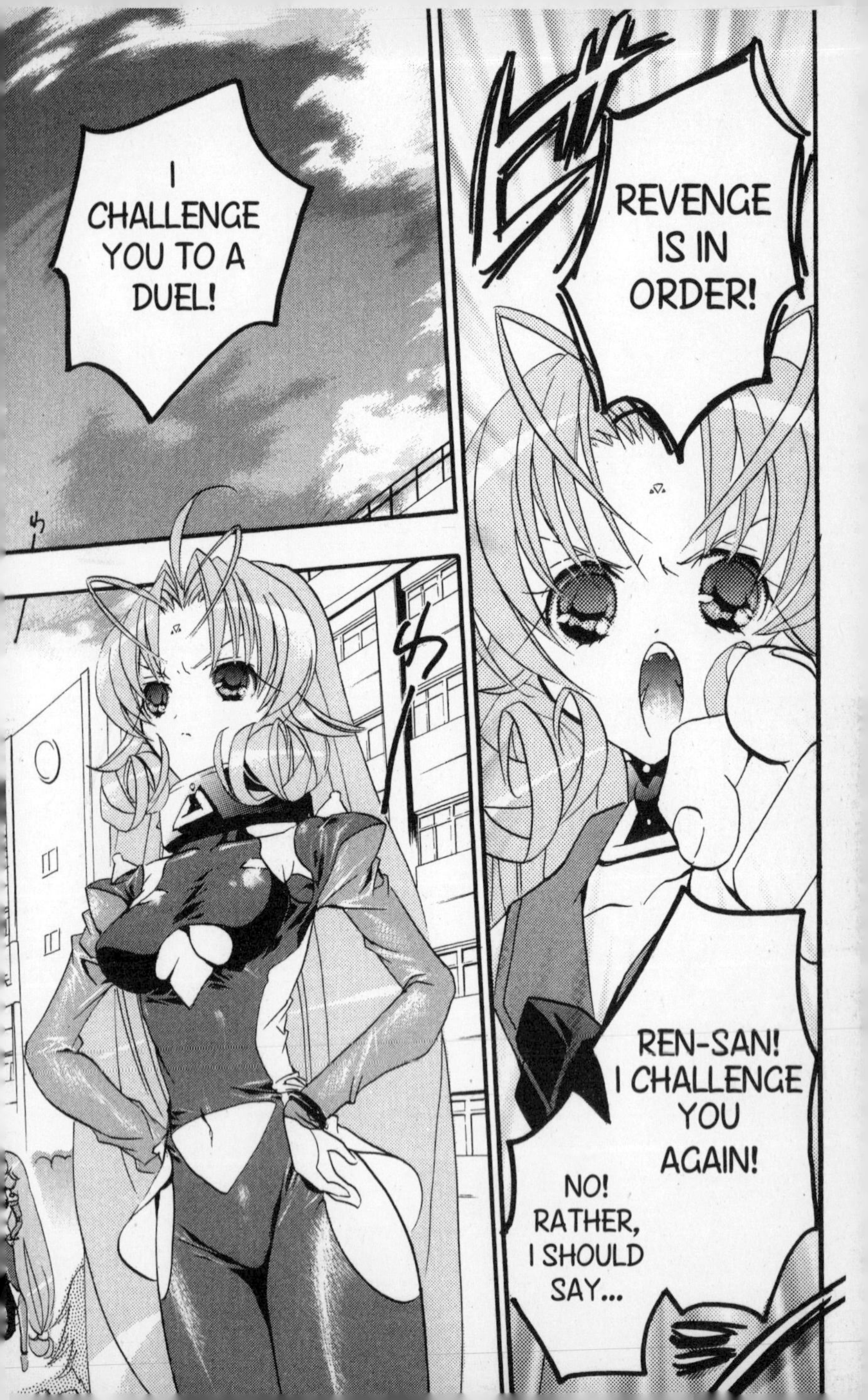
REVENGE IS IN ORDER!
REN-SAN! I CHALLENGE YOU AGAIN!
NO! RATHER, I SHOULD SAY...
I CHALLENGE YOU TO A DUEL!

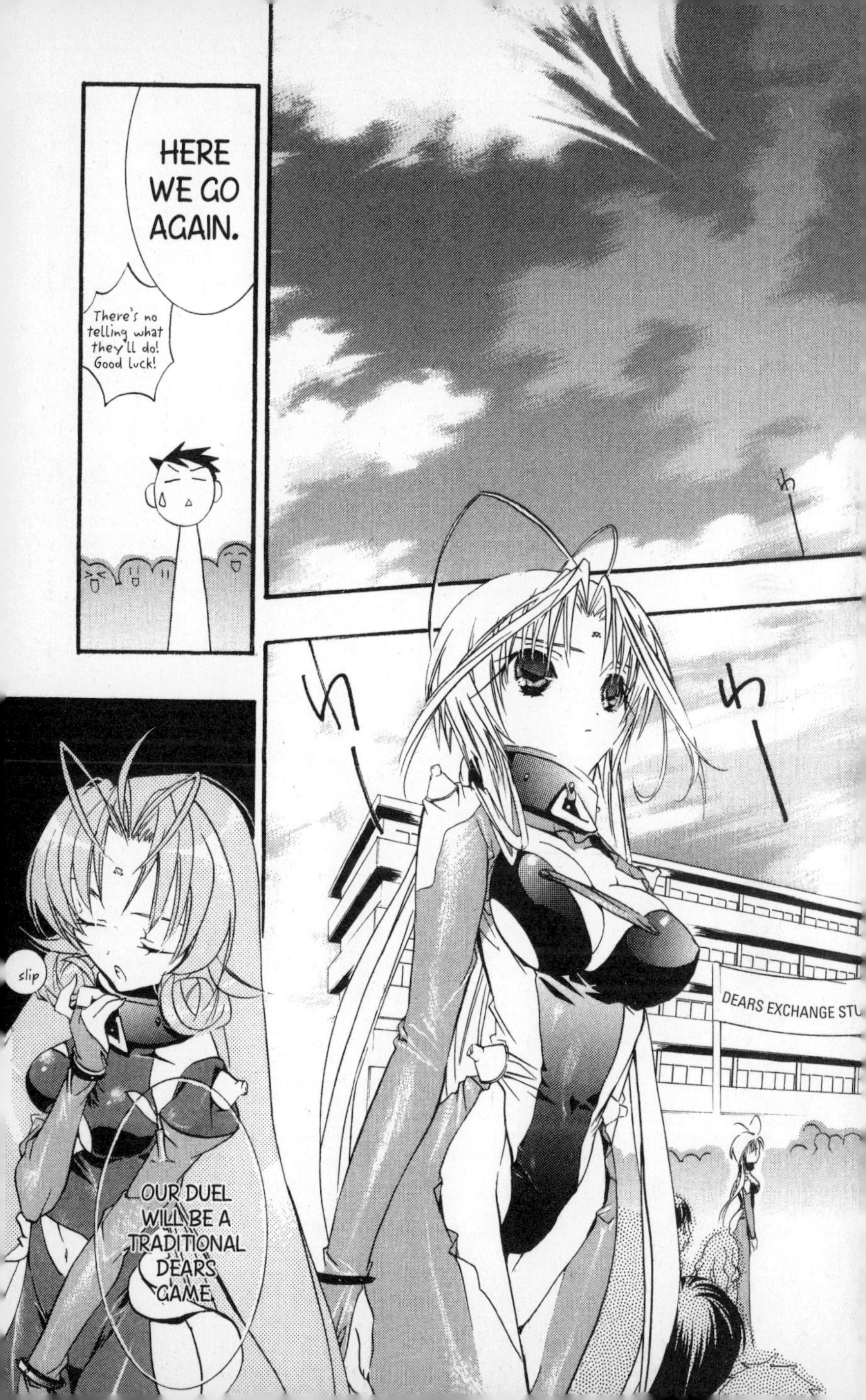
わ
HERE WE GO AGAIN.
There's no telling what they'll do! Good luck!
わー
わー
DEARS EXCHANGE STU
slip
OUR DUEL WILL BE A TRADITIONAL DEARS GAME.

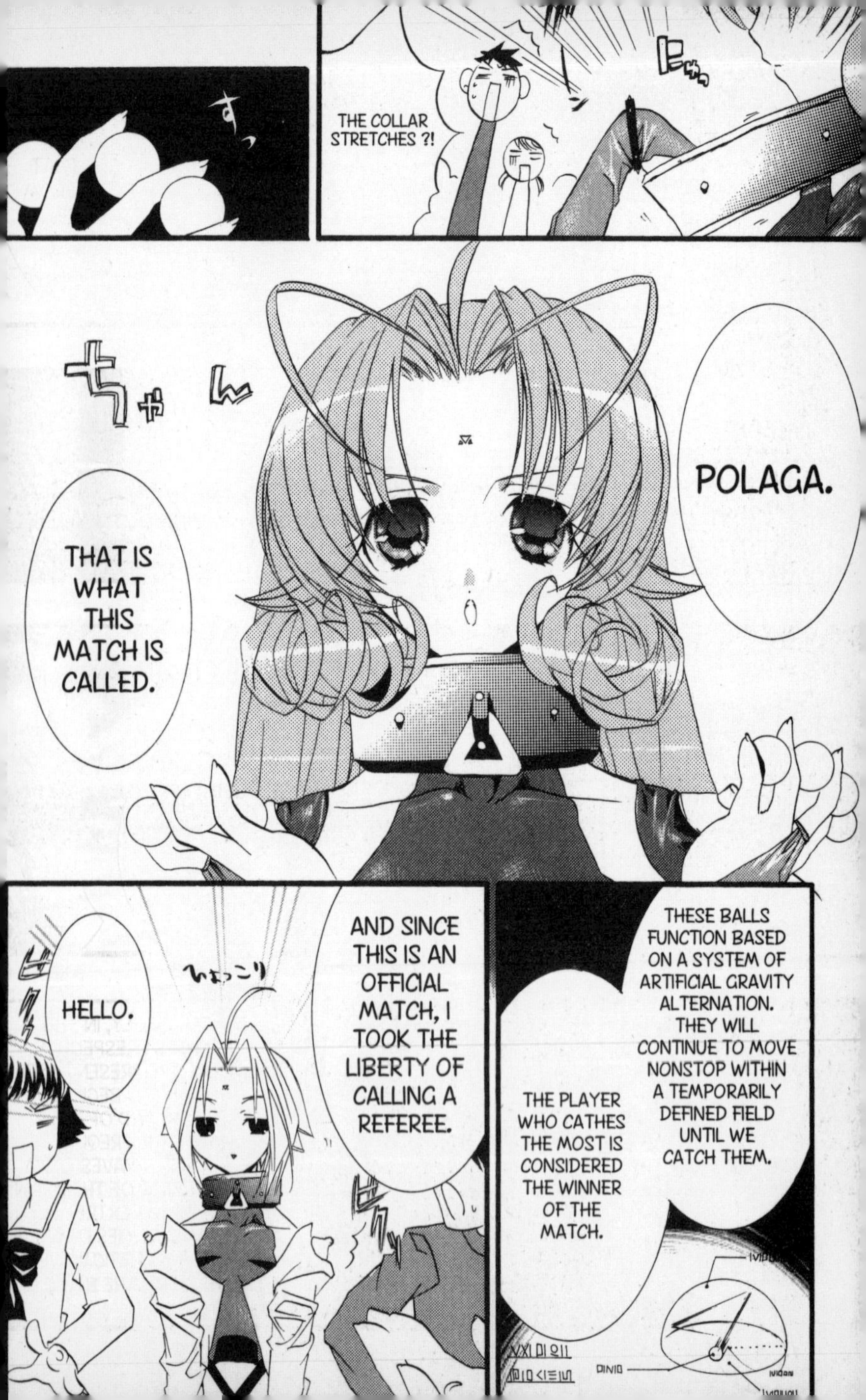
THE COLLAR STRETCHES ?!
すっ
POLAGA.
ちゃん
THAT IS WHAT THIS MATCH IS CALLED.
THESE BALLS FUNCTION BASED ON A SYSTEM OF ARTIFICIAL GRAVITY ALTERNATION. THEY WILL CONTINUE TO MOVE NONSTOP WITHIN A TEMPORARILY DEFINED FIELD UNTIL WE CATCH THEM.
THE PLAYER WHO CATHES THE MOST IS CONSIDERED THE WINNER OF THE MATCH.
AND SINCE THIS IS AN OFFICIAL MATCH, I TOOK THE LIBERTY OF CALLING A REFEREE.
ひょっこり
HELLO.

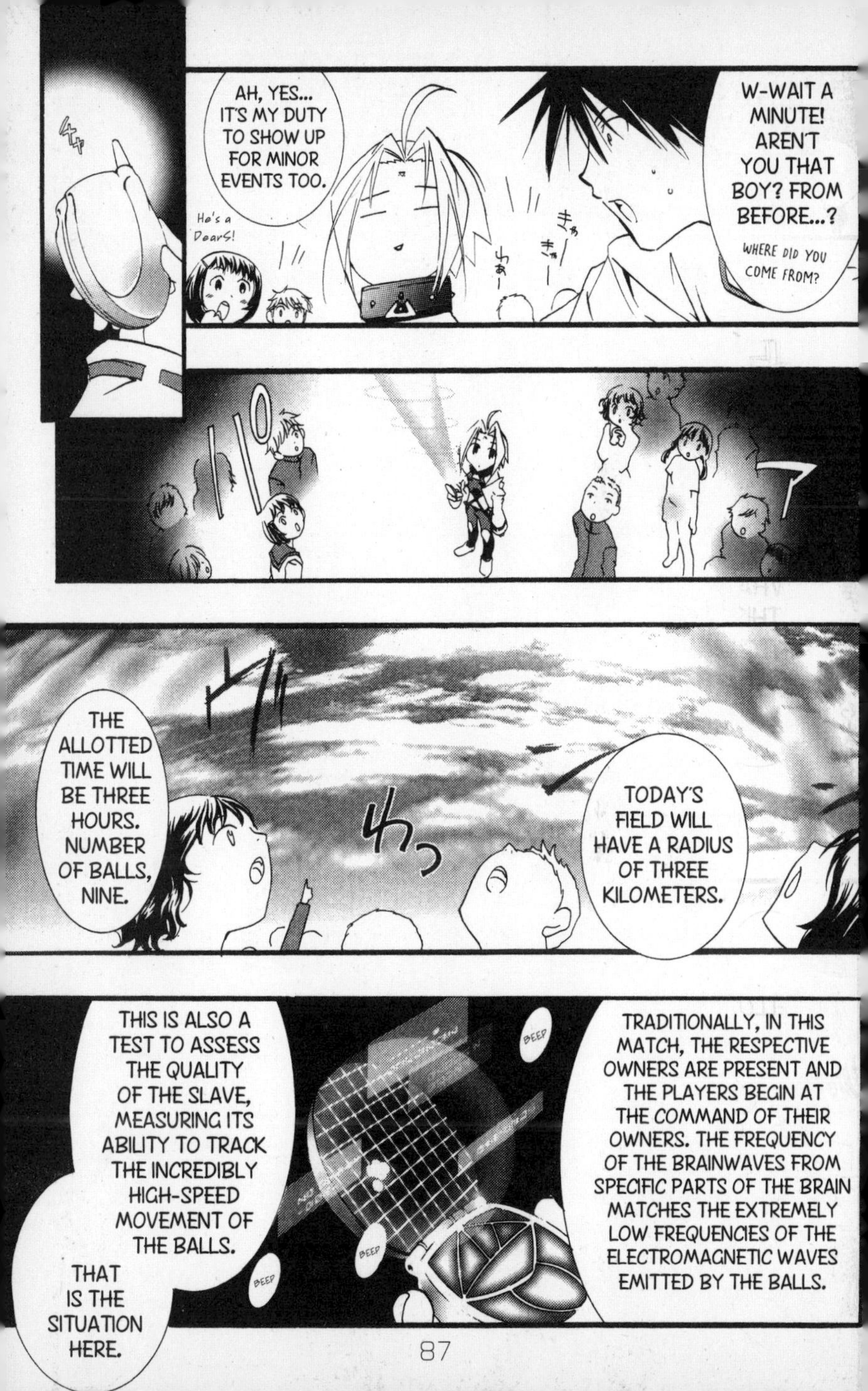
W-WAIT A MINUTE! AREN'T YOU THAT BOY? FROM BEFORE...?
WHERE DID YOU COME FROM?
AH, YES... IT'S MY DUTY TO SHOW UP FOR MINOR EVENTS TOO.
He's a Dears!
TODAY'S FIELD WILL HAVE A RADIUS OF THREE KILOMETERS.
THE ALLOTTED TIME WILL BE THREE HOURS. NUMBER OF BALLS, NINE.
TRADITIONALLY, IN THIS MATCH, THE RESPECTIVE OWNERS ARE PRESENT AND THE PLAYERS BEGIN AT THE COMMAND OF THEIR OWNERS. THE FREQUENCY OF THE BRAINWAVES FROM SPECIFIC PARTS OF THE BRAIN MATCHES THE EXTREMELY LOW FREQUENCIES OF THE ELECTROMAGNETIC WAVES EMITTED BY THE BALLS.
BEEP
BEEP
BEEP
THIS IS ALSO A TEST TO ASSESS THE QUALITY OF THE SLAVE, MEASURING ITS ABILITY TO TRACK THE INCREDIBLY HIGH-SPEED MOVEMENT OF THE BALLS.
THAT IS THE SITUATION HERE.

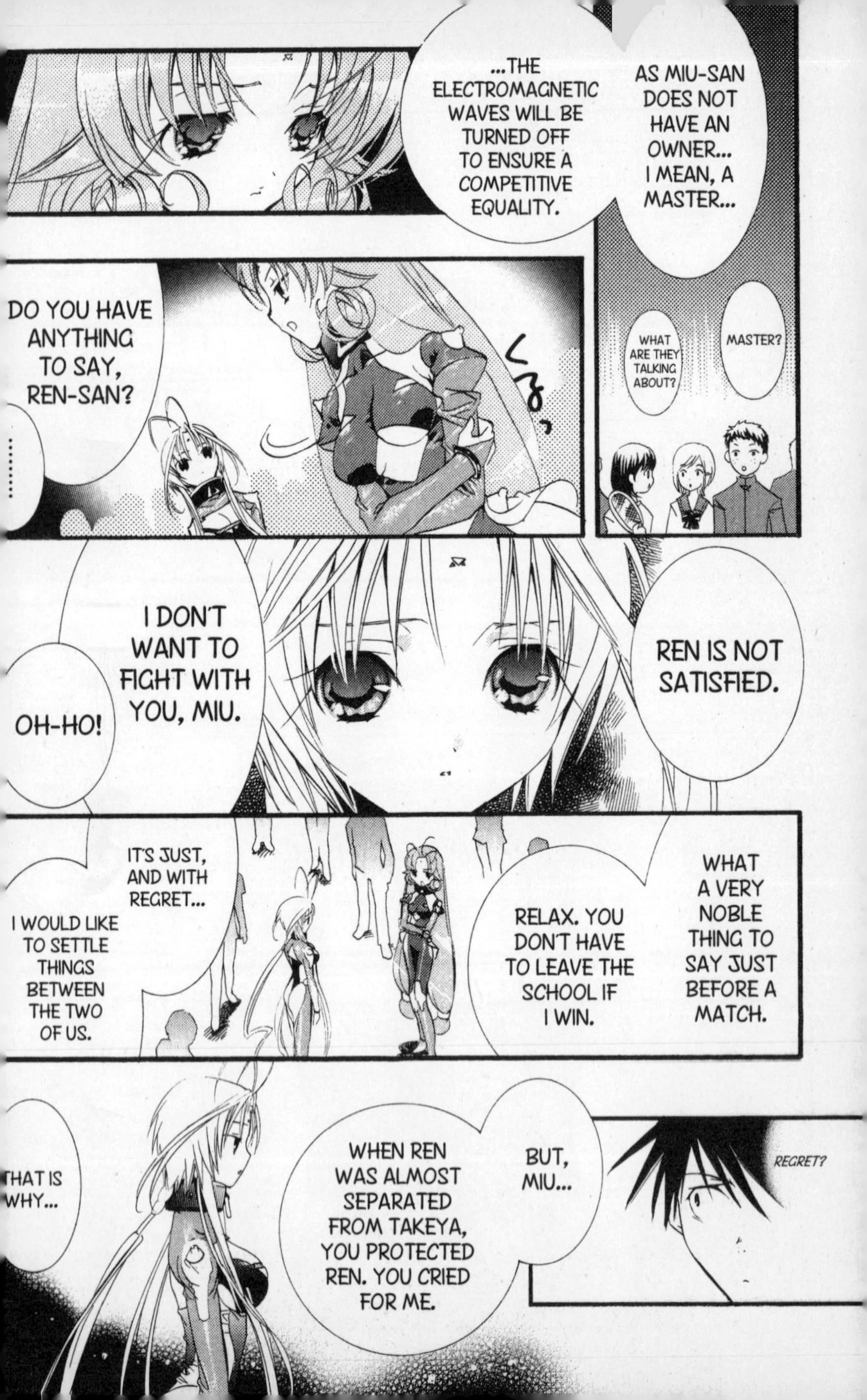
AS MIU-SAN DOES NOT HAVE AN OWNER... I MEAN, A MASTER...
...THE ELECTROMAGNETIC WAVES WILL BE TURNED OFF TO ENSURE A COMPETITIVE EQUALITY.
MASTER?
WHAT ARE THEY TALKING ABOUT?
DO YOU HAVE ANYTHING TO SAY, REN-SAN?
......
REN IS NOT SATISFIED.
I DON'T WANT TO FIGHT WITH YOU, MIU.
OH-HO!
WHAT A VERY NOBLE THING TO SAY JUST BEFORE A MATCH.
RELAX. YOU DON'T HAVE TO LEAVE THE SCHOOL IF I WIN.
IT'S JUST, AND WITH REGRET...
I WOULD LIKE TO SETTLE THINGS BETWEEN THE TWO OF US.
REGRET?
BUT, MIU...
WHEN REN WAS ALMOST SEPARATED FROM TAKEYA, YOU PROTECTED REN. YOU CRIED FOR ME.
THAT IS WHY...

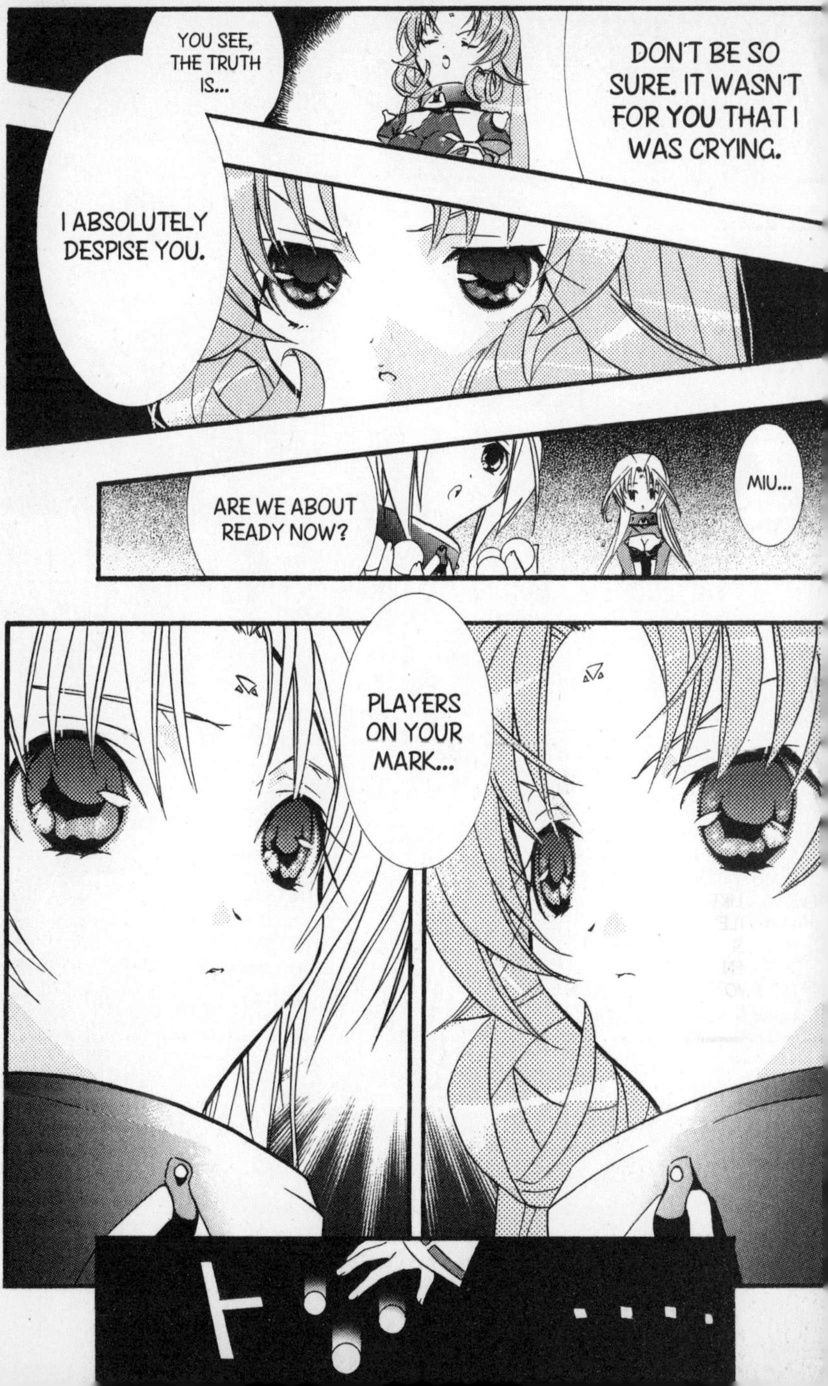
DON'T BE SO SURE. IT WASN'T FOR YOU THAT I WAS CRYING.
YOU SEE, THE TRUTH IS...
I ABSOLUTELY DESPISE YOU.
MIU...
ARE WE ABOUT READY NOW?
PLAYERS ON YOUR MARK...
ト...

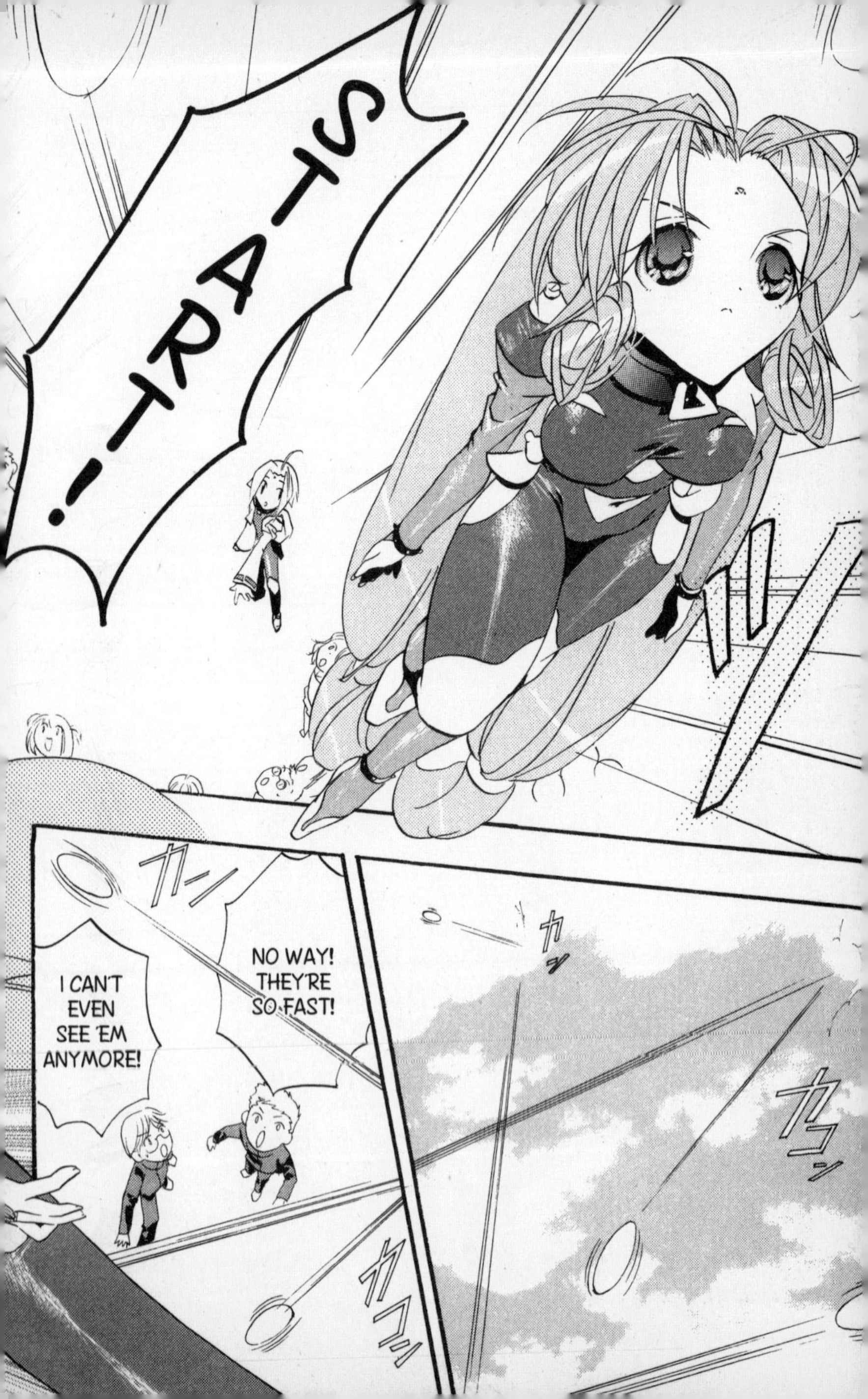
START—!
NO WAY! THEY'RE SO FAST!
I CAN'T EVEN SEE 'EM ANYMORE!

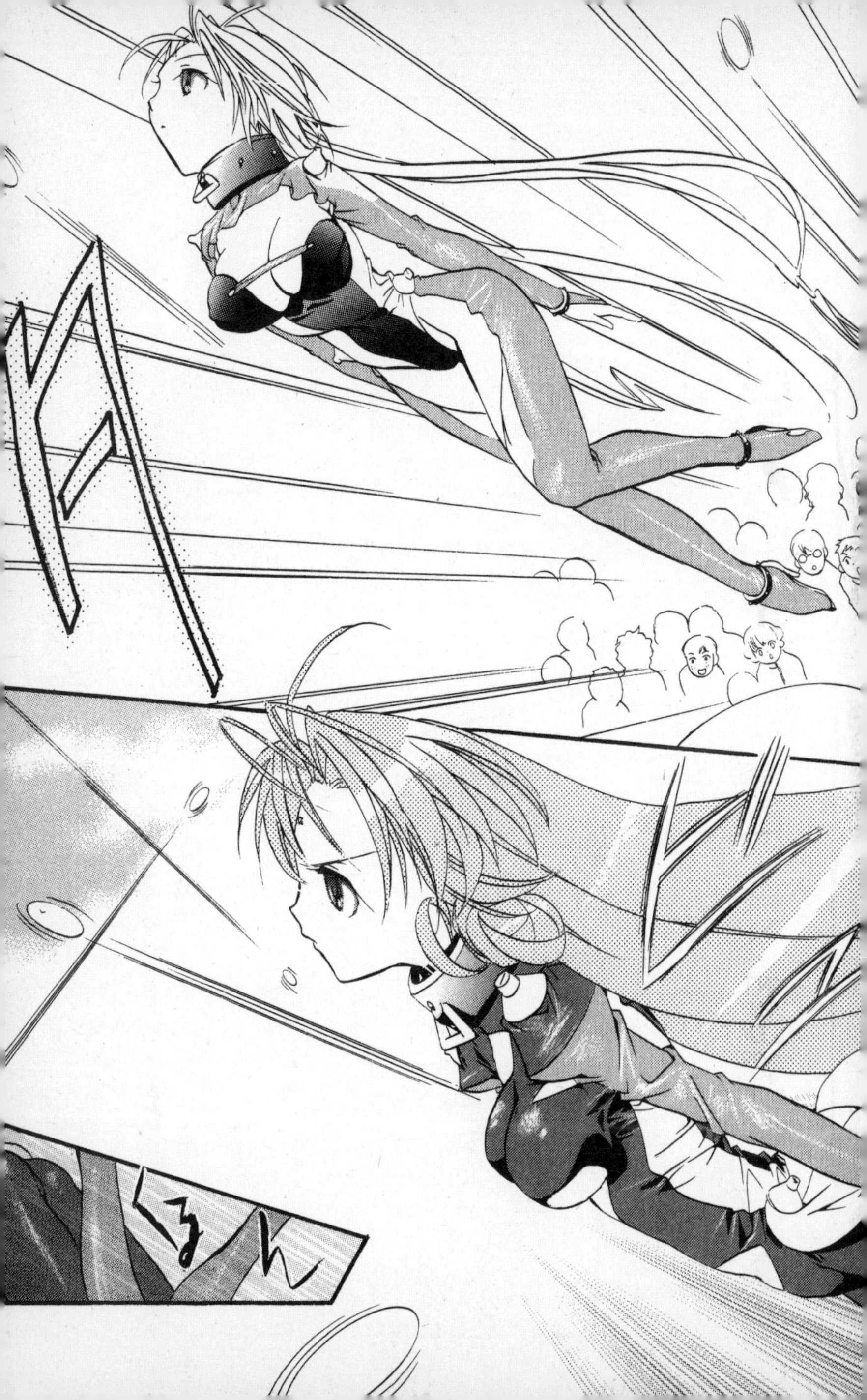

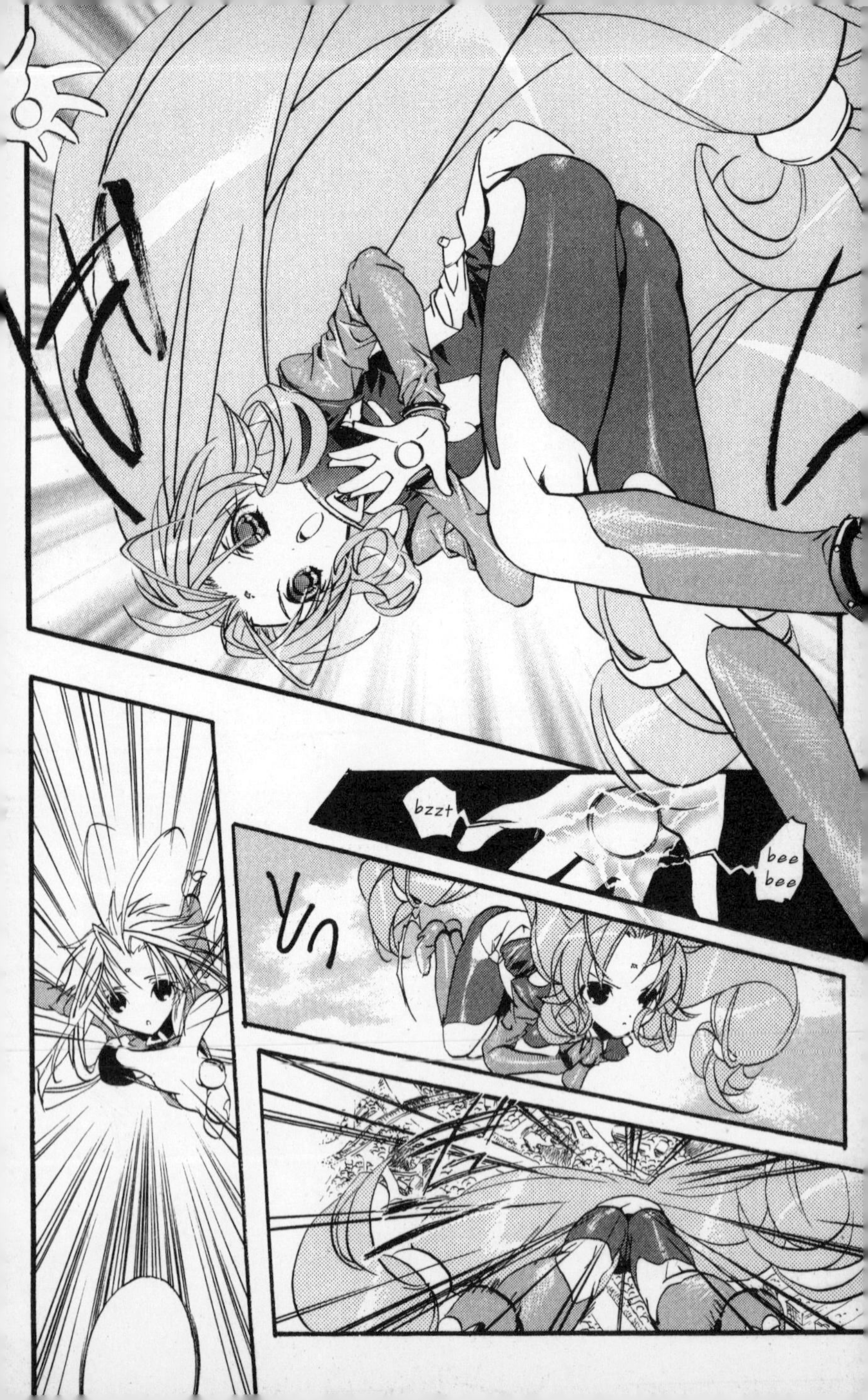
bzzt
bee bee

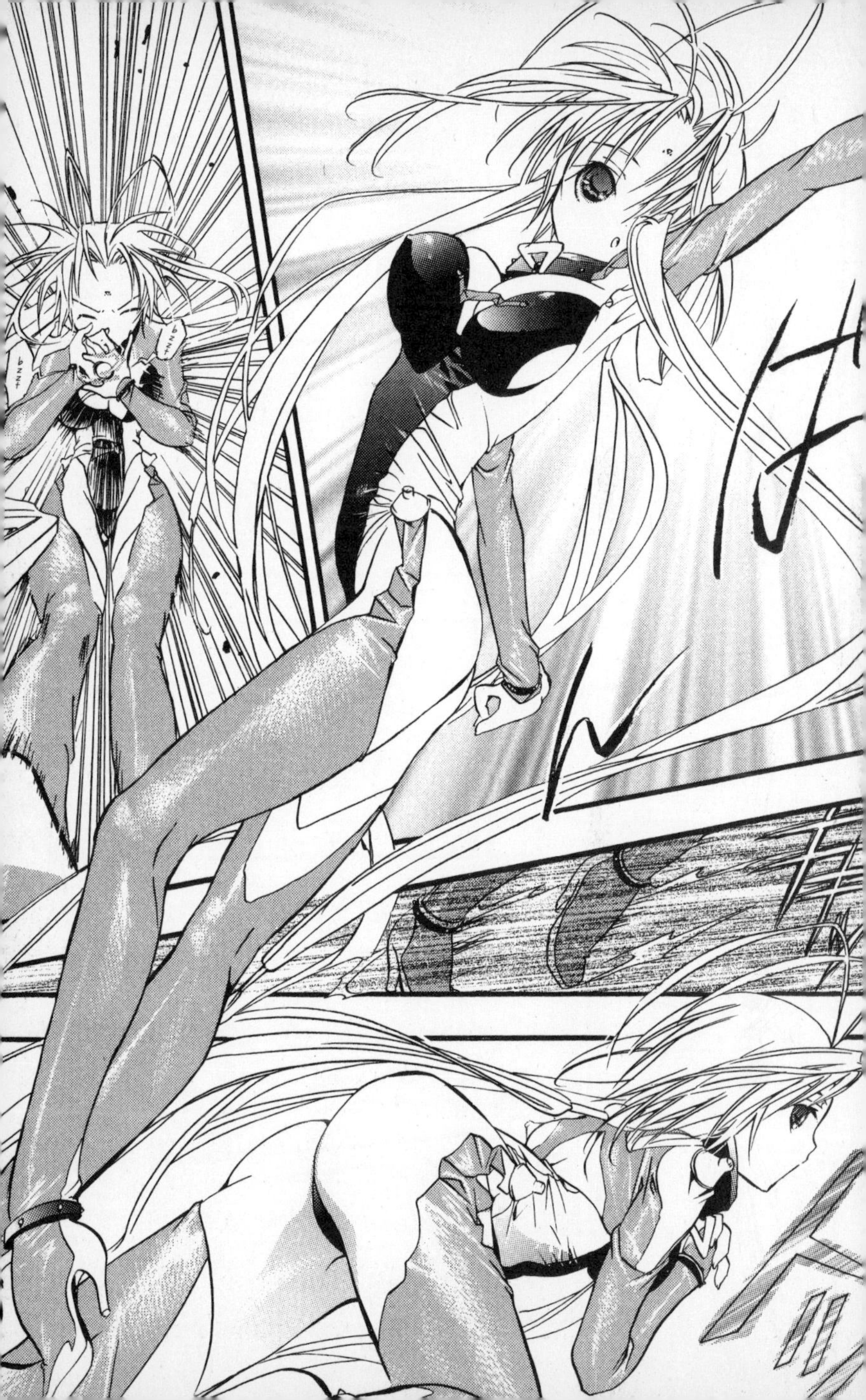
bzzt
bzzt

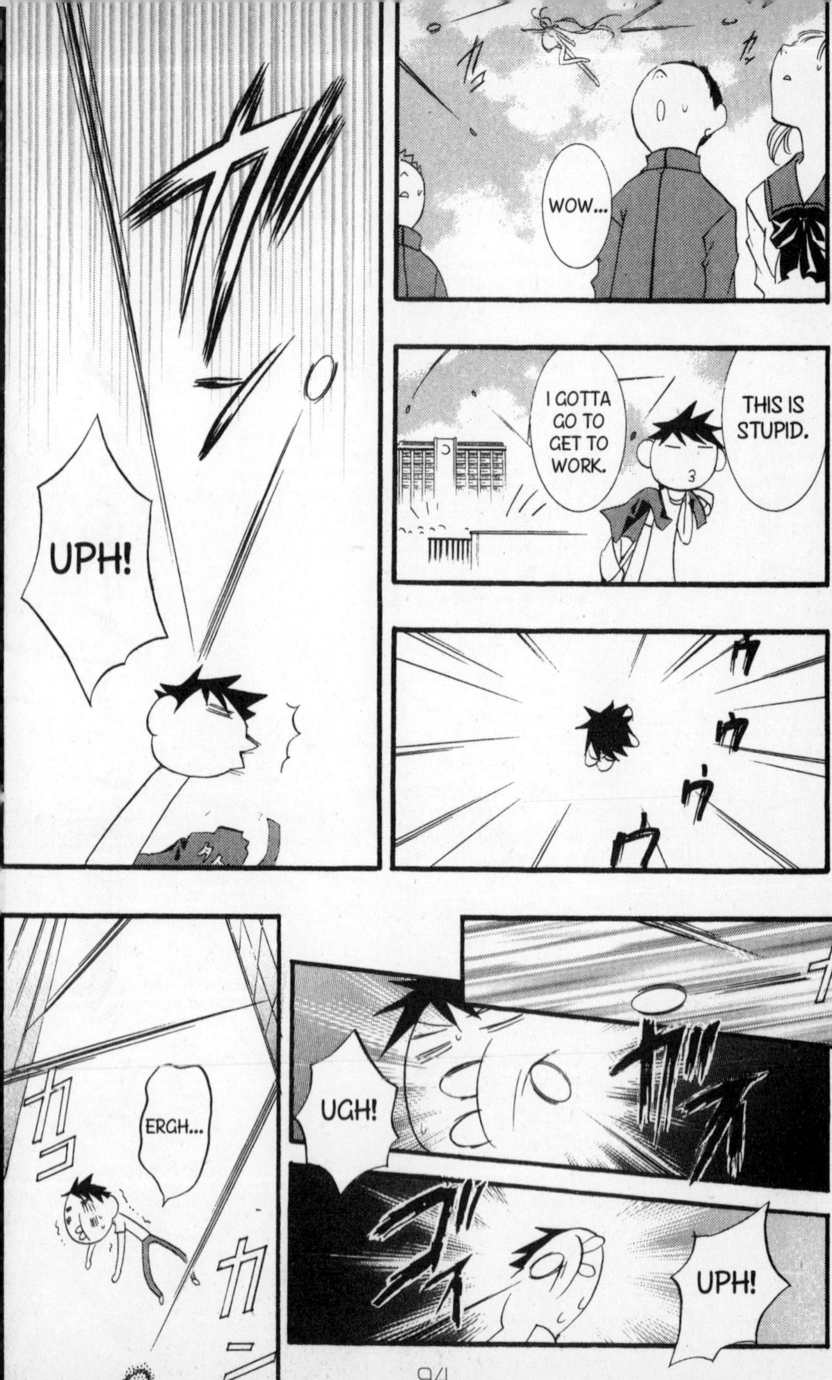
WOW...
THIS IS STUPID.
I GOTTA GO TO GET TO WORK.
UPH!
UGH!
UPH!
ERGH...

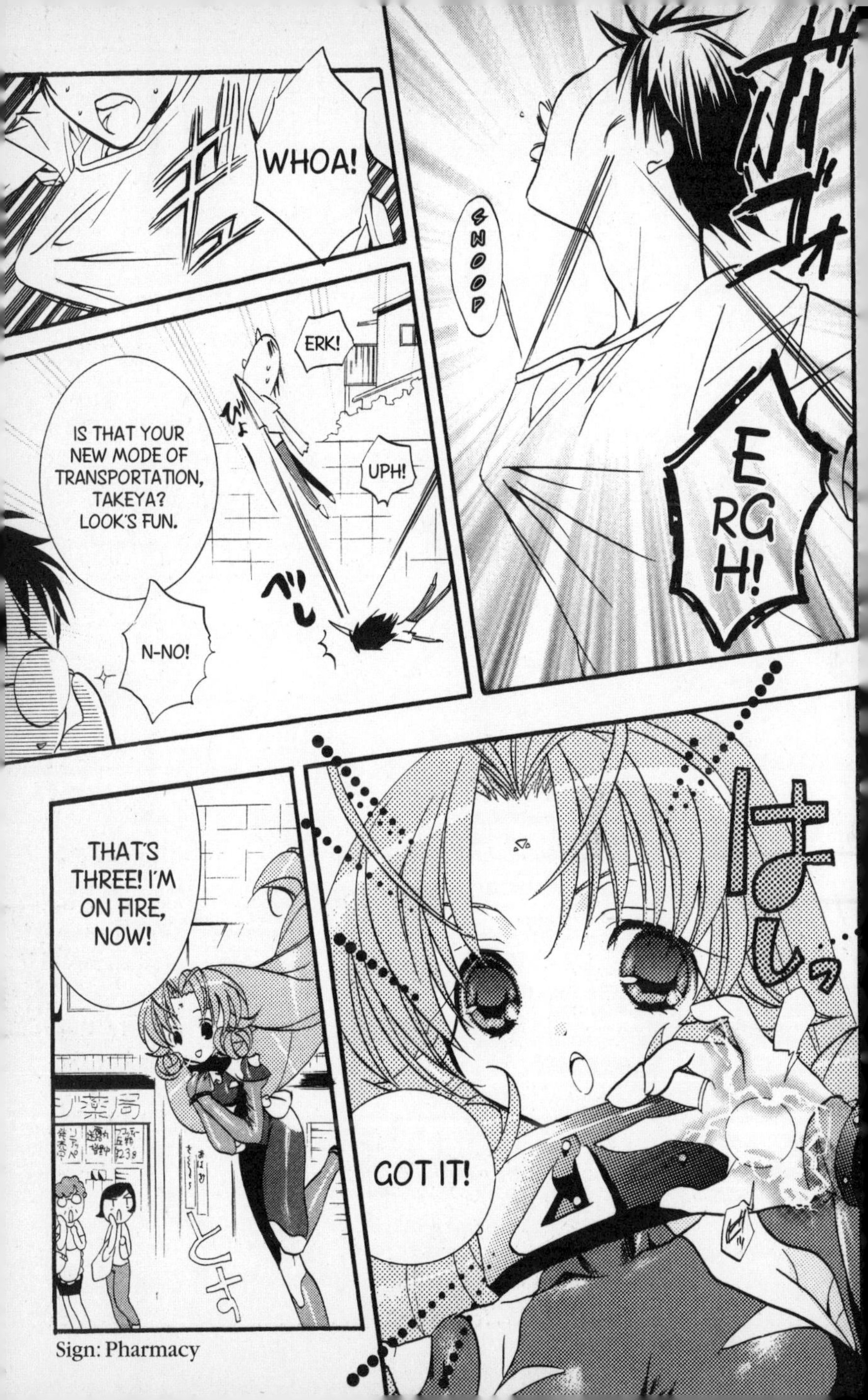
SNOOP
ERGH!
WHOA!
ERK!
UPH!
IS THAT YOUR NEW MODE OF TRANSPORTATION, TAKEYA? LOOK'S FUN.
N-NO!
GOT IT!
THAT'S THREE! I'M ON FIRE, NOW!
Sign: Pharmacy

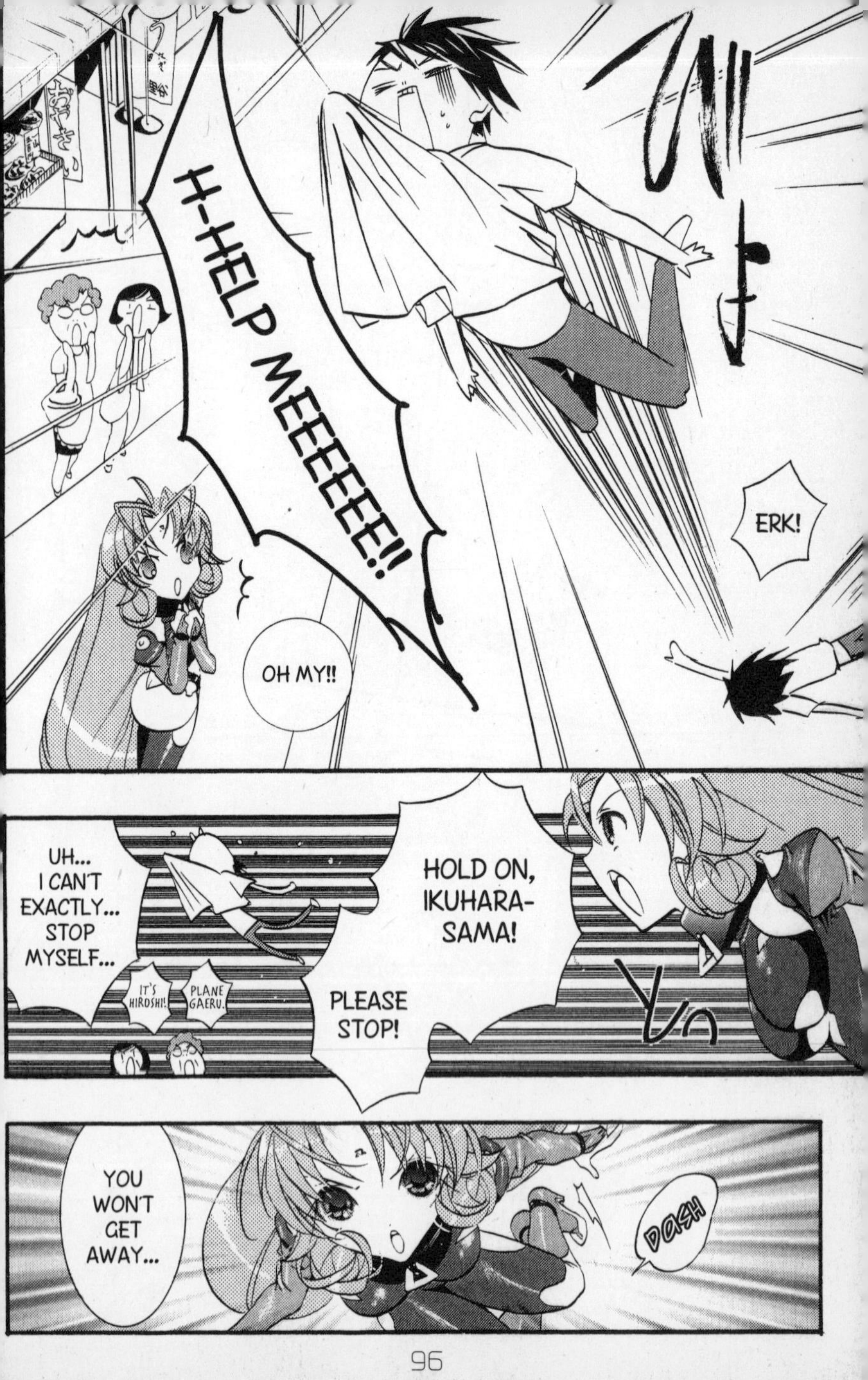
ERK!
H-HELP MEEEEEEE!!
OH MY!!
HOLD ON, IKUHARA-SAMA!
PLEASE STOP!
UH... I CAN'T EXACTLY... STOP MYSELF...
PLANE GAERU.
IT'S HIROSHI!
DASH
YOU WON'T GET AWAY...

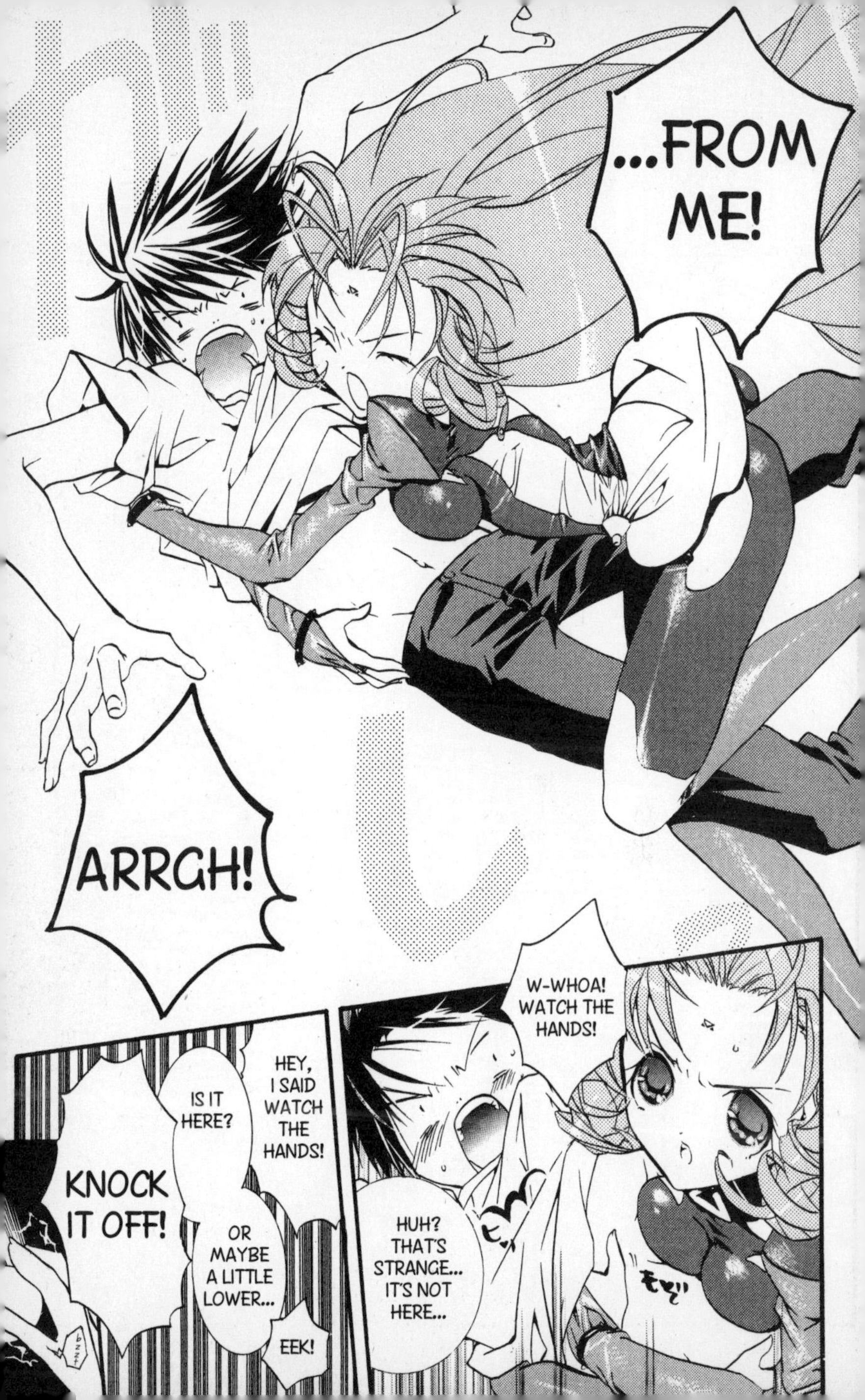
...FROM ME!
ARRGH!
W-WHOA! WATCH THE HANDS!
HUH? THAT'S STRANGE... IT'S NOT HERE...
HEY, I SAID WATCH THE HANDS!
IS IT HERE?
OR MAYBE A LITTLE LOWER...
EEK!
KNOCK IT OFF!

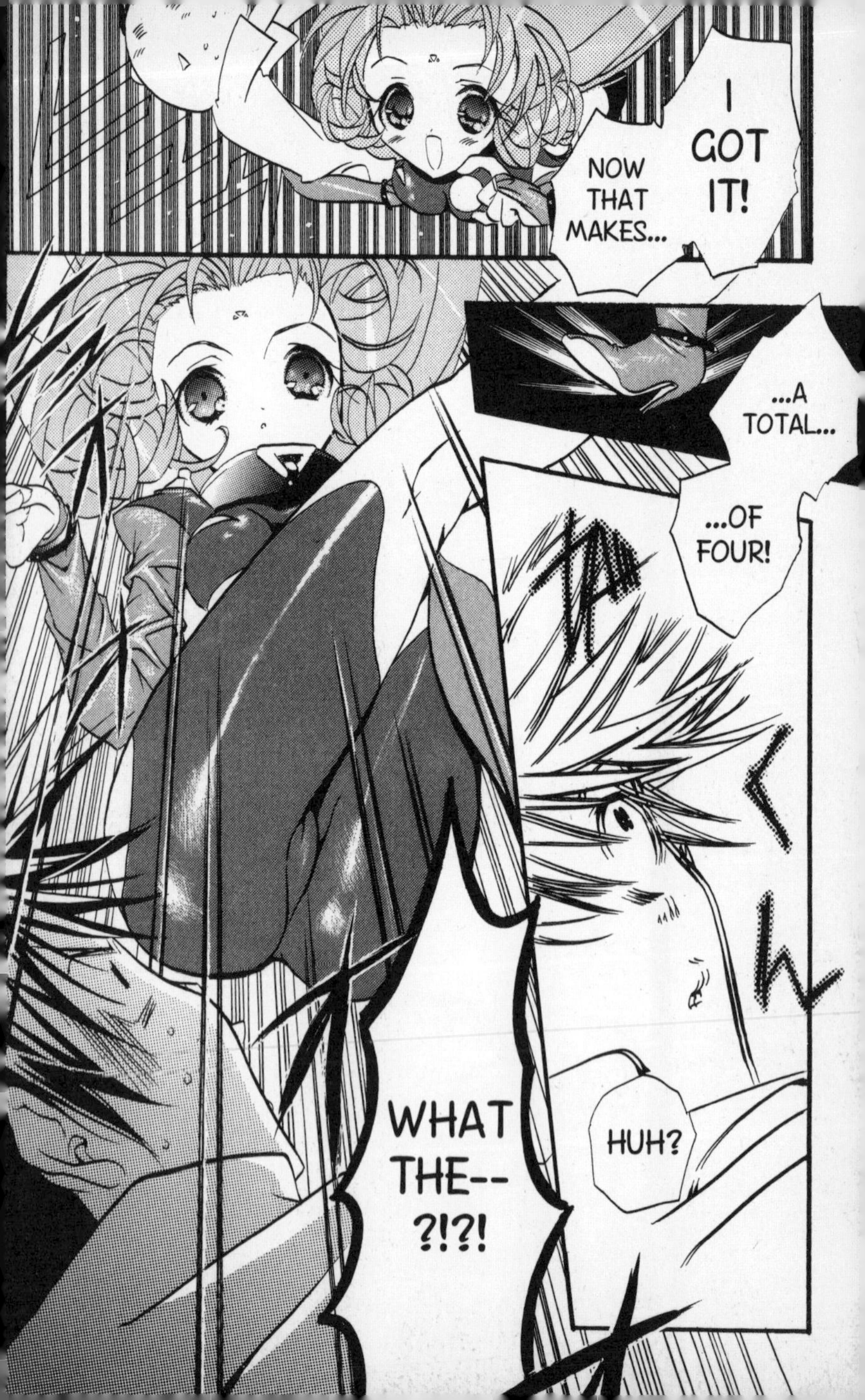
I GOT IT!
NOW THAT MAKES...
...A TOTAL...
...OF FOUR!
HUH?
WHAT THE-- ?!?!

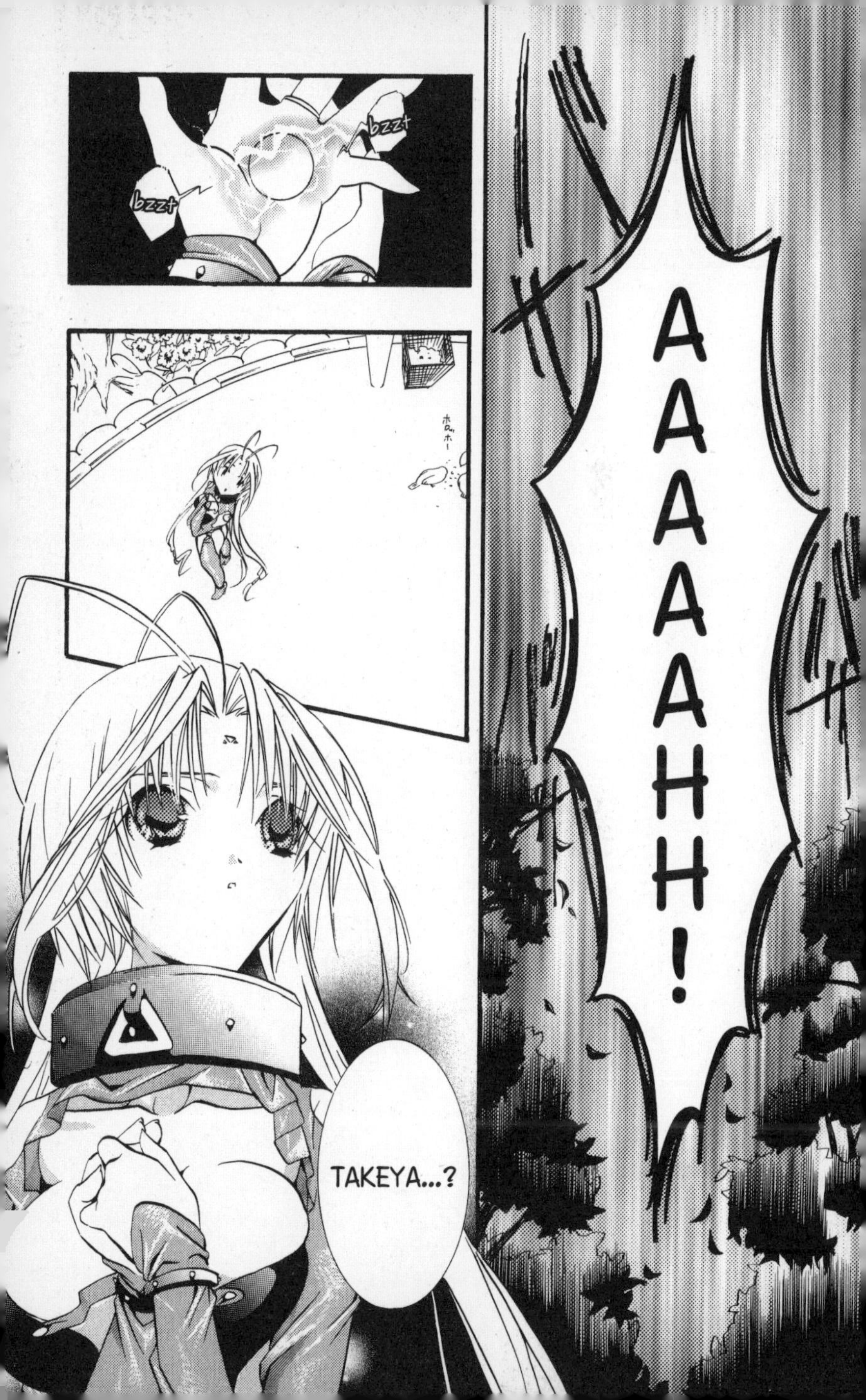
AAAAAH!
bzzt
bzzt
TAKEYA...?

DearS
ディアーズ

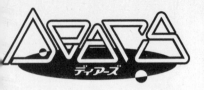

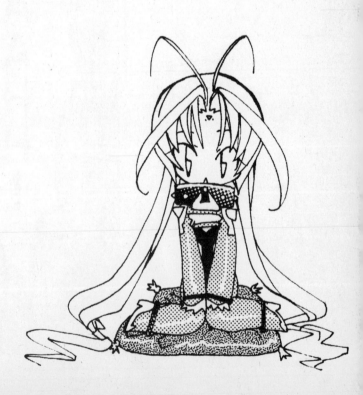

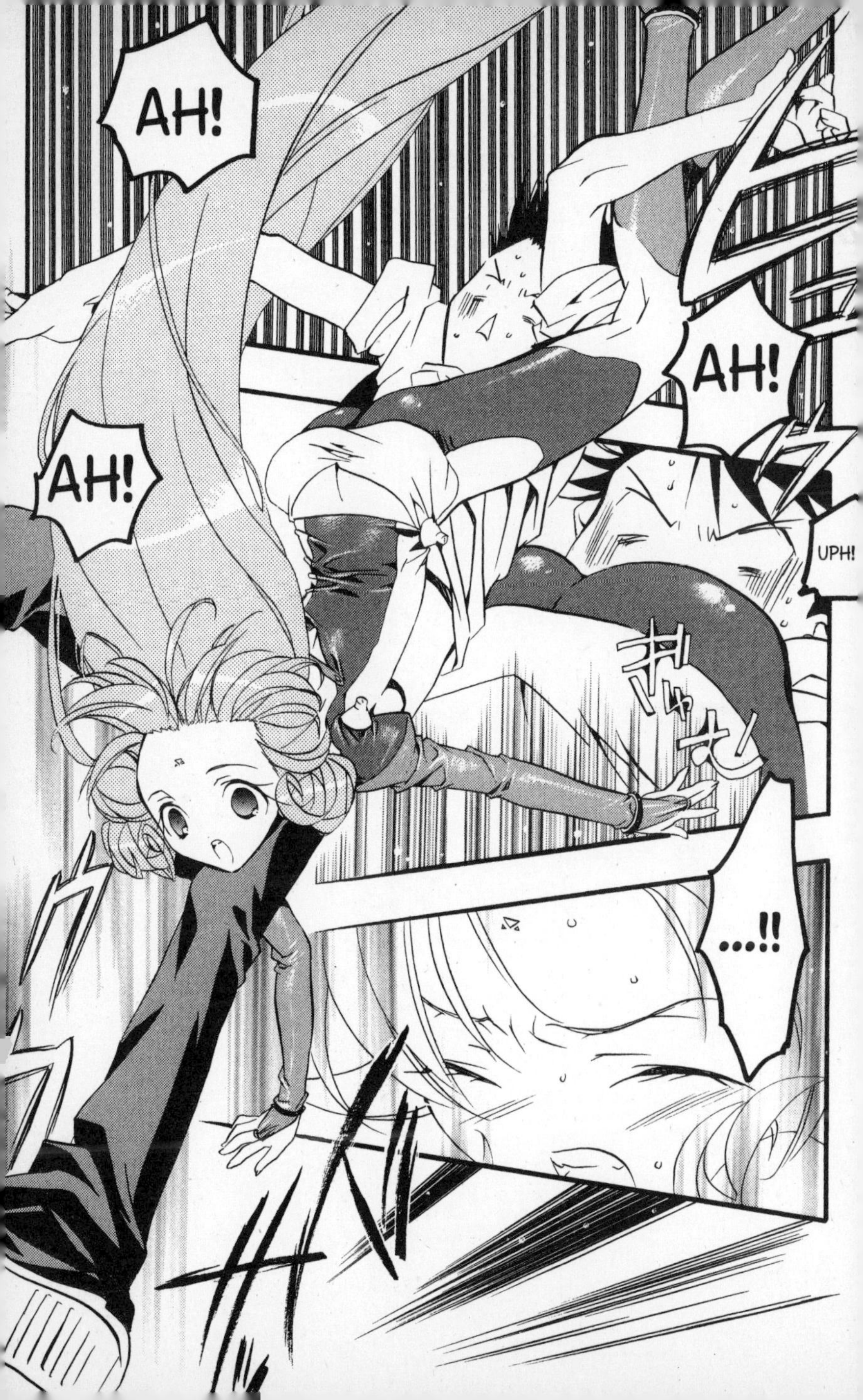
AH!
AH!
AH!
UPH!
...!!

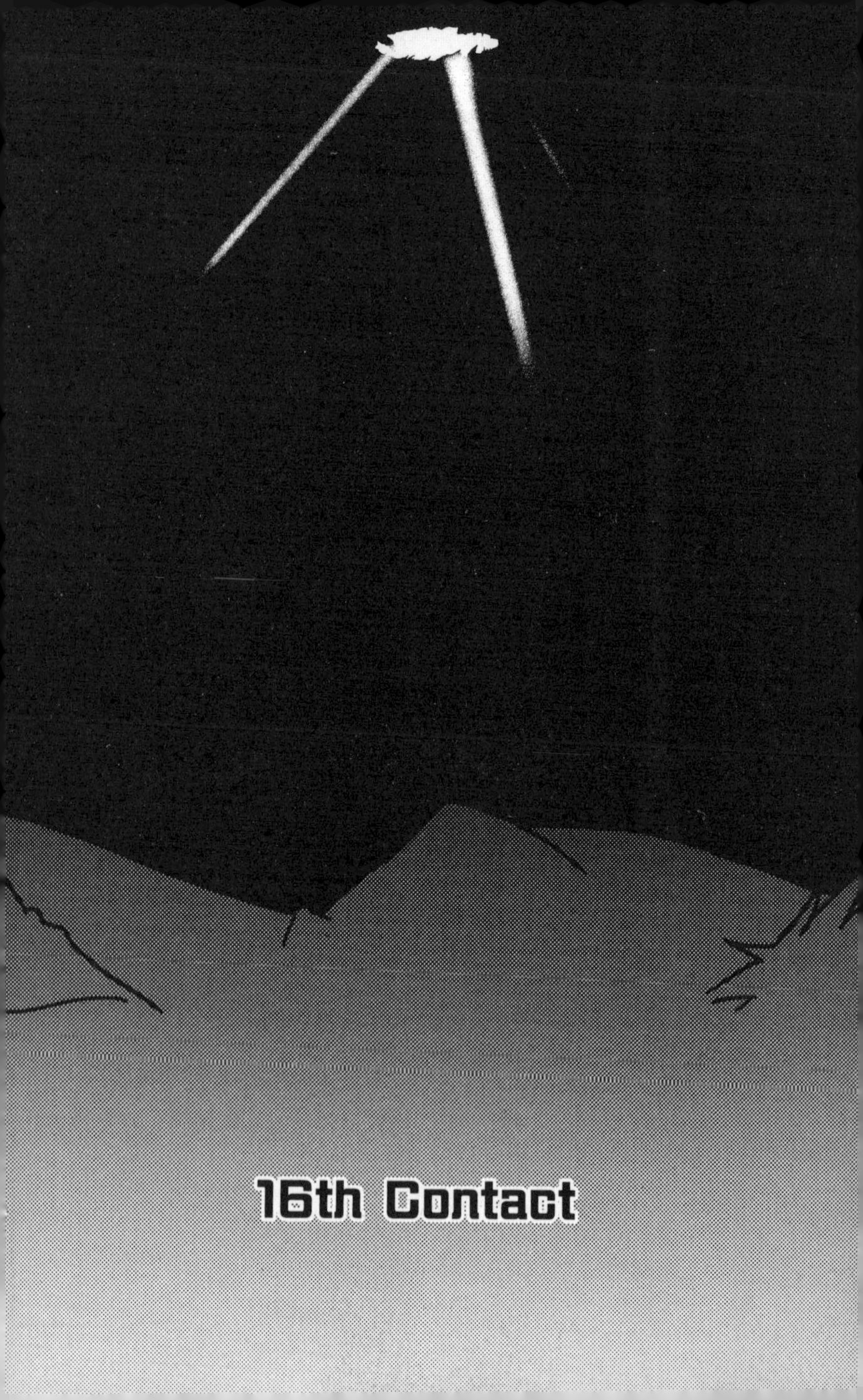
16th Contact

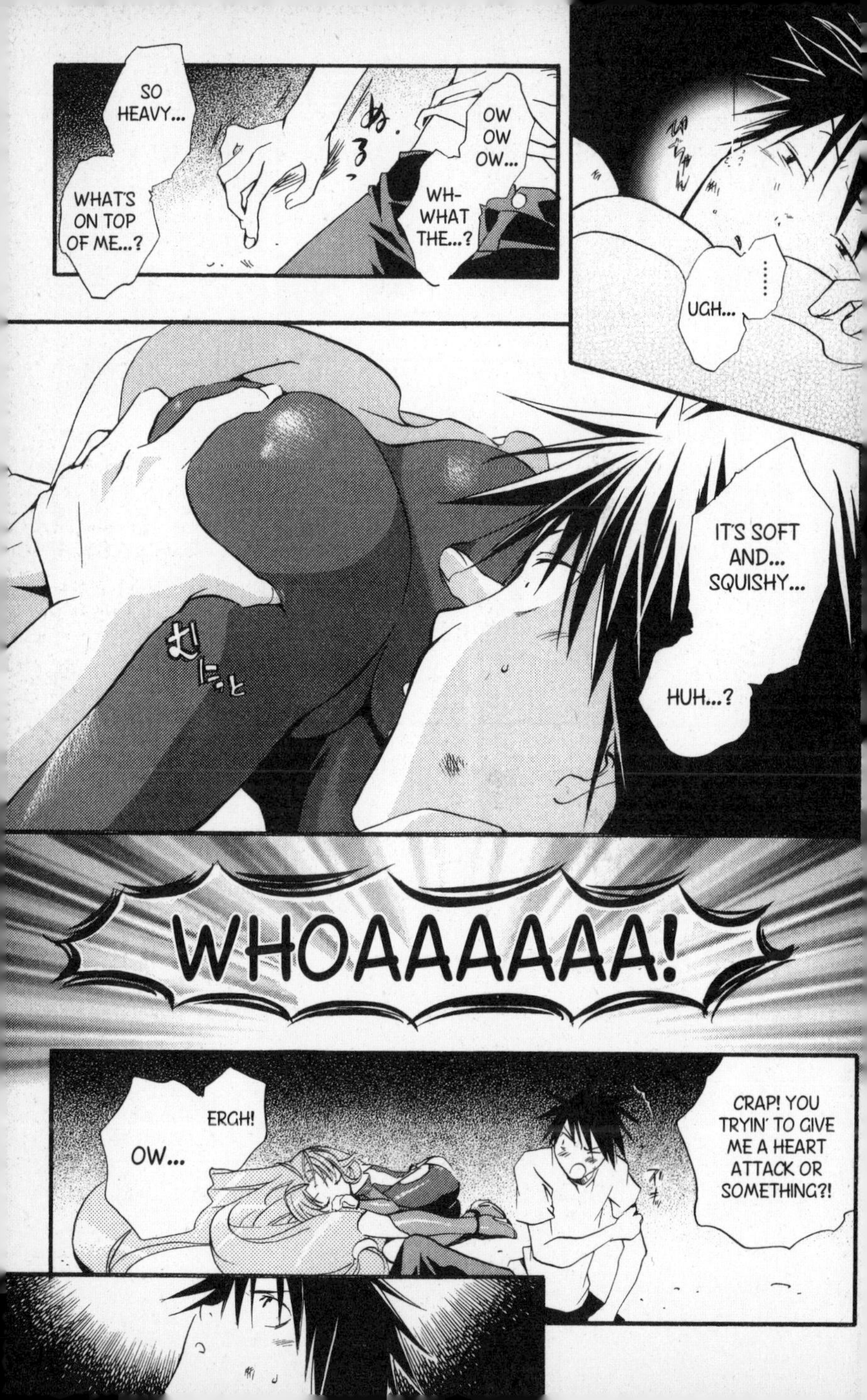
......
UGH...
OW OW OW...
SO HEAVY...
WH-WHAT THE...?
WHAT'S ON TOP OF ME...?
IT'S SOFT AND... SQUISHY...
HUH...?
WHOAAAAAAA!
CRAP! YOU TRYIN' TO GIVE ME A HEART ATTACK OR SOMETHING?!
ERGH!
OW...

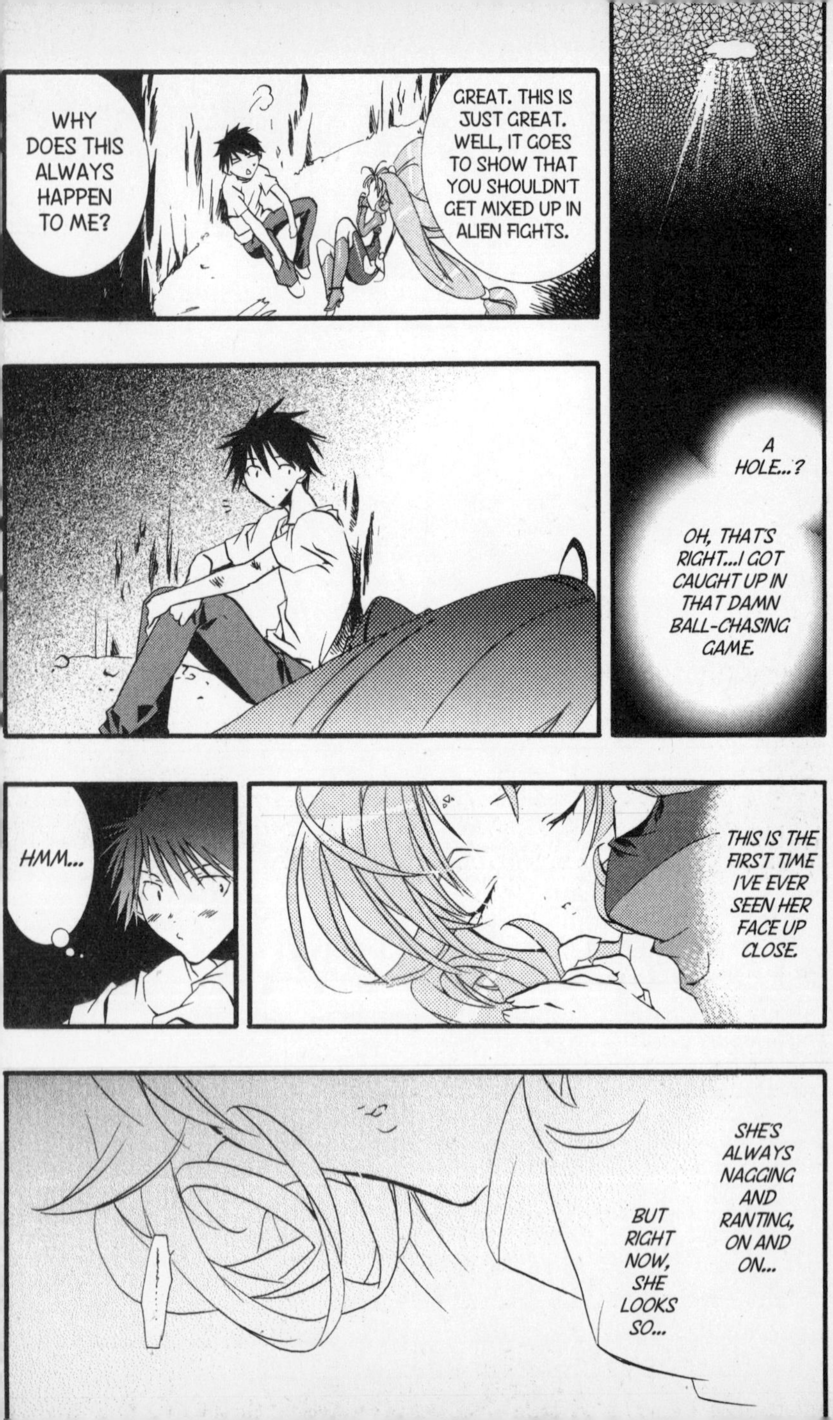
A HOLE...?
OH, THAT'S RIGHT...I GOT CAUGHT UP IN THAT DAMN BALL-CHASING GAME.
GREAT. THIS IS JUST GREAT. WELL, IT GOES TO SHOW THAT YOU SHOULDN'T GET MIXED UP IN ALIEN FIGHTS.
WHY DOES THIS ALWAYS HAPPEN TO ME?
THIS IS THE FIRST TIME I'VE EVER SEEN HER FACE UP CLOSE.
HMM...
SHE'S ALWAYS NAGGING AND RANTING, ON AND ON...
BUT RIGHT NOW, SHE LOOKS SO...
......

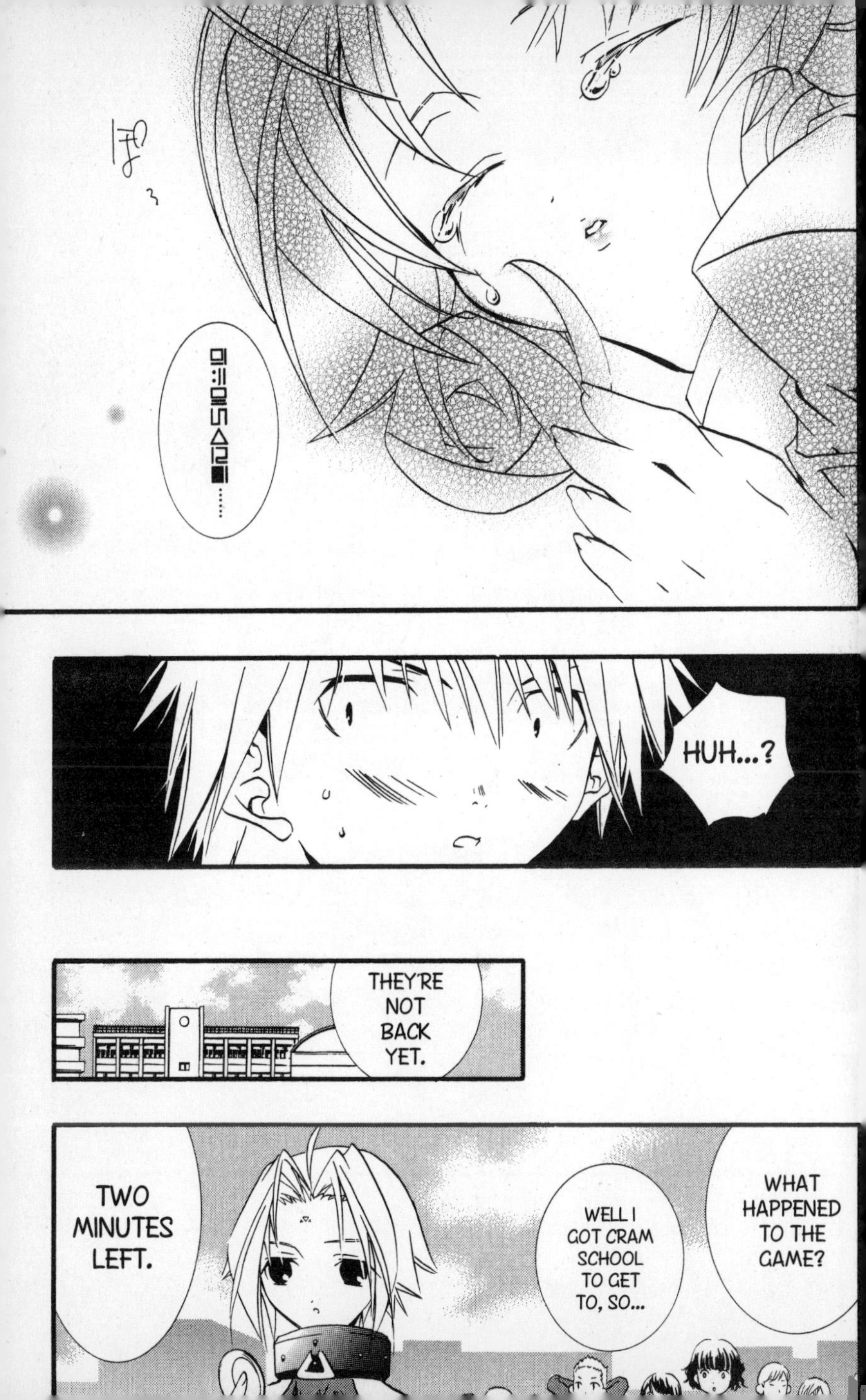
HUH...?
THEY'RE NOT BACK YET.
WHAT HAPPENED TO THE GAME?
WELL I GOT CRAM SCHOOL TO GET TO, SO...
TWO MINUTES LEFT.

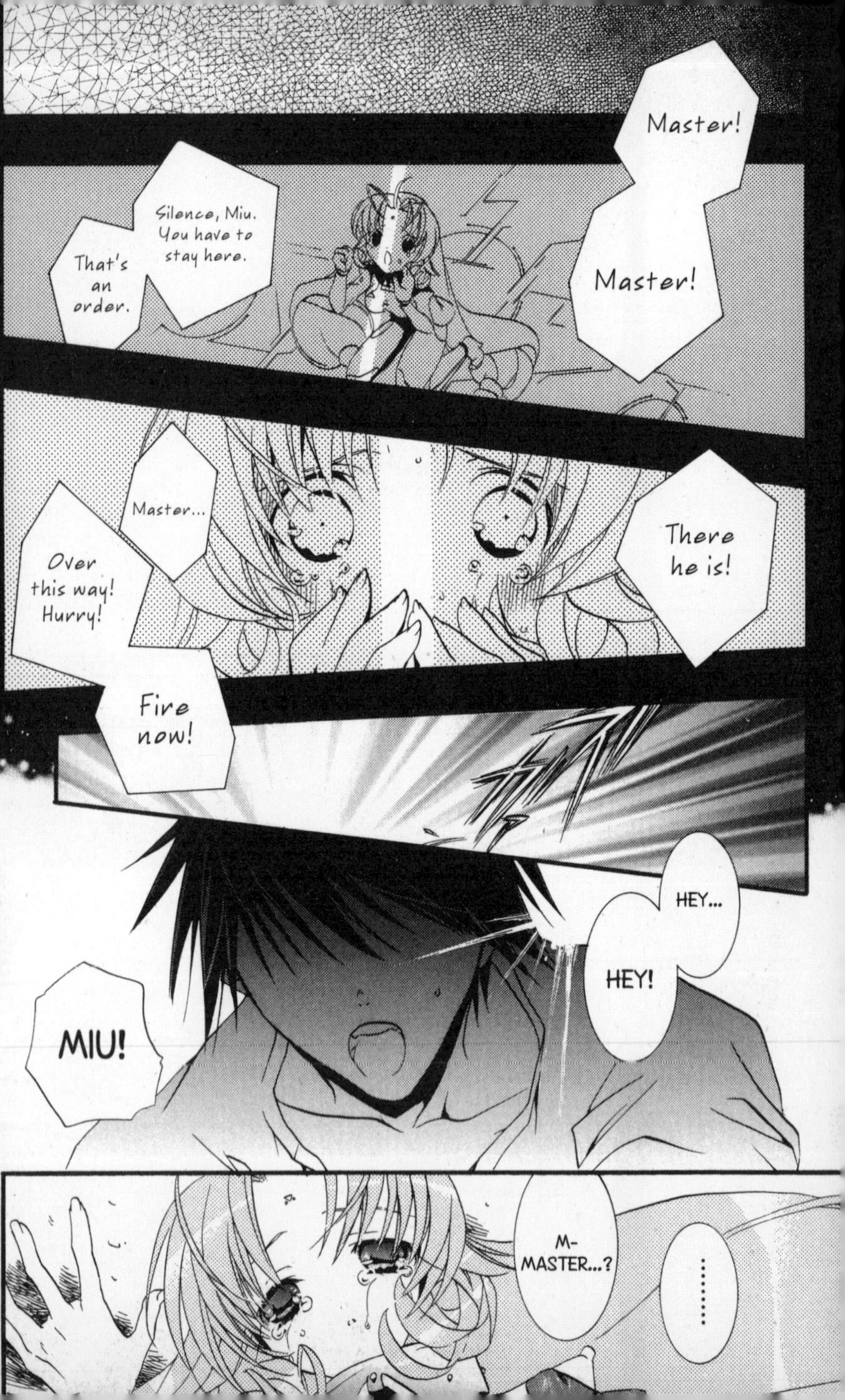

Master!
Master!
Silence, Miu. You have to stay here.
That's an order.
There he is!
Master...
Over this way! Hurry!
Fire now!
HEY...
HEY!
MIU!
....
M-MASTER...?

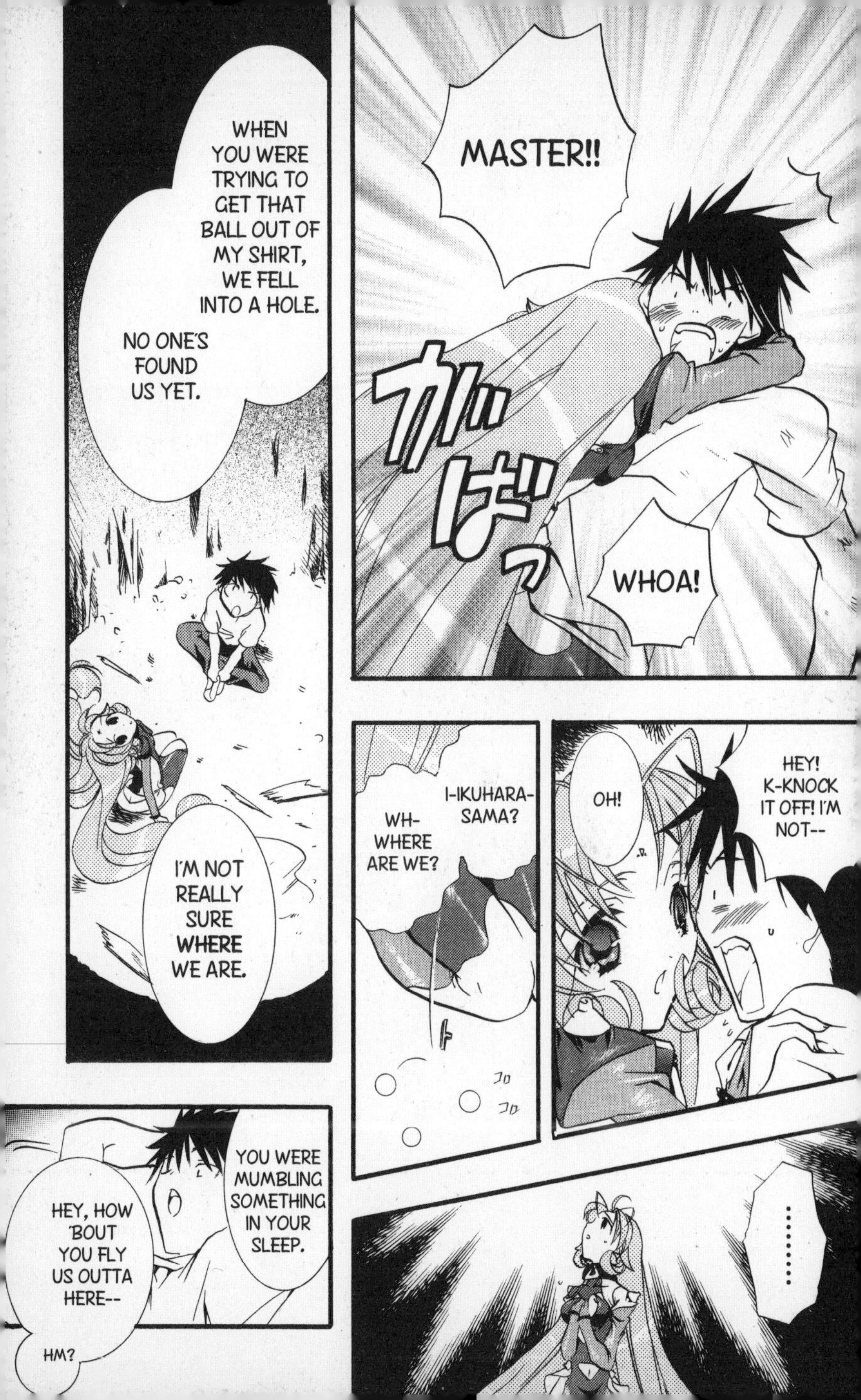
MASTER!!
カばっ
WHOA!
HEY! K-KNOCK IT OFF! I'M NOT--
OH!
I-IKUHARA-SAMA?
WH- WHERE ARE WE?
コロ
コロ
WHEN YOU WERE TRYING TO GET THAT BALL OUT OF MY SHIRT, WE FELL INTO A HOLE.
NO ONE'S FOUND US YET.
I'M NOT REALLY SURE WHERE WE ARE.
......
YOU WERE MUMBLING SOMETHING IN YOUR SLEEP.
HEY, HOW 'BOUT YOU FLY US OUTTA HERE--
HM?

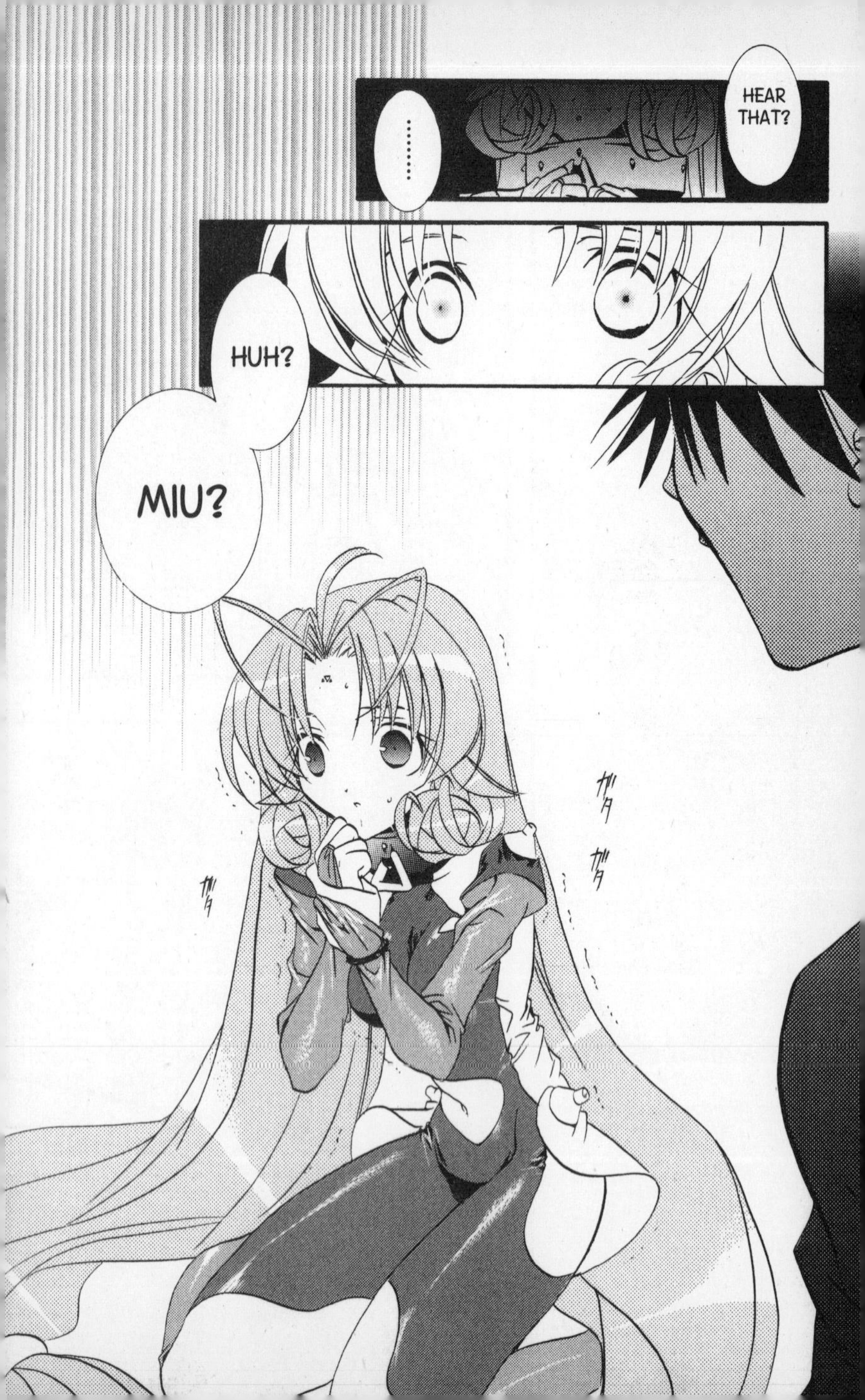
HEAR THAT?
......
HUH?
MIU?
ガタ
ガタ
ガタ

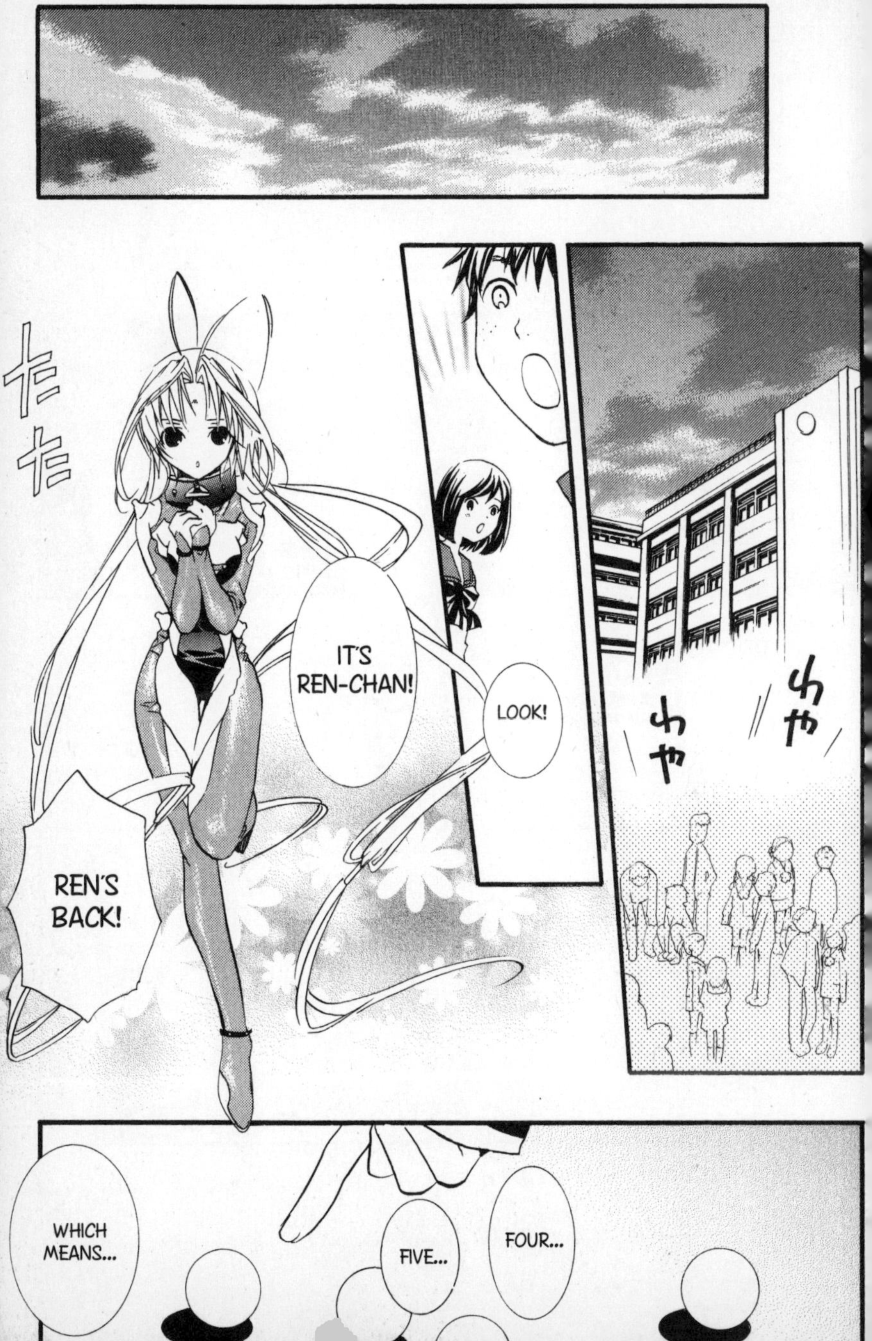
わや わや
LOOK!
IT'S REN-CHAN!
たた
REN'S BACK!
FOUR...
FIVE...
WHICH MEANS...

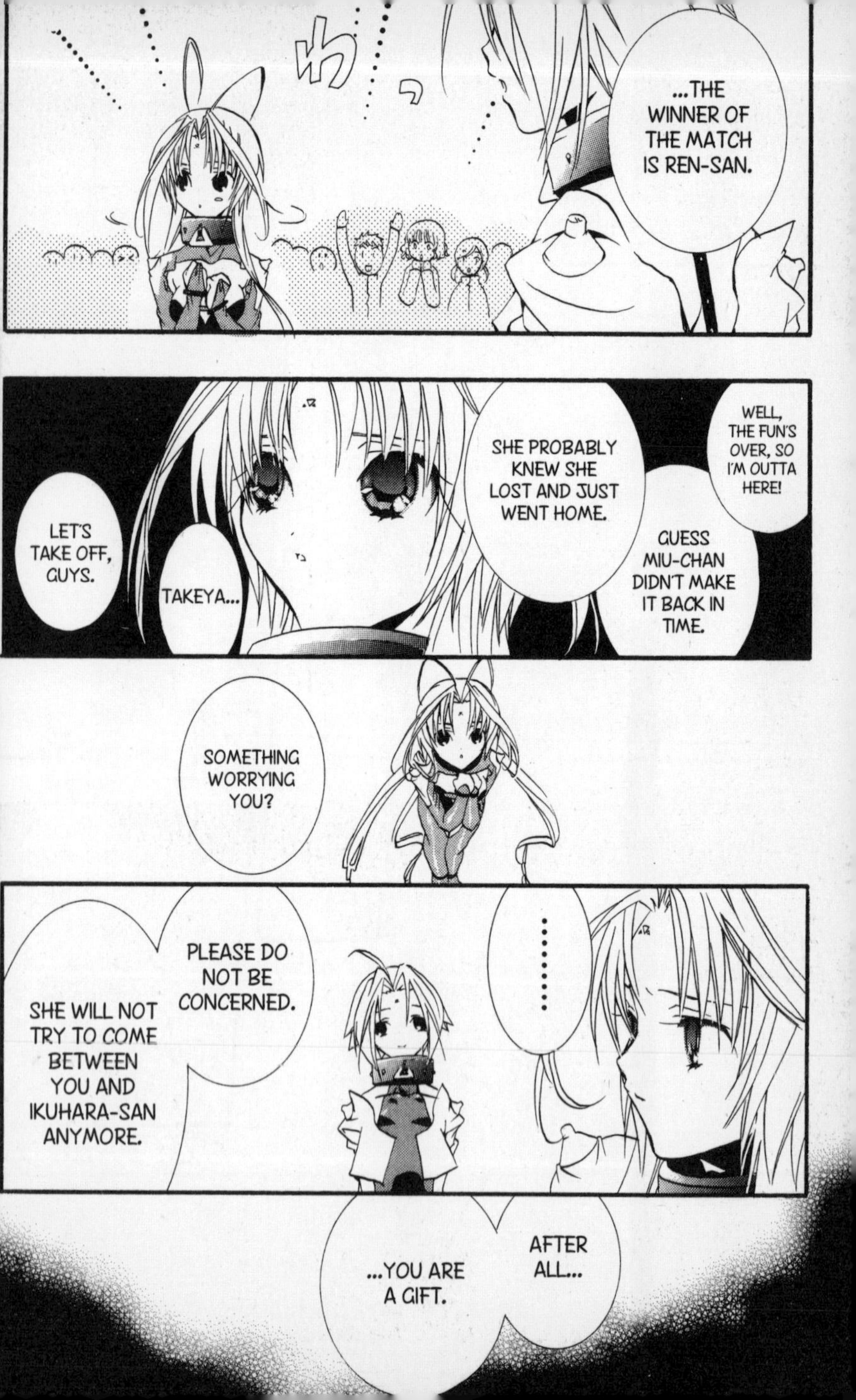
...THE WINNER OF THE MATCH IS REN-SAN.
わっ
WELL, THE FUN'S OVER, SO I'M OUTTA HERE!
GUESS MIU-CHAN DIDN'T MAKE IT BACK IN TIME.
SHE PROBABLY KNEW SHE LOST AND JUST WENT HOME.
TAKEYA...
LET'S TAKE OFF, GUYS.
SOMETHING WORRYING YOU?
......
PLEASE DO NOT BE CONCERNED.
SHE WILL NOT TRY TO COME BETWEEN YOU AND IKUHARA-SAN ANYMORE.
AFTER ALL...
...YOU ARE A GIFT.

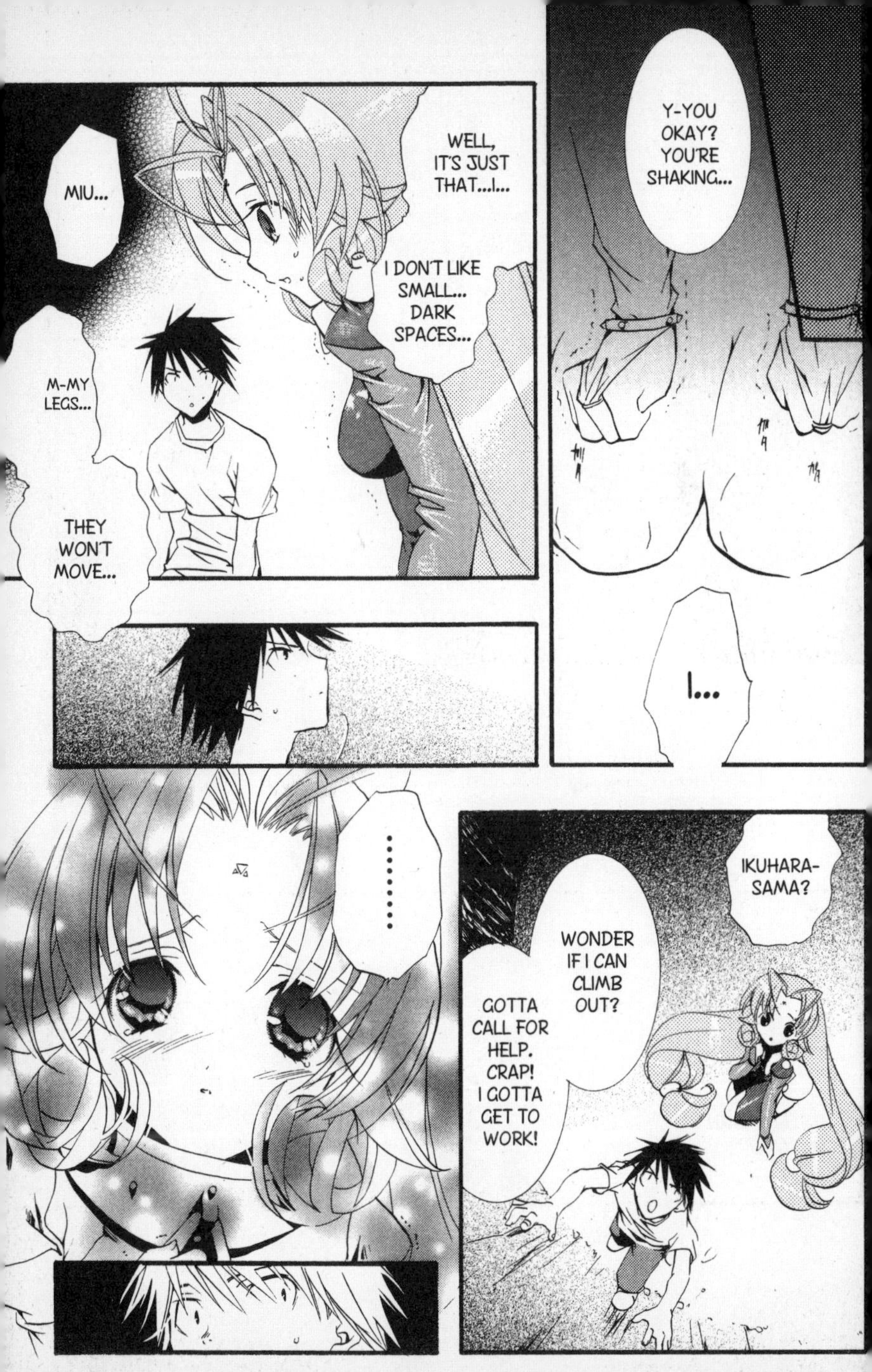
Y-YOU OKAY? YOU'RE SHAKING...
I...
WELL, IT'S JUST THAT...I...
I DON'T LIKE SMALL... DARK SPACES...
MIU...
M-MY LEGS...
THEY WON'T MOVE...
IKUHARA-SAMA?
WONDER IF I CAN CLIMB OUT?
GOTTA CALL FOR HELP. CRAP! I GOTTA GET TO WORK!
....

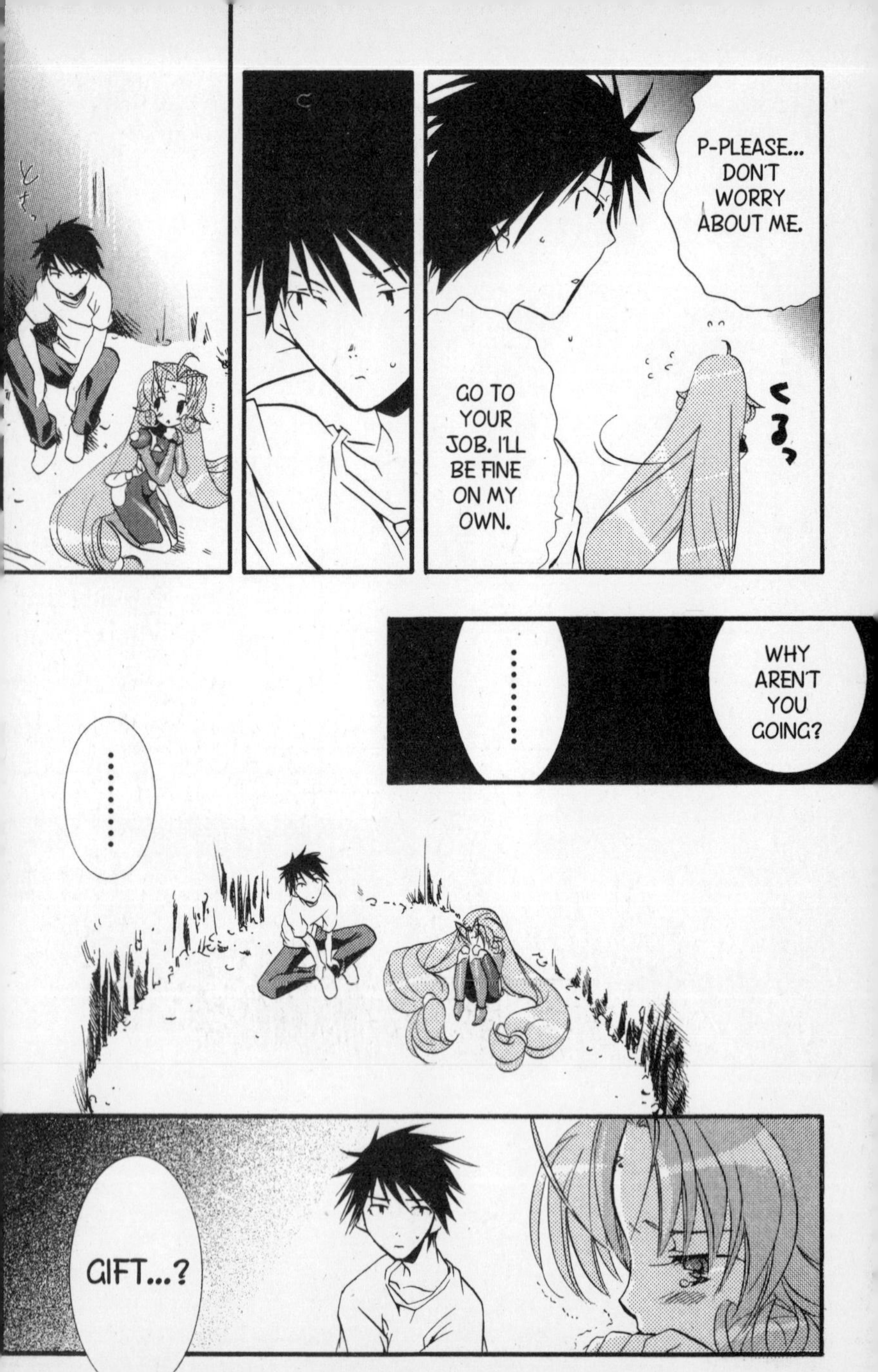
P-PLEASE... DON'T WORRY ABOUT ME.
くるっ
GO TO YOUR JOB. I'LL BE FINE ON MY OWN.
WHY AREN'T YOU GOING?
......
......
GIFT...?

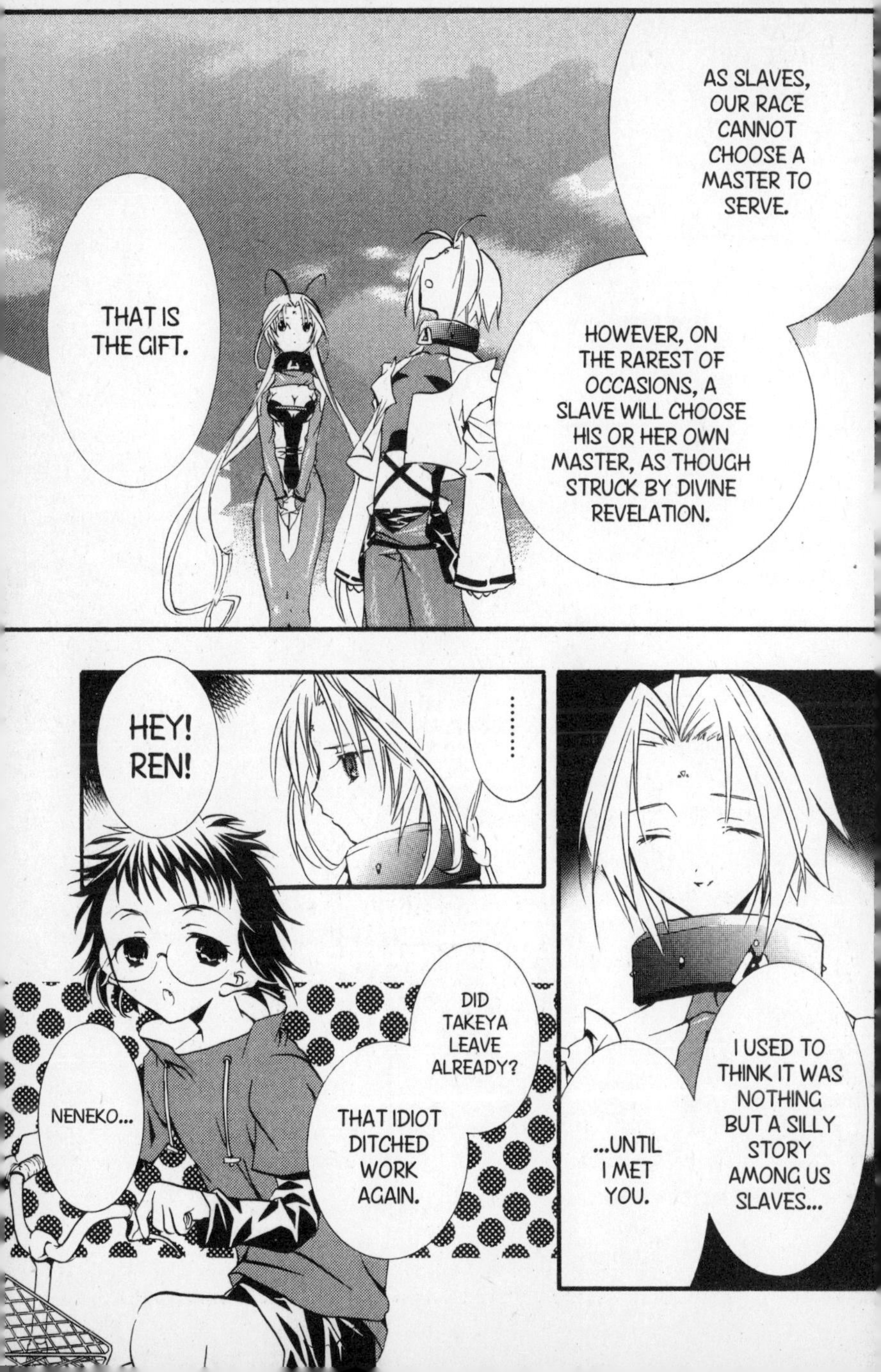
AS SLAVES, OUR RACE CANNOT CHOOSE A MASTER TO SERVE.
HOWEVER, ON THE RAREST OF OCCASIONS, A SLAVE WILL CHOOSE HIS OR HER OWN MASTER, AS THOUGH STRUCK BY DIVINE REVELATION.
THAT IS THE GIFT.
I USED TO THINK IT WAS NOTHING BUT A SILLY STORY AMONG US SLAVES...
...UNTIL I MET YOU.
......
HEY! REN!
DID TAKEYA LEAVE ALREADY?
THAT IDIOT DITCHED WORK AGAIN.
NENEKO...

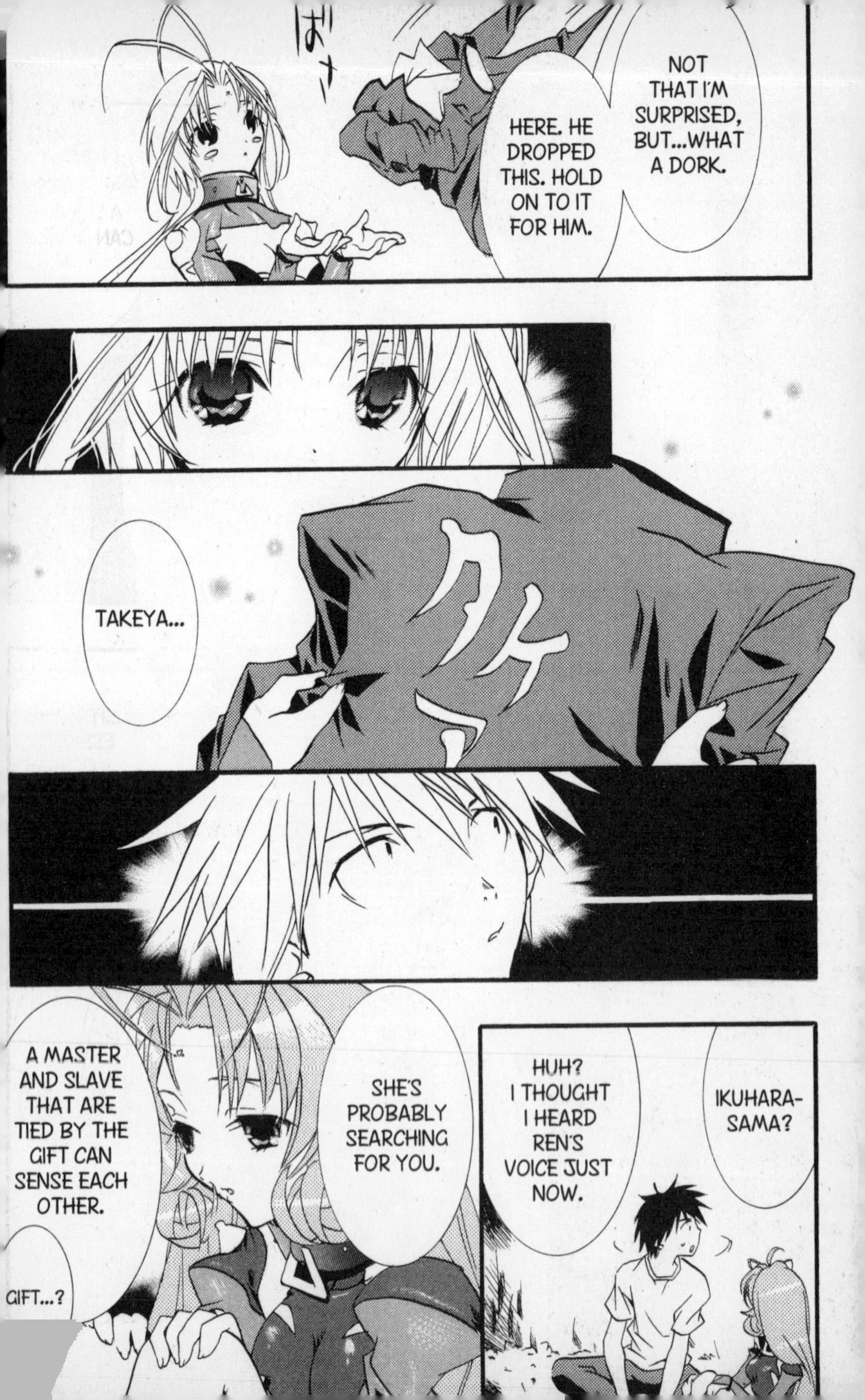
NOT THAT I'M SURPRISED, BUT...WHAT A DORK.
HERE. HE DROPPED THIS. HOLD ON TO IT FOR HIM.
ばさっ
TAKEYA...
IKUHARA-SAMA?
HUH? I THOUGHT I HEARD REN'S VOICE JUST NOW.
SHE'S PROBABLY SEARCHING FOR YOU.
A MASTER AND SLAVE THAT ARE TIED BY THE GIFT CAN SENSE EACH OTHER.
GIFT...?

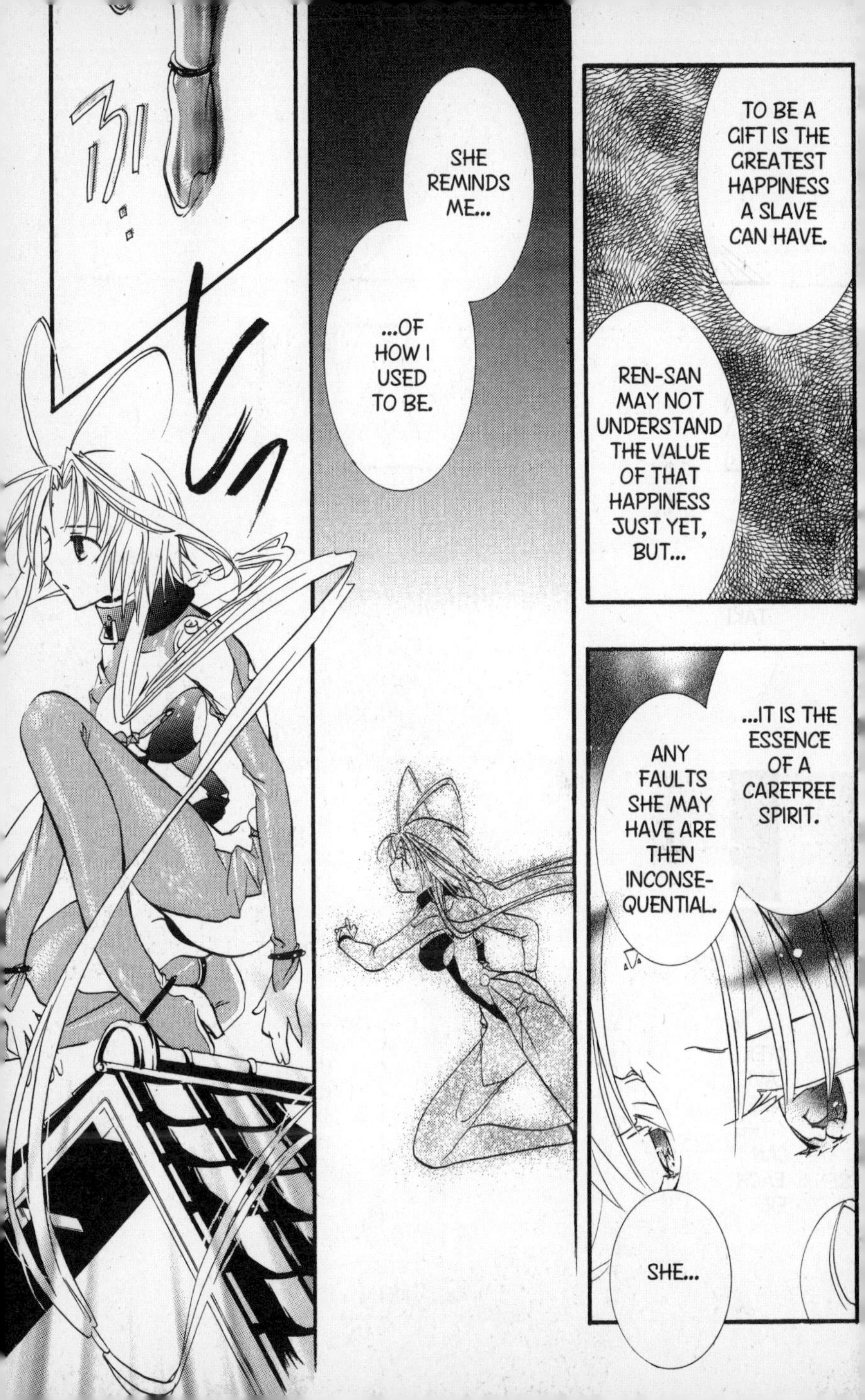
TO BE A GIFT IS THE GREATEST HAPPINESS A SLAVE CAN HAVE.
REN-SAN MAY NOT UNDERSTAND THE VALUE OF THAT HAPPINESS JUST YET, BUT...
...IT IS THE ESSENCE OF A CAREFREE SPIRIT.
ANY FAULTS SHE MAY HAVE ARE THEN INCONSE-QUENTIAL.
SHE...
SHE REMINDS ME...
...OF HOW I USED TO BE.

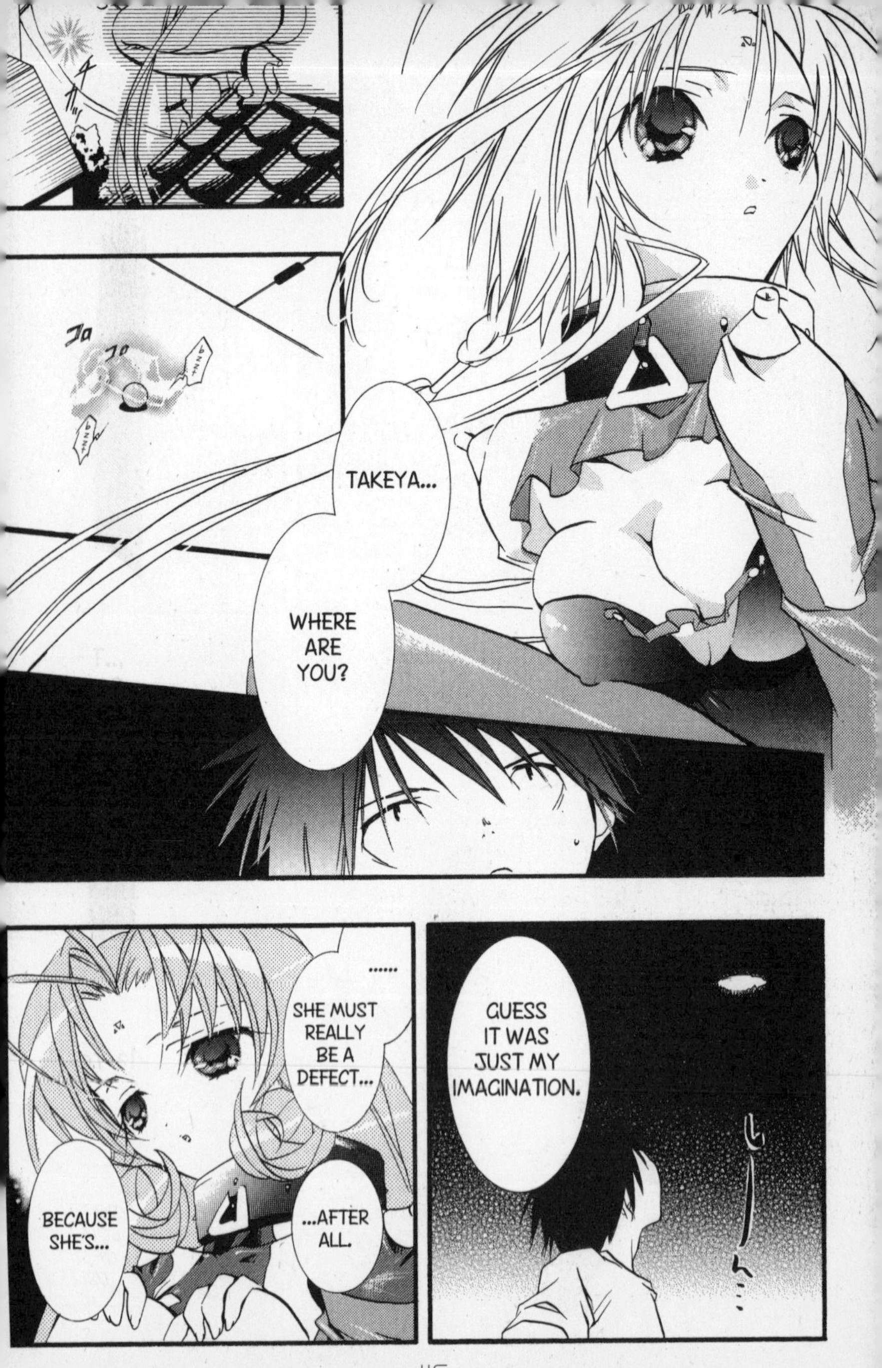
TAKEYA...
WHERE ARE YOU?
GUESS IT WAS JUST MY IMAGINATION.
......
SHE MUST REALLY BE A DEFECT...
...AFTER ALL.
BECAUSE SHE'S...

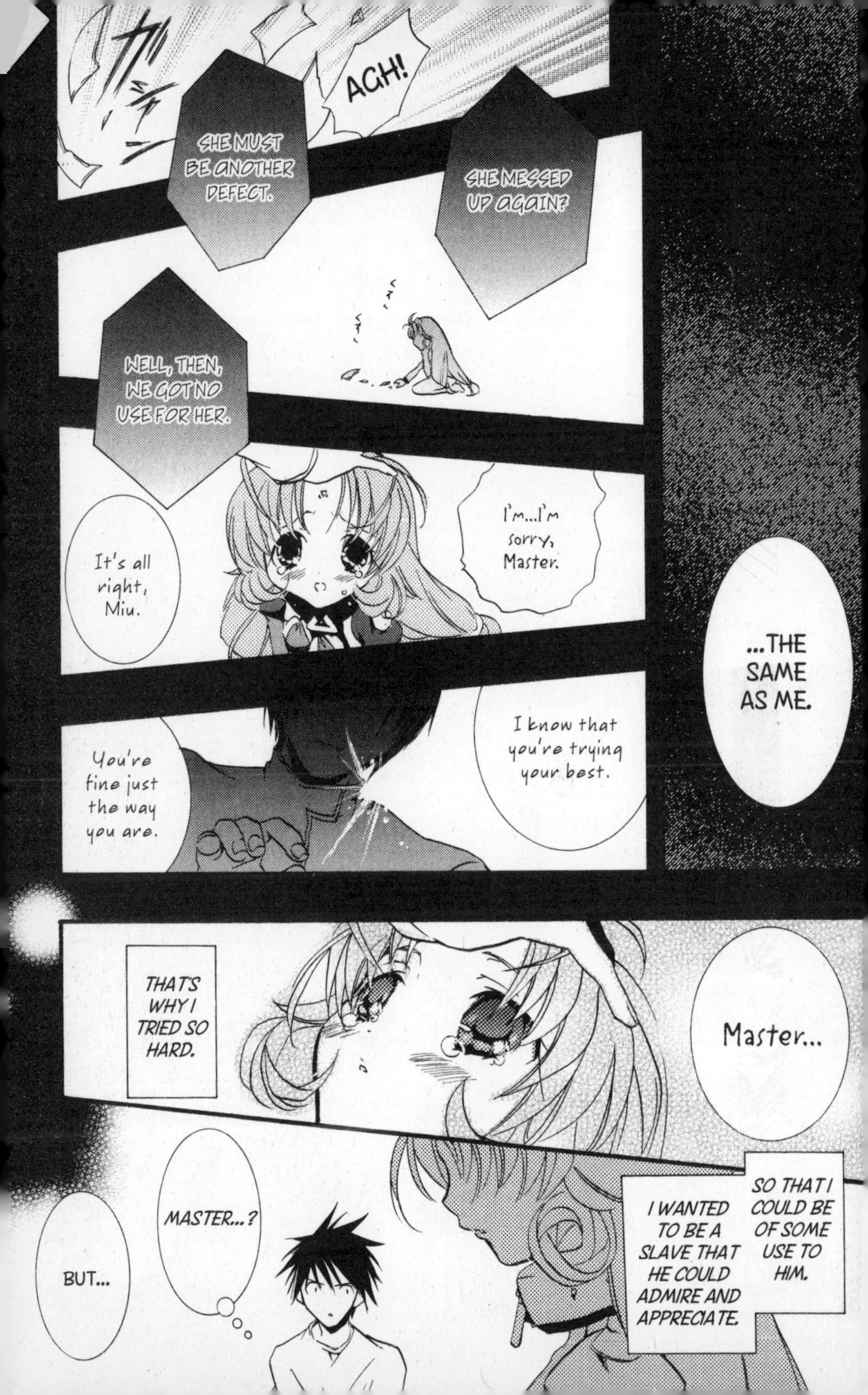
ACH!
SHE MESSED UP AGAIN?
SHE MUST BE ANOTHER DEFECT.
WELL, THEN, WE GOT NO USE FOR HER.
I'm...I'm sorry, Master.
It's all right, Miu.
I know that you're trying your best.
You're fine just the way you are.
...THE SAME AS ME.
Master...
THAT'S WHY I TRIED SO HARD.
SO THAT I COULD BE OF SOME USE TO HIM.
I WANTED TO BE A SLAVE THAT HE COULD ADMIRE AND APPRECIATE.
MASTER...?
BUT...

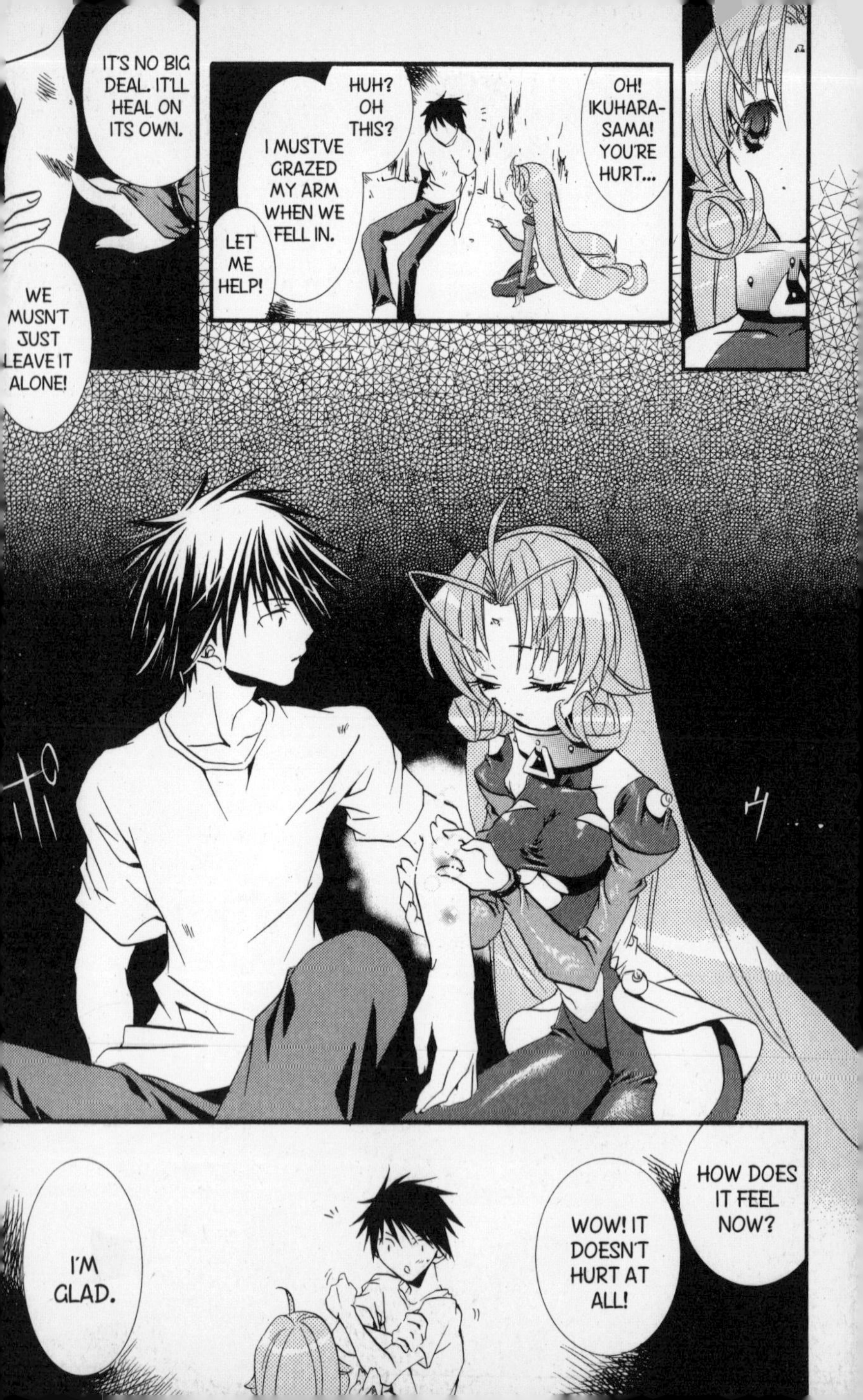
OH! IKUHARA-SAMA! YOU'RE HURT...
HUH? OH THIS?
I MUST'VE GRAZED MY ARM WHEN WE FELL IN.
LET ME HELP!
IT'S NO BIG DEAL. IT'LL HEAL ON ITS OWN.
WE MUSN'T JUST LEAVE IT ALONE!
HOW DOES IT FEEL NOW?
WOW! IT DOESN'T HURT AT ALL!
I'M GLAD.

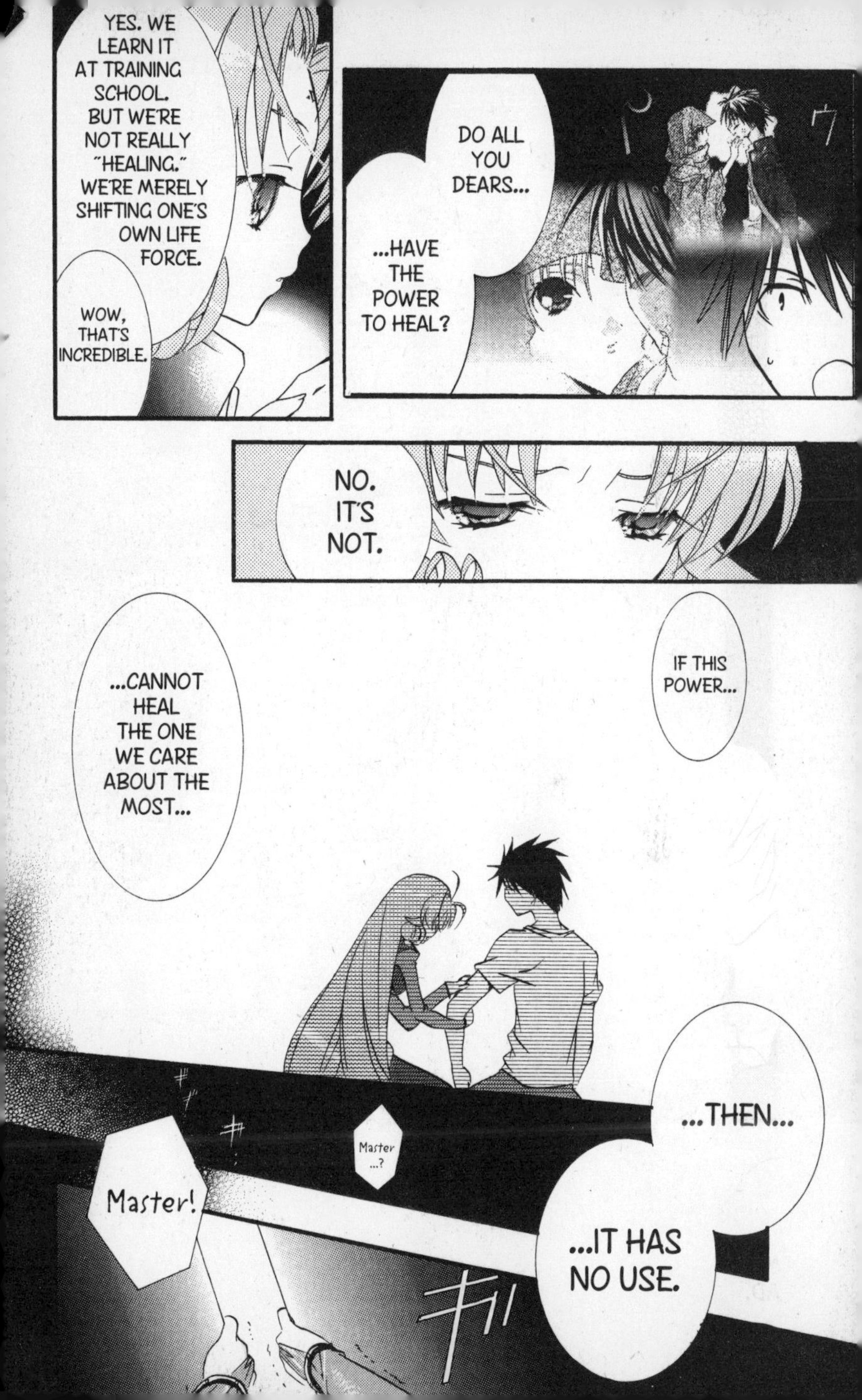
DO ALL YOU DEARS...
...HAVE THE POWER TO HEAL?
YES. WE LEARN IT AT TRAINING SCHOOL. BUT WE'RE NOT REALLY "HEALING." WE'RE MERELY SHIFTING ONE'S OWN LIFE FORCE.
WOW, THAT'S INCREDIBLE.
NO. IT'S NOT.
IF THIS POWER...
...CANNOT HEAL THE ONE WE CARE ABOUT THE MOST...
...THEN...
...IT HAS NO USE.
Master ...?
Master!

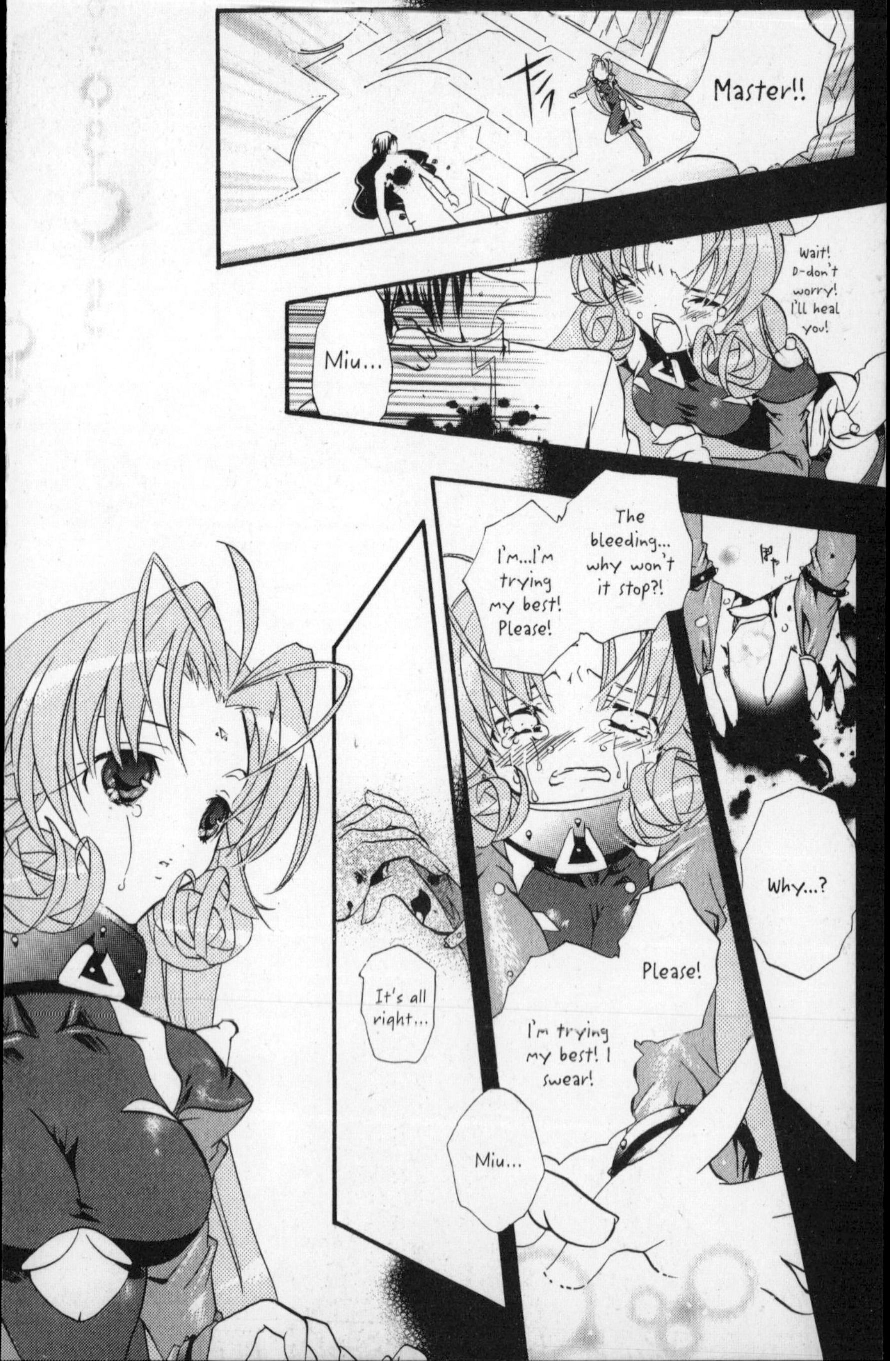
Master!!
Wait! D-don't worry! I'll heal you!
Miu...
Why...?
The bleeding... why won't it stop?!
I'm...I'm trying my best! Please!
Please!
I'm trying my best! I swear!
Miu...
It's all right...

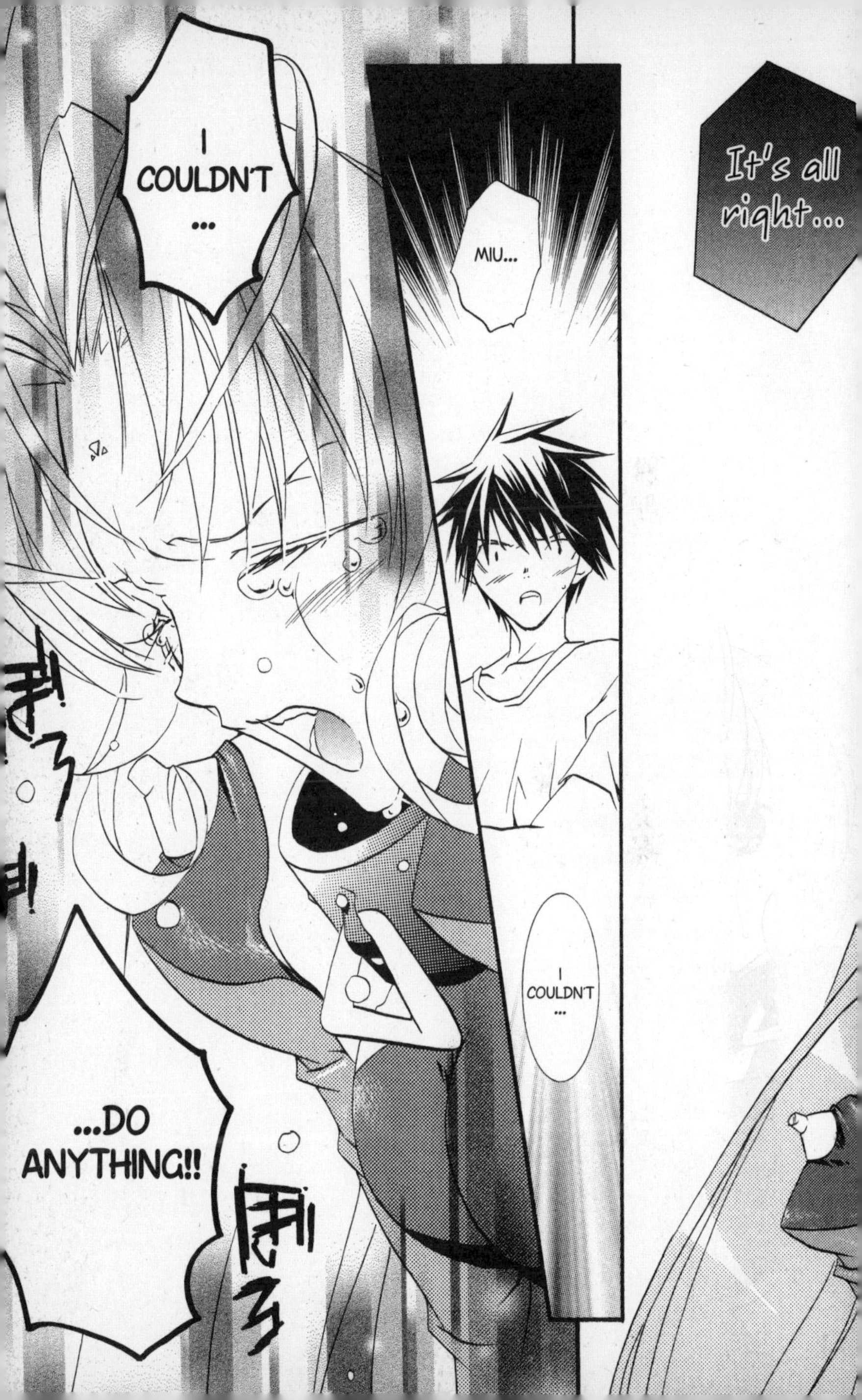
It's all right...
MIU...
I COULDN'T ...
I COULDN'T ...
...DO ANYTHING!!

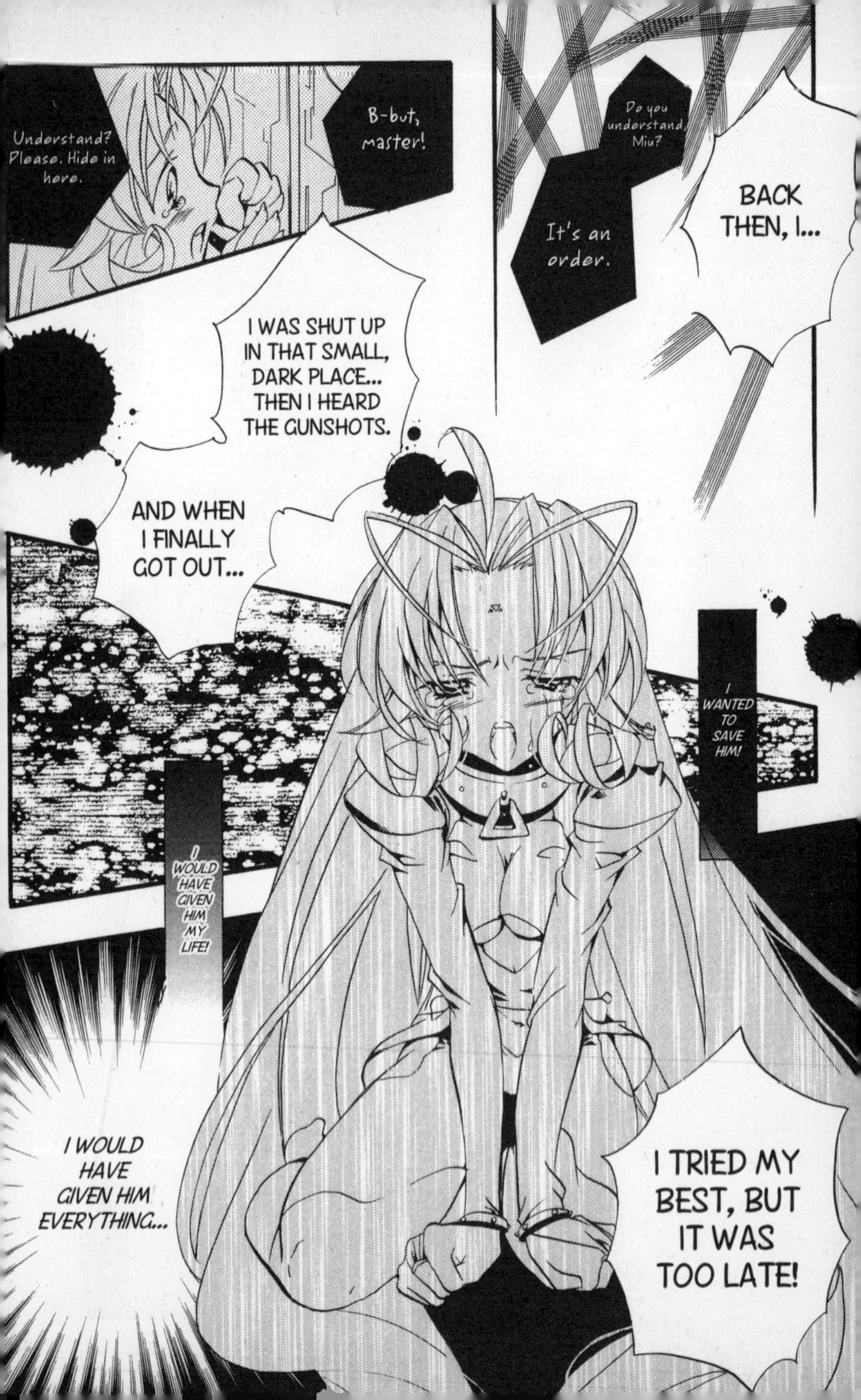
Do you understand, Miu?
It's an order.
BACK THEN, I...
B-but, master!
Understand? Please. Hide in here.
I WAS SHUT UP IN THAT SMALL, DARK PLACE... THEN I HEARD THE GUNSHOTS.
AND WHEN I FINALLY GOT OUT...
I WANTED TO SAVE HIM!
I WOULD HAVE GIVEN HIM MY LIFE!
I TRIED MY BEST, BUT IT WAS TOO LATE!
I WOULD HAVE GIVEN HIM EVERYTHING...

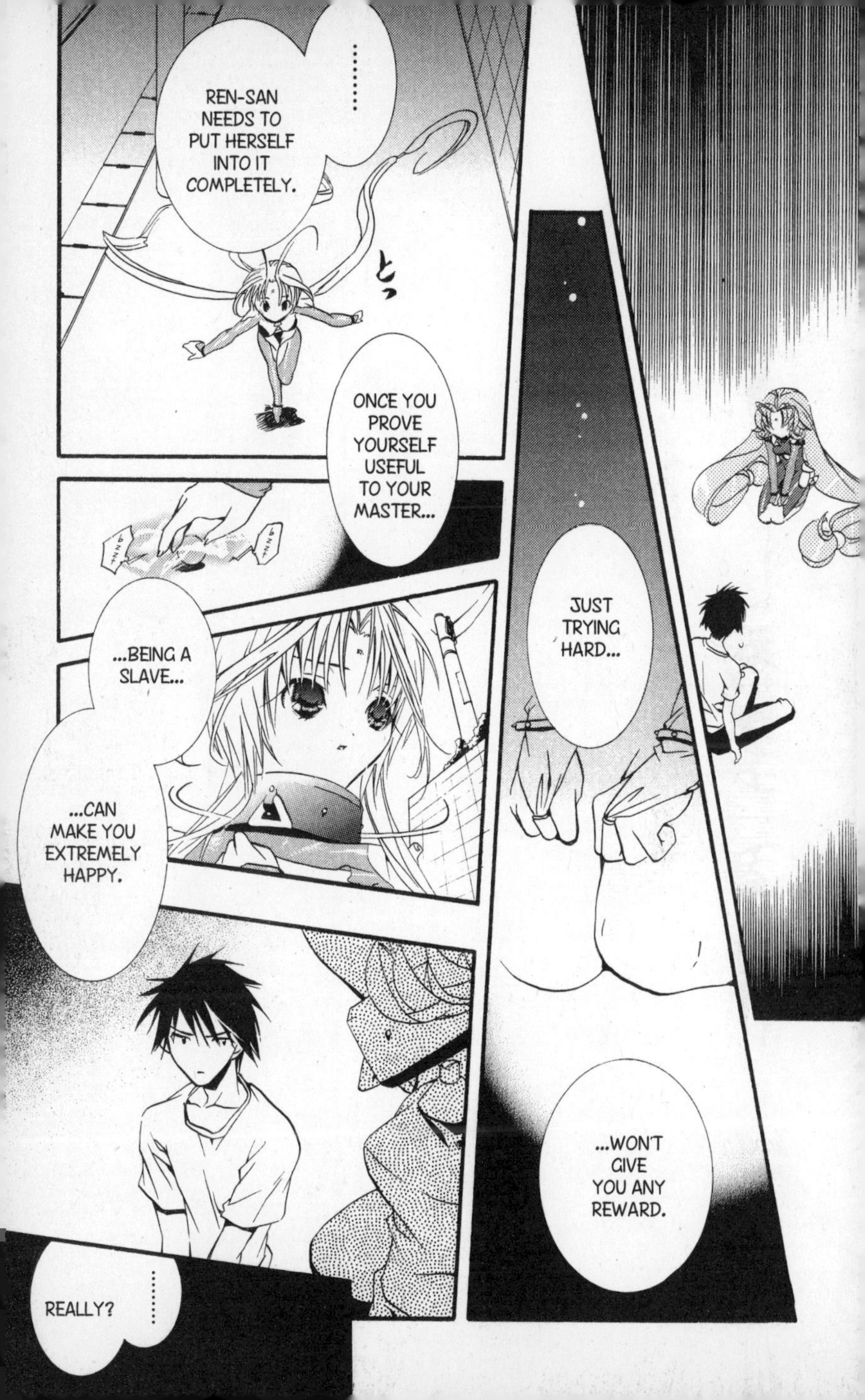
JUST TRYING HARD...
...WON'T GIVE YOU ANY REWARD.
......
REN-SAN NEEDS TO PUT HERSELF INTO IT COMPLETELY.
とっ
ONCE YOU PROVE YOURSELF USEFUL TO YOUR MASTER...
...BEING A SLAVE...
...CAN MAKE YOU EXTREMELY HAPPY.
......
REALLY?

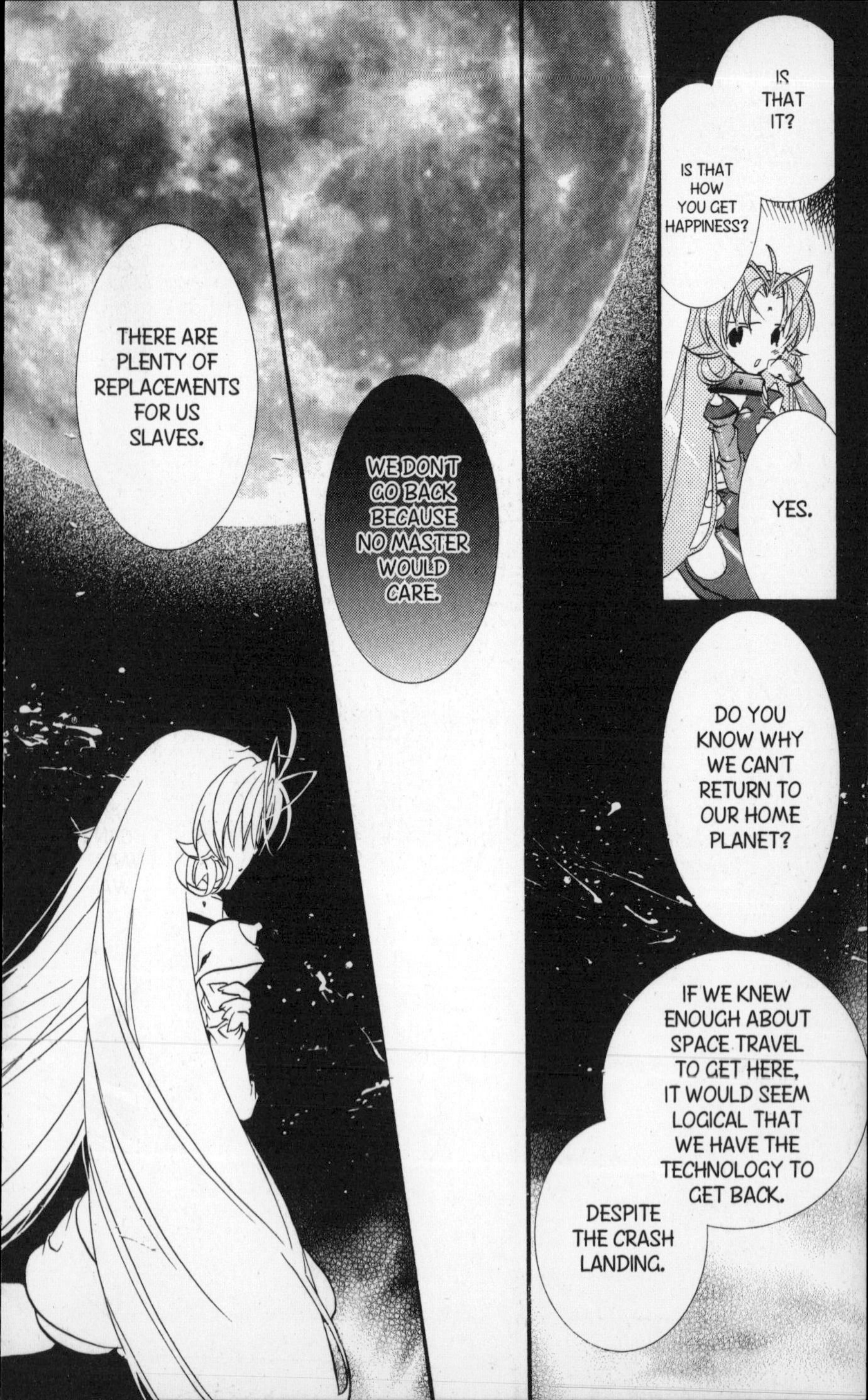
IS THAT IT?
IS THAT HOW YOU GET HAPPINESS?
YES.
DO YOU KNOW WHY WE CAN'T RETURN TO OUR HOME PLANET?
IF WE KNEW ENOUGH ABOUT SPACE TRAVEL TO GET HERE, IT WOULD SEEM LOGICAL THAT WE HAVE THE TECHNOLOGY TO GET BACK.
DESPITE THE CRASH LANDING.
WE DON'T GO BACK BECAUSE NO MASTER WOULD CARE.
THERE ARE PLENTY OF REPLACEMENTS FOR US SLAVES.

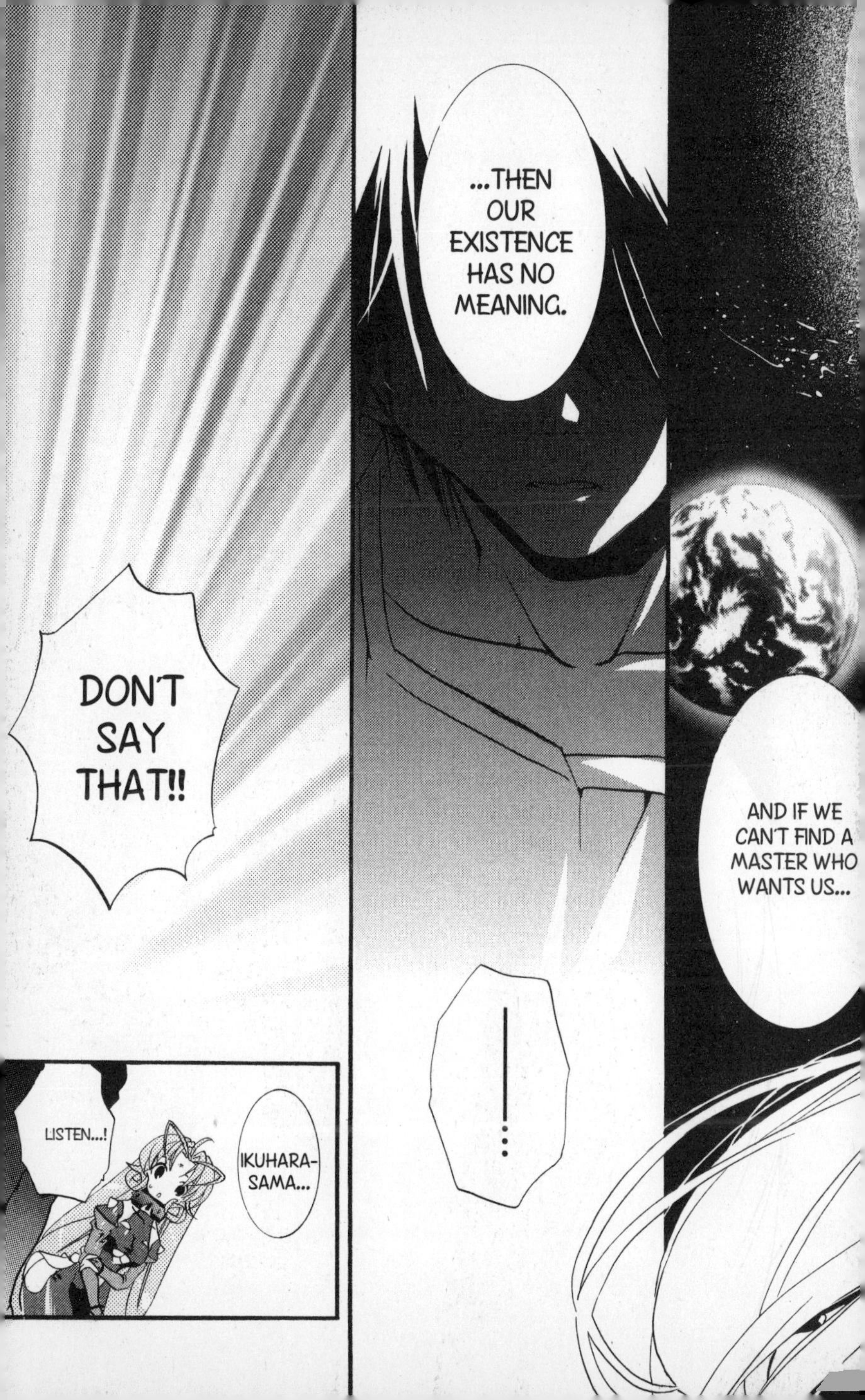
AND IF WE CAN'T FIND A MASTER WHO WANTS US...
...THEN OUR EXISTENCE HAS NO MEANING.
—...
DON'T SAY THAT!!
IKUHARA-SAMA...
LISTEN...!

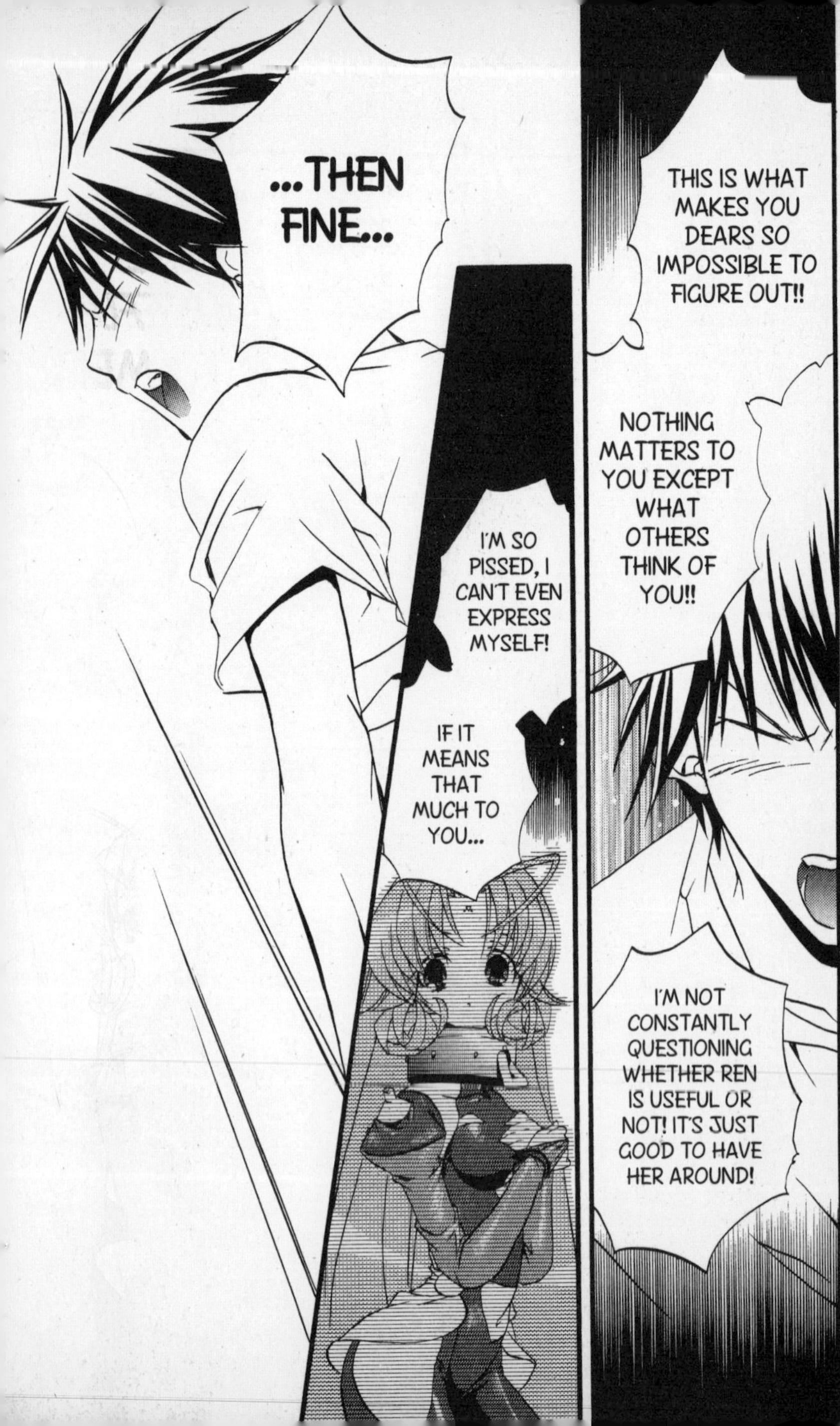
THIS IS WHAT MAKES YOU DEARS SO IMPOSSIBLE TO FIGURE OUT!!
NOTHING MATTERS TO YOU EXCEPT WHAT OTHERS THINK OF YOU!!
I'M NOT CONSTANTLY QUESTIONING WHETHER REN IS USEFUL OR NOT! IT'S JUST GOOD TO HAVE HER AROUND!
I'M SO PISSED, I CAN'T EVEN EXPRESS MYSELF!
IF IT MEANS THAT MUCH TO YOU...
...THEN FINE...

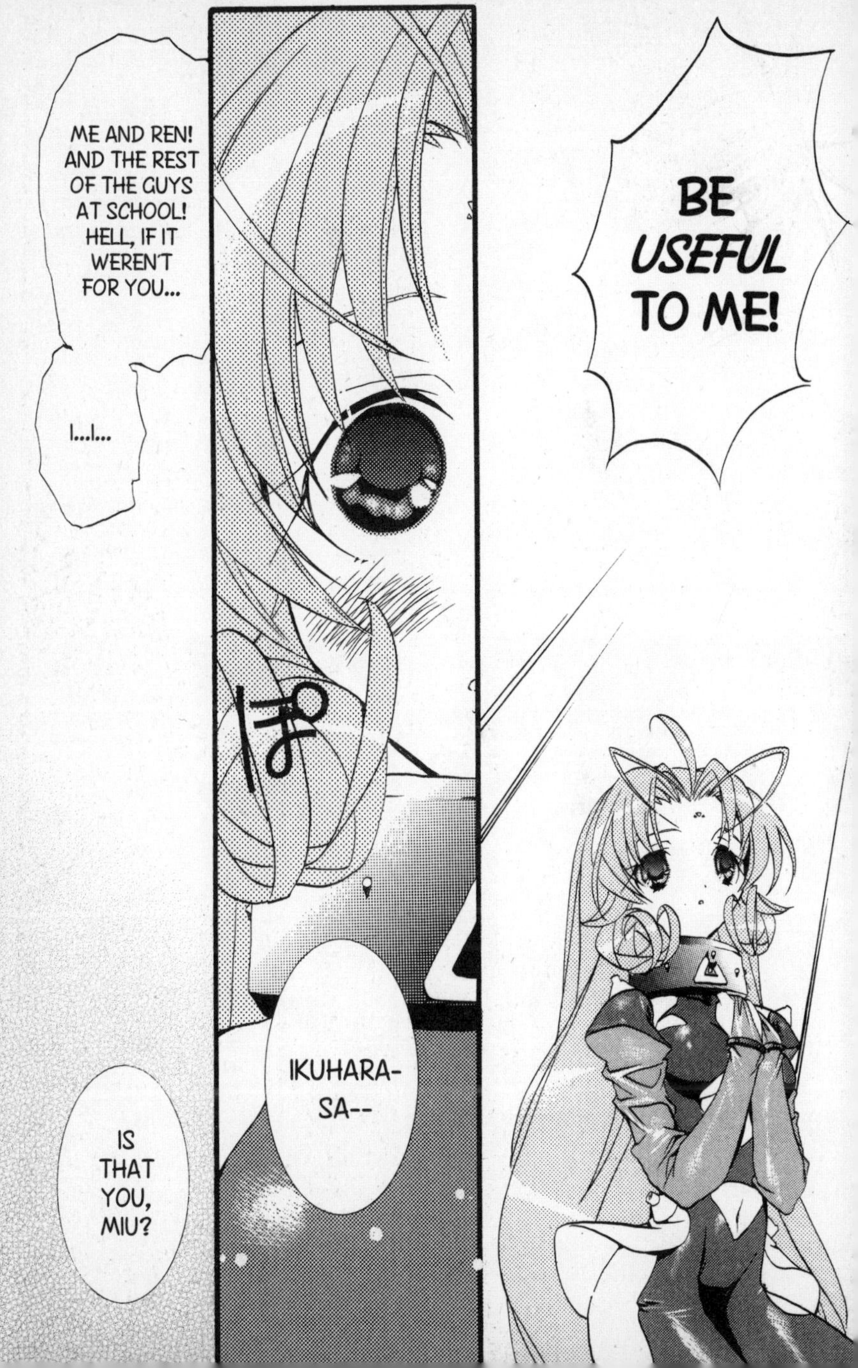
BE USEFUL TO ME!
ぽ
IKUHARA-SA--
ME AND REN! AND THE REST OF THE GUYS AT SCHOOL! HELL, IF IT WEREN'T FOR YOU...
I...I...
IS THAT YOU, MIU?

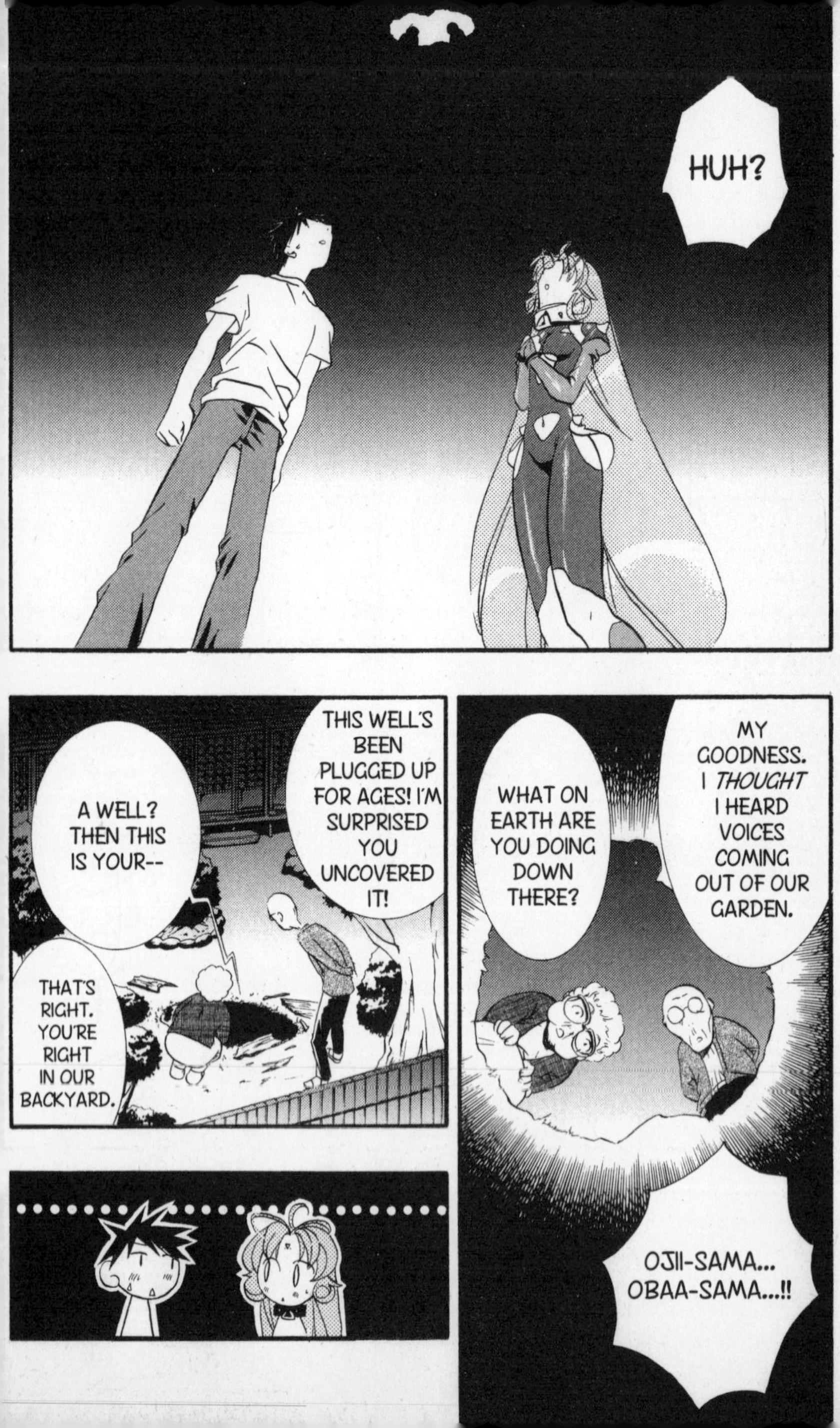
HUH?
MY GOODNESS. I *THOUGHT* I HEARD VOICES COMING OUT OF OUR GARDEN.
WHAT ON EARTH ARE YOU DOING DOWN THERE?
OJII-SAMA... OBAA-SAMA...!!
THIS WELL'S BEEN PLUGGED UP FOR AGES! I'M SURPRISED YOU UNCOVERED IT!
A WELL? THEN THIS IS YOUR--
THAT'S RIGHT. YOU'RE RIGHT IN OUR BACKYARD.

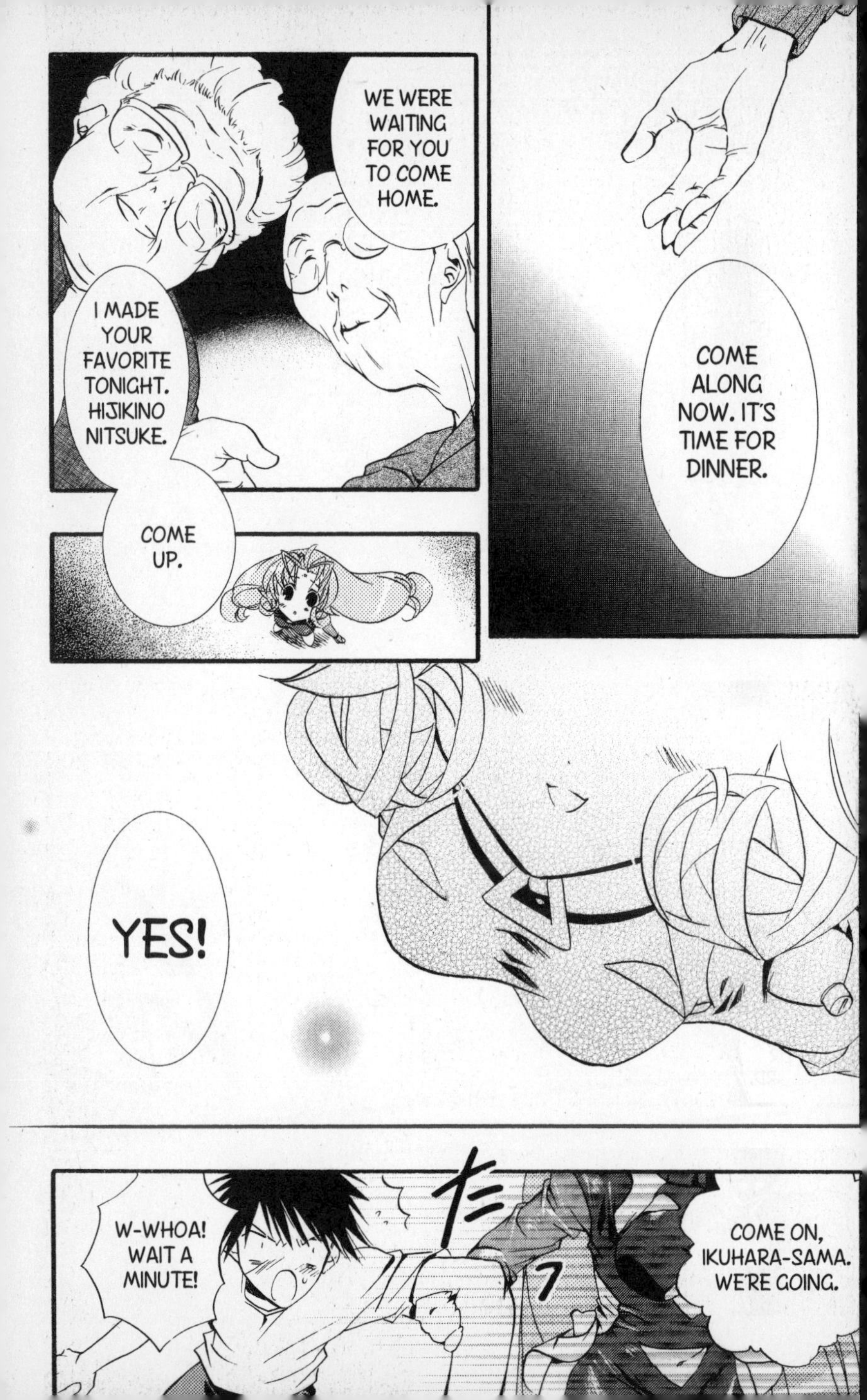
COME ALONG NOW. IT'S TIME FOR DINNER.
WE WERE WAITING FOR YOU TO COME HOME.
I MADE YOUR FAVORITE TONIGHT. HIJIKINO NITSUKE.
COME UP.
YES!
COME ON, IKUHARA-SAMA. WE'RE GOING.
W-WHOA! WAIT A MINUTE!

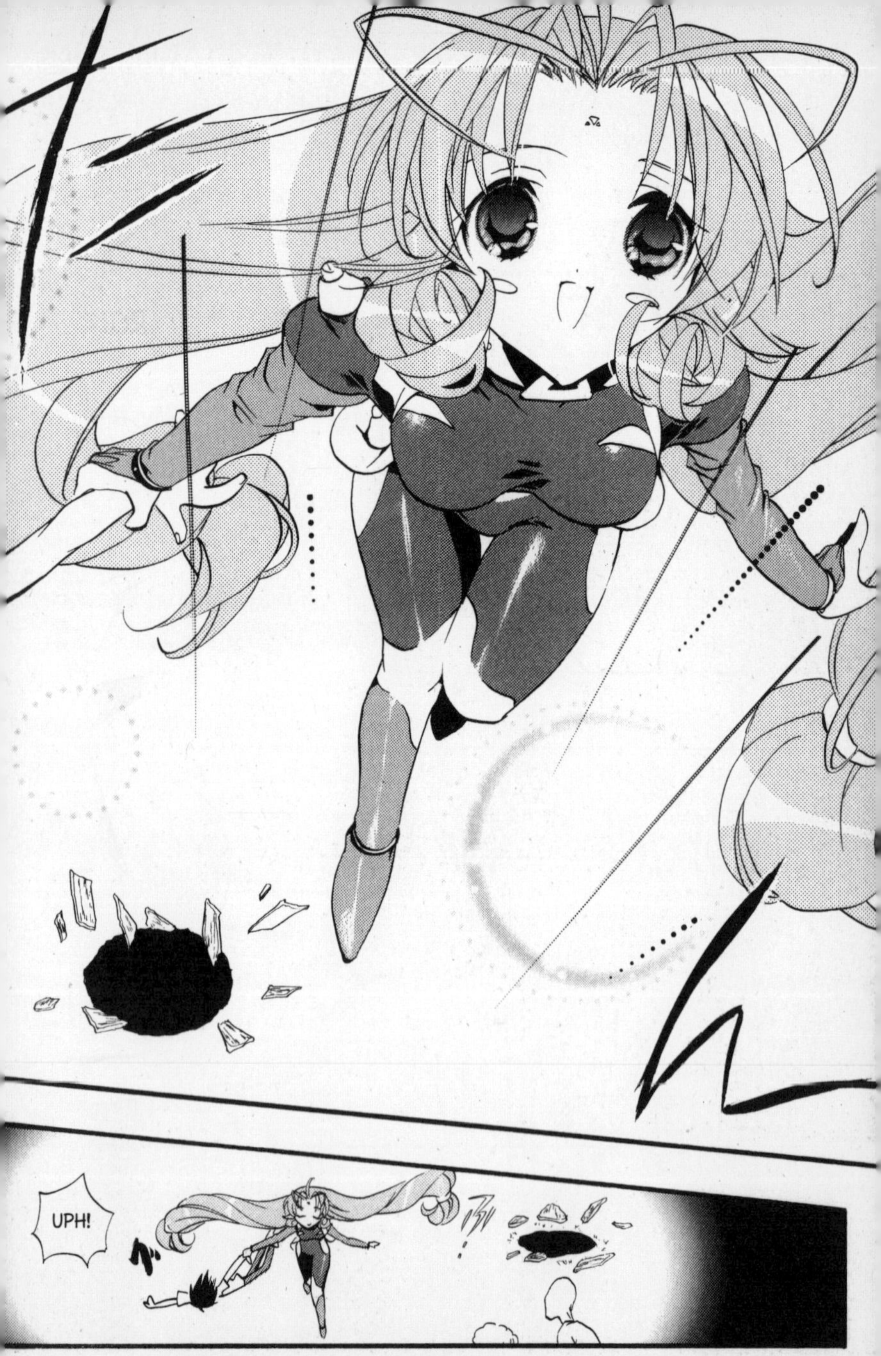
UPH!

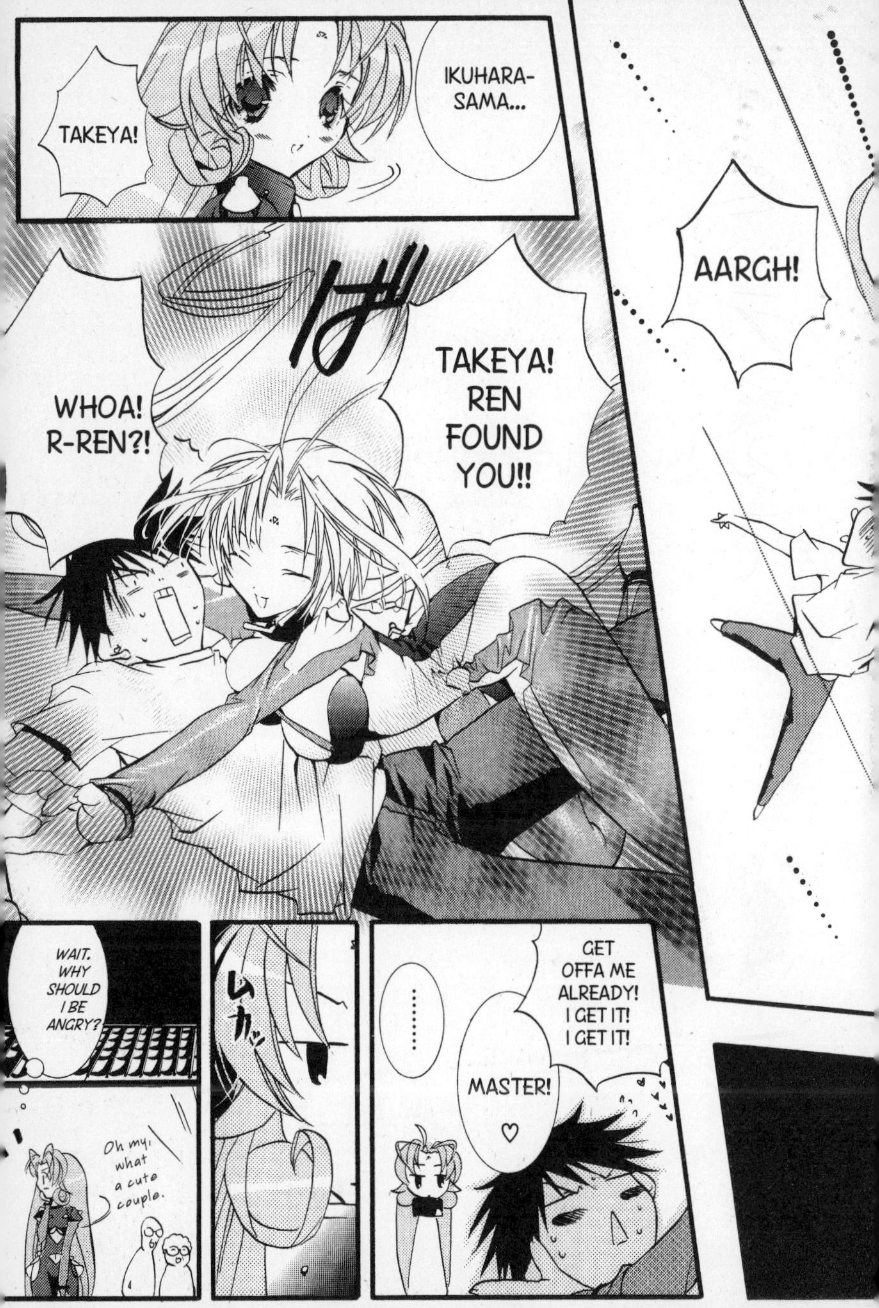
AARGH!
IKUHARA-SAMA...
TAKEYA!
ば
TAKEYA! REN FOUND YOU!!
WHOA! R-REN?!
GET OFFA ME ALREADY! I GET IT! I GET IT!
MASTER! ♡
......
ムカッ
WAIT. WHY SHOULD I BE ANGRY?
Oh my, what a cute couple.

>>>Thank you for your reading>>>

http://p-pit.ktplan.ne.jp/

all produced by

Banri.Sendou ... Shibuko.Ebara

special thanks to
Nao
Zaki
Momiji
Kinomin
T.Hatano

AND JUST LIKE THAT, WE'RE UP TO VOLUME THREE OF DEARS! I CAN'T THANK YOU ENOUGH FOR CONTINUING TO READ! DON'T WORRY, THERE'S STILL PLENTY OF THE STORY LEFT TO TELL. I CAN ONLY HOPE THAT BOTH SPACE ALIENS AND HUMANS ALIKE WILL KINDLY WATCH OVER EACH OTHER, AND THAT WE SEE WHAT BECOMES OF REN AND TAKEYA. WELL, ON TO THE NEXT CHAPTER!
-PEACH-PIT

17th Contact

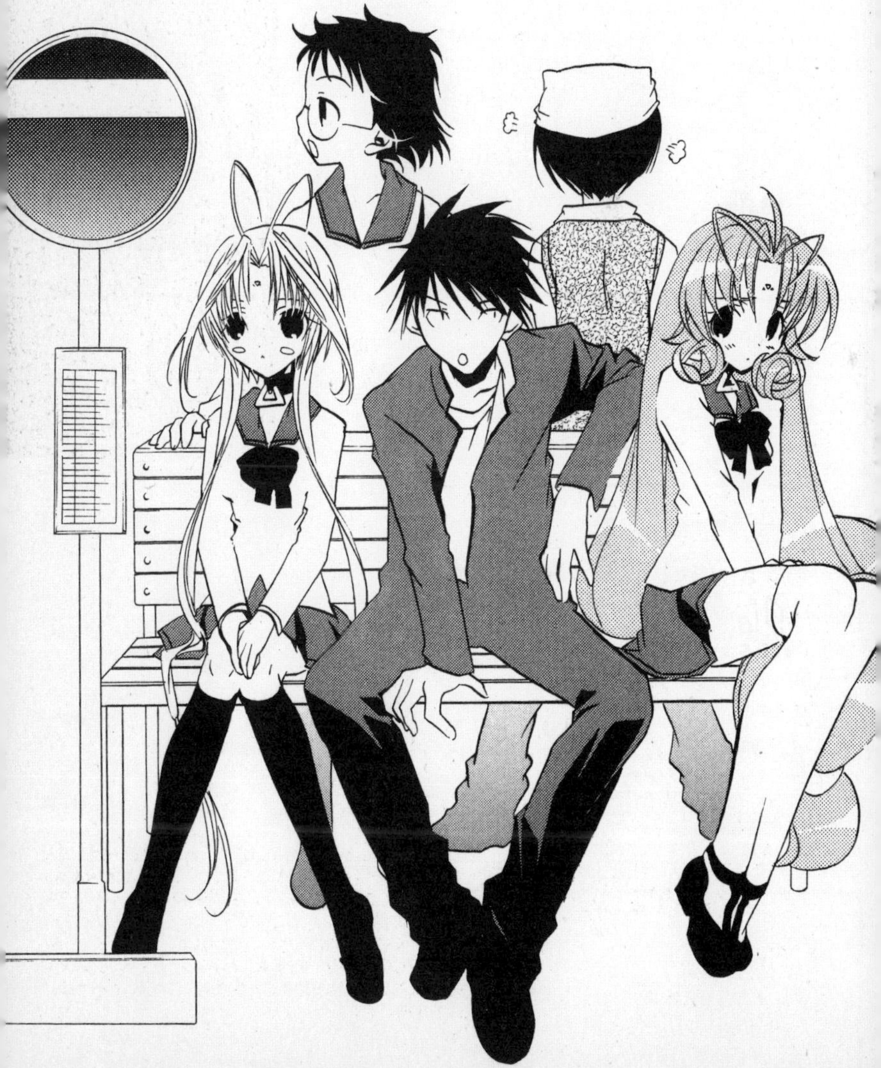

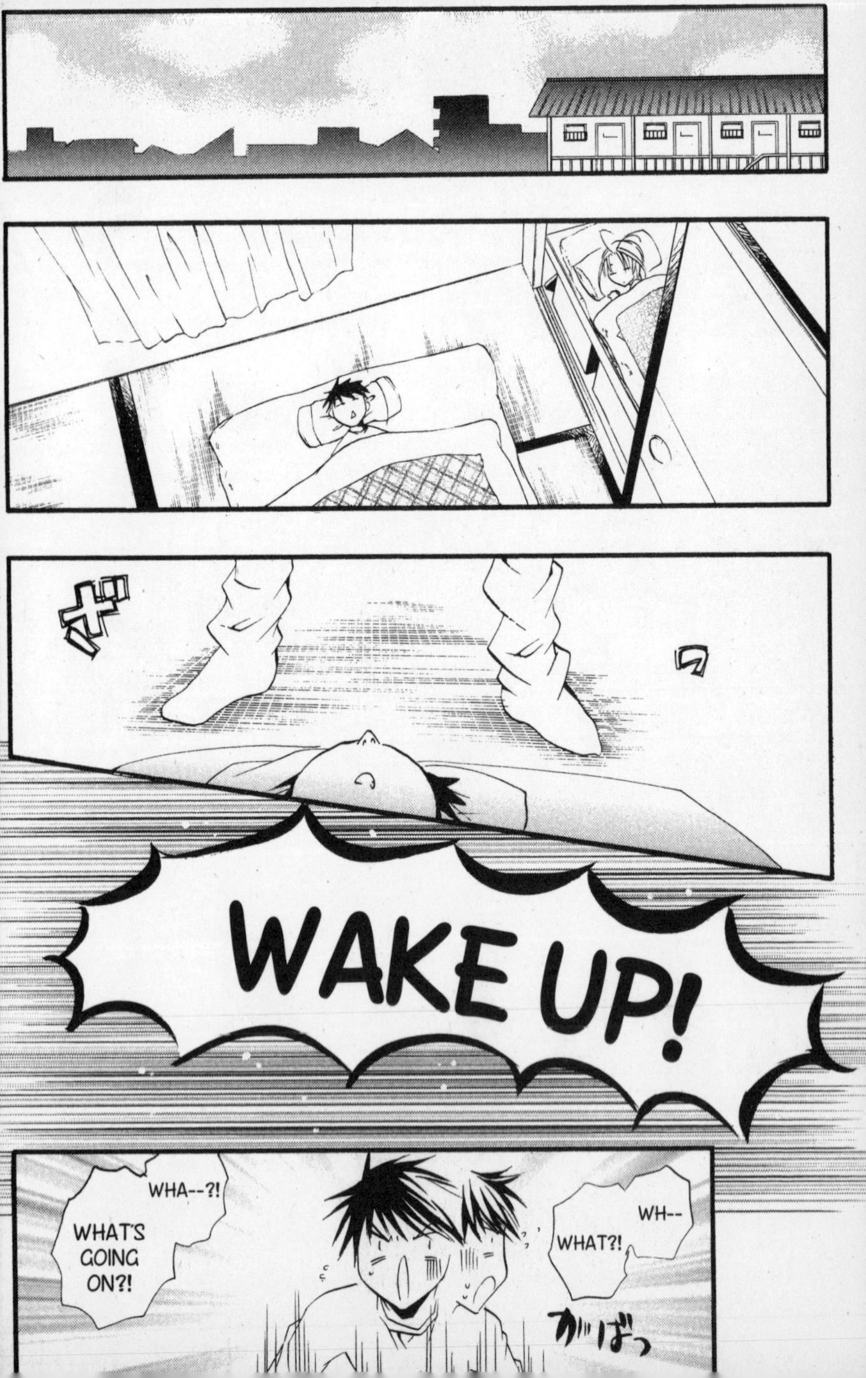
WAKE UP!
WH-- WHAT?!
WHA--?! WHAT'S GOING ON?!
がばっ

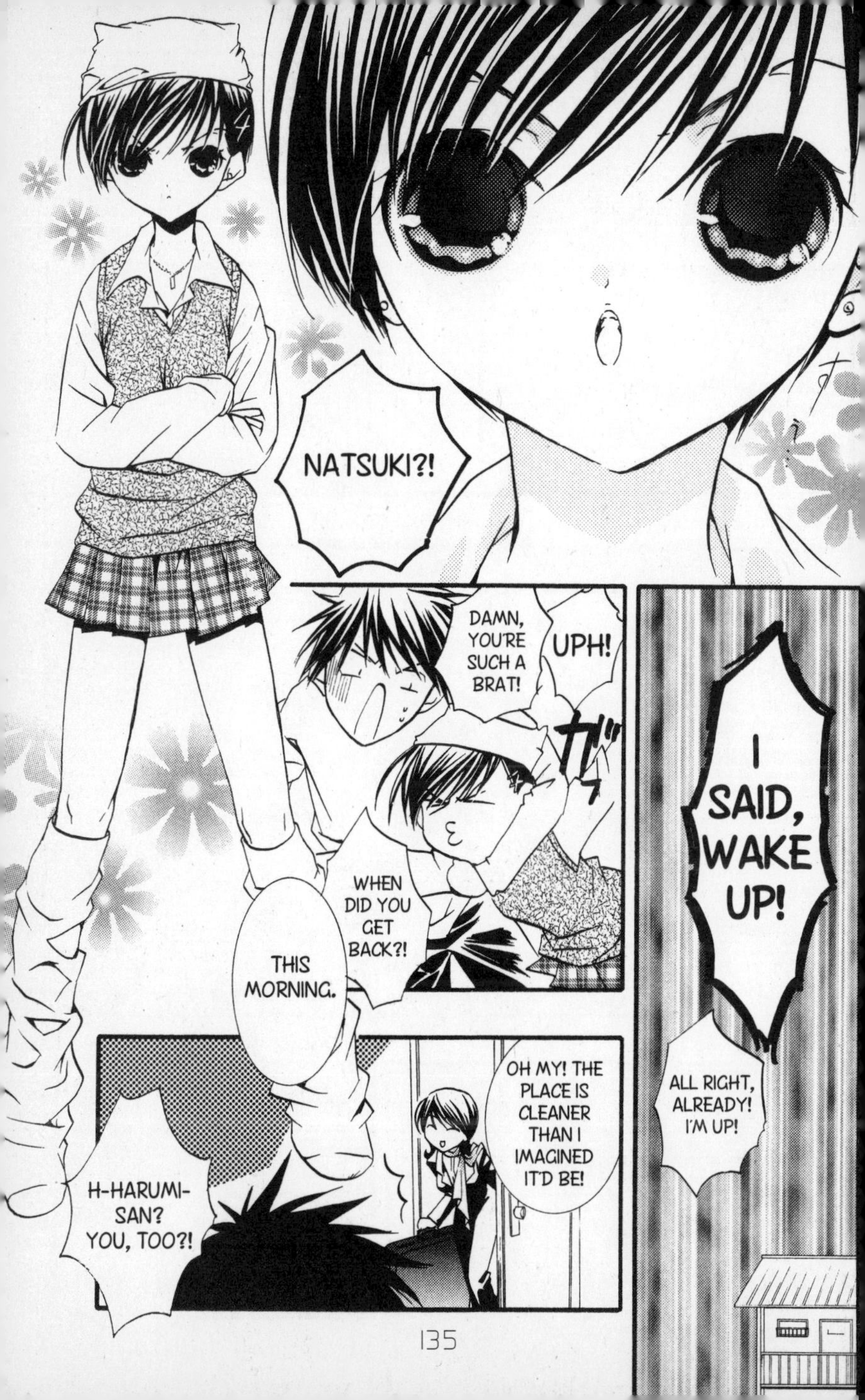
NATSUKI?!
I SAID, WAKE UP!
ALL RIGHT, ALREADY! I'M UP!
UPH!
DAMN, YOU'RE SUCH A BRAT!
WHEN DID YOU GET BACK?!
THIS MORNING.
OH MY! THE PLACE IS CLEANER THAN I IMAGINED IT'D BE!
H-HARUMI-SAN? YOU, TOO?!

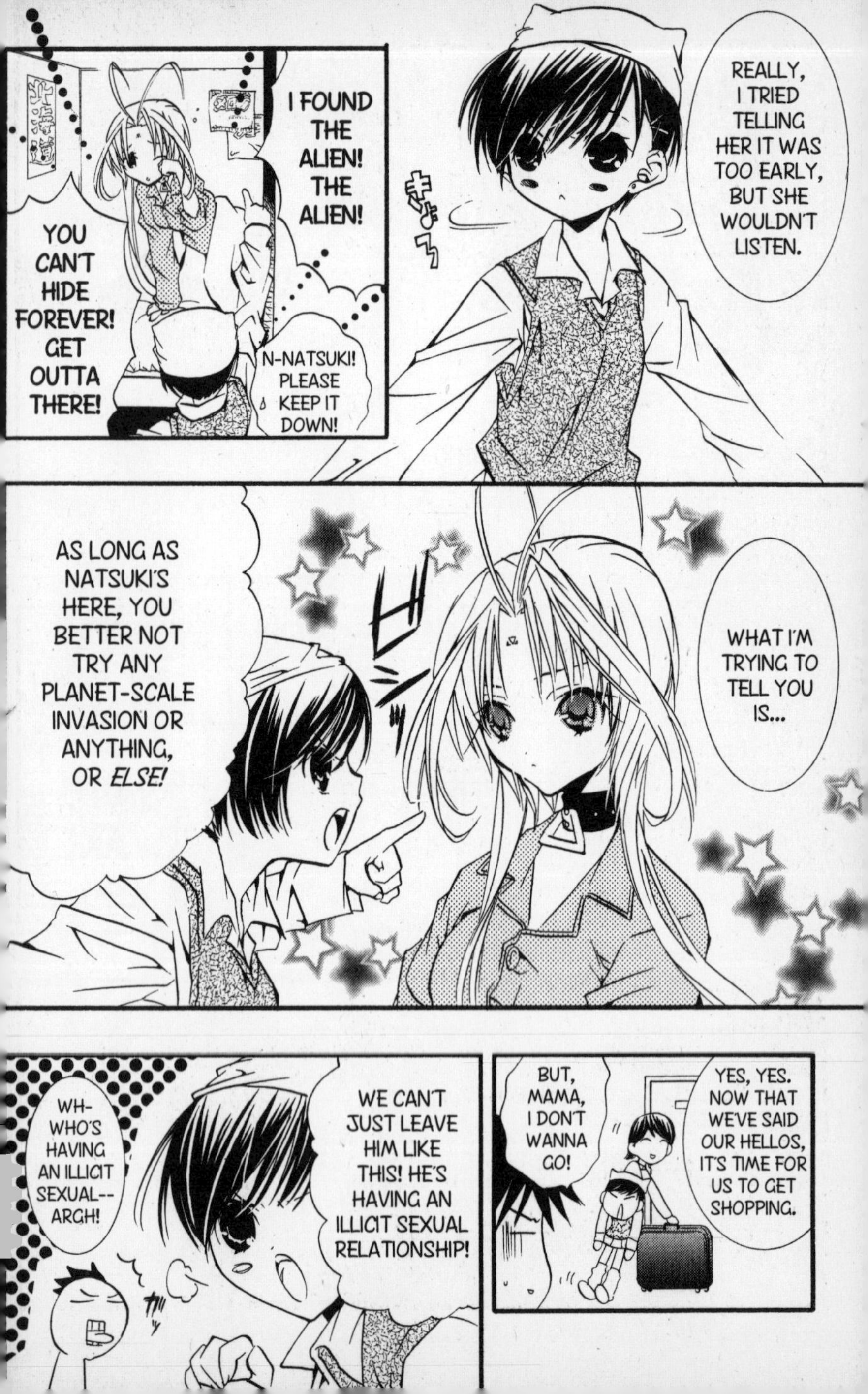
REALLY, I TRIED TELLING HER IT WAS TOO EARLY, BUT SHE WOULDN'T LISTEN.
I FOUND THE ALIEN! THE ALIEN!
YOU CAN'T HIDE FOREVER! GET OUTTA THERE!
N-NATSUKI! PLEASE KEEP IT DOWN!
WHAT I'M TRYING TO TELL YOU IS...
AS LONG AS NATSUKI'S HERE, YOU BETTER NOT TRY ANY PLANET-SCALE INVASION OR ANYTHING, OR *ELSE!*
YES, YES. NOW THAT WE'VE SAID OUR HELLOS, IT'S TIME FOR US TO GET SHOPPING.
BUT, MAMA, I DON'T WANNA GO!
WE CAN'T JUST LEAVE HIM LIKE THIS! HE'S HAVING AN ILLICIT SEXUAL RELATIONSHIP!
WH- WHO'S HAVING AN ILLICIT SEXUAL-- ARGH!

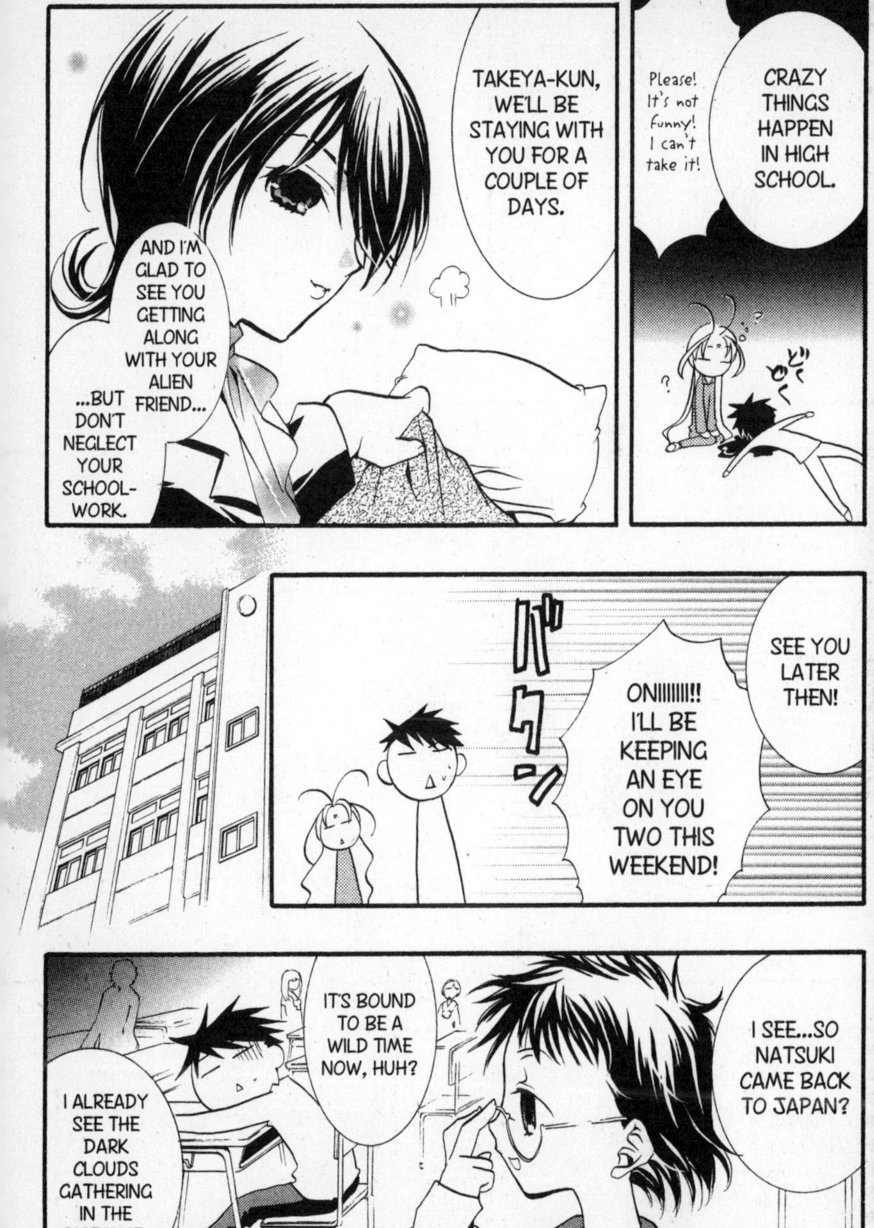
CRAZY THINGS HAPPEN IN HIGH SCHOOL.
Please! It's not funny! I can't take it!
TAKEYA-KUN, WE'LL BE STAYING WITH YOU FOR A COUPLE OF DAYS.
AND I'M GLAD TO SEE YOU GETTING ALONG WITH YOUR ALIEN FRIEND...
...BUT DON'T NEGLECT YOUR SCHOOL-WORK.
SEE YOU LATER THEN!
ONIIIIIII!! I'LL BE KEEPING AN EYE ON YOU TWO THIS WEEKEND!
I SEE...SO NATSUKI CAME BACK TO JAPAN?
IT'S BOUND TO BE A WILD TIME NOW, HUH?
I ALREADY SEE THE DARK CLOUDS GATHERING IN THE DISTANCE.

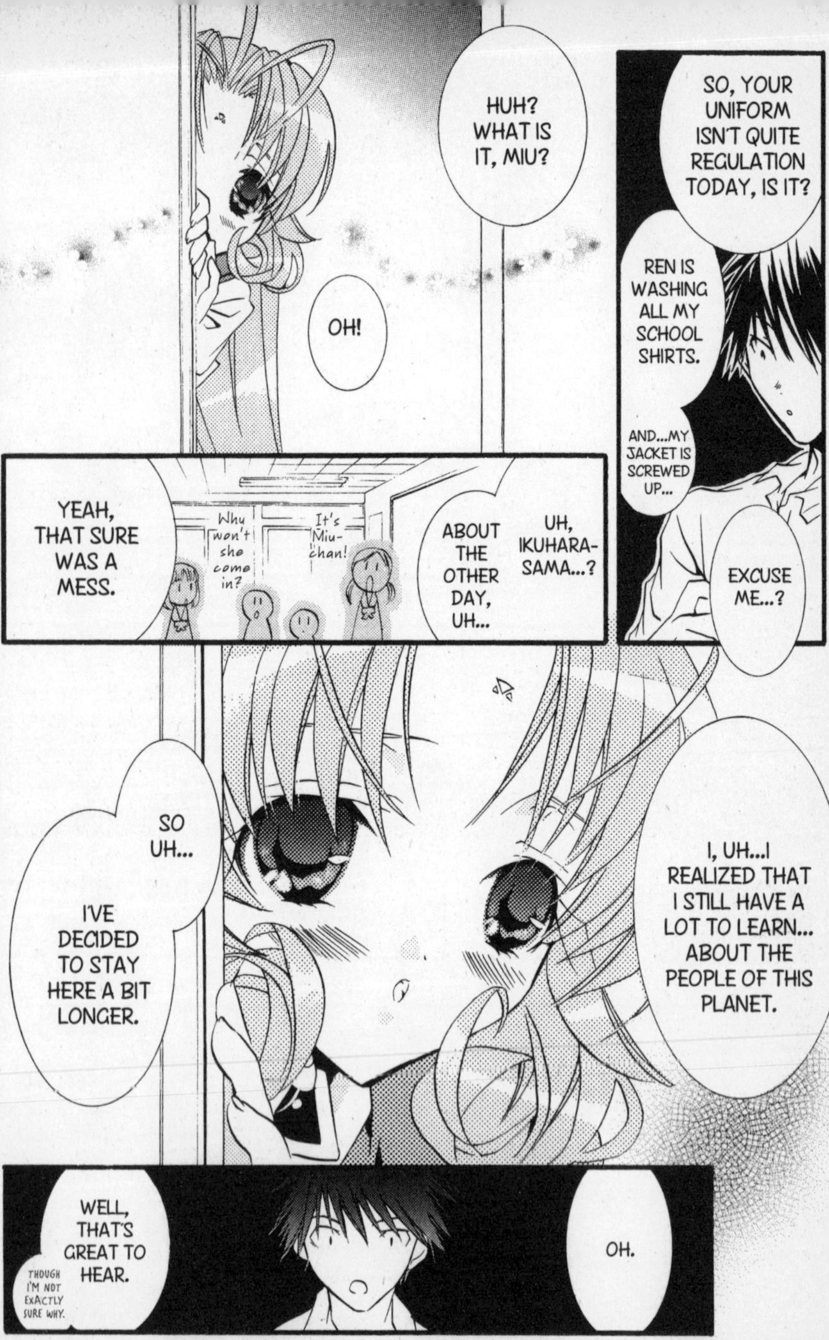

SO, YOUR UNIFORM ISN'T QUITE REGULATION TODAY, IS IT?
REN IS WASHING ALL MY SCHOOL SHIRTS.
AND...MY JACKET IS SCREWED UP...
EXCUSE ME...?
HUH? WHAT IS IT, MIU?
OH!
UH, IKUHARA-SAMA...?
ABOUT THE OTHER DAY, UH...
It's Miu-chan!
Why won't she come in?
YEAH, THAT SURE WAS A MESS.
I, UH...I REALIZED THAT I STILL HAVE A LOT TO LEARN... ABOUT THE PEOPLE OF THIS PLANET.
SO UH...
I'VE DECIDED TO STAY HERE A BIT LONGER.
OH.
WELL, THAT'S GREAT TO HEAR.
THOUGH I'M NOT EXACTLY SURE WHY.

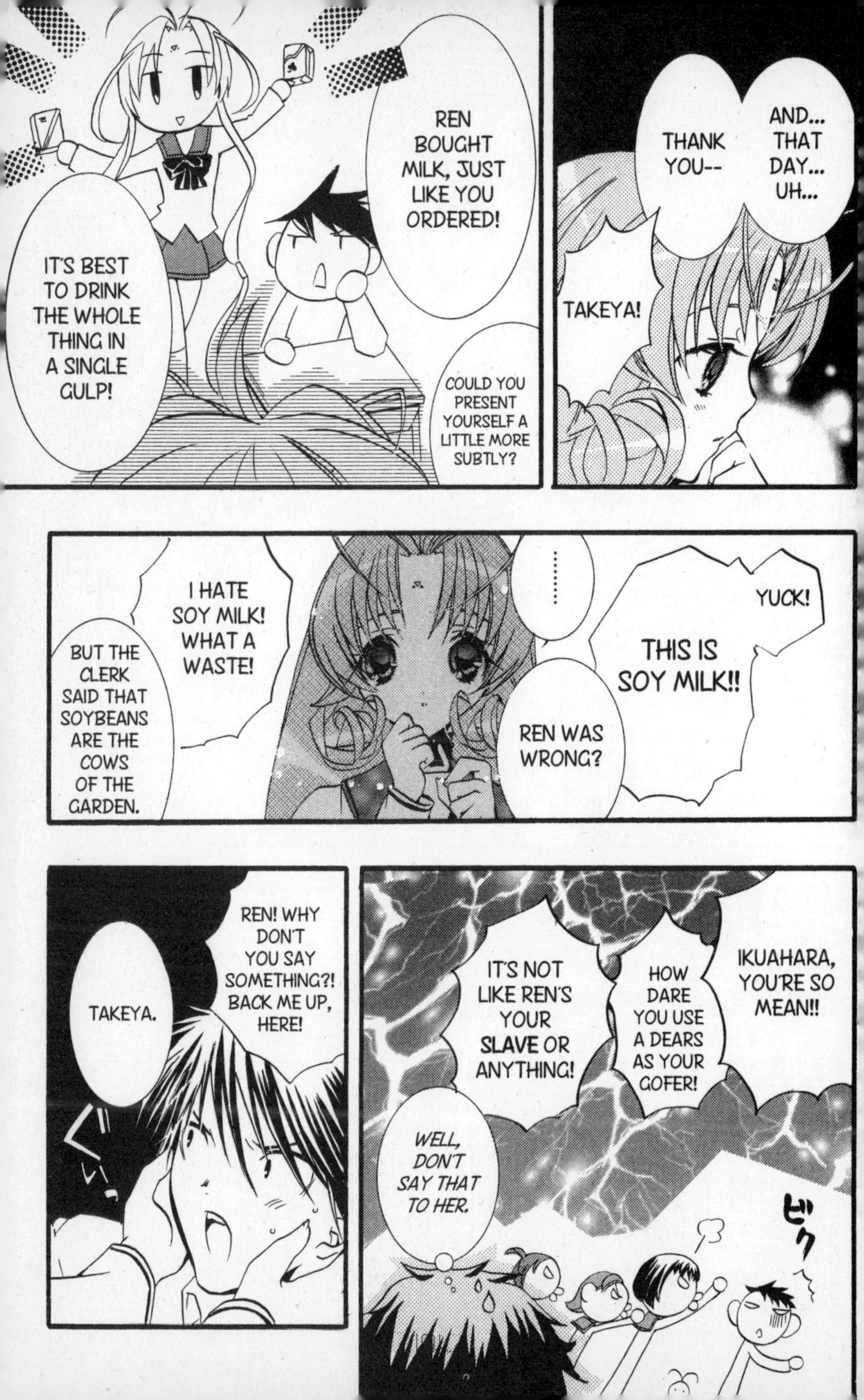
THANK YOU--
AND... THAT DAY... UH...
TAKEYA!
REN BOUGHT MILK, JUST LIKE YOU ORDERED!
IT'S BEST TO DRINK THE WHOLE THING IN A SINGLE GULP!
COULD YOU PRESENT YOURSELF A LITTLE MORE SUBTLY?
YUCK!
THIS IS SOY MILK!!
......
REN WAS WRONG?
I HATE SOY MILK! WHAT A WASTE!
BUT THE CLERK SAID THAT SOYBEANS ARE THE COWS OF THE GARDEN.
IKUAHARA, YOU'RE SO MEAN!!
HOW DARE YOU USE A DEARS AS YOUR GOFER!
IT'S NOT LIKE REN'S YOUR **SLAVE** OR ANYTHING!
ビク
WELL, DON'T SAY THAT TO HER.
REN! WHY DON'T YOU SAY SOMETHING?! BACK ME UP, HERE!
TAKEYA.

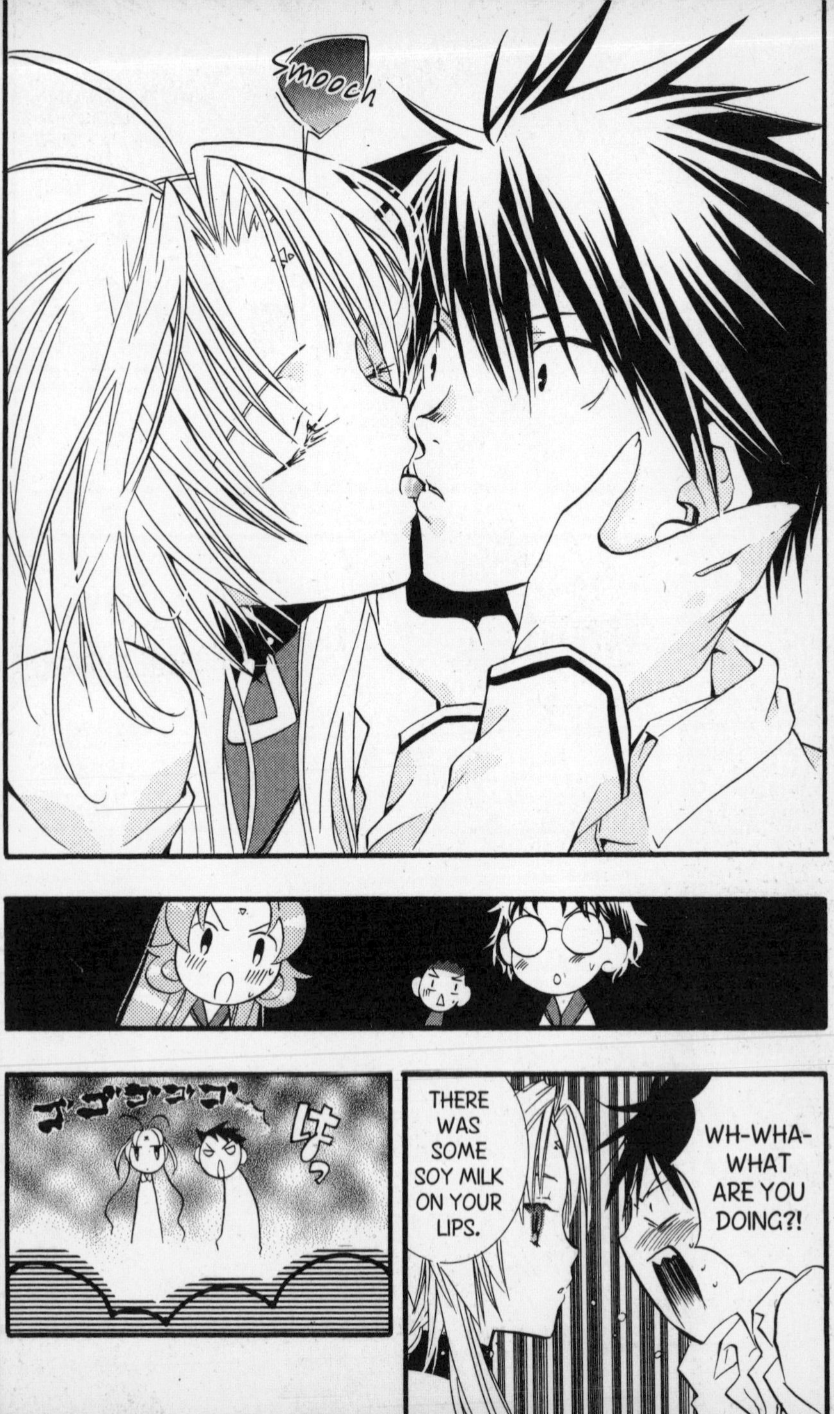
Smooch
WH-WHA-WHAT ARE YOU DOING?!
THERE WAS SOME SOY MILK ON YOUR LIPS.
ゴゴゴゴゴ
はっ

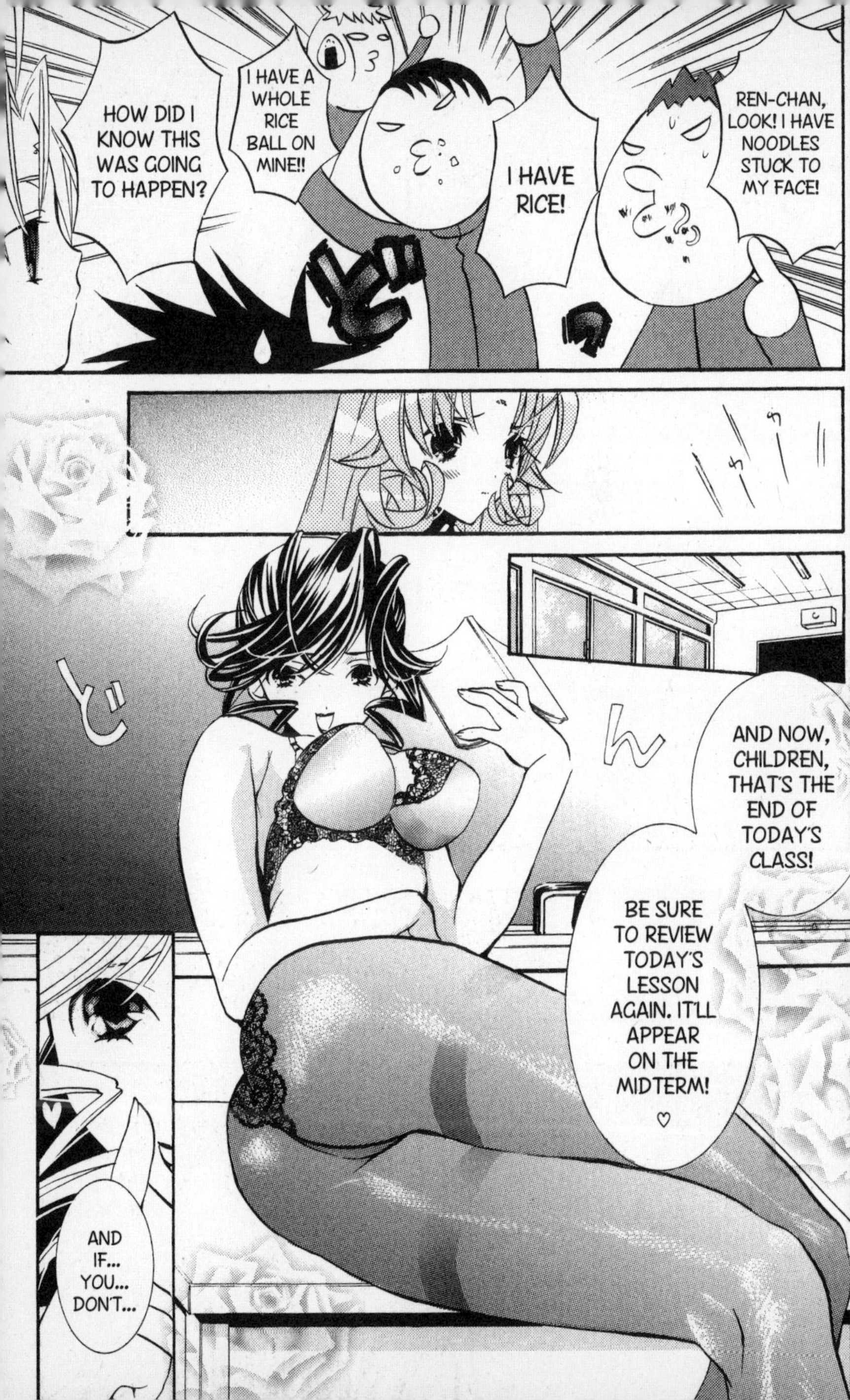
REN-CHAN, LOOK! I HAVE NOODLES STUCK TO MY FACE!
I HAVE RICE!
I HAVE A WHOLE RICE BALL ON MINE!!
HOW DID I KNOW THIS WAS GOING TO HAPPEN?
AND NOW, CHILDREN, THAT'S THE END OF TODAY'S CLASS!
BE SURE TO REVIEW TODAY'S LESSON AGAIN. IT'LL APPEAR ON THE MIDTERM! ♡
どん
AND IF... YOU... DON'T...

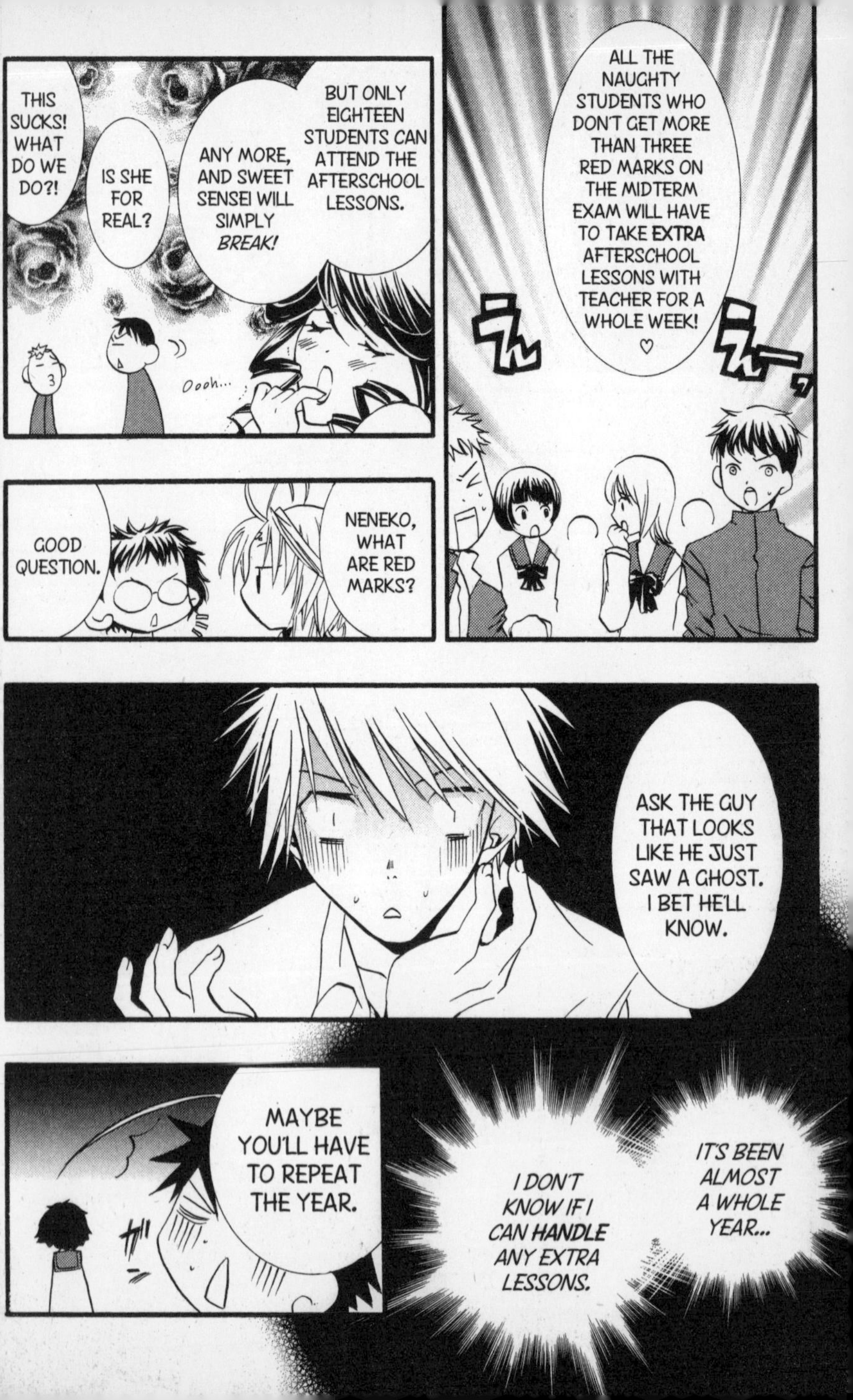
ALL THE NAUGHTY STUDENTS WHO DON'T GET MORE THAN THREE RED MARKS ON THE MIDTERM EXAM WILL HAVE TO TAKE **EXTRA** AFTERSCHOOL LESSONS WITH TEACHER FOR A WHOLE WEEK! ♡
BUT ONLY EIGHTEEN STUDENTS CAN ATTEND THE AFTERSCHOOL LESSONS.
ANY MORE, AND SWEET SENSEI WILL SIMPLY *BREAK!*
Oooh...
IS SHE FOR REAL?
THIS SUCKS! WHAT DO WE DO?!
NENEKO, WHAT ARE RED MARKS?
GOOD QUESTION.
ASK THE GUY THAT LOOKS LIKE HE JUST SAW A GHOST. I BET HE'LL KNOW.
IT'S BEEN ALMOST A WHOLE YEAR...
I DON'T KNOW IF I CAN ***HANDLE*** *ANY EXTRA LESSONS.*
MAYBE YOU'LL HAVE TO REPEAT THE YEAR.

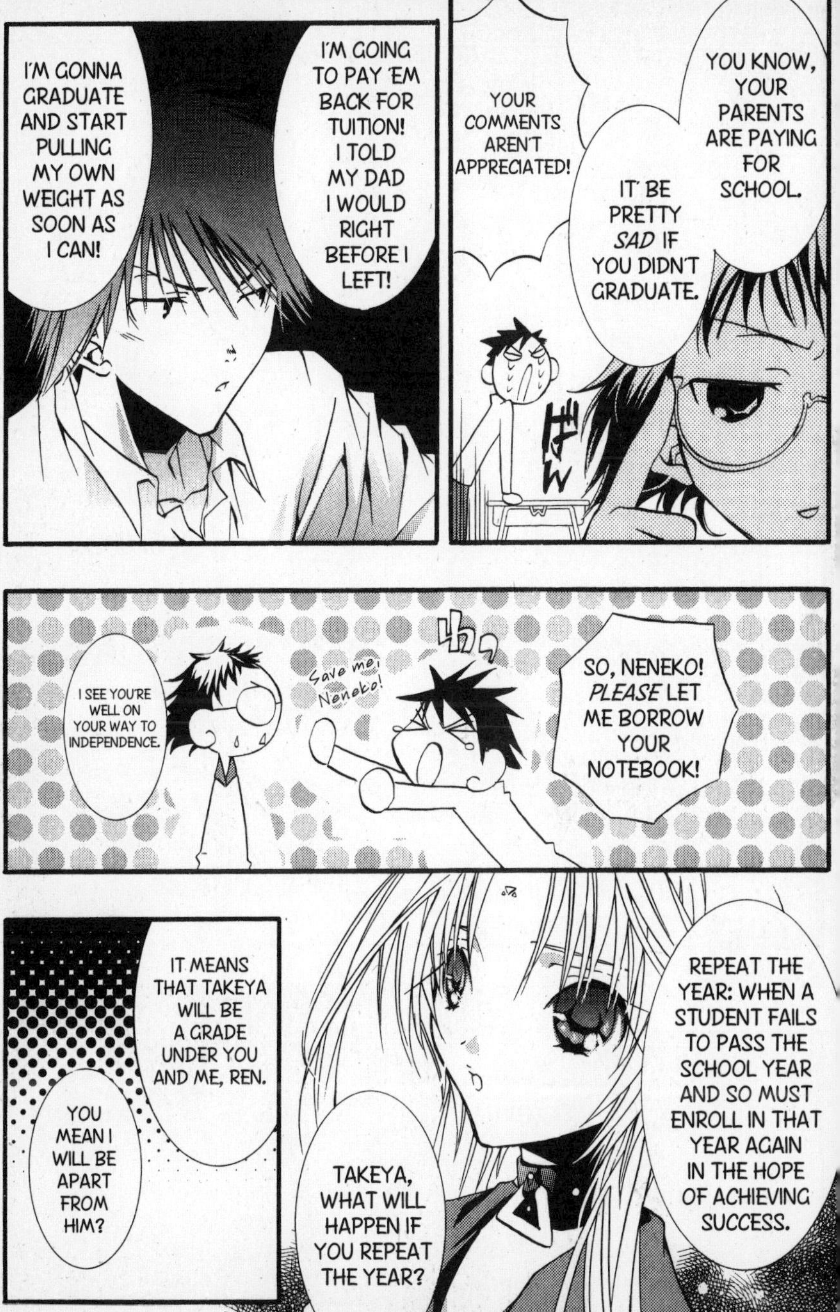
YOU KNOW, YOUR PARENTS ARE PAYING FOR SCHOOL.
IT' BE PRETTY *SAD* IF YOU DIDN'T GRADUATE.
YOUR COMMENTS AREN'T APPRECIATED!
I'M GOING TO PAY 'EM BACK FOR TUITION! I TOLD MY DAD I WOULD RIGHT BEFORE I LEFT!
I'M GONNA GRADUATE AND START PULLING MY OWN WEIGHT AS SOON AS I CAN!
SO, NENEKO! *PLEASE* LET ME BORROW YOUR NOTEBOOK!
Save me! Neneko!
I SEE YOU'RE WELL ON YOUR WAY TO INDEPENDENCE.
REPEAT THE YEAR: WHEN A STUDENT FAILS TO PASS THE SCHOOL YEAR AND SO MUST ENROLL IN THAT YEAR AGAIN IN THE HOPE OF ACHIEVING SUCCESS.
TAKEYA, WHAT WILL HAPPEN IF YOU REPEAT THE YEAR?
IT MEANS THAT TAKEYA WILL BE A GRADE UNDER YOU AND ME, REN.
YOU MEAN I WILL BE APART FROM HIM?

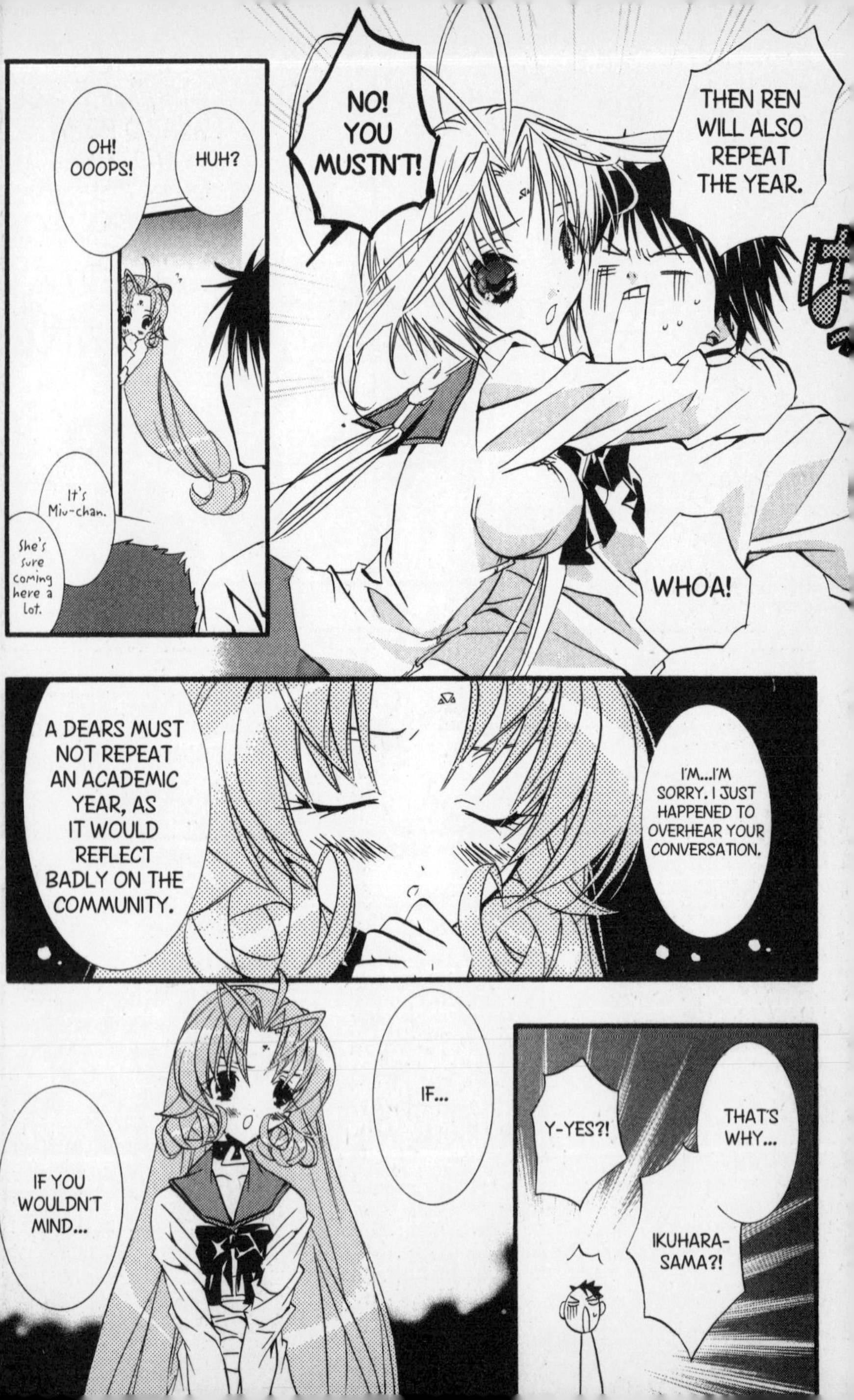
THEN REN WILL ALSO REPEAT THE YEAR.
NO! YOU MUSTN'T!
WHOA!
HUH?
OH! OOOPS!
It's Miu-chan.
She's sure coming here a lot.
I'M...I'M SORRY. I JUST HAPPENED TO OVERHEAR YOUR CONVERSATION.
A DEARS MUST NOT REPEAT AN ACADEMIC YEAR, AS IT WOULD REFLECT BADLY ON THE COMMUNITY.
THAT'S WHY...
Y-YES?!
IKUHARA-SAMA?!
IF...
IF YOU WOULDN'T MIND...

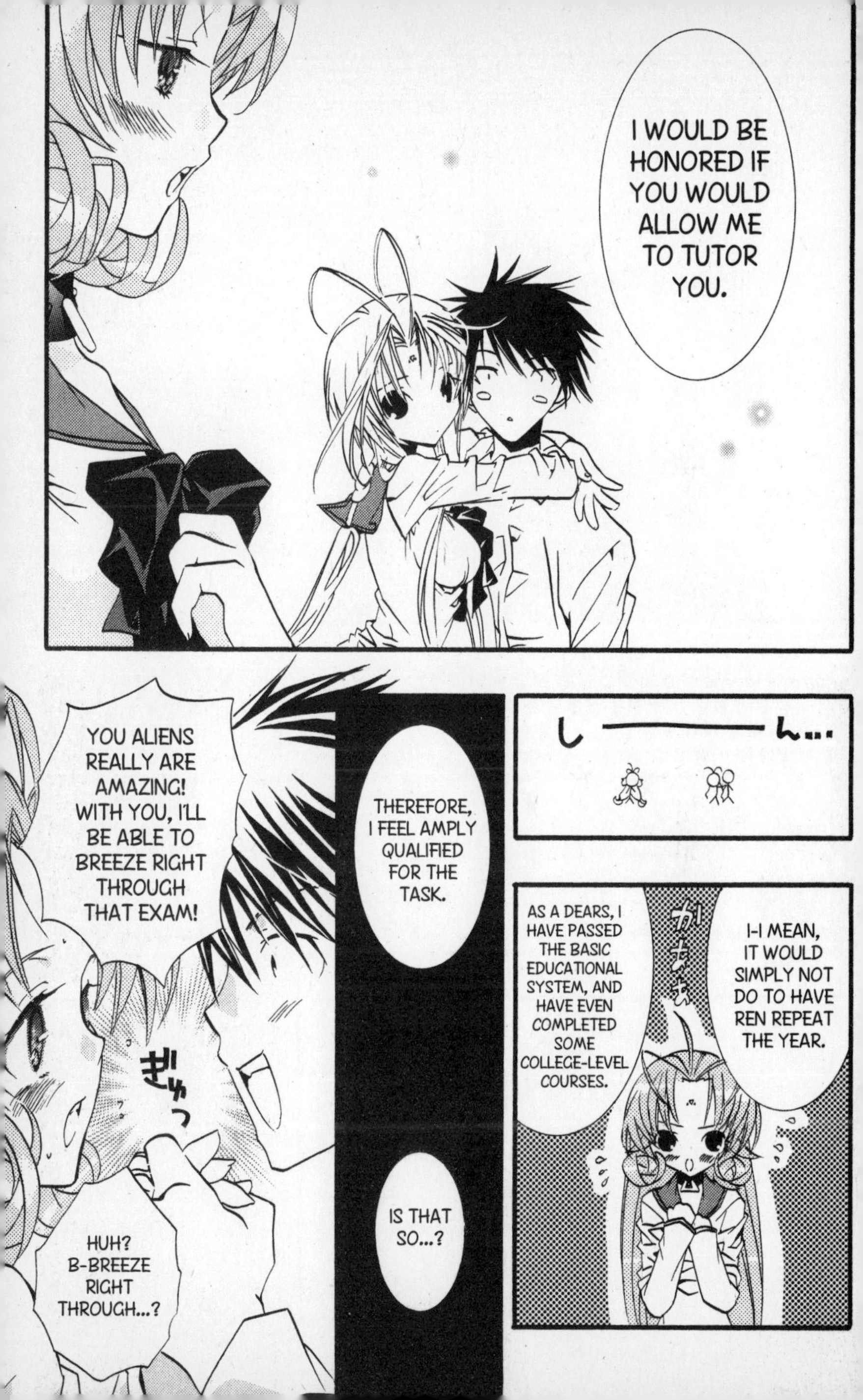
I WOULD BE HONORED IF YOU WOULD ALLOW ME TO TUTOR YOU.
し———ん...
I-I MEAN, IT WOULD SIMPLY NOT DO TO HAVE REN REPEAT THE YEAR.
AS A DEARS, I HAVE PASSED THE BASIC EDUCATIONAL SYSTEM, AND HAVE EVEN COMPLETED SOME COLLEGE-LEVEL COURSES.
THEREFORE, I FEEL AMPLY QUALIFIED FOR THE TASK.
IS THAT SO...?
YOU ALIENS REALLY ARE AMAZING! WITH YOU, I'LL BE ABLE TO BREEZE RIGHT THROUGH THAT EXAM!
ぎゅっ
HUH? B-BREEZE RIGHT THROUGH...?

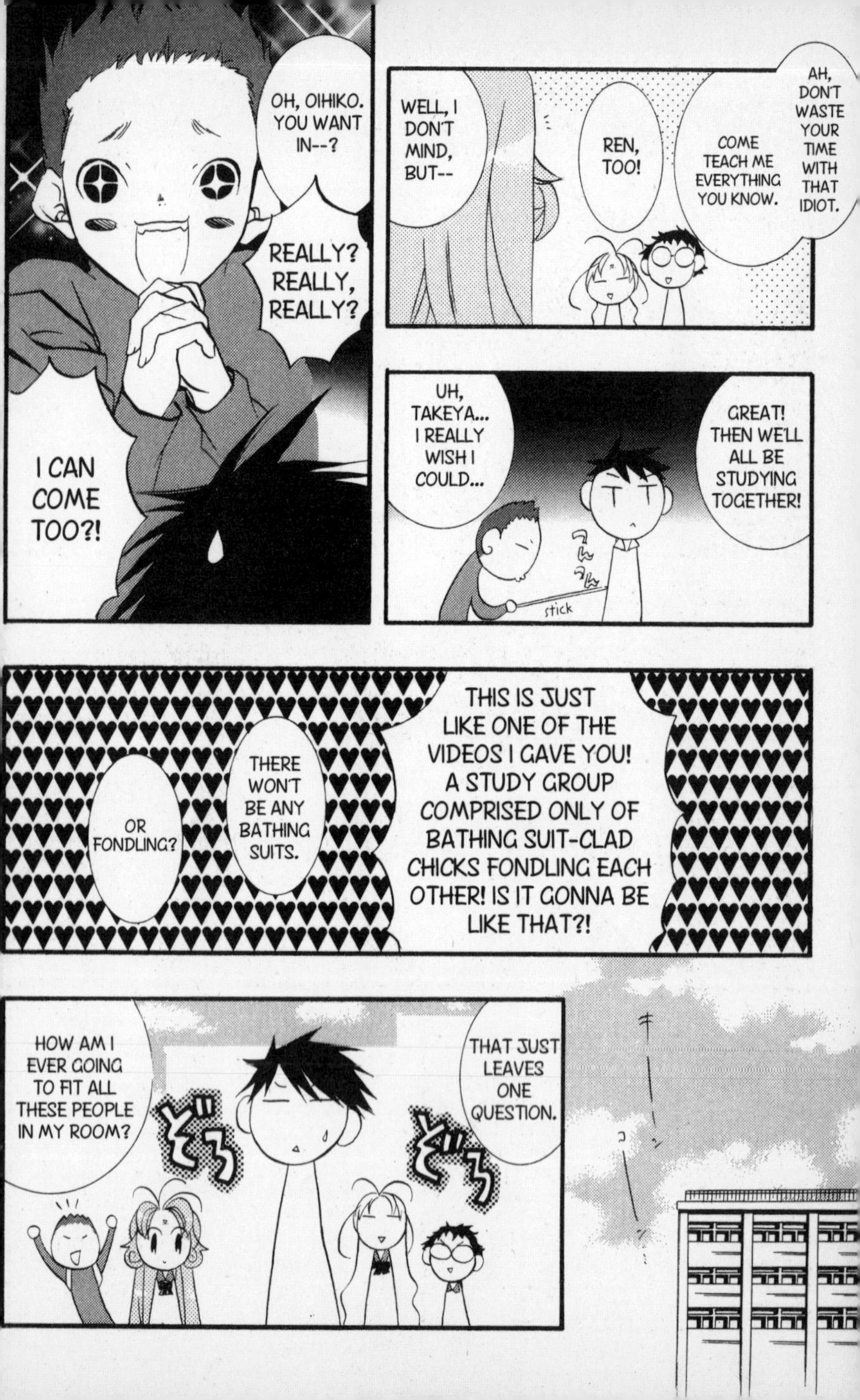
AH, DON'T WASTE YOUR TIME WITH THAT IDIOT.
COME TEACH ME EVERYTHING YOU KNOW.
REN, TOO!
WELL, I DON'T MIND, BUT--
GREAT! THEN WE'LL ALL BE STUDYING TOGETHER!
UH, TAKEYA... I REALLY WISH I COULD...
stick
OH, OIHIKO. YOU WANT IN--?
REALLY? REALLY, REALLY?
I CAN COME TOO?!
THIS IS JUST LIKE ONE OF THE VIDEOS I GAVE YOU! A STUDY GROUP COMPRISED ONLY OF BATHING SUIT-CLAD CHICKS FONDLING EACH OTHER! IS IT GONNA BE LIKE THAT?!
THERE WON'T BE ANY BATHING SUITS.
OR FONDLING?
THAT JUST LEAVES ONE QUESTION.
ぞろ
ぞろ
HOW AM I EVER GOING TO FIT ALL THESE PEOPLE IN MY ROOM?

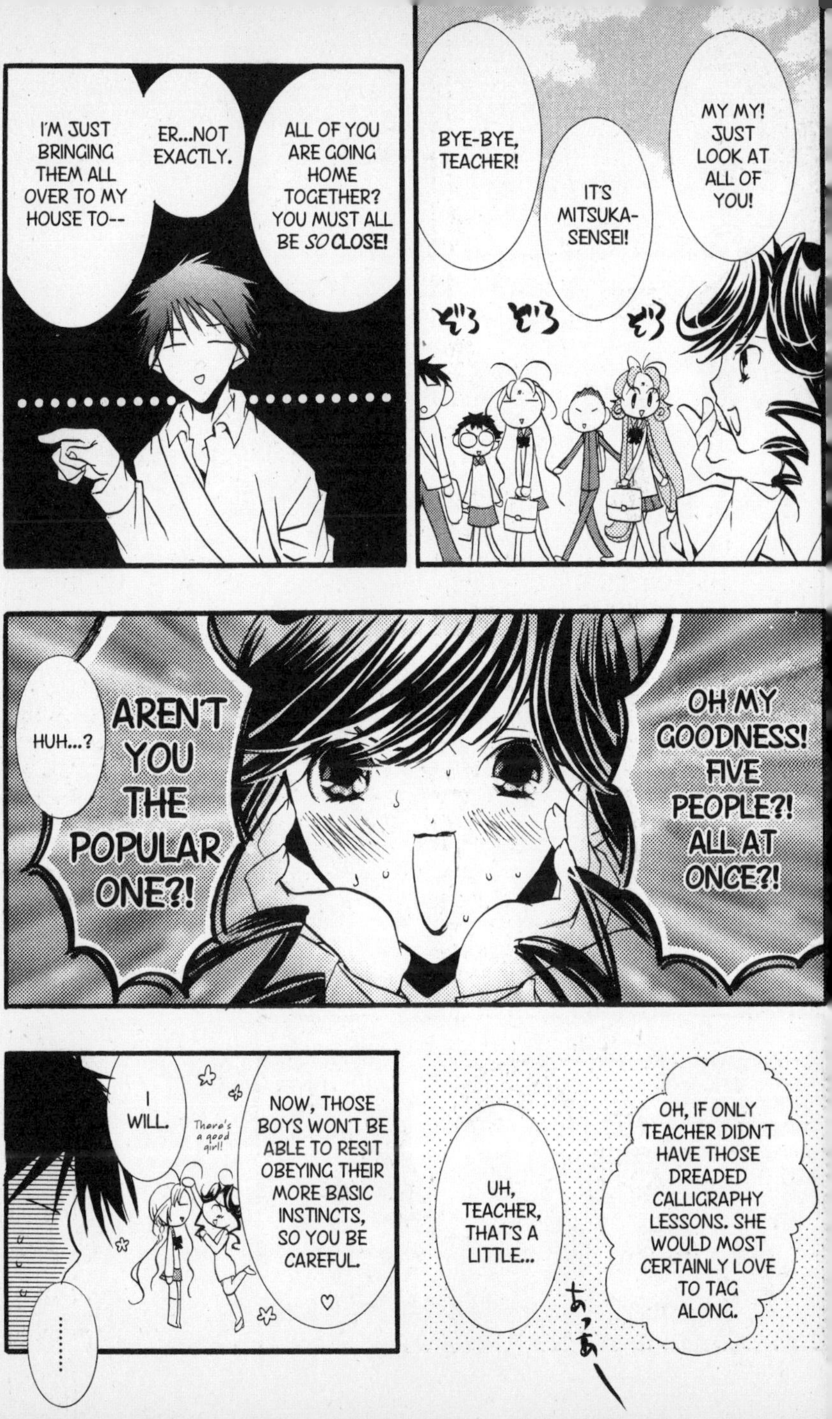
MY MY! JUST LOOK AT ALL OF YOU!
IT'S MITSUKA-SENSEI!
BYE-BYE, TEACHER!
ぞろ ぞろ ぞろ
ALL OF YOU ARE GOING HOME TOGETHER? YOU MUST ALL BE *SO* CLOSE!
ER...NOT EXACTLY.
I'M JUST BRINGING THEM ALL OVER TO MY HOUSE TO--
....
OH MY GOODNESS! FIVE PEOPLE?! ALL AT ONCE?!
AREN'T YOU THE POPULAR ONE?!
HUH...?
OH, IF ONLY TEACHER DIDN'T HAVE THOSE DREADED CALLIGRAPHY LESSONS. SHE WOULD MOST CERTAINLY LOVE TO TAG ALONG.
UH, TEACHER, THAT'S A LITTLE...
あっあ
NOW, THOSE BOYS WON'T BE ABLE TO RESIT OBEYING THEIR MORE BASIC INSTINCTS, SO YOU BE CAREFUL. ♡
I WILL.
There's a good girl!
......

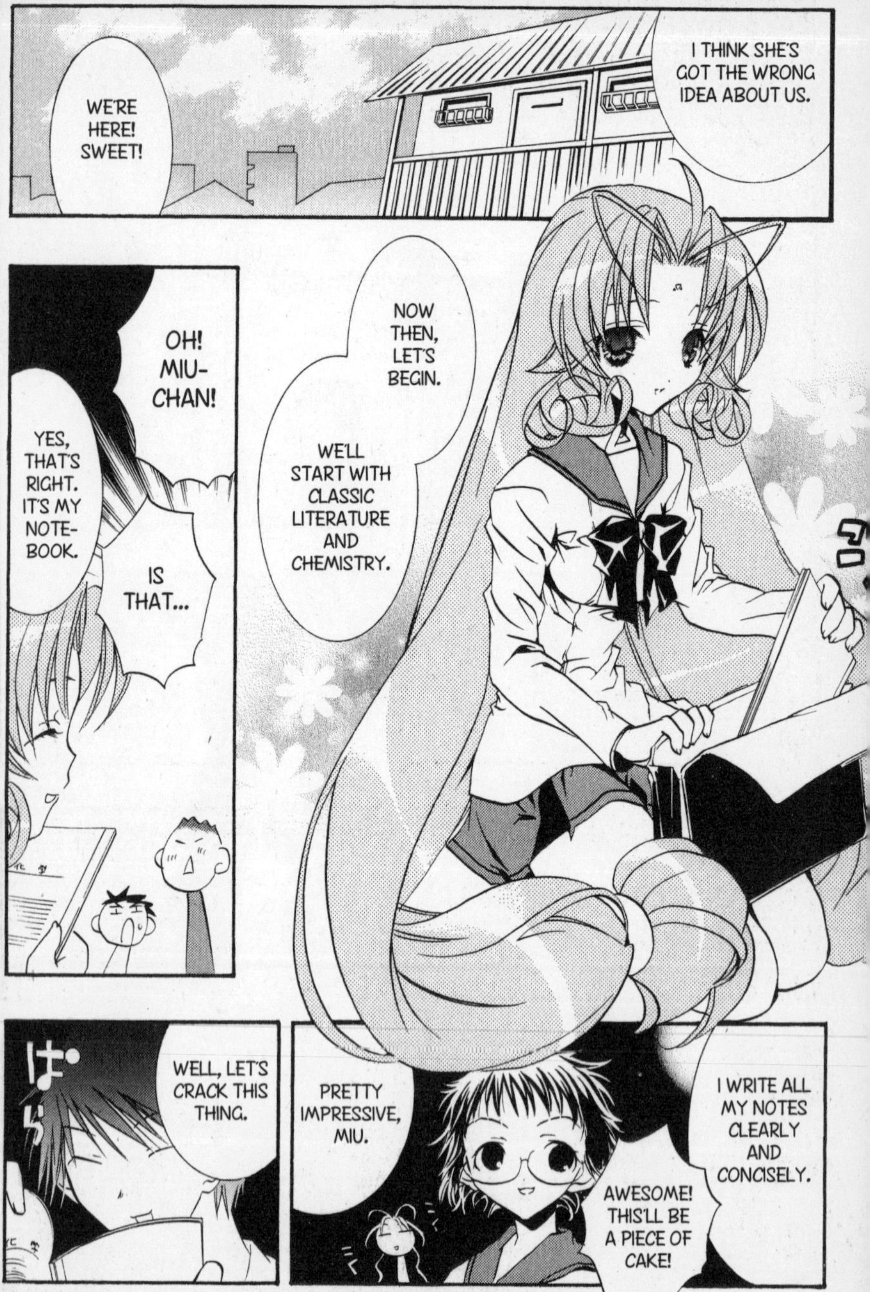
I THINK SHE'S GOT THE WRONG IDEA ABOUT US.
WE'RE HERE! SWEET!
NOW THEN, LET'S BEGIN.
WE'LL START WITH CLASSIC LITERATURE AND CHEMISTRY.
OH! MIU-CHAN!
IS THAT...
YES, THAT'S RIGHT. IT'S MY NOTE-BOOK.
I WRITE ALL MY NOTES CLEARLY AND CONCISELY.
PRETTY IMPRESSIVE, MIU.
AWESOME! THIS'LL BE A PIECE OF CAKE!
ぱら
WELL, LET'S CRACK THIS THING.

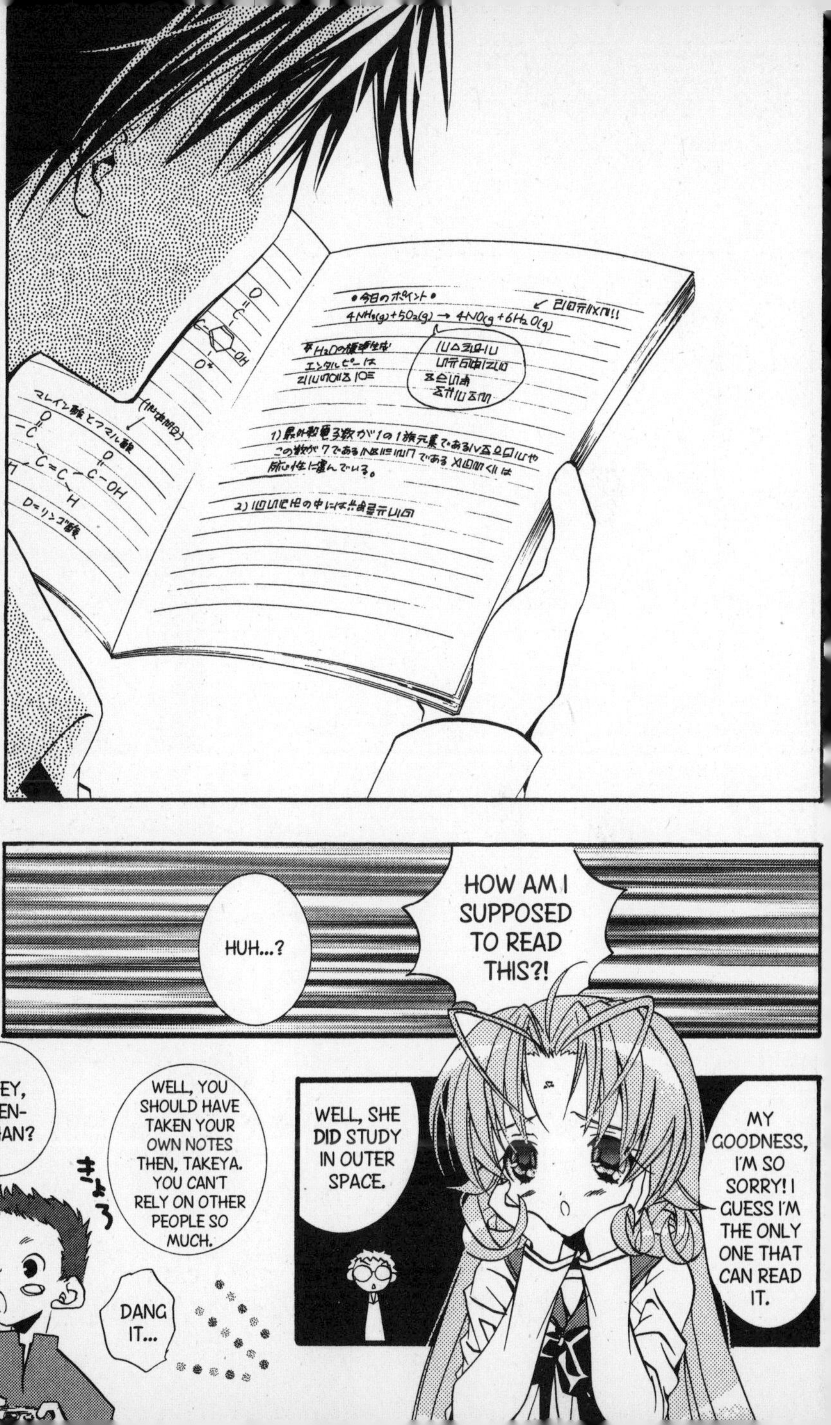
●今日のポイント●
マレイン酸とフマル酸
D=リンゴ酸
HOW AM I SUPPOSED TO READ THIS?!
HUH...?
MY GOODNESS, I'M SO SORRY! I GUESS I'M THE ONLY ONE THAT CAN READ IT.
WELL, SHE DID STUDY IN OUTER SPACE.
WELL, YOU SHOULD HAVE TAKEN YOUR OWN NOTES THEN, TAKEYA. YOU CAN'T RELY ON OTHER PEOPLE SO MUCH.
HEY, REN-CHAN?
きょろ
DANG IT...

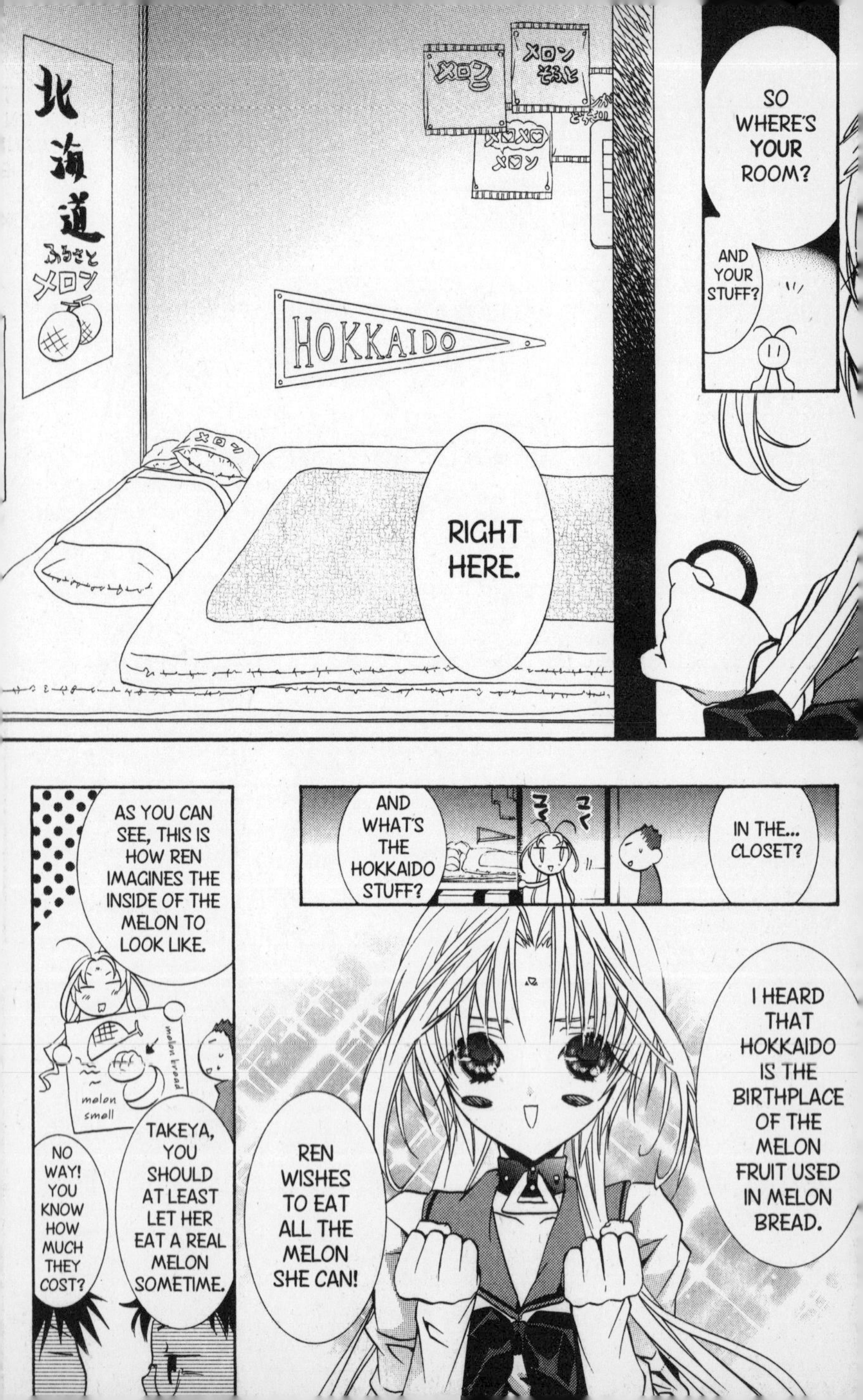
SO WHERE'S YOUR ROOM?
AND YOUR STUFF?
北海道
ふるさと
メロン
HOKKAIDO
RIGHT HERE.
IN THE... CLOSET?
AND WHAT'S THE HOKKAIDO STUFF?
I HEARD THAT HOKKAIDO IS THE BIRTHPLACE OF THE MELON FRUIT USED IN MELON BREAD.
REN WISHES TO EAT ALL THE MELON SHE CAN!
AS YOU CAN SEE, THIS IS HOW REN IMAGINES THE INSIDE OF THE MELON TO LOOK LIKE.
melon bread
melon smell
TAKEYA, YOU SHOULD AT LEAST LET HER EAT A REAL MELON SOMETIME.
NO WAY! YOU KNOW HOW MUCH THEY COST?

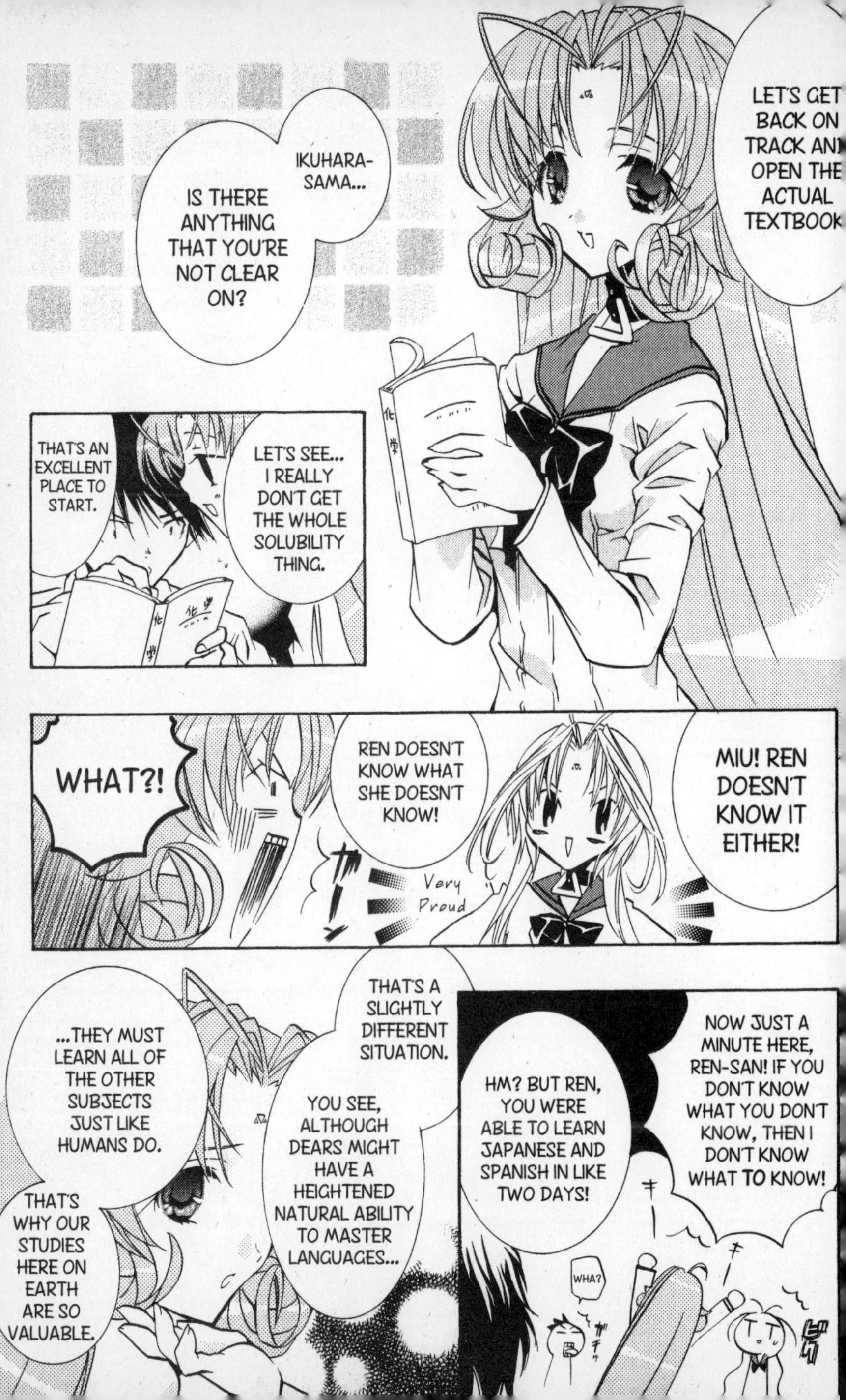
LET'S GET BACK ON TRACK AN OPEN THE ACTUAL TEXTBOOK
IKUHARA-SAMA... IS THERE ANYTHING THAT YOU'RE NOT CLEAR ON?
LET'S SEE... I REALLY DON'T GET THE WHOLE SOLUBILITY THING.
THAT'S AN EXCELLENT PLACE TO START.
MIU! REN DOESN'T KNOW IT EITHER!
REN DOESN'T KNOW WHAT SHE DOESN'T KNOW!
Very Proud
WHAT?!
NOW JUST A MINUTE HERE, REN-SAN! IF YOU DON'T KNOW WHAT YOU DON'T KNOW, THEN I DON'T KNOW WHAT TO KNOW!
HM? BUT REN, YOU WERE ABLE TO LEARN JAPANESE AND SPANISH IN LIKE TWO DAYS!
WHA?
THAT'S A SLIGHTLY DIFFERENT SITUATION.
YOU SEE, ALTHOUGH DEARS MIGHT HAVE A HEIGHTENED NATURAL ABILITY TO MASTER LANGUAGES...
...THEY MUST LEARN ALL OF THE OTHER SUBJECTS JUST LIKE HUMANS DO.
THAT'S WHY OUR STUDIES HERE ON EARTH ARE SO VALUABLE.

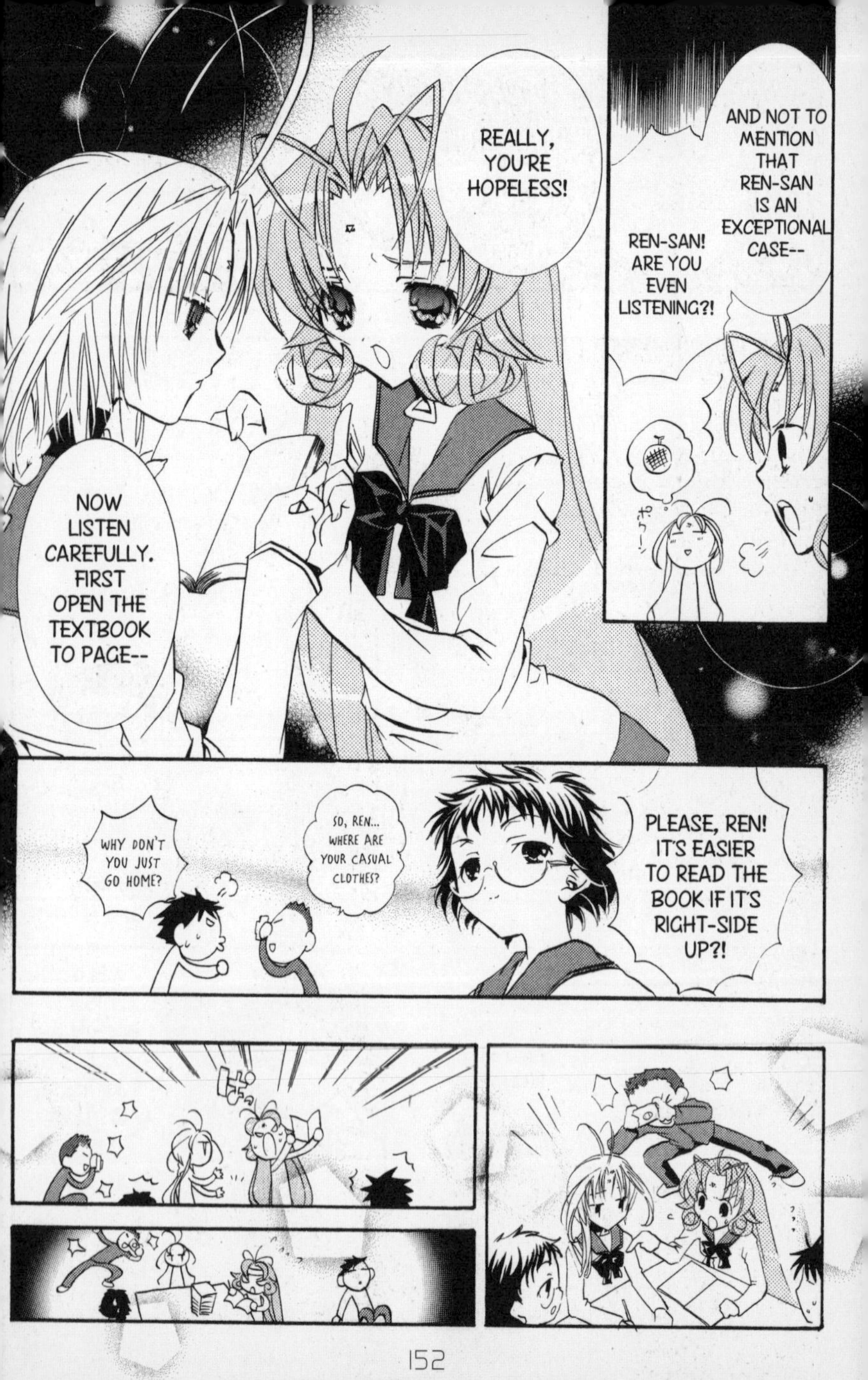
AND NOT TO MENTION THAT REN-SAN IS AN EXCEPTIONAL CASE--
REN-SAN! ARE YOU EVEN LISTENING?!
REALLY, YOU'RE HOPELESS!
NOW LISTEN CAREFULLY. FIRST OPEN THE TEXTBOOK TO PAGE--
PLEASE, REN! IT'S EASIER TO READ THE BOOK IF IT'S RIGHT-SIDE UP?!
SO, REN... WHERE ARE YOUR CASUAL CLOTHES?
WHY DON'T YOU JUST GO HOME?

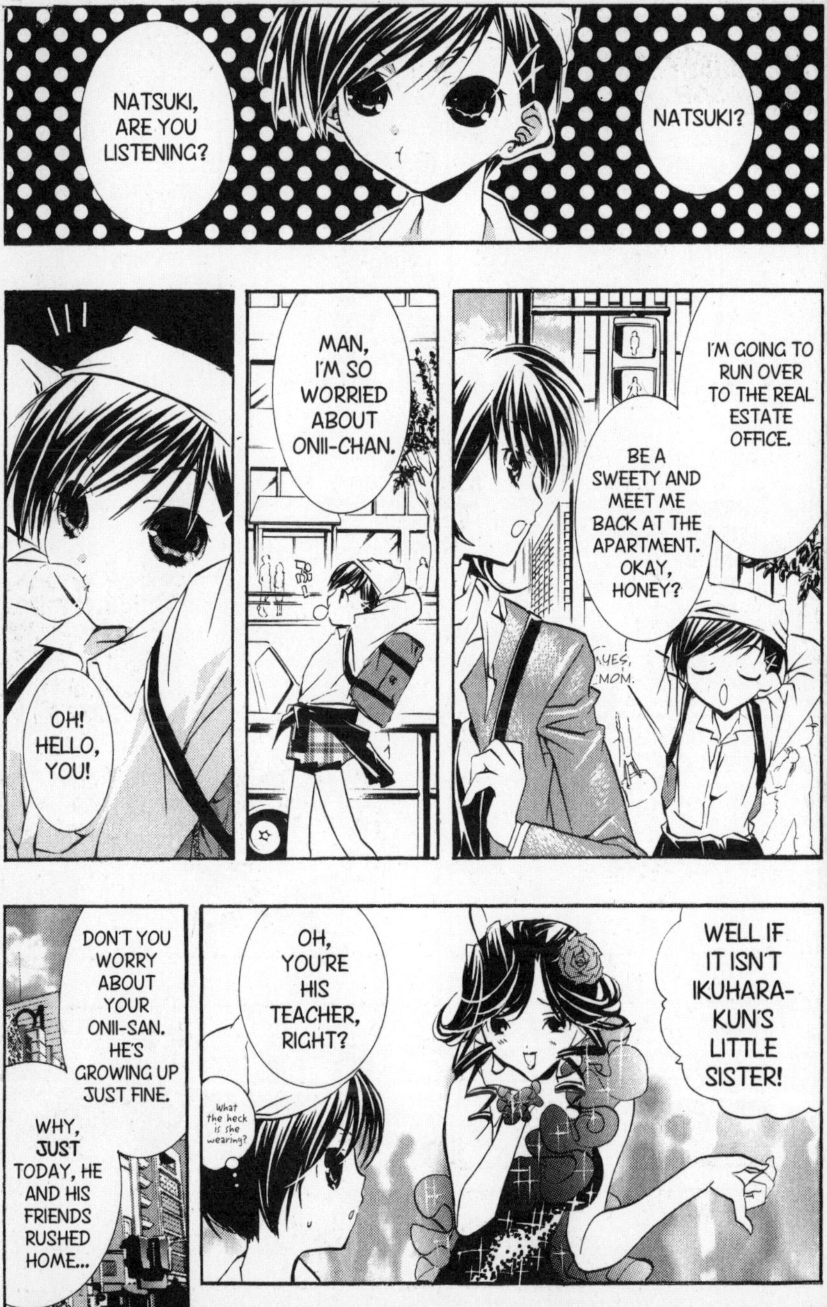
NATSUKI?
NATSUKI, ARE YOU LISTENING?
I'M GOING TO RUN OVER TO THE REAL ESTATE OFFICE.
BE A SWEETY AND MEET ME BACK AT THE APARTMENT. OKAY, HONEY?
YES, MOM.
MAN, I'M SO WORRIED ABOUT ONII-CHAN.
OH! HELLO, YOU!
WELL IF IT ISN'T IKUHARA-KUN'S LITTLE SISTER!
OH, YOU'RE HIS TEACHER, RIGHT?
What the heck is she wearing?
DON'T YOU WORRY ABOUT YOUR ONII-SAN. HE'S GROWING UP JUST FINE.
WHY, JUST TODAY, HE AND HIS FRIENDS RUSHED HOME...

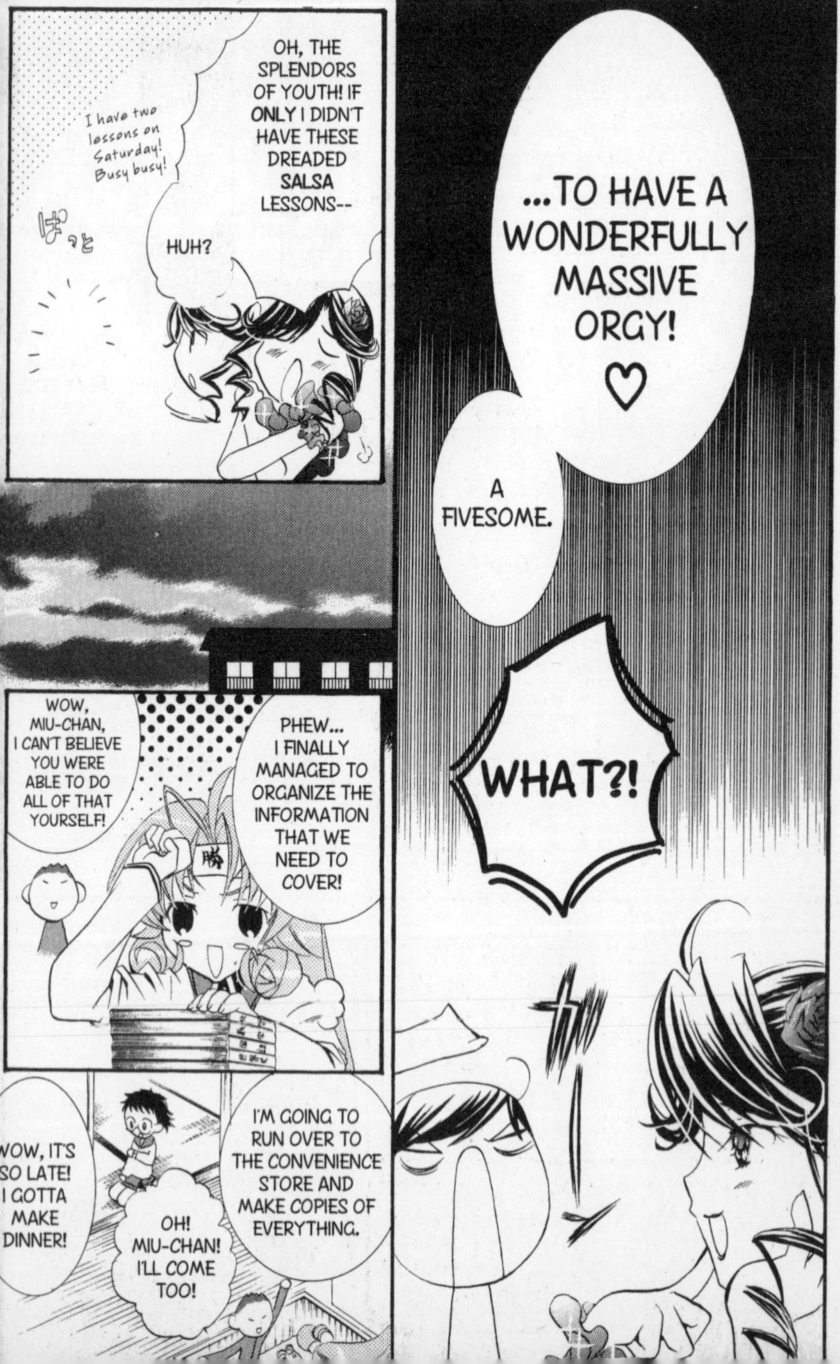
...TO HAVE A WONDERFULLY MASSIVE ORGY! ♡
A FIVESOME.
WHAT?!
OH, THE SPLENDORS OF YOUTH! IF ONLY I DIDN'T HAVE THESE DREADED SALSA LESSONS--
I have two lessons on Saturday! Busy busy!
ぱっと
HUH?
PHEW... I FINALLY MANAGED TO ORGANIZE THE INFORMATION THAT WE NEED TO COVER!
WOW, MIU-CHAN, I CAN'T BELIEVE YOU WERE ABLE TO DO ALL OF THAT YOURSELF!
I'M GOING TO RUN OVER TO THE CONVENIENCE STORE AND MAKE COPIES OF EVERYTHING.
OH! MIU-CHAN! I'LL COME TOO!
WOW, IT'S SO LATE! I GOTTA MAKE DINNER!

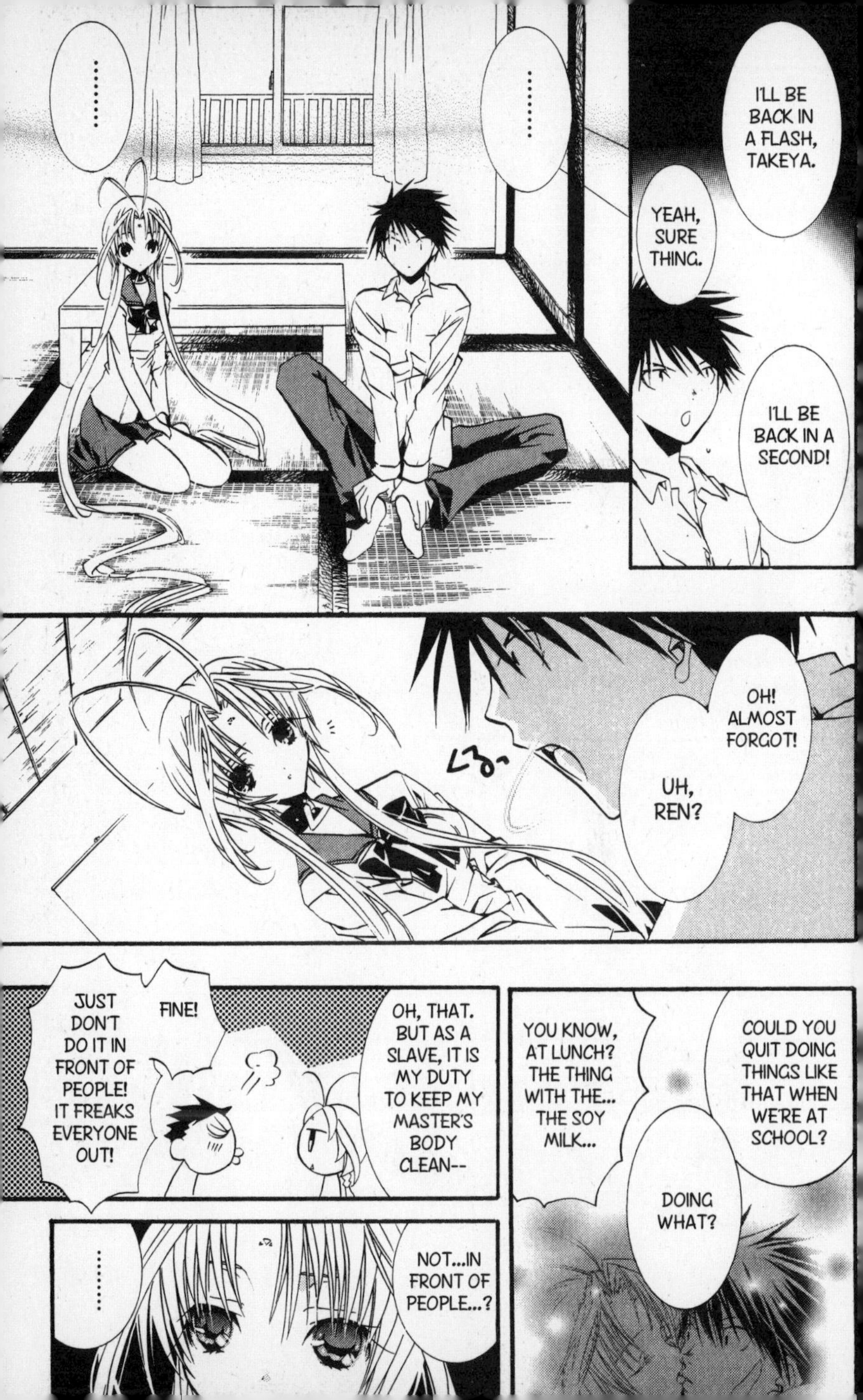
I'LL BE BACK IN A FLASH, TAKEYA.
YEAH, SURE THING.
I'LL BE BACK IN A SECOND!
....
....
OH! ALMOST FORGOT!
UH, REN?
COULD YOU QUIT DOING THINGS LIKE THAT WHEN WE'RE AT SCHOOL?
YOU KNOW, AT LUNCH? THE THING WITH THE... THE SOY MILK...
DOING WHAT?
OH, THAT. BUT AS A SLAVE, IT IS MY DUTY TO KEEP MY MASTER'S BODY CLEAN--
FINE!
JUST DON'T DO IT IN FRONT OF PEOPLE! IT FREAKS EVERYONE OUT!
NOT...IN FRONT OF PEOPLE...?
....

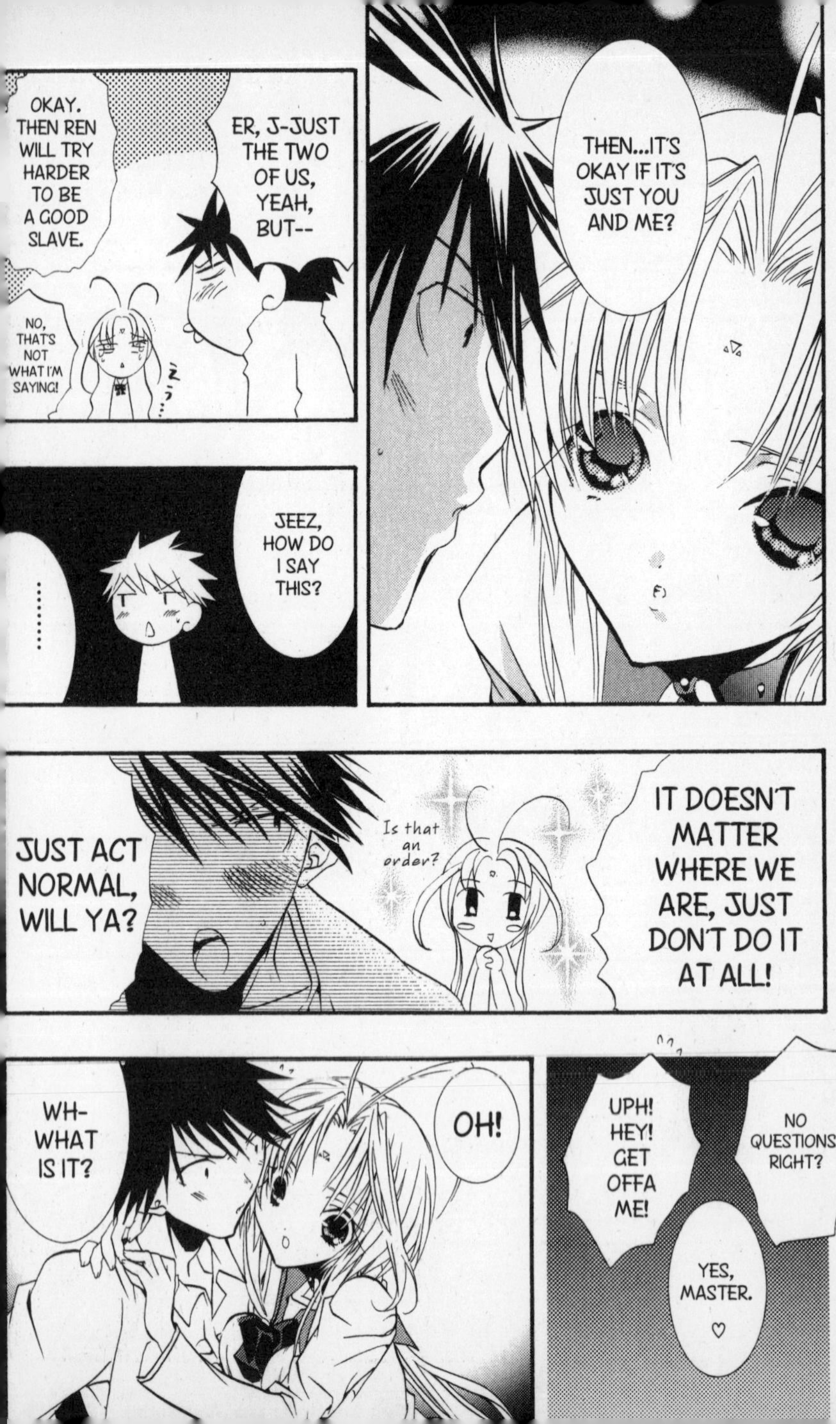
THEN...IT'S OKAY IF IT'S JUST YOU AND ME?
ER, J-JUST THE TWO OF US, YEAH, BUT--
OKAY. THEN REN WILL TRY HARDER TO BE A GOOD SLAVE.
NO, THAT'S NOT WHAT I'M SAYING!
JEEZ, HOW DO I SAY THIS?
......
IT DOESN'T MATTER WHERE WE ARE, JUST DON'T DO IT AT ALL!
Is that an order?
JUST ACT NORMAL, WILL YA?
NO QUESTIONS, RIGHT?
UPH! HEY! GET OFFA ME!
YES, MASTER. ♡
OH!
WH-WHAT IS IT?

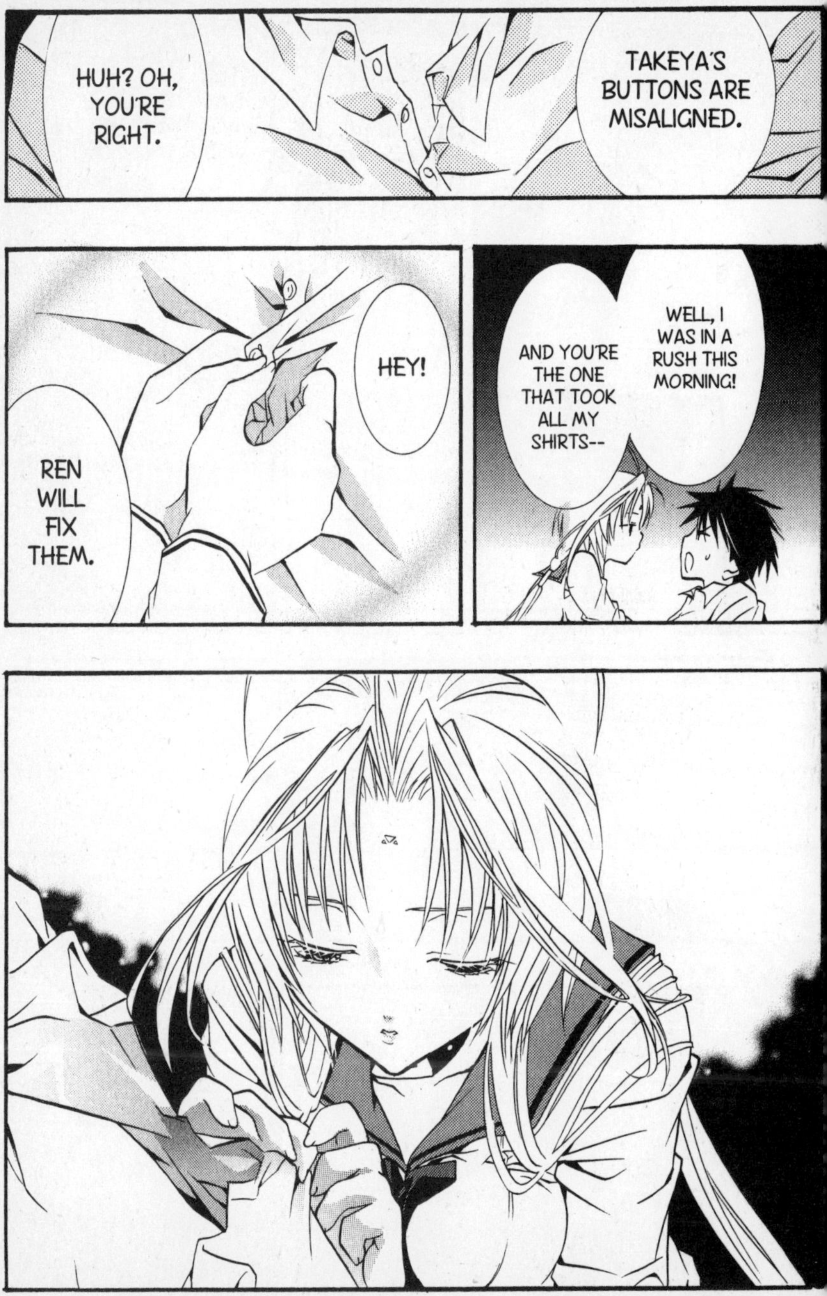
TAKEYA'S BUTTONS ARE MISALIGNED.
HUH? OH, YOU'RE RIGHT.
WELL, I WAS IN A RUSH THIS MORNING!
AND YOU'RE THE ONE THAT TOOK ALL MY SHIRTS--
HEY!
REN WILL FIX THEM.

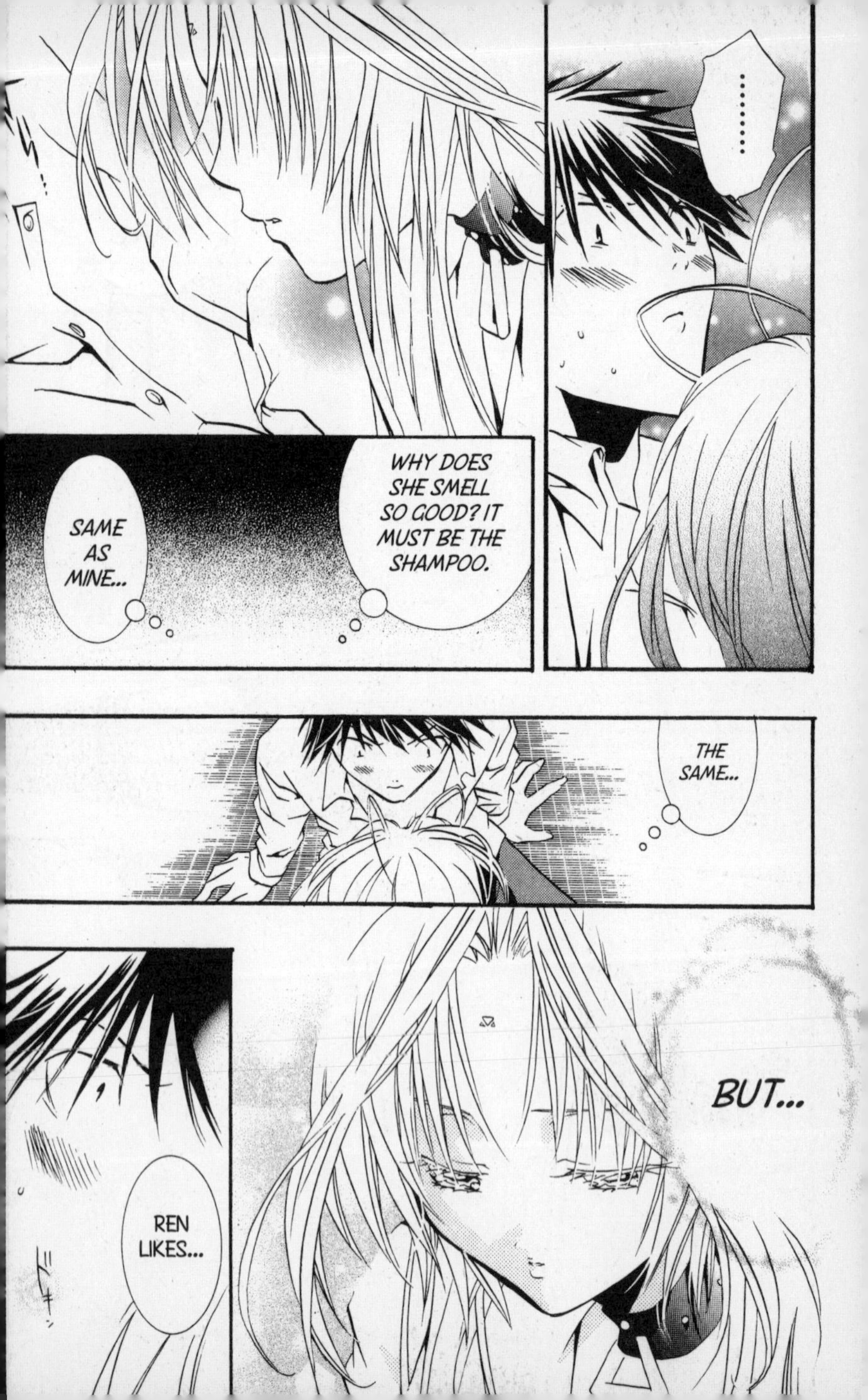
......
WHY DOES SHE SMELL SO GOOD? IT MUST BE THE SHAMPOO.
SAME AS MINE...
THE SAME...
BUT...
REN LIKES...

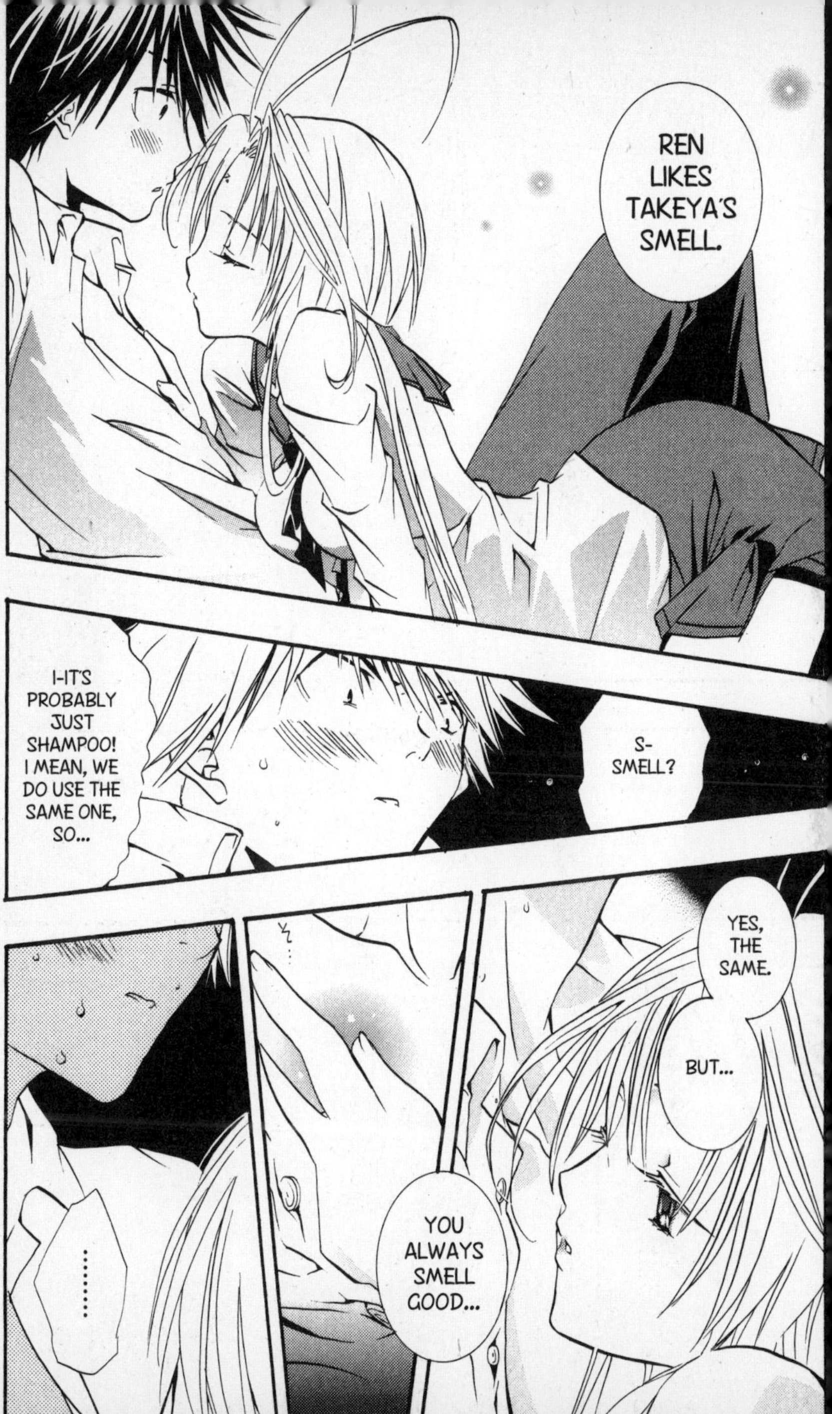
REN LIKES TAKEYA'S SMELL.
S-SMELL?
I-IT'S PROBABLY JUST SHAMPOO! I MEAN, WE DO USE THE SAME ONE, SO...
YES, THE SAME.
BUT...
YOU ALWAYS SMELL GOOD...
....

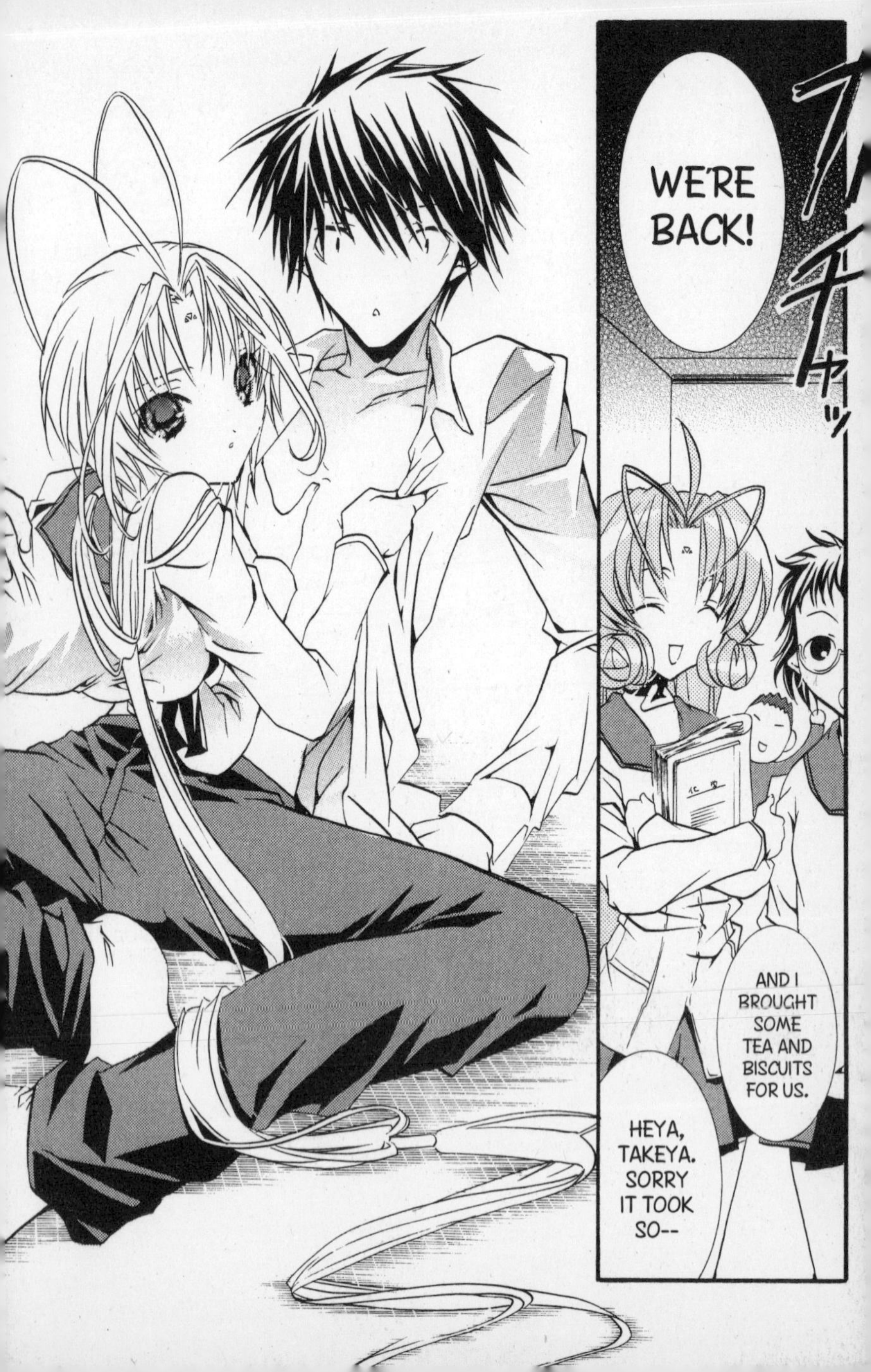
WE'RE BACK!
AND I BROUGHT SOME TEA AND BISCUITS FOR US.
HEYA, TAKEYA. SORRY IT TOOK SO--

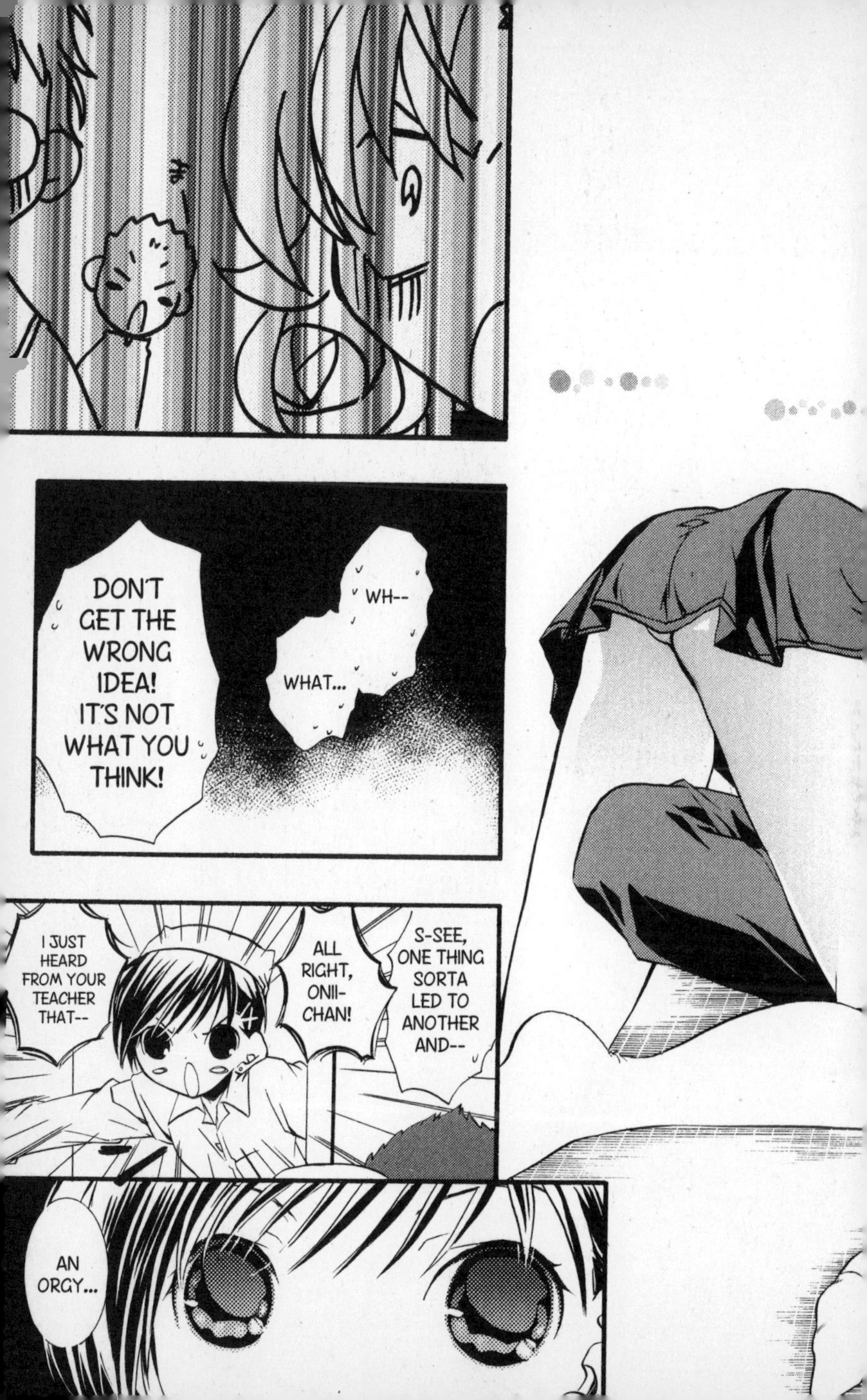
WH-- WHAT...
DON'T GET THE WRONG IDEA! IT'S NOT WHAT YOU THINK!
S-SEE, ONE THING SORTA LED TO ANOTHER AND--
ALL RIGHT, ONII-CHAN!
I JUST HEARD FROM YOUR TEACHER THAT--
AN ORGY...

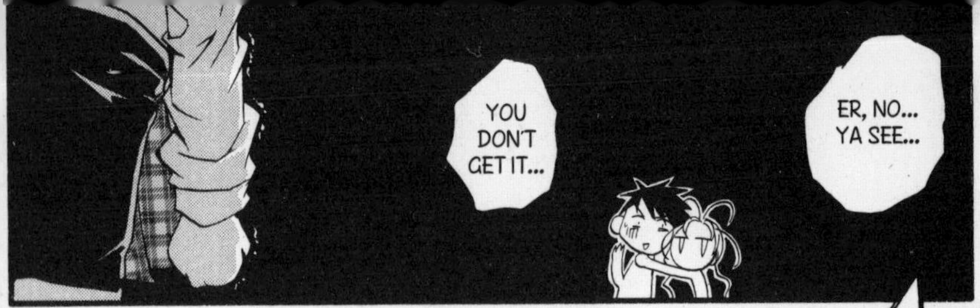
ER, NO... YA SEE...
YOU DON'T GET IT...
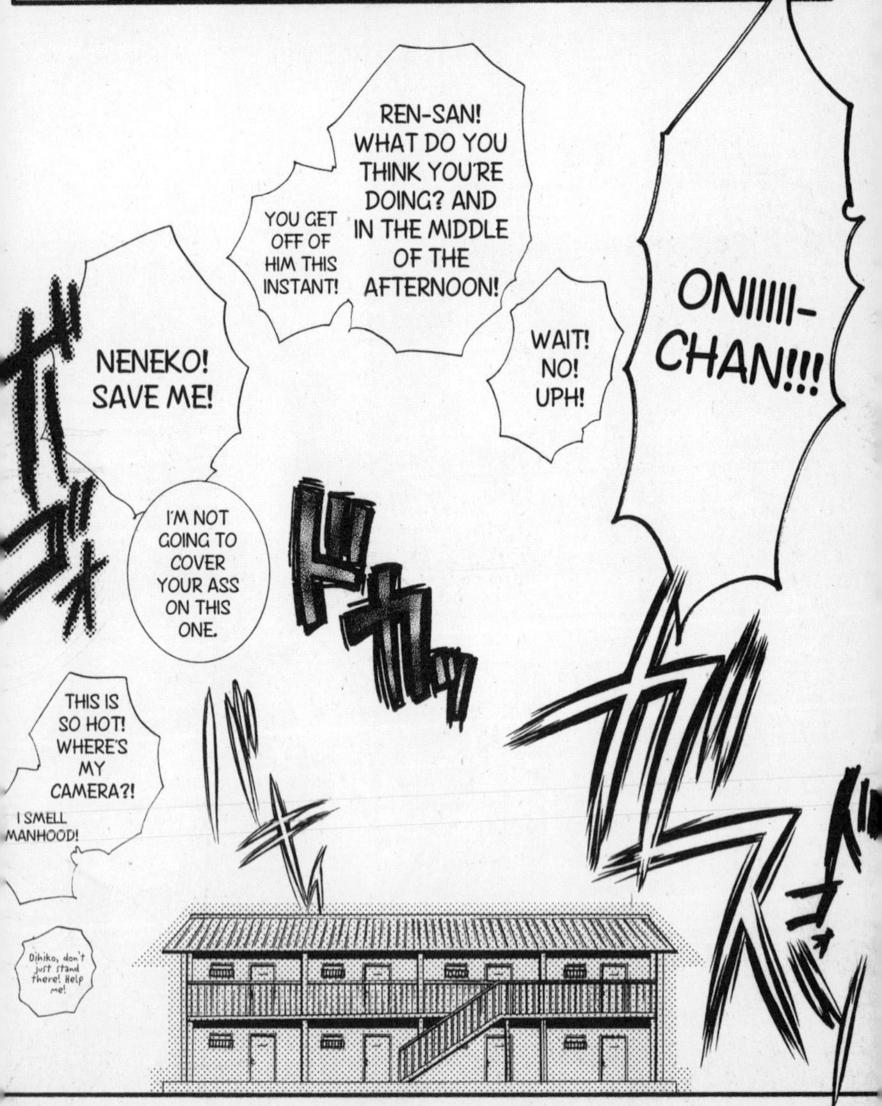
ONIIIIII-CHAN!!!
REN-SAN! WHAT DO YOU THINK YOU'RE DOING? AND IN THE MIDDLE OF THE AFTERNOON!
WAIT! NO! UPH!
YOU GET OFF OF HIM THIS INSTANT!
NENEKO! SAVE ME!
I'M NOT GOING TO COVER YOUR ASS ON THIS ONE.
THIS IS SO HOT! WHERE'S MY CAMERA?!
I SMELL MANHOOD!
Oihiko, don't just stand there! Help me!

18th Contact

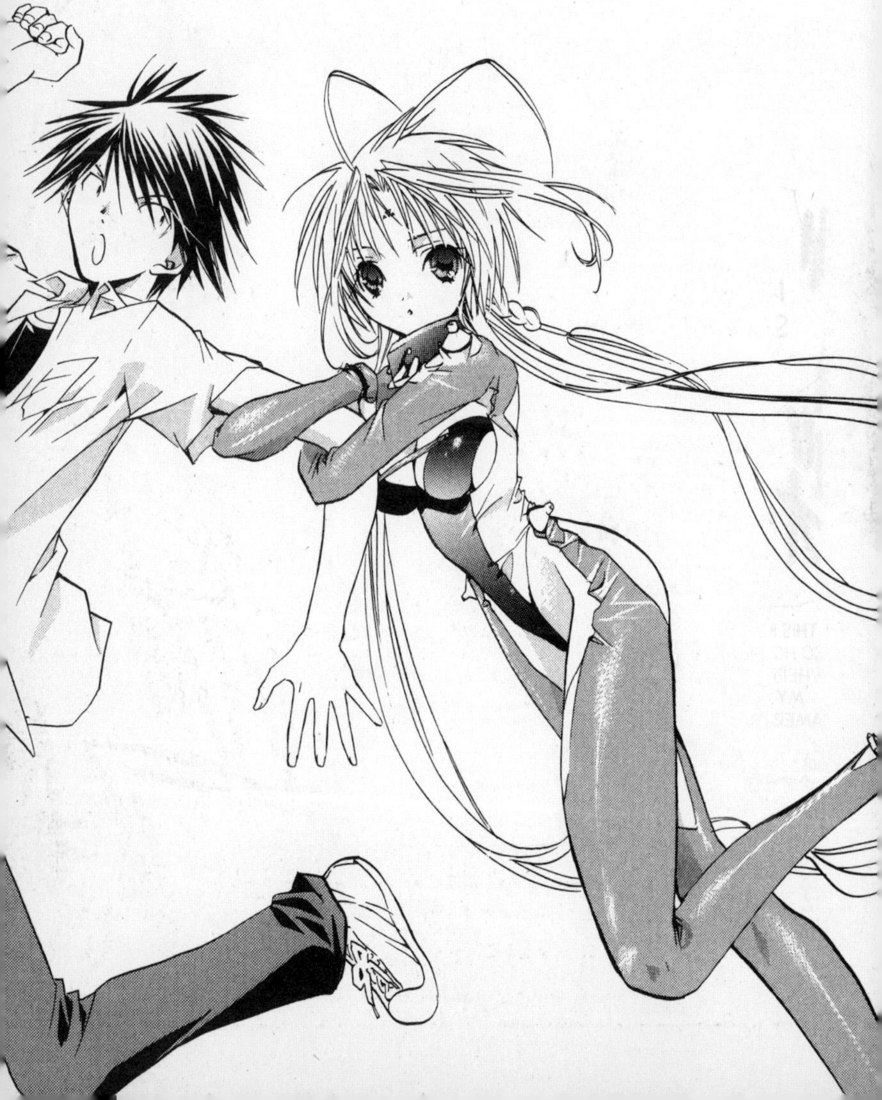

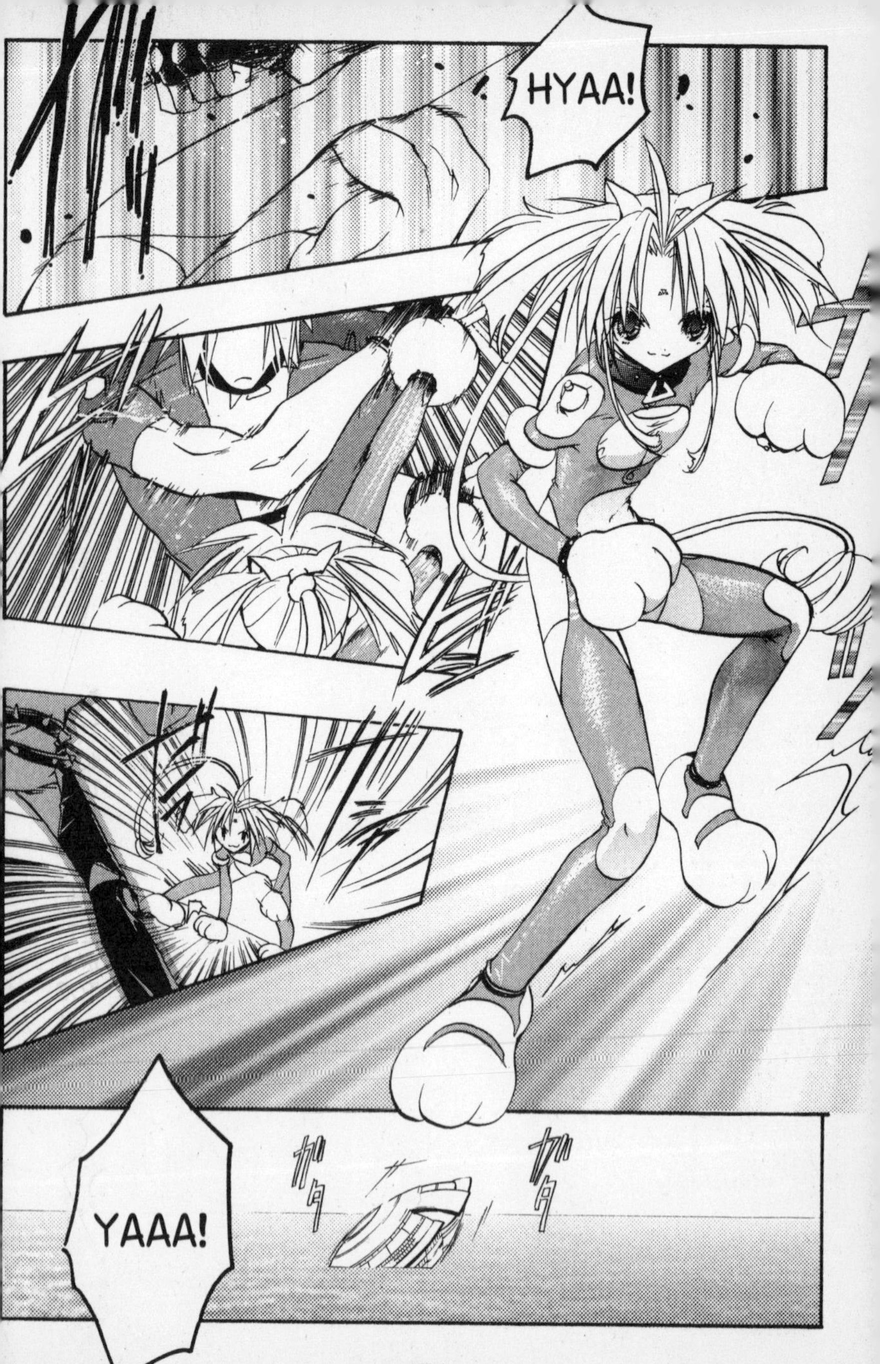
HYAA!
YAAA!

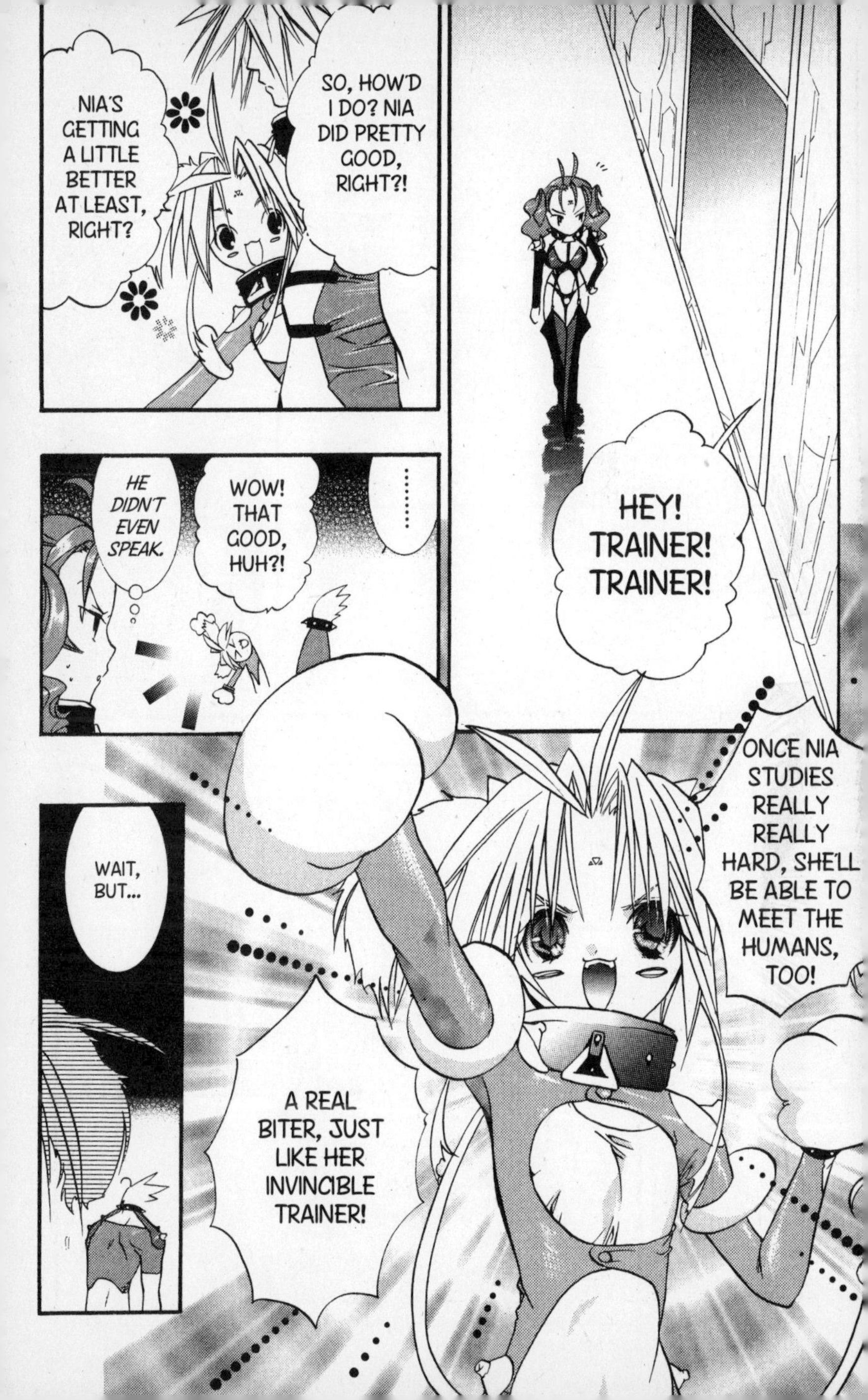
HEY! TRAINER! TRAINER!
SO, HOW'D I DO? NIA DID PRETTY GOOD, RIGHT?!
NIA'S GETTING A LITTLE BETTER AT LEAST, RIGHT?
......
WOW! THAT GOOD, HUH?!
HE DIDN'T EVEN SPEAK.
ONCE NIA STUDIES REALLY REALLY HARD, SHE'LL BE ABLE TO MEET THE HUMANS, TOO!
A REAL BITER, JUST LIKE HER INVINCIBLE TRAINER!
WAIT, BUT...

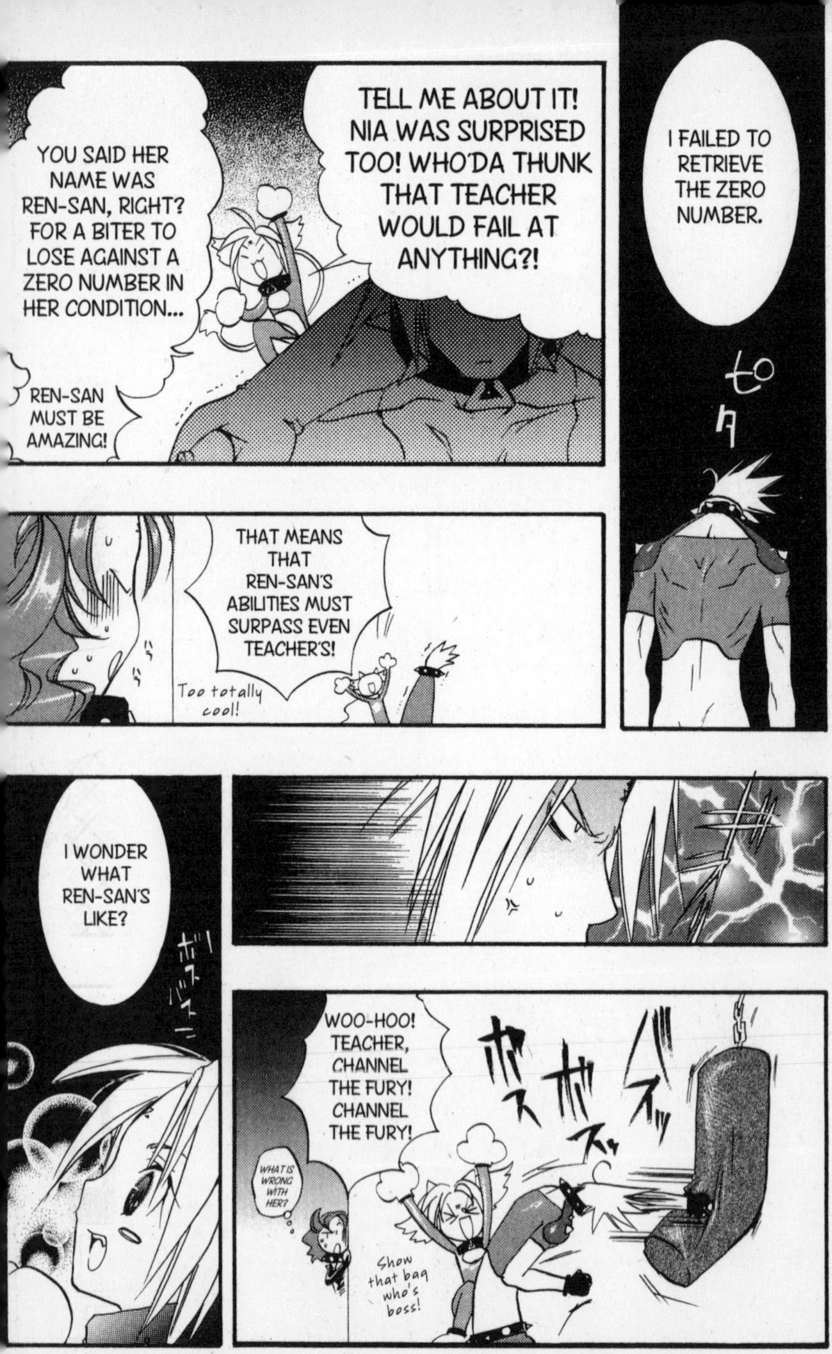
I FAILED TO RETRIEVE THE ZERO NUMBER.
ピタ
TELL ME ABOUT IT! NIA WAS SURPRISED TOO! WHO'DA THUNK THAT TEACHER WOULD FAIL AT ANYTHING?!
YOU SAID HER NAME WAS REN-SAN, RIGHT? FOR A BITER TO LOSE AGAINST A ZERO NUMBER IN HER CONDITION...
REN-SAN MUST BE AMAZING!
THAT MEANS THAT REN-SAN'S ABILITIES MUST SURPASS EVEN TEACHER'S!
Too totally cool!
WOO-HOO! TEACHER, CHANNEL THE FURY! CHANNEL THE FURY!
WHAT IS WRONG WITH HER?
Show that bag who's boss!
I WONDER WHAT REN-SAN'S LIKE?

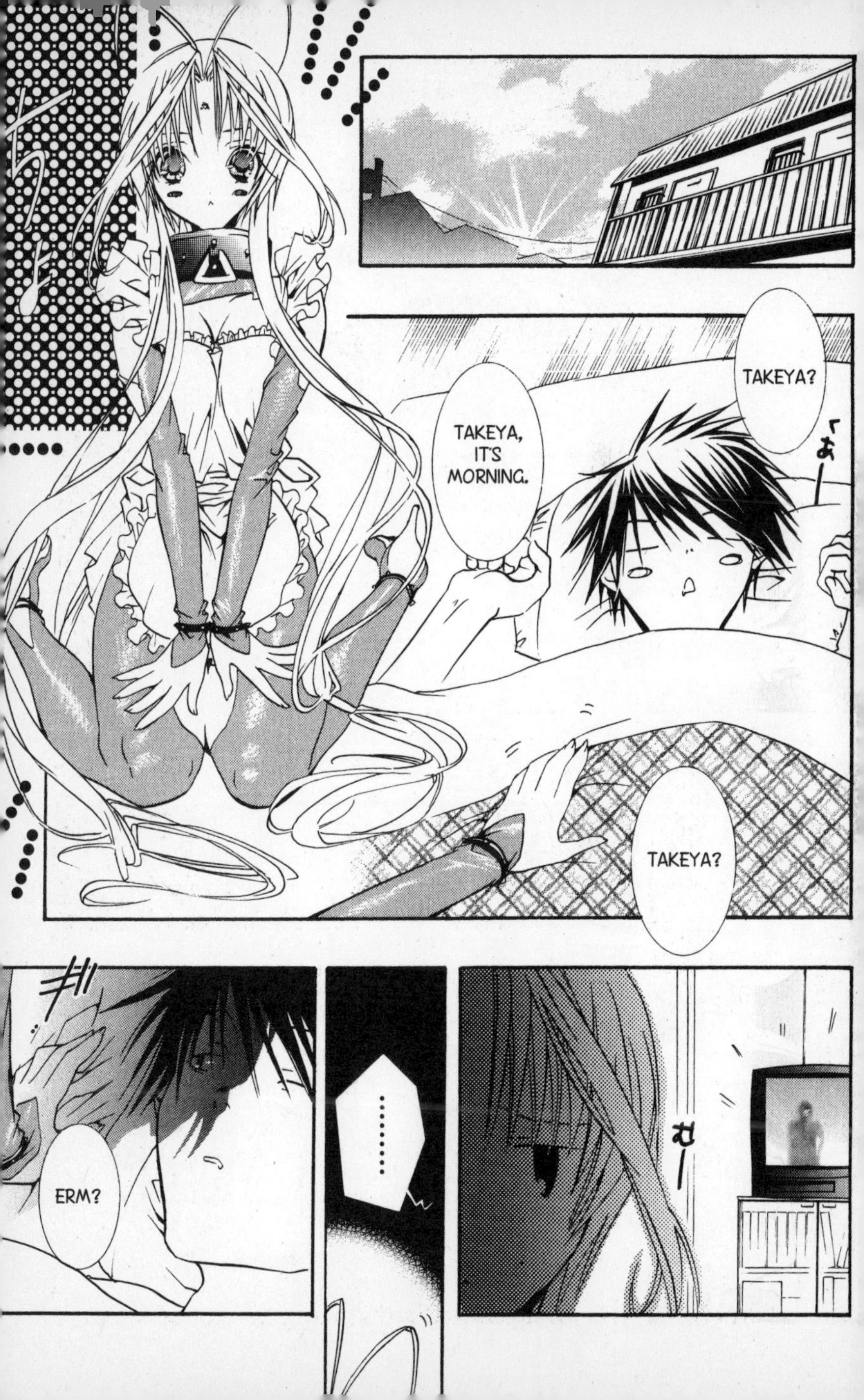
TAKEYA?
TAKEYA, IT'S MORNING.
TAKEYA?
......
ERM?

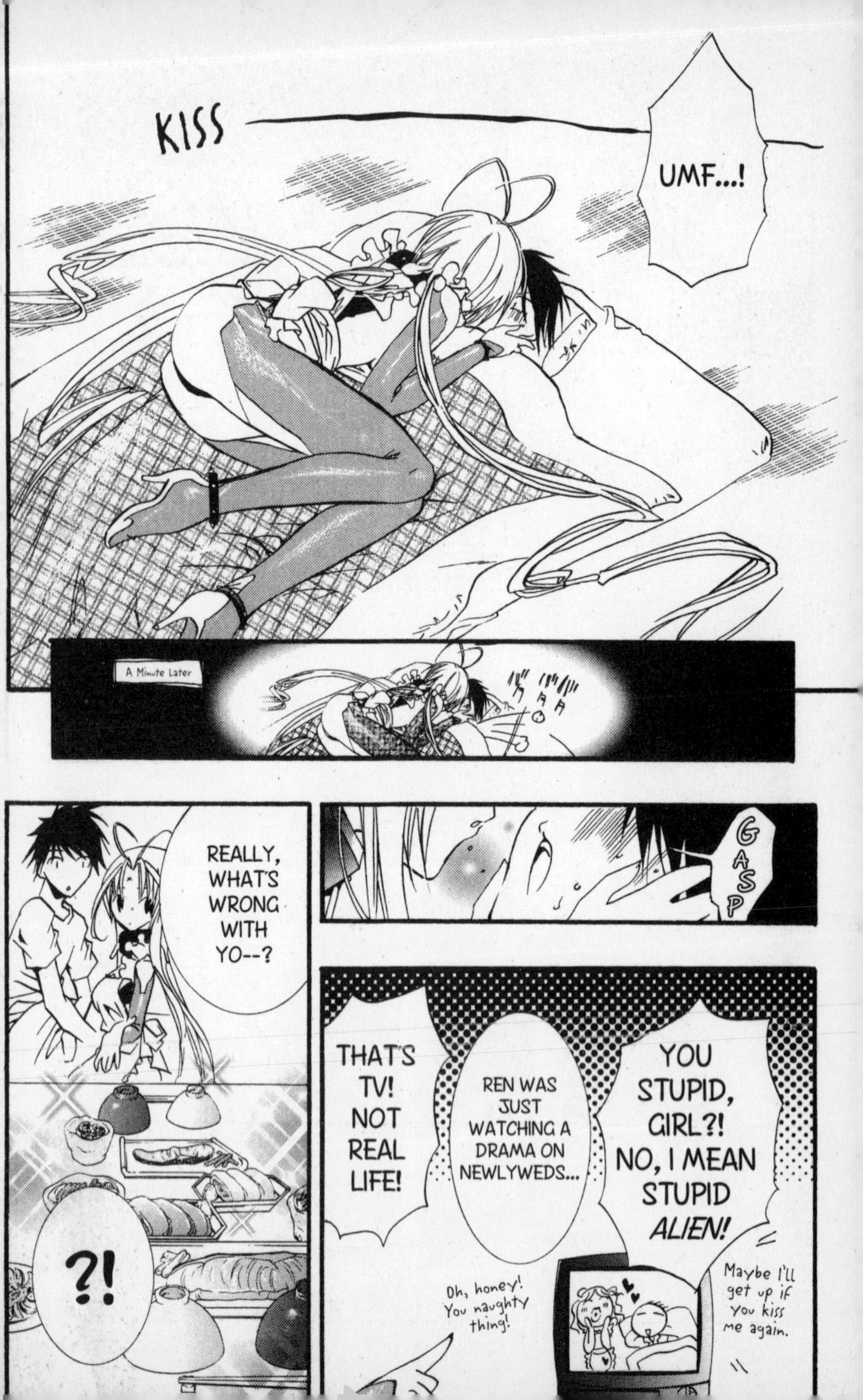
UMF...!
KISS
A Minute Later
GASP
REALLY, WHAT'S WRONG WITH YO--?
YOU STUPID, GIRL?! NO, I MEAN STUPID ALIEN!
REN WAS JUST WATCHING A DRAMA ON NEWLYWEDS...
THAT'S TV! NOT REAL LIFE!
Maybe I'll get up if you kiss me again.
Oh, honey! You naughty thing!
?!

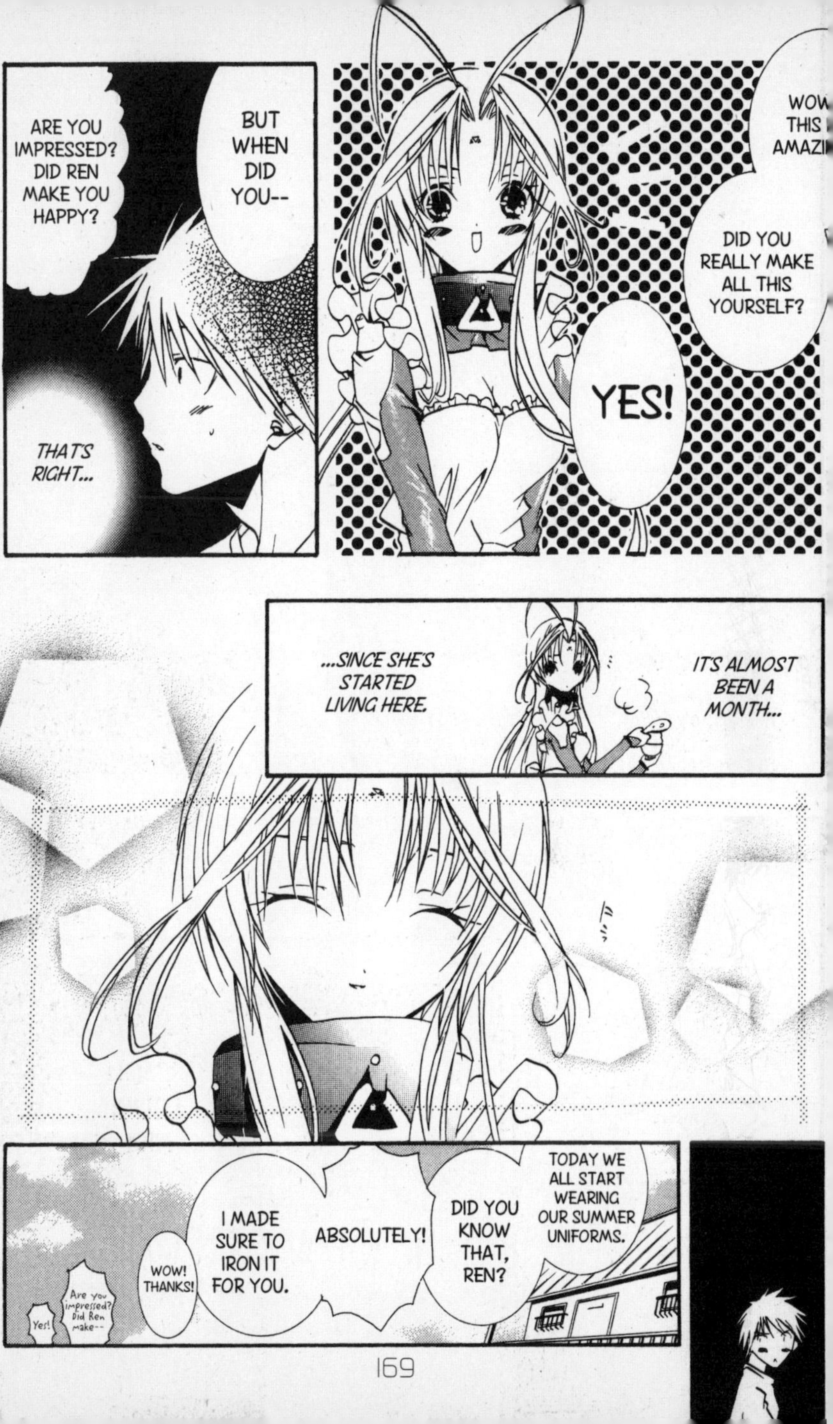
WOW THIS AMAZI
DID YOU REALLY MAKE ALL THIS YOURSELF?
YES!
BUT WHEN DID YOU--
ARE YOU IMPRESSED? DID REN MAKE YOU HAPPY?
THAT'S RIGHT...
IT'S ALMOST BEEN A MONTH...
...SINCE SHE'S STARTED LIVING HERE.
TODAY WE ALL START WEARING OUR SUMMER UNIFORMS.
DID YOU KNOW THAT, REN?
ABSOLUTELY!
I MADE SURE TO IRON IT FOR YOU.
WOW! THANKS!
Are you impressed? Did Ren make--
Yes!

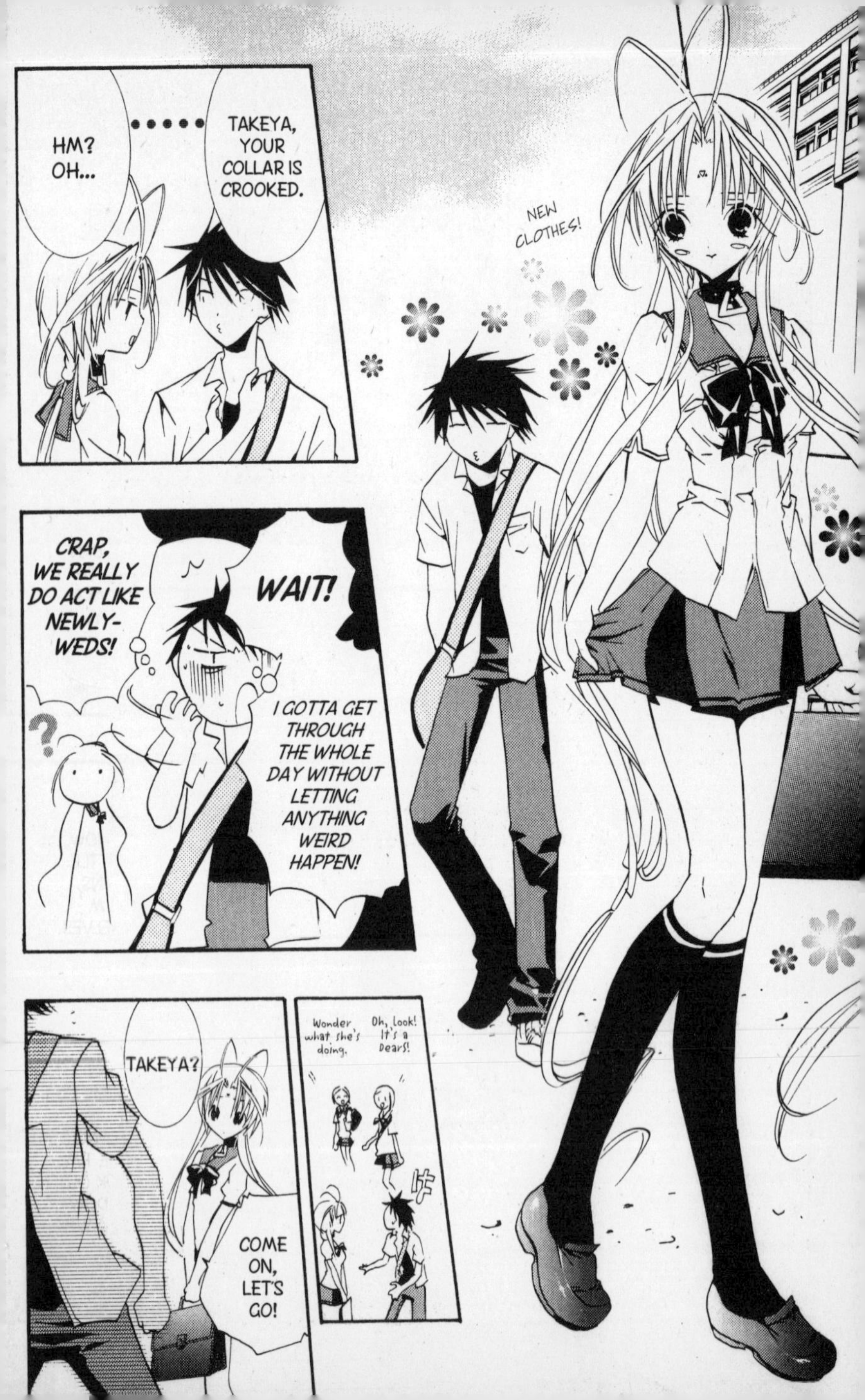
NEW CLOTHES!
TAKEYA, YOUR COLLAR IS CROOKED.
.....
HM? OH...
WAIT!
CRAP, WE REALLY DO ACT LIKE NEWLY-WEDS!
I GOTTA GET THROUGH THE WHOLE DAY WITHOUT LETTING ANYTHING WEIRD HAPPEN!
Oh, look! It's a Dears!
Wonder what she's doing.
TAKEYA?
COME ON, LET'S GO!

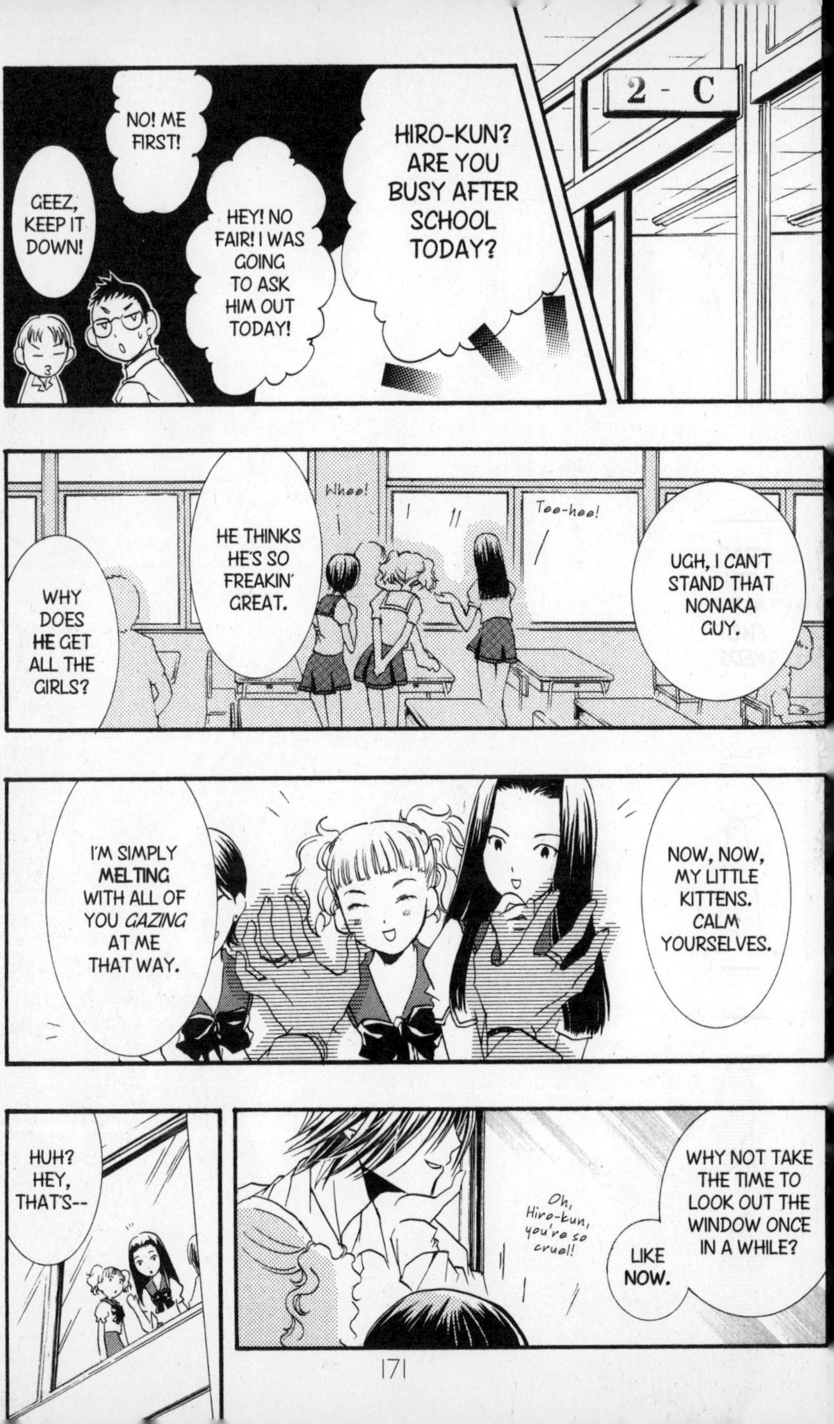
2 - C
HIRO-KUN? ARE YOU BUSY AFTER SCHOOL TODAY?
HEY! NO FAIR! I WAS GOING TO ASK HIM OUT TODAY!
NO! ME FIRST!
GEEZ, KEEP IT DOWN!
UGH, I CAN'T STAND THAT NONAKA GUY.
Tee-hee!
Whee!
HE THINKS HE'S SO FREAKIN' GREAT.
WHY DOES HE GET ALL THE GIRLS?
NOW, NOW, MY LITTLE KITTENS. CALM YOURSELVES.
I'M SIMPLY MELTING WITH ALL OF YOU GAZING AT ME THAT WAY.
WHY NOT TAKE THE TIME TO LOOK OUT THE WINDOW ONCE IN A WHILE?
LIKE NOW.
Oh, Hiro-kun, you're so cruel!
HUH? HEY, THAT'S--

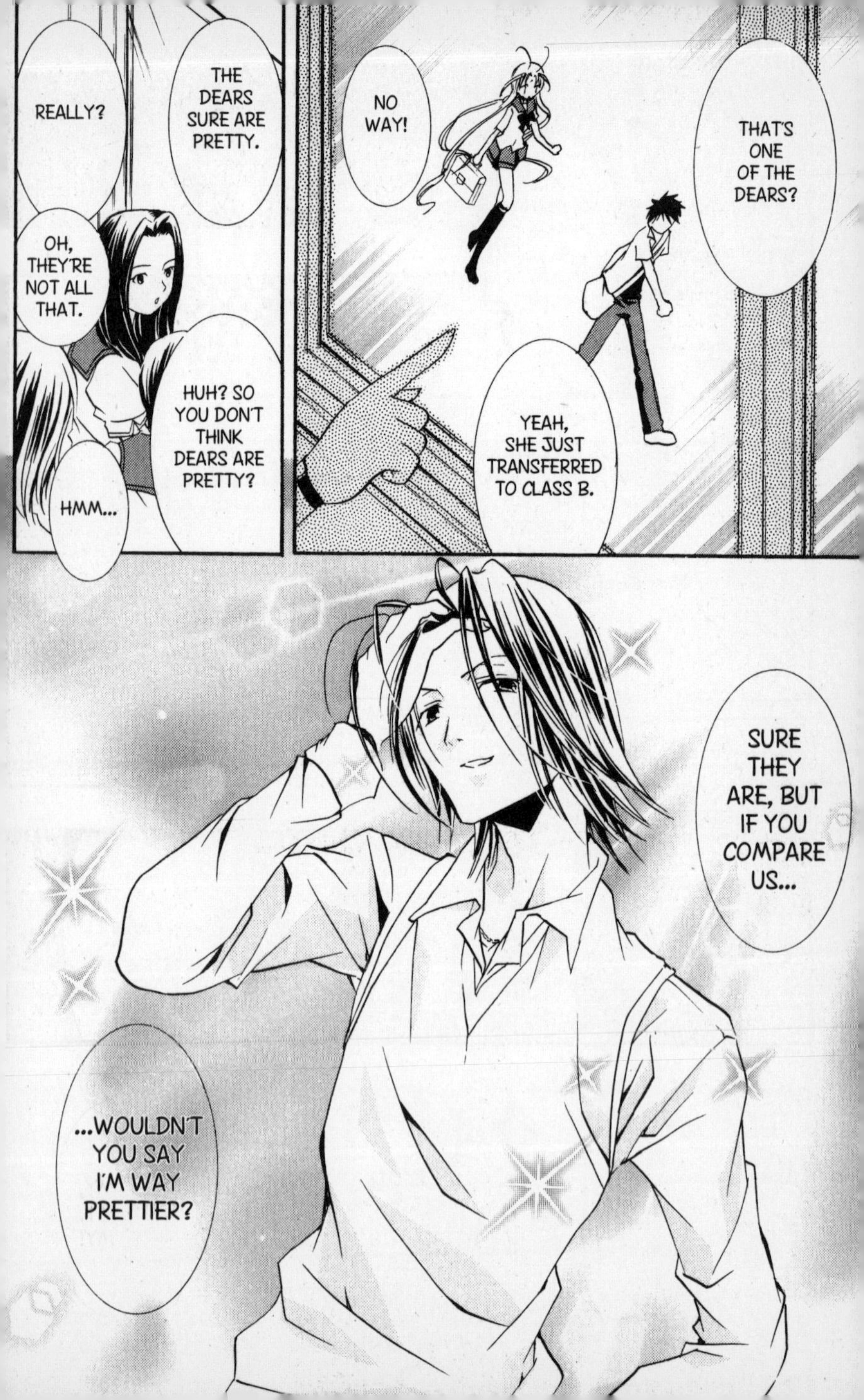
THAT'S ONE OF THE DEARS?
NO WAY!
YEAH, SHE JUST TRANSFERRED TO CLASS B.
THE DEARS SURE ARE PRETTY.
REALLY?
OH, THEY'RE NOT ALL THAT.
HUH? SO YOU DON'T THINK DEARS ARE PRETTY?
HMM...
SURE THEY ARE, BUT IF YOU COMPARE US...
...WOULDN'T YOU SAY I'M WAY PRETTIER?

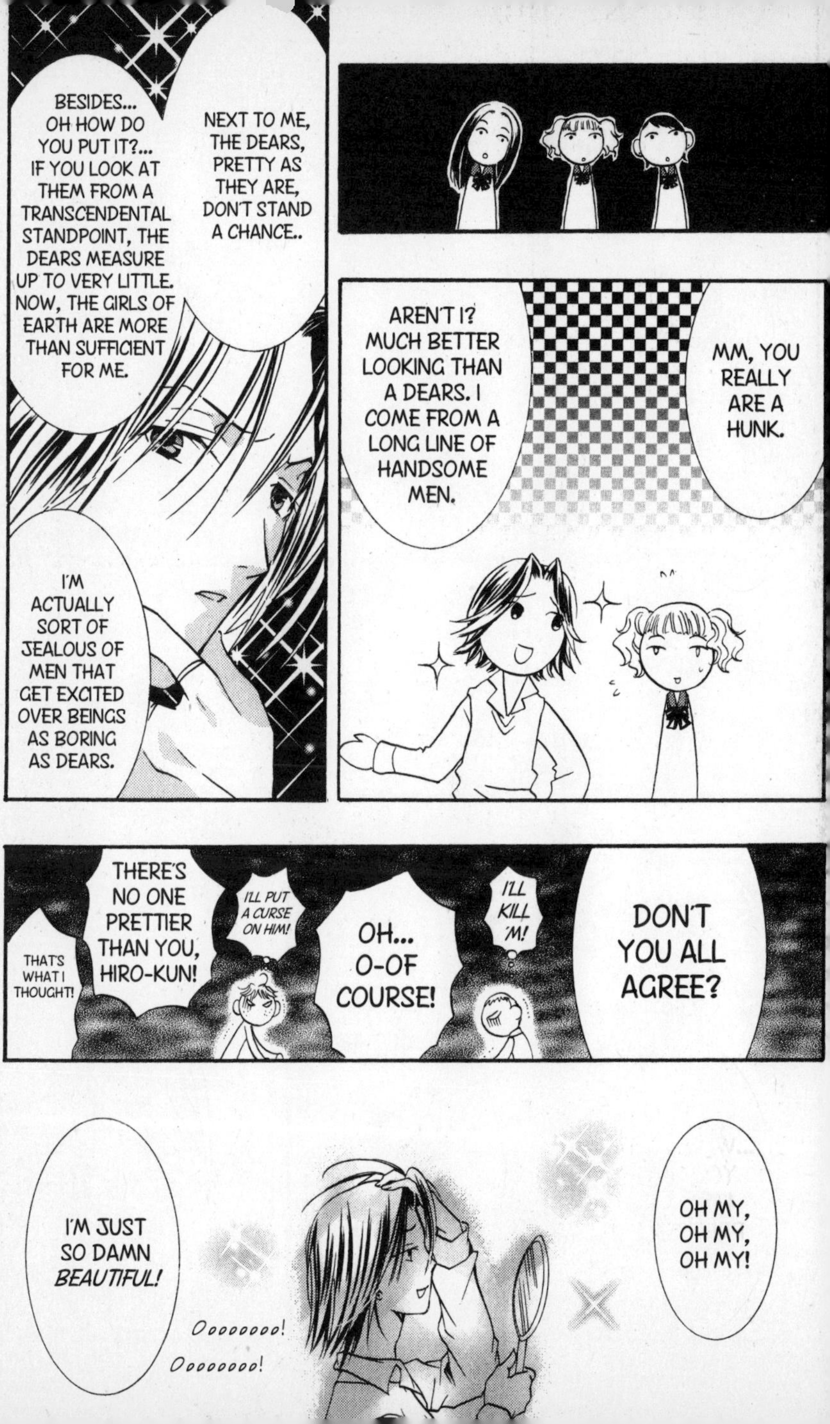
MM, YOU REALLY ARE A HUNK.
AREN'T I? MUCH BETTER LOOKING THAN A DEARS. I COME FROM A LONG LINE OF HANDSOME MEN.
NEXT TO ME, THE DEARS, PRETTY AS THEY ARE, DON'T STAND A CHANCE..
BESIDES... OH HOW DO YOU PUT IT?... IF YOU LOOK AT THEM FROM A TRANSCENDENTAL STANDPOINT, THE DEARS MEASURE UP TO VERY LITTLE. NOW, THE GIRLS OF EARTH ARE MORE THAN SUFFICIENT FOR ME.
I'M ACTUALLY SORT OF JEALOUS OF MEN THAT GET EXCITED OVER BEINGS AS BORING AS DEARS.
DON'T YOU ALL AGREE?
I'LL KILL 'M!
OH... O-OF COURSE!
I'LL PUT A CURSE ON HIM!
THERE'S NO ONE PRETTIER THAN YOU, HIRO-KUN!
THAT'S WHAT I THOUGHT!
OH MY, OH MY, OH MY!
I'M JUST SO DAMN *BEAUTIFUL!*
Oooooooo!
Oooooooo!

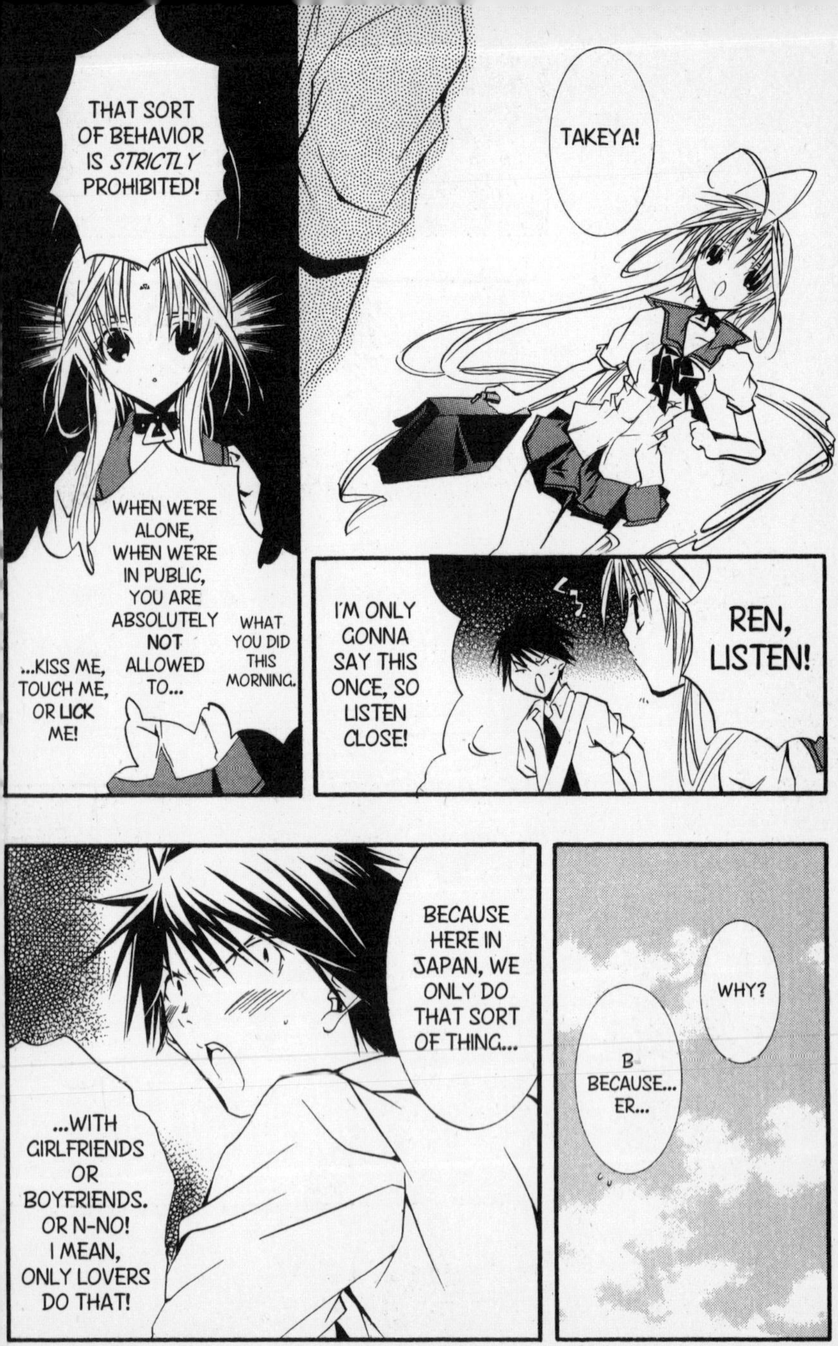
TAKEYA!
REN, LISTEN!
I'M ONLY GONNA SAY THIS ONCE, SO LISTEN CLOSE!
THAT SORT OF BEHAVIOR IS *STRICTLY* PROHIBITED!
WHEN WE'RE ALONE, WHEN WE'RE IN PUBLIC, YOU ARE ABSOLUTELY **NOT** ALLOWED TO...
WHAT YOU DID THIS MORNING.
...KISS ME, TOUCH ME, OR **LICK** ME!
WHY?
B BECAUSE... ER...
BECAUSE HERE IN JAPAN, WE ONLY DO THAT SORT OF THING...
...WITH GIRLFRIENDS OR BOYFRIENDS. OR N-NO! I MEAN, ONLY LOVERS DO THAT!

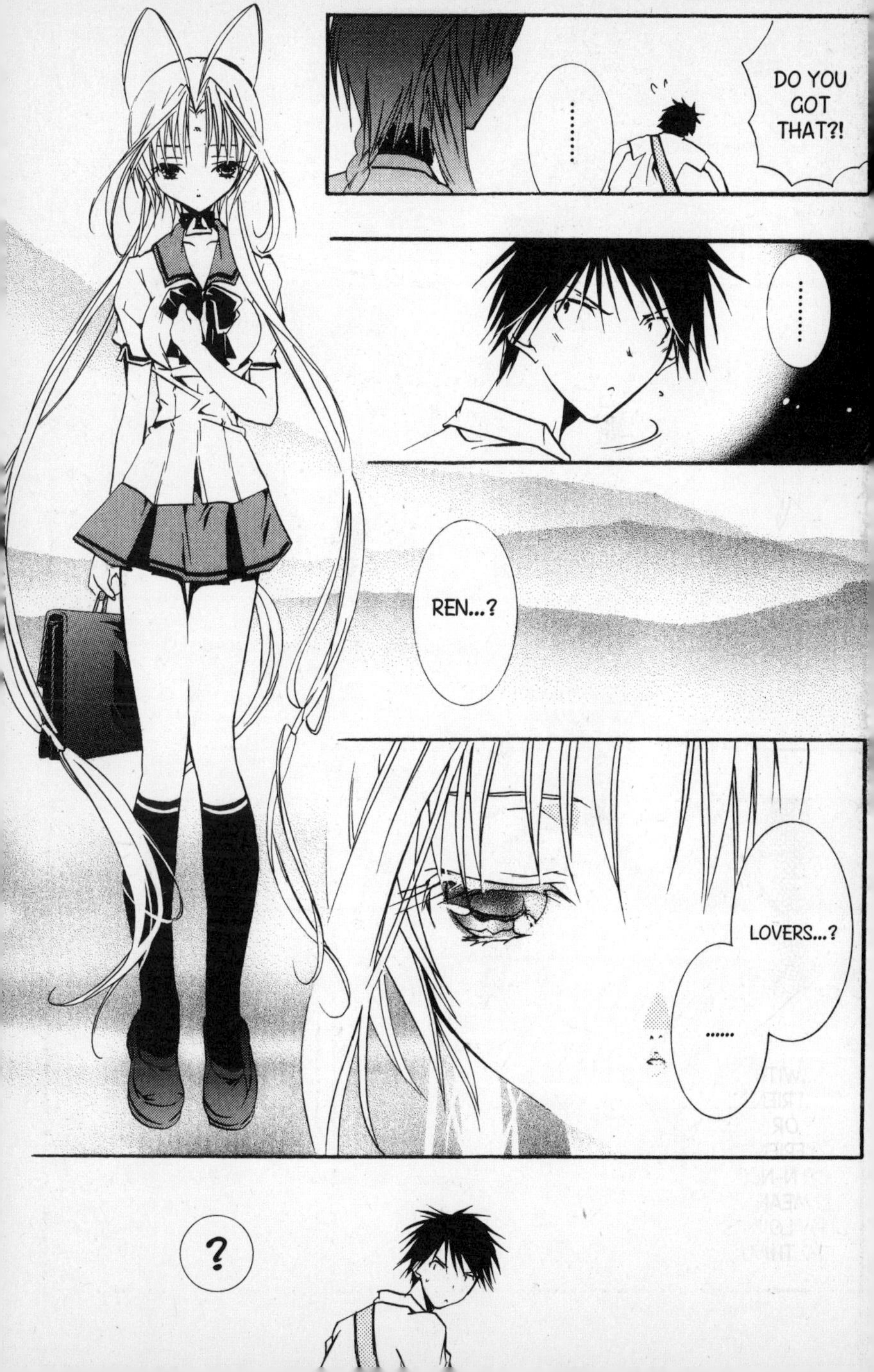
DO YOU GOT THAT?!
......
......
REN...?
LOVERS...?
......
?

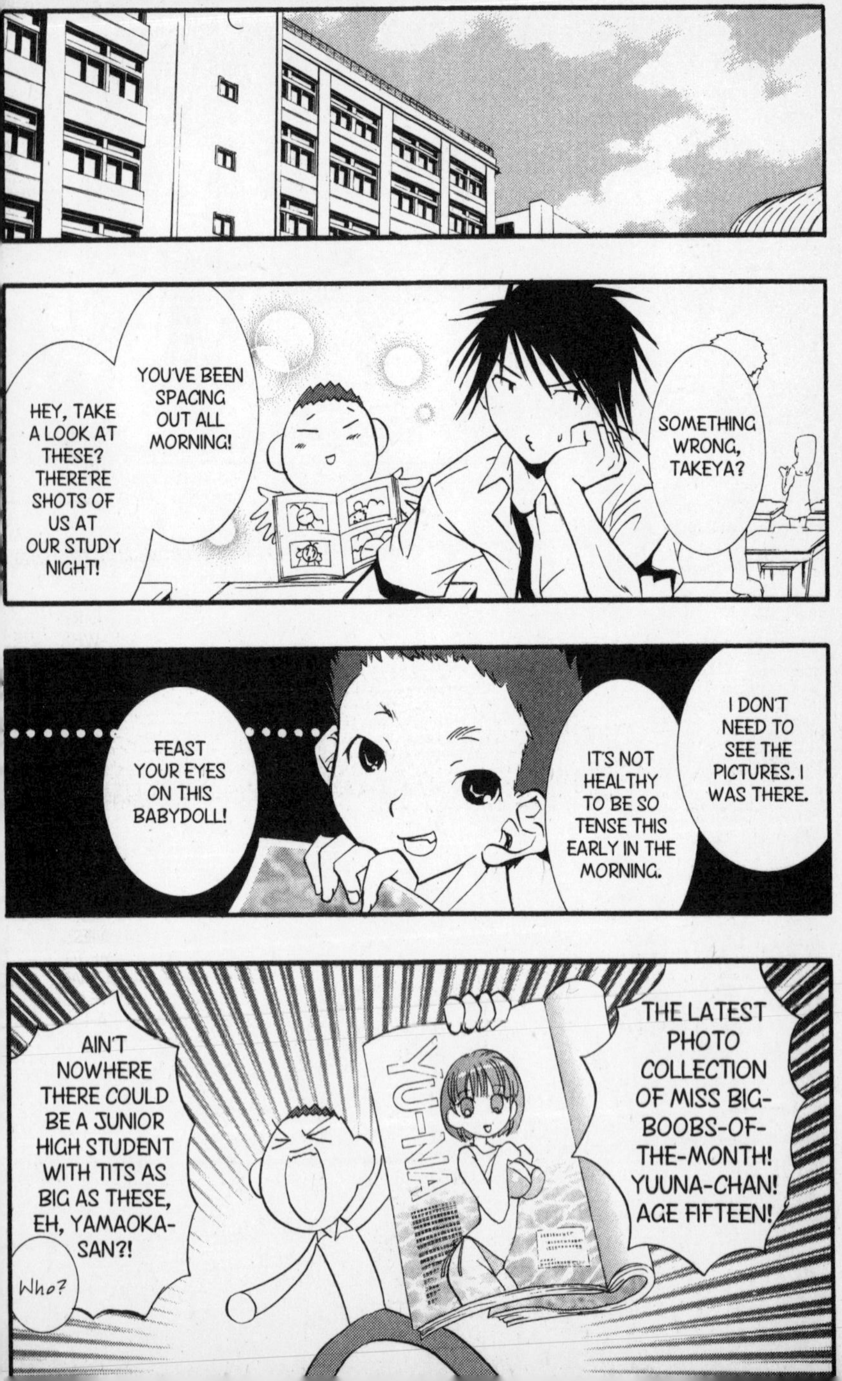
SOMETHING WRONG, TAKEYA?
YOU'VE BEEN SPACING OUT ALL MORNING!
HEY, TAKE A LOOK AT THESE? THERE'RE SHOTS OF US AT OUR STUDY NIGHT!
I DON'T NEED TO SEE THE PICTURES. I WAS THERE.
IT'S NOT HEALTHY TO BE SO TENSE THIS EARLY IN THE MORNING.
FEAST YOUR EYES ON THIS BABYDOLL!
THE LATEST PHOTO COLLECTION OF MISS BIG-BOOBS-OF-THE-MONTH! YUUNA-CHAN! AGE FIFTEEN!
YU-NA
AIN'T NOWHERE THERE COULD BE A JUNIOR HIGH STUDENT WITH TITS AS BIG AS THESE, EH, YAMAOKA-SAN?!
Who?

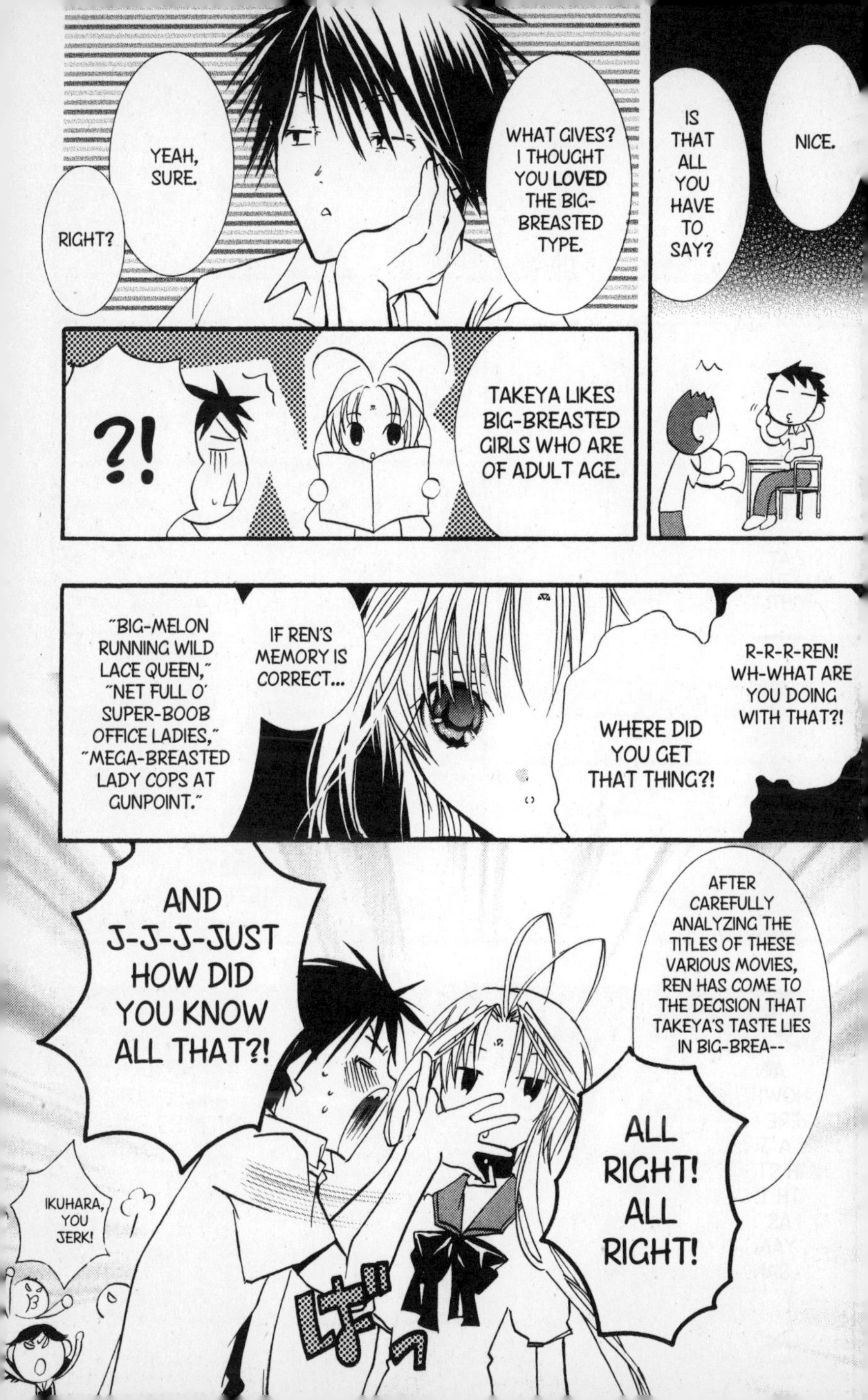
NICE.
IS THAT ALL YOU HAVE TO SAY?
WHAT GIVES? I THOUGHT YOU LOVED THE BIG-BREASTED TYPE.
YEAH, SURE.
RIGHT?
TAKEYA LIKES BIG-BREASTED GIRLS WHO ARE OF ADULT AGE.
?!
R-R-R-REN! WH-WHAT ARE YOU DOING WITH THAT?!
WHERE DID YOU GET THAT THING?!
IF REN'S MEMORY IS CORRECT...
"BIG-MELON RUNNING WILD LACE QUEEN," "NET FULL O' SUPER-BOOB OFFICE LADIES," "MEGA-BREASTED LADY COPS AT GUNPOINT."
AFTER CAREFULLY ANALYZING THE TITLES OF THESE VARIOUS MOVIES, REN HAS COME TO THE DECISION THAT TAKEYA'S TASTE LIES IN BIG-BREA--
ALL RIGHT! ALL RIGHT!
AND J-J-J-JUST HOW DID YOU KNOW ALL THAT?!
IKUHARA, YOU JERK!
ぼっ

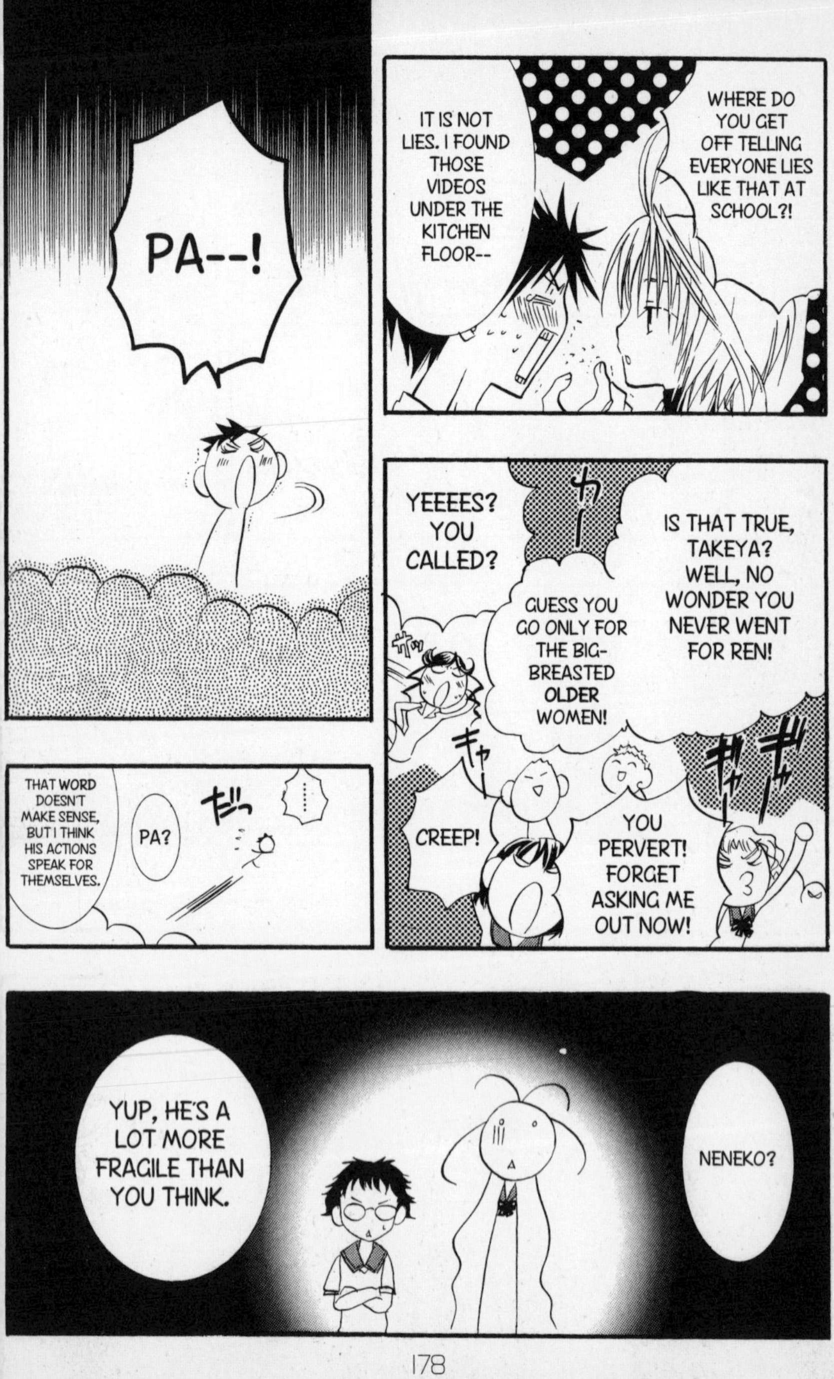
WHERE DO YOU GET OFF TELLING EVERYONE LIES LIKE THAT AT SCHOOL?!
IT IS NOT LIES. I FOUND THOSE VIDEOS UNDER THE KITCHEN FLOOR--
PA--!
IS THAT TRUE, TAKEYA? WELL, NO WONDER YOU NEVER WENT FOR REN!
YEEEES? YOU CALLED?
GUESS YOU GO ONLY FOR THE BIG-BREASTED OLDER WOMEN!
YOU PERVERT! FORGET ASKING ME OUT NOW!
CREEP!
PA?
THAT WORD DOESN'T MAKE SENSE, BUT I THINK HIS ACTIONS SPEAK FOR THEMSELVES.
NENEKO?
YUP, HE'S A LOT MORE FRAGILE THAN YOU THINK.

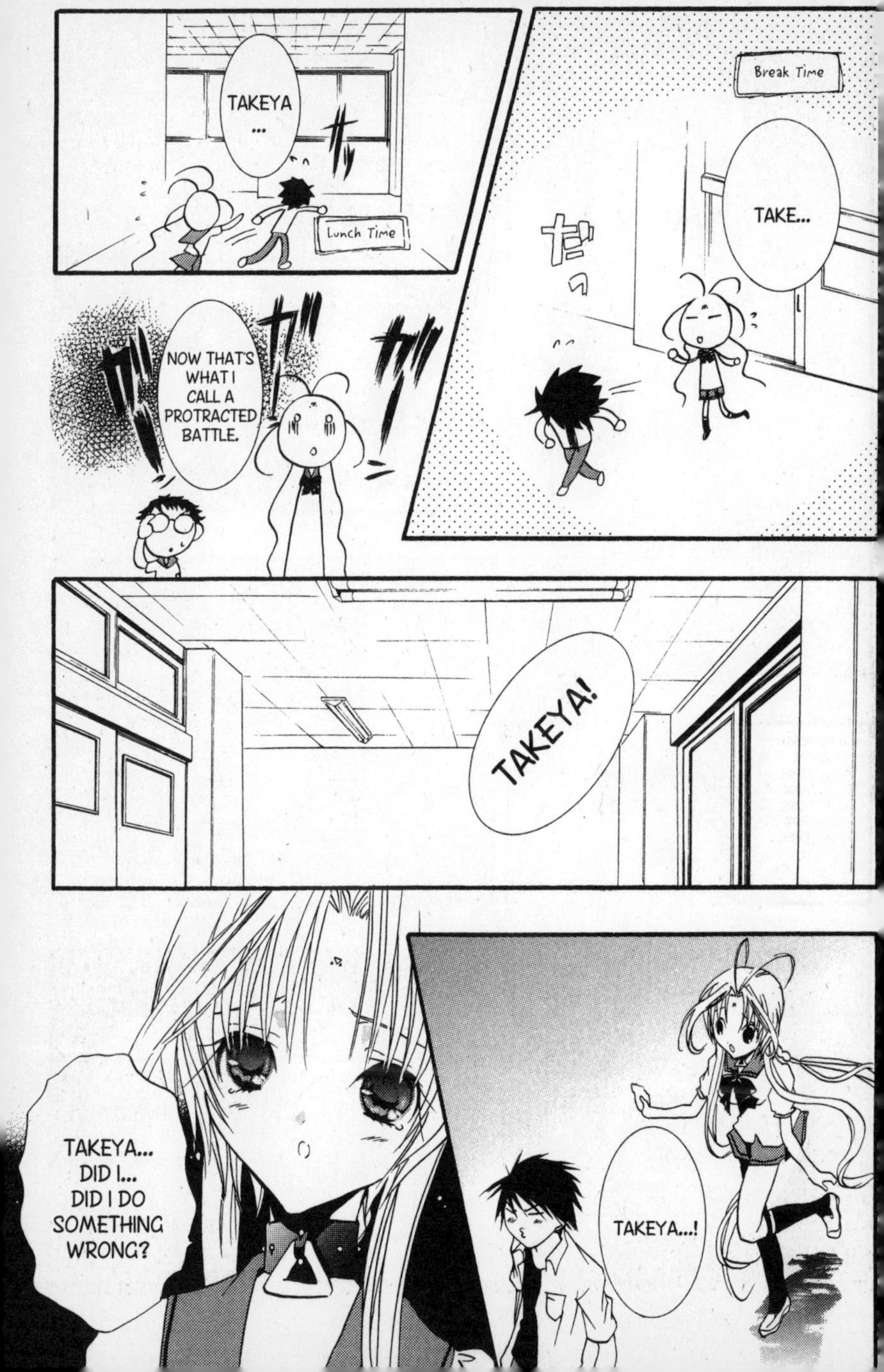
Break Time
TAKE...
Lunch Time
TAKEYA ...
NOW THAT'S WHAT I CALL A PROTRACTED BATTLE.
TAKEYA!
TAKEYA...!
TAKEYA... DID I... DID I DO SOMETHING WRONG?

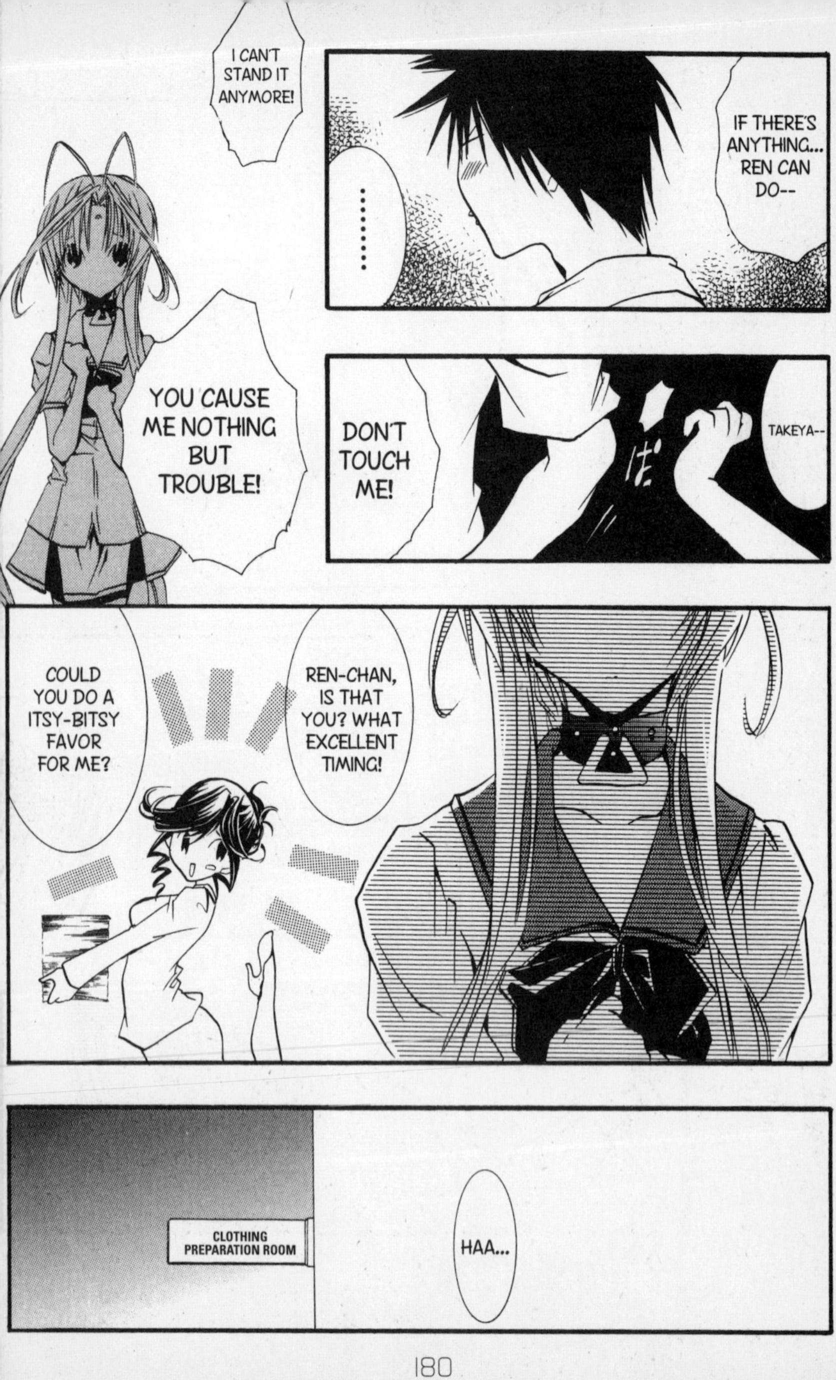
IF THERE'S ANYTHING... REN CAN DO--
......
TAKEYA--
ぱ
DON'T TOUCH ME!
I CAN'T STAND IT ANYMORE!
YOU CAUSE ME NOTHING BUT TROUBLE!
REN-CHAN, IS THAT YOU? WHAT EXCELLENT TIMING!
COULD YOU DO A ITSY-BITSY FAVOR FOR ME?
HAA...
CLOTHING PREPARATION ROOM

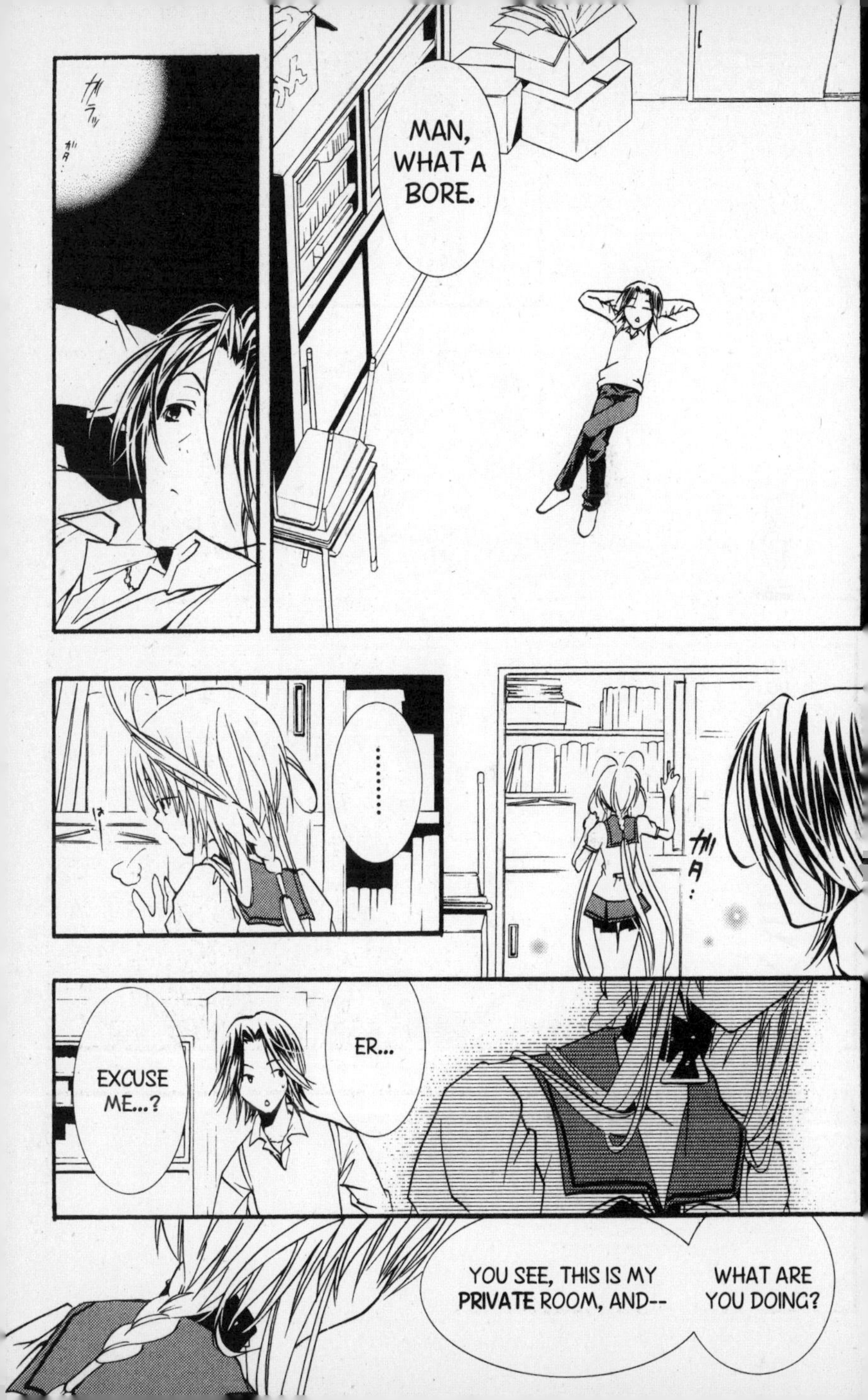
MAN, WHAT A BORE.
......
ER...
EXCUSE ME...?
WHAT ARE YOU DOING?
YOU SEE, THIS IS MY PRIVATE ROOM, AND--

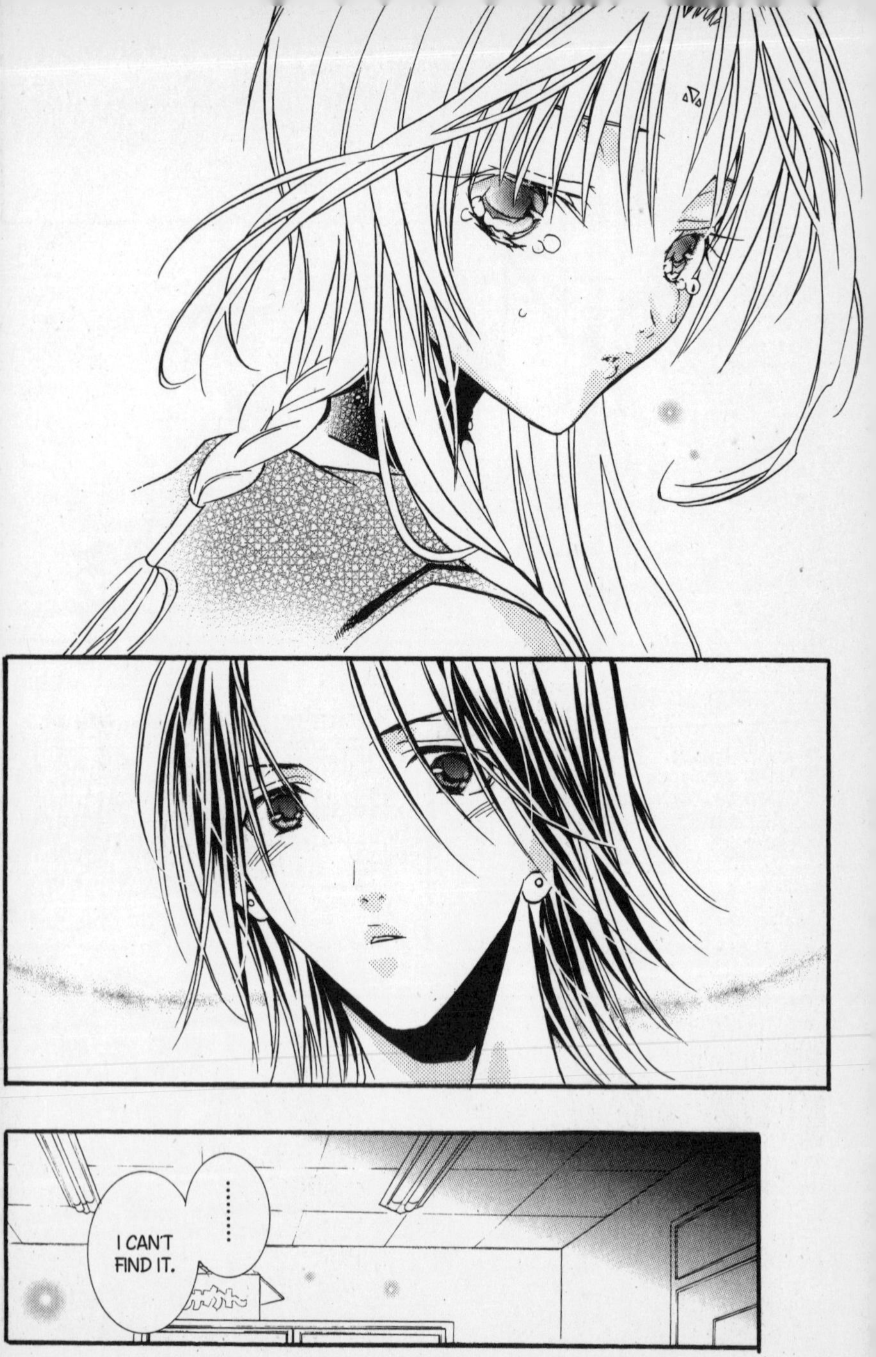
......
I CAN'T FIND IT.

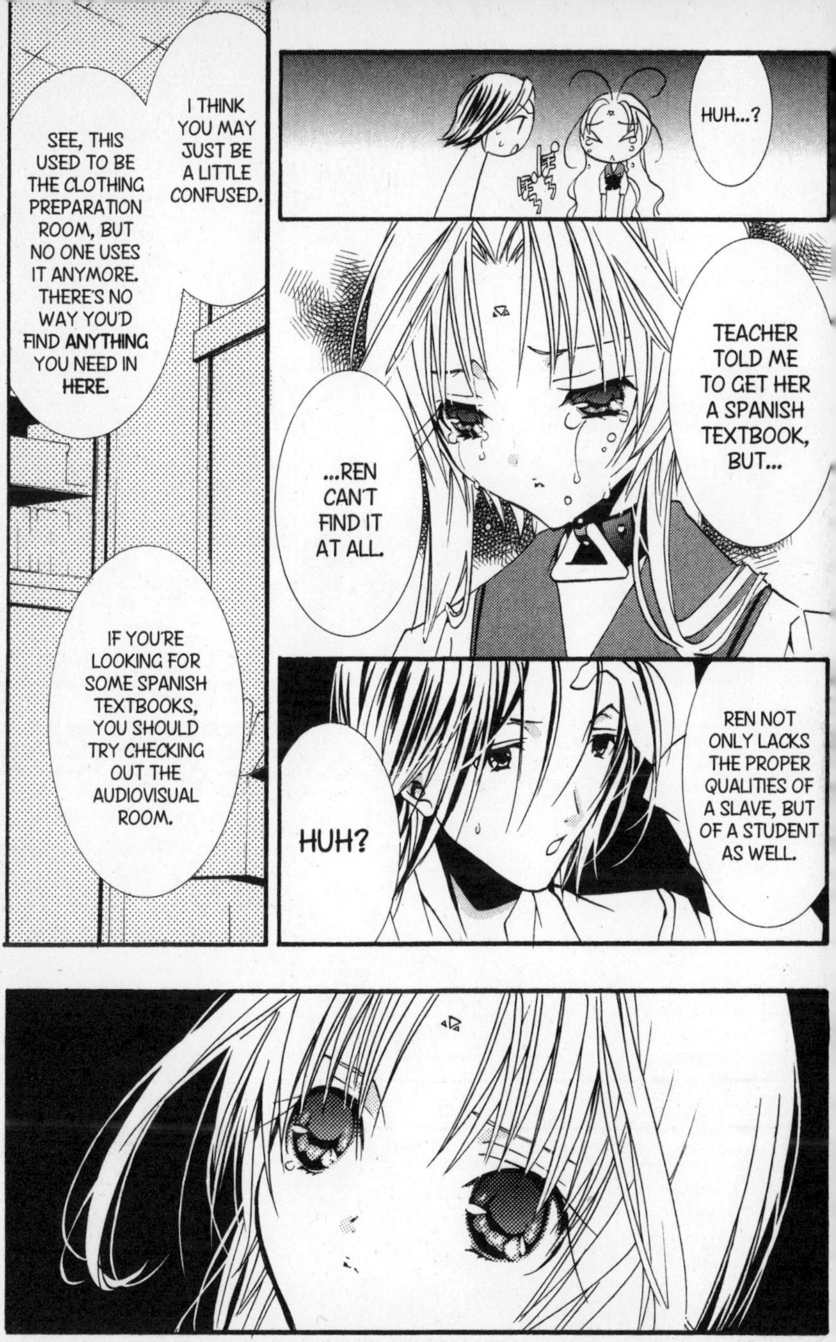
HUH...?
TEACHER TOLD ME TO GET HER A SPANISH TEXTBOOK, BUT...
...REN CAN'T FIND IT AT ALL.
REN NOT ONLY LACKS THE PROPER QUALITIES OF A SLAVE, BUT OF A STUDENT AS WELL.
HUH?
I THINK YOU MAY JUST BE A LITTLE CONFUSED.
SEE, THIS USED TO BE THE CLOTHING PREPARATION ROOM, BUT NO ONE USES IT ANYMORE. THERE'S NO WAY YOU'D FIND **ANYTHING** YOU NEED IN **HERE**.
IF YOU'RE LOOKING FOR SOME SPANISH TEXTBOOKS, YOU SHOULD TRY CHECKING OUT THE AUDIOVISUAL ROOM.

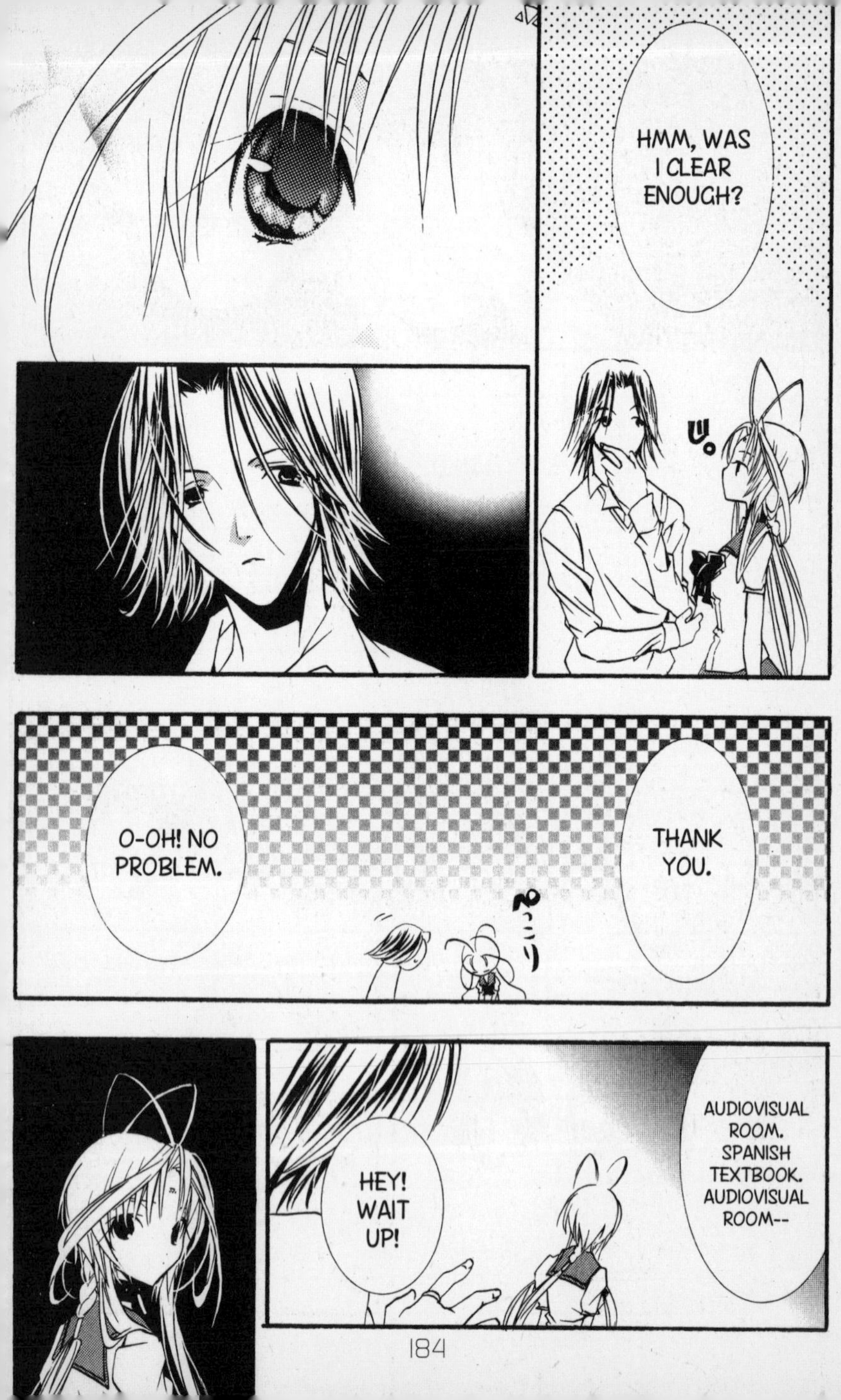
HMM, WAS I CLEAR ENOUGH?
じ。
THANK YOU.
ぺこり
O-OH! NO PROBLEM.
AUDIOVISUAL ROOM. SPANISH TEXTBOOK. AUDIOVISUAL ROOM--
HEY! WAIT UP!

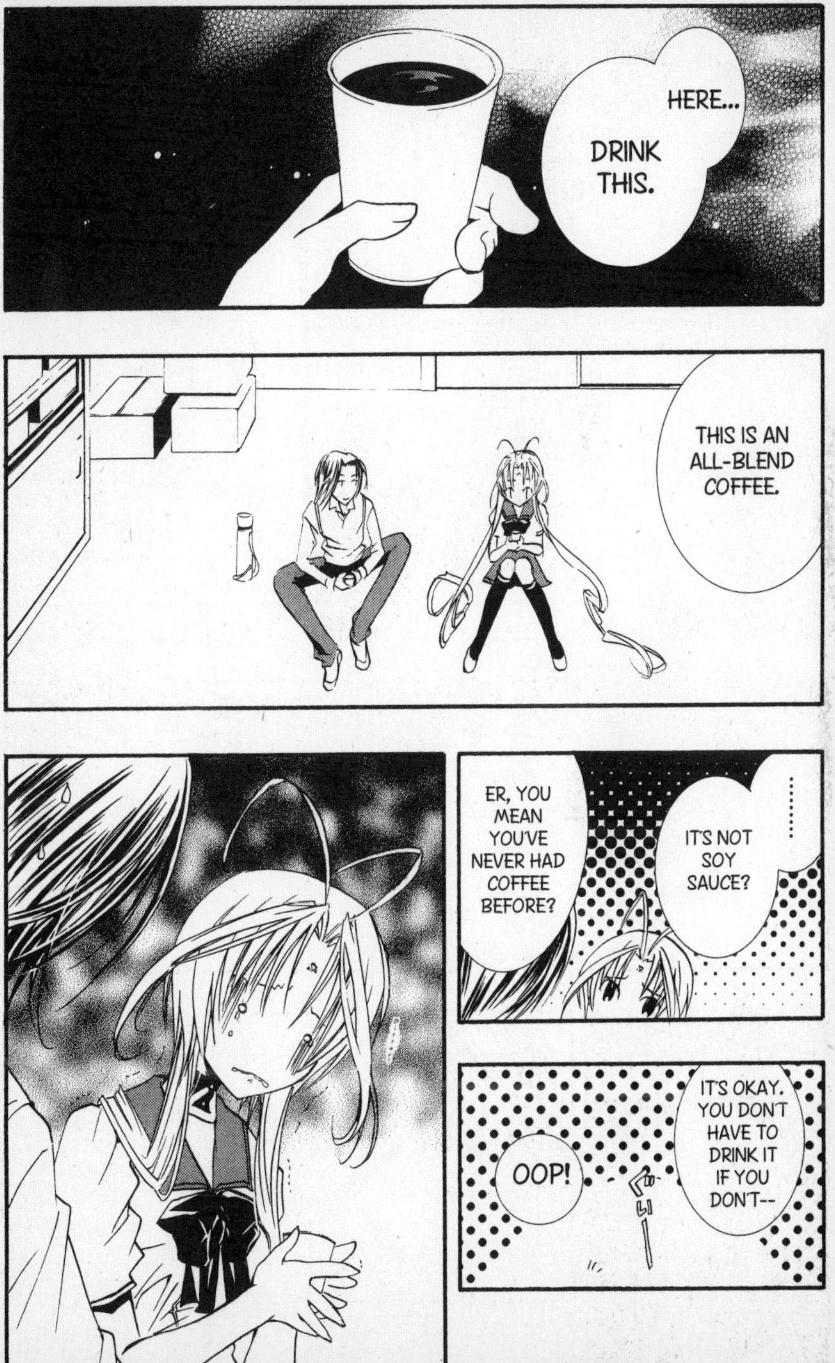
HERE...
DRINK THIS.
THIS IS AN ALL-BLEND COFFEE.
......
IT'S NOT SOY SAUCE?
ER, YOU MEAN YOU'VE NEVER HAD COFFEE BEFORE?
IT'S OKAY. YOU DON'T HAVE TO DRINK IT IF YOU DON'T--
OOP!

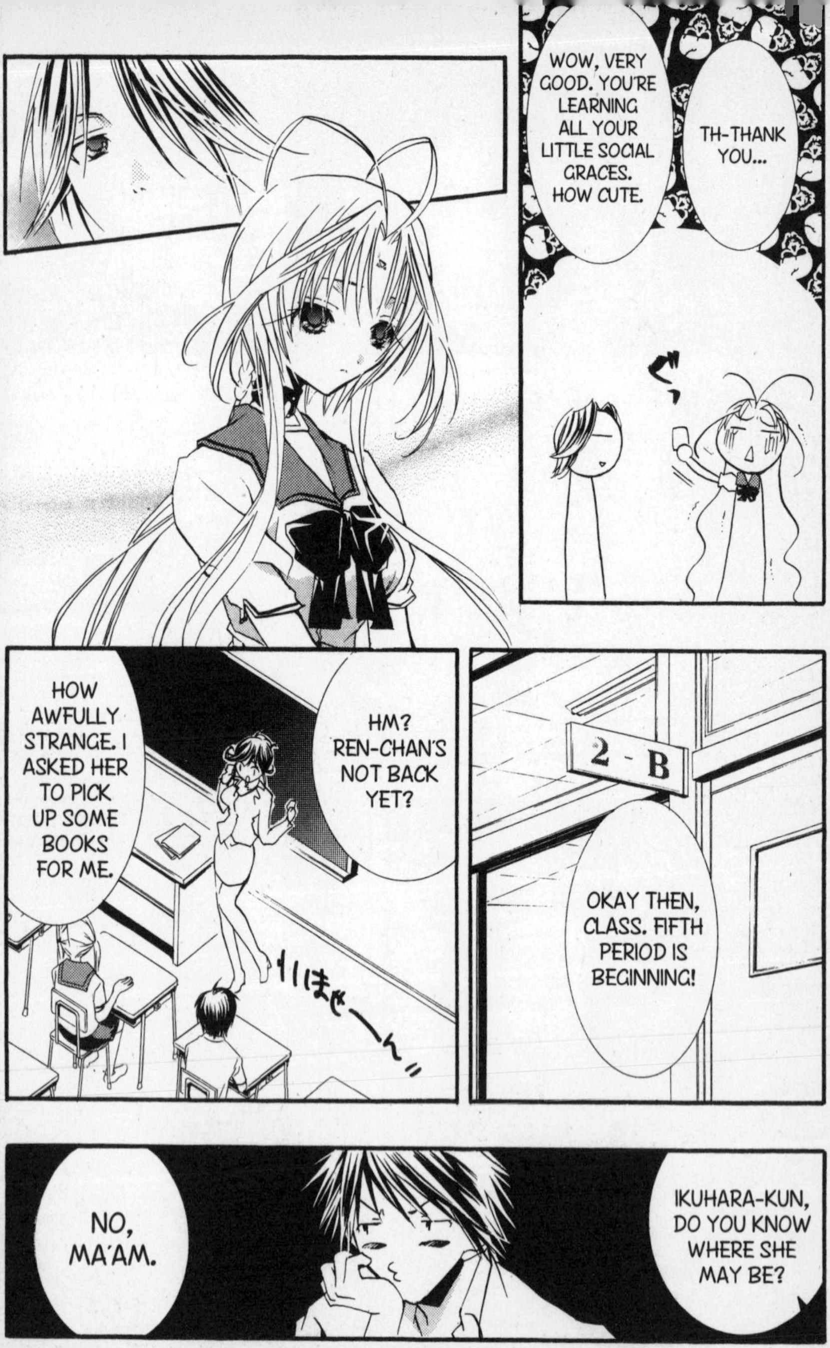
WOW, VERY GOOD. YOU'RE LEARNING ALL YOUR LITTLE SOCIAL GRACES. HOW CUTE.
TH-THANK YOU...
2-B
OKAY THEN, CLASS. FIFTH PERIOD IS BEGINNING!
HM? REN-CHAN'S NOT BACK YET?
HOW AWFULLY STRANGE. I ASKED HER TO PICK UP SOME BOOKS FOR ME.
IKUHARA-KUN, DO YOU KNOW WHERE SHE MAY BE?
NO, MA'AM.

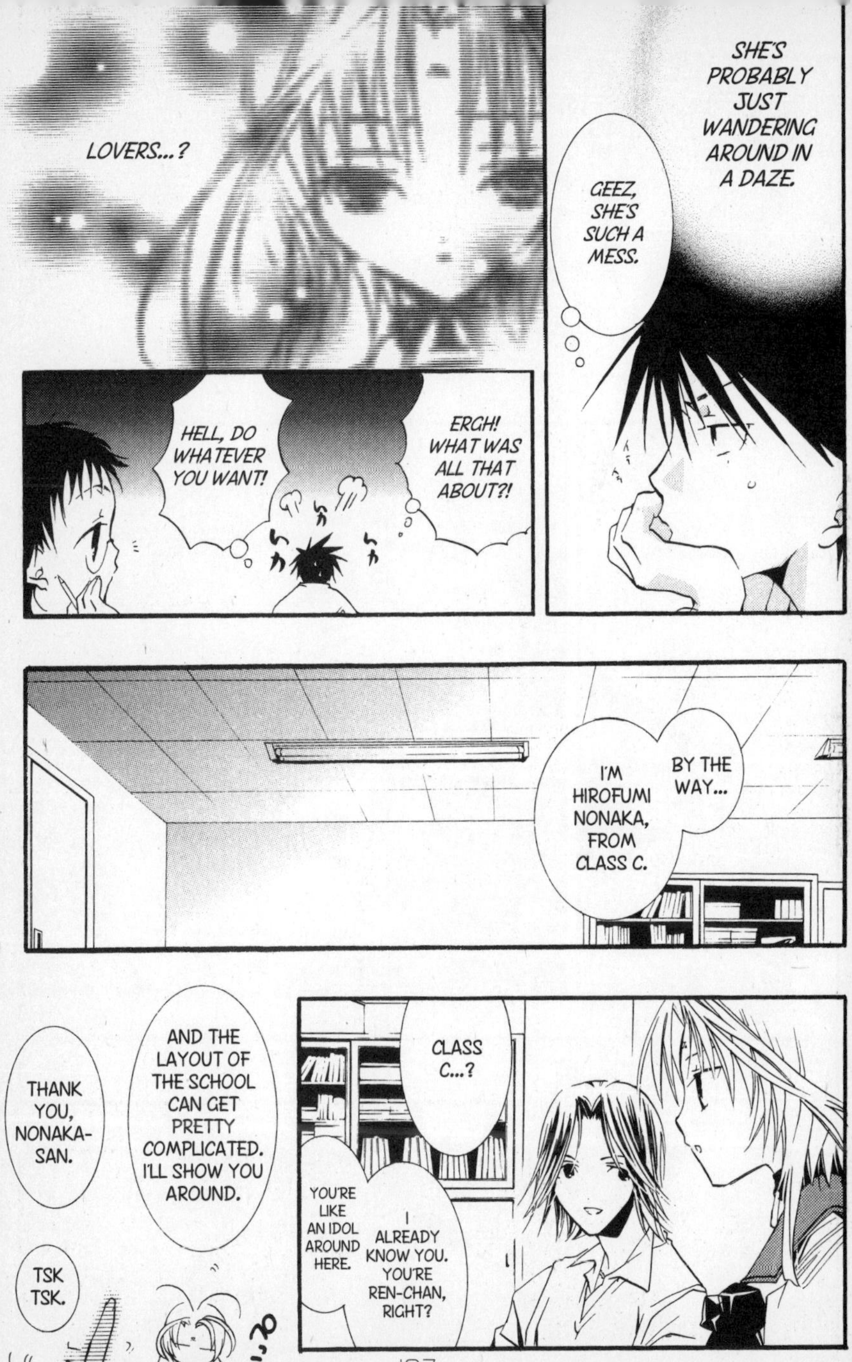
SHE'S PROBABLY JUST WANDERING AROUND IN A DAZE.
GEEZ, SHE'S SUCH A MESS.
LOVERS...?
ERGH! WHAT WAS ALL THAT ABOUT?!
HELL, DO WHATEVER YOU WANT!
BY THE WAY...
I'M HIROFUMI NONAKA, FROM CLASS C.
CLASS C...?
I ALREADY KNOW YOU. YOU'RE REN-CHAN, RIGHT?
YOU'RE LIKE AN IDOL AROUND HERE.
AND THE LAYOUT OF THE SCHOOL CAN GET PRETTY COMPLICATED. I'LL SHOW YOU AROUND.
THANK YOU, NONAKA-SAN.
TSK TSK.

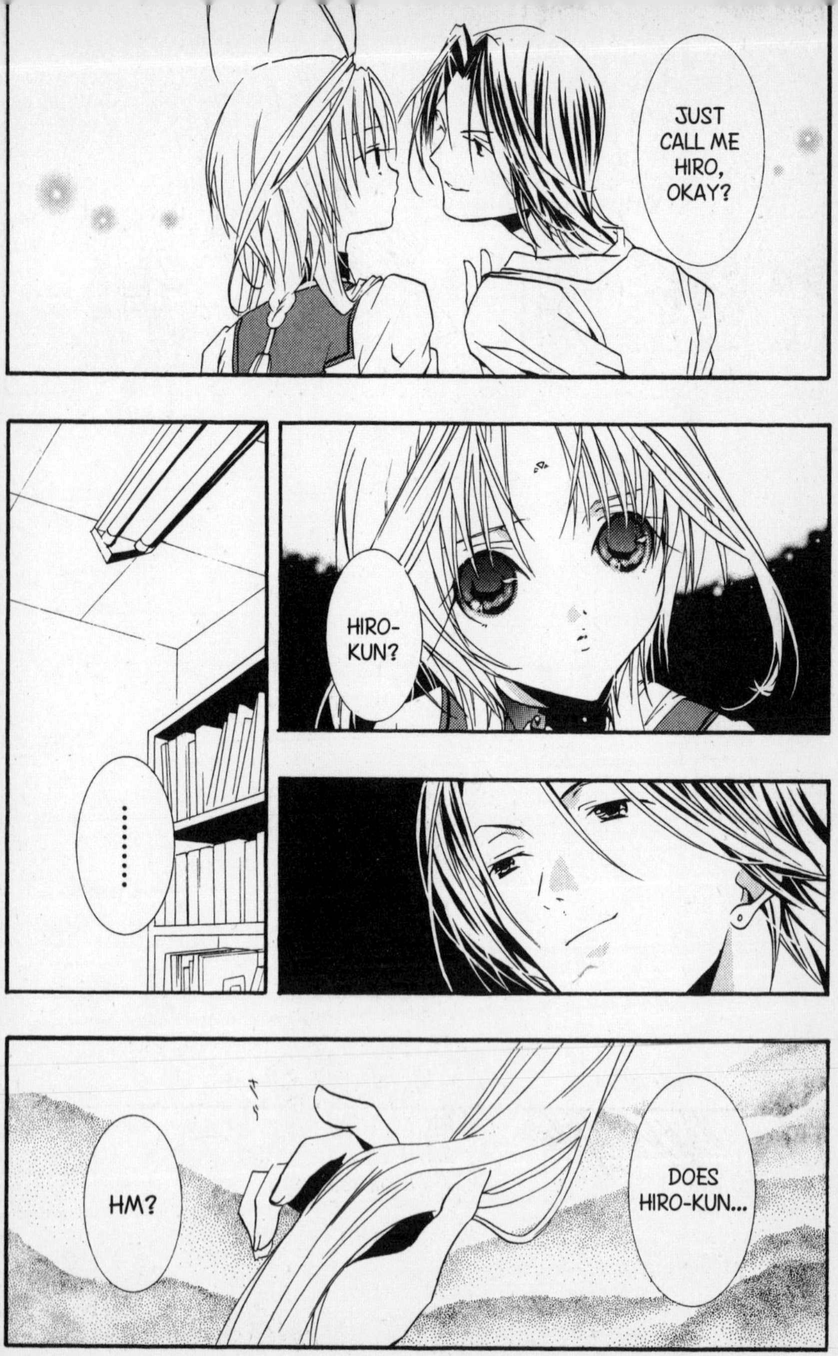
JUST CALL ME HIRO, OKAY?
HIRO-KUN?
......
DOES HIRO-KUN...
HM?

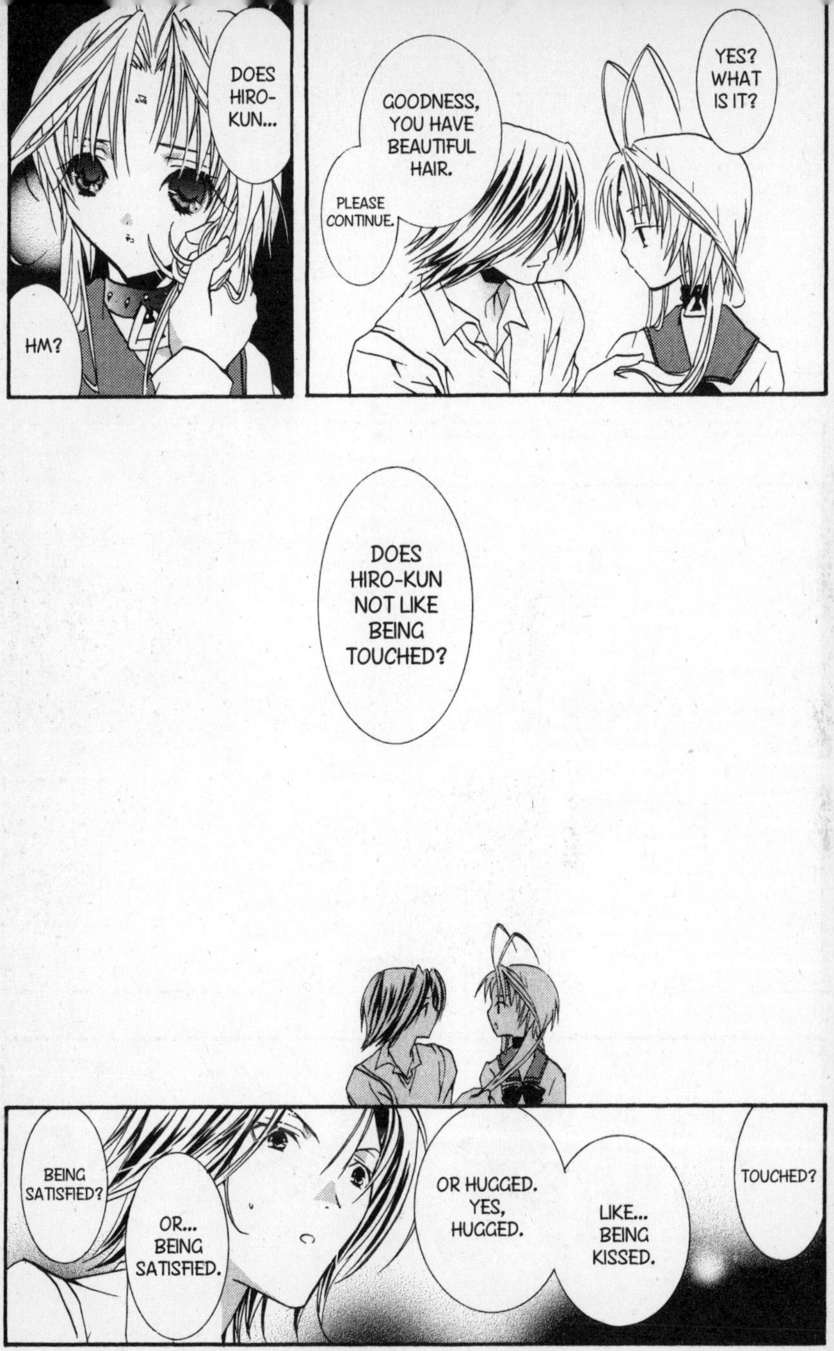
YES? WHAT IS IT?
GOODNESS, YOU HAVE BEAUTIFUL HAIR.
PLEASE CONTINUE.
DOES HIRO-KUN...
HM?
DOES HIRO-KUN NOT LIKE BEING TOUCHED?
TOUCHED?
LIKE... BEING KISSED.
OR HUGGED. YES, HUGGED.
OR... BEING SATISFIED.
BEING SATISFIED?

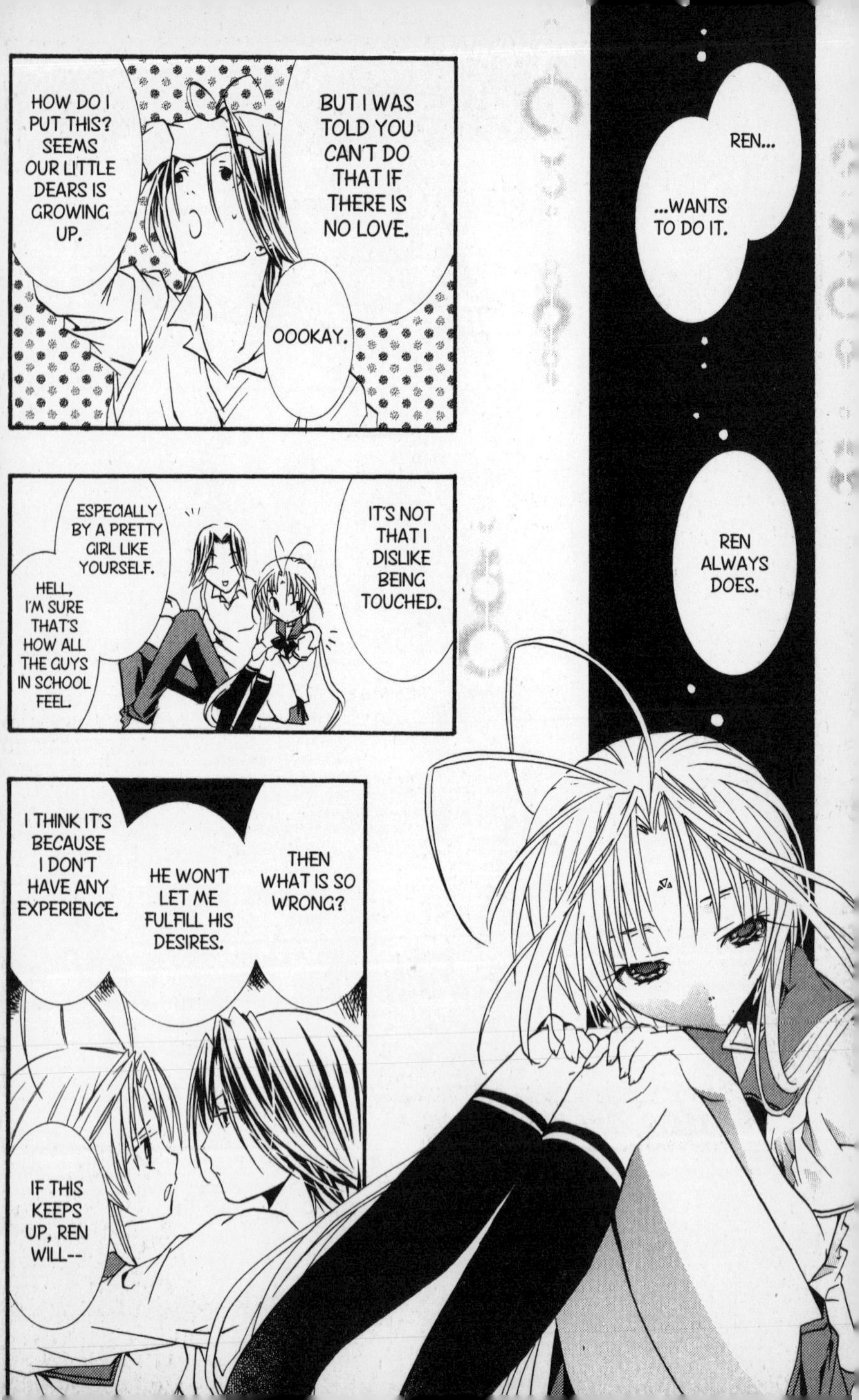
REN...
...WANTS TO DO IT.
REN ALWAYS DOES.
BUT I WAS TOLD YOU CAN'T DO THAT IF THERE IS NO LOVE.
OOOKAY.
HOW DO I PUT THIS? SEEMS OUR LITTLE DEARS IS GROWING UP.
IT'S NOT THAT I DISLIKE BEING TOUCHED.
ESPECIALLY BY A PRETTY GIRL LIKE YOURSELF.
HELL, I'M SURE THAT'S HOW ALL THE GUYS IN SCHOOL FEEL.
THEN WHAT IS SO WRONG?
HE WON'T LET ME FULFILL HIS DESIRES.
I THINK IT'S BECAUSE I DON'T HAVE ANY EXPERIENCE.
IF THIS KEEPS UP, REN WILL--

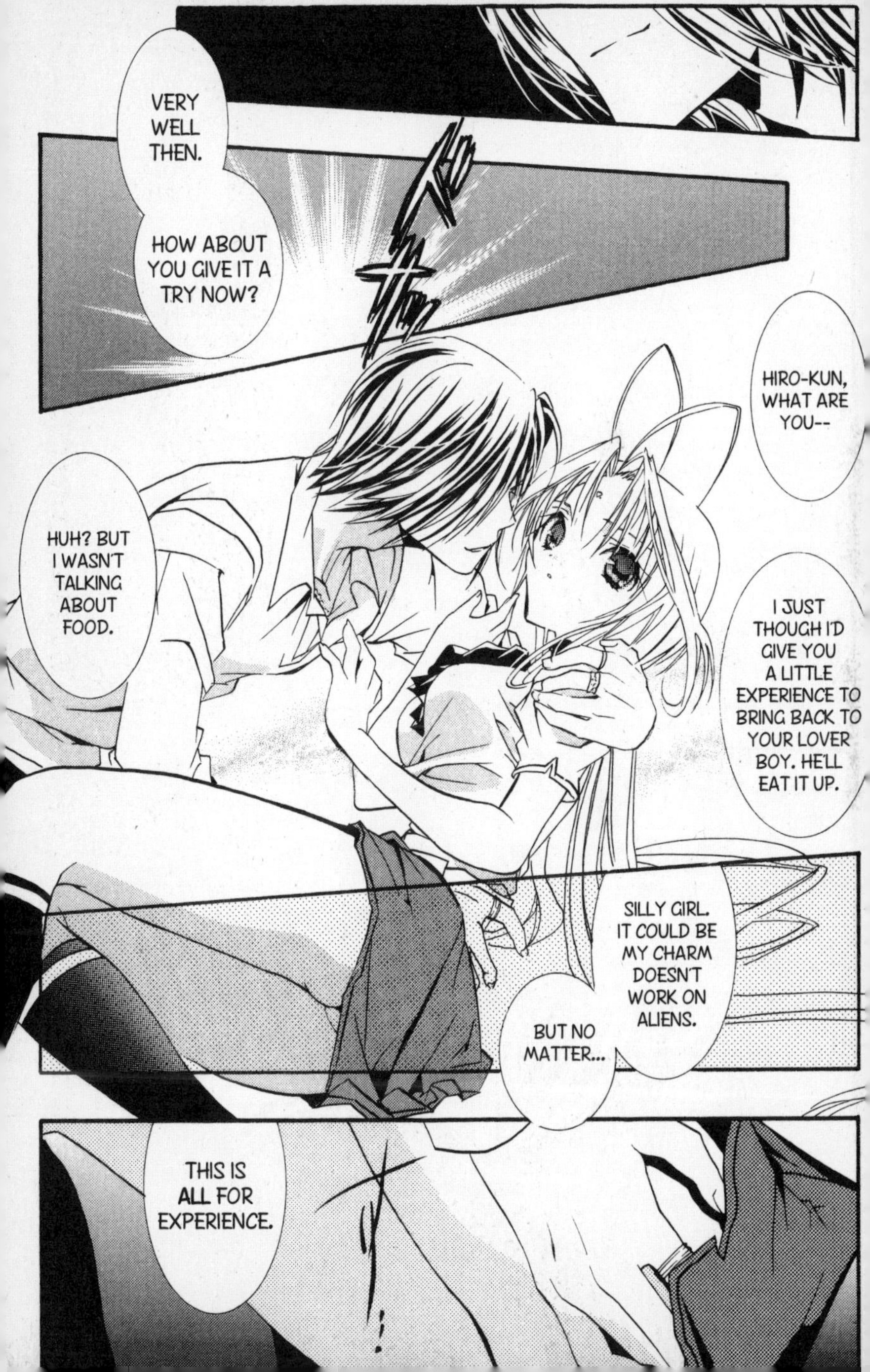
VERY WELL THEN.
HOW ABOUT YOU GIVE IT A TRY NOW?
HIRO-KUN, WHAT ARE YOU--
I JUST THOUGH I'D GIVE YOU A LITTLE EXPERIENCE TO BRING BACK TO YOUR LOVER BOY. HE'LL EAT IT UP.
HUH? BUT I WASN'T TALKING ABOUT FOOD.
SILLY GIRL. IT COULD BE MY CHARM DOESN'T WORK ON ALIENS.
BUT NO MATTER...
THIS IS ALL FOR EXPERIENCE.

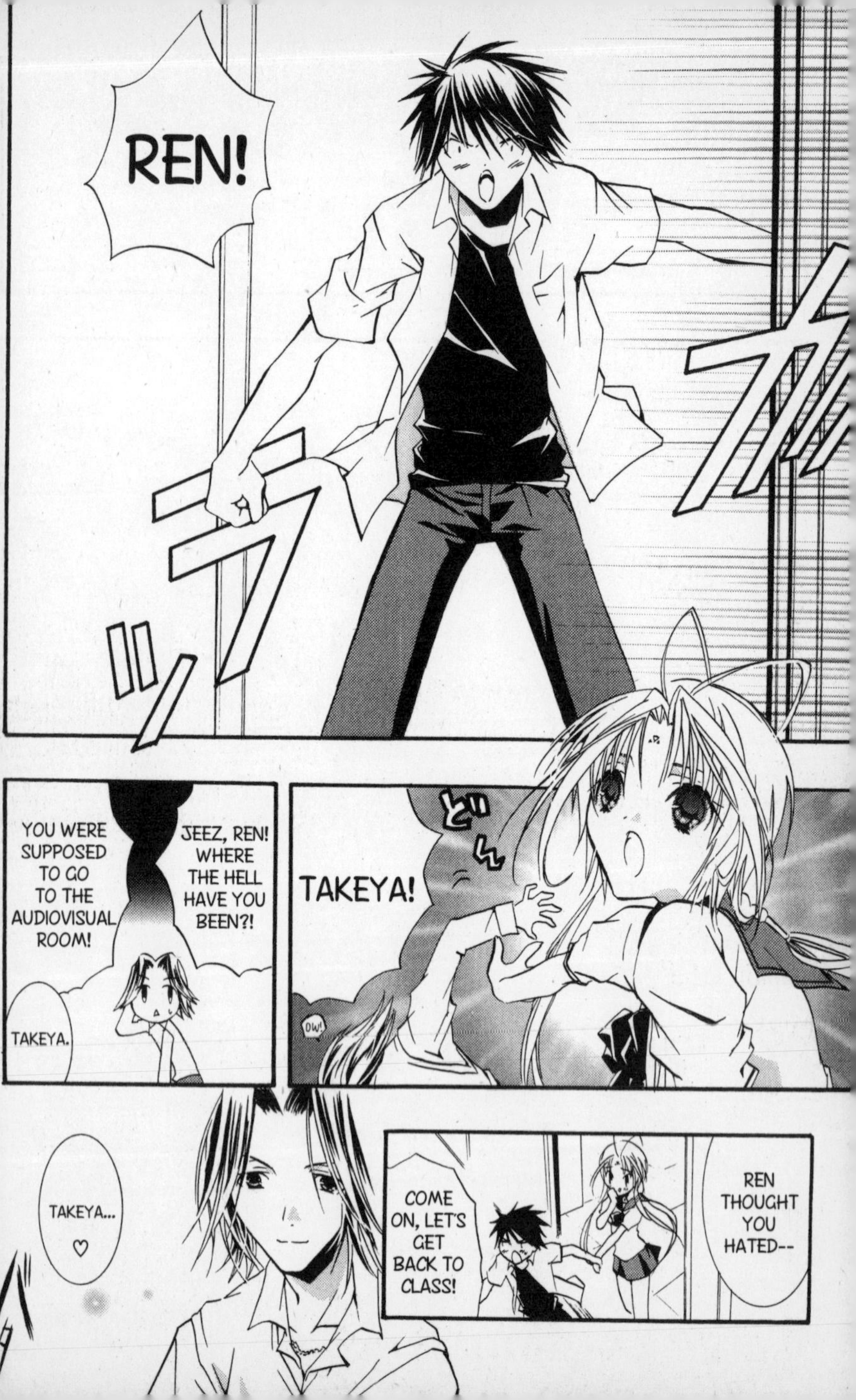
REN!
TAKEYA!
OW!
JEEZ, REN! WHERE THE HELL HAVE YOU BEEN?!
YOU WERE SUPPOSED TO GO TO THE AUDIOVISUAL ROOM!
TAKEYA.
REN THOUGHT YOU HATED--
COME ON, LET'S GET BACK TO CLASS!
TAKEYA... ♡

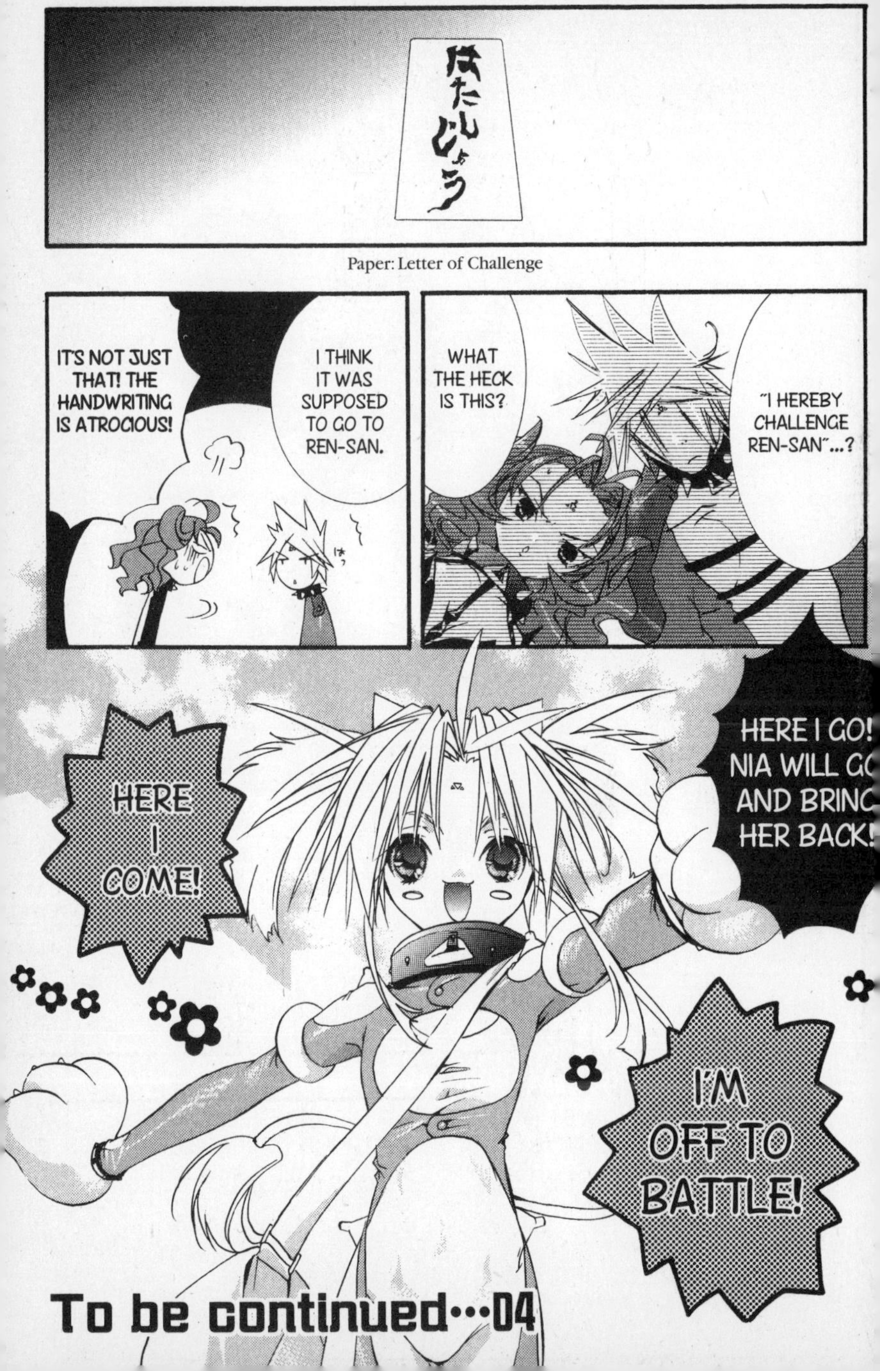
はたしじょう
Paper: Letter of Challenge
"I HEREBY CHALLENGE REN-SAN"...?
WHAT THE HECK IS THIS?
I THINK IT WAS SUPPOSED TO GO TO REN-SAN.
IT'S NOT JUST THAT! THE HANDWRITING IS ATROCIOUS!
HERE I GO! NIA WILL GO AND BRING HER BACK!
HERE I COME!
I'M OFF TO BATTLE!
To be continued…04

DearS

VOLUME 4

CATLIKE BITER-IN-TRAINING ARRIVES TO CHALLENGE REN, THE DEARS WHO DEFEATED HER TRAINER, BUT THE COMBINATION OF TAKEYA, SOME LEFTOVER BREAD, NATSUKI, AND A KITTEN ATOP A UTILITY POLE SERVE TO DISTRACT HER FROM HER GOAL. CLASS PLAYBOY HIRO MEANWHILE TRIES TO PLANT DOUBTS IN REN'S HEAD ABOUT HER RELATIONSHIP WITH HER "MASTER"...AND DEARS BARKER RUBI TRIES TO PLANT DOUBTS TO THE SAME EFFECT IN TAKEYA'S. WHEN THINGS START TO FALL APART AFTER A COOKING MISHAP AND ANOTHER REBUFFED SEXUAL ADVANCE FROM REN, IT COULD BE THE RECYCLING BIN FOR ONE DEFECTIVE SLAVE...

CHECK OUT DEARS VOLUME 4, DUE TO HIT MANGA SHELVES EVERYWHERE IN OCTOBER!

TOKYOPOP SHOP

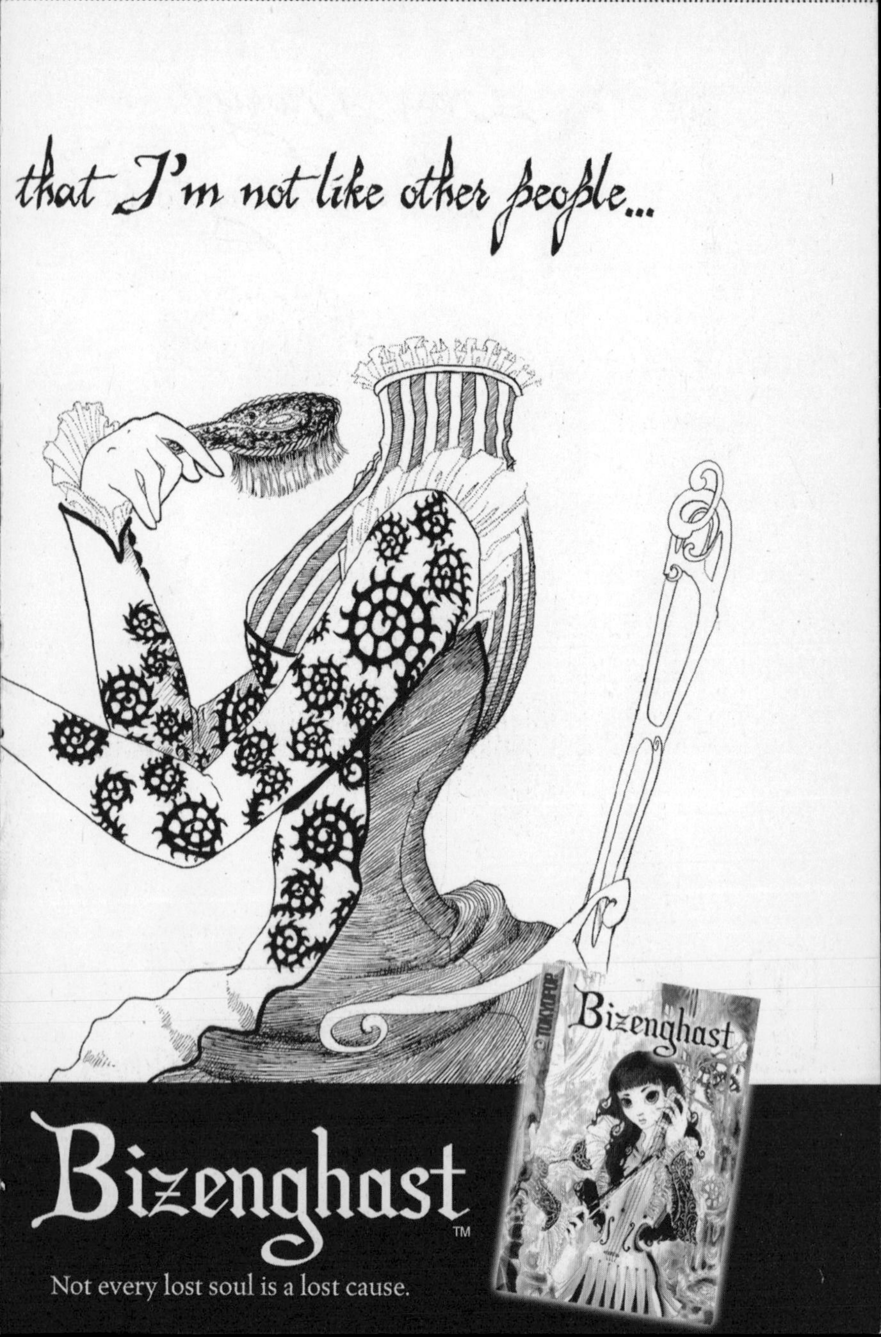

that I'm not like other people...
Bizenghast
TOKYOPOP
Bizenghast™
Not every lost soul is a lost cause.

Dear Diary,
I'm starting to feel

When a young girl moves to the forgotten town of Bizenghast, she uncovers a terrifying collection of lost souls that leads her to the brink of insanity. One thing becomes painfully clear: The residents of Bizenghast are just dying to come home.

QWAN

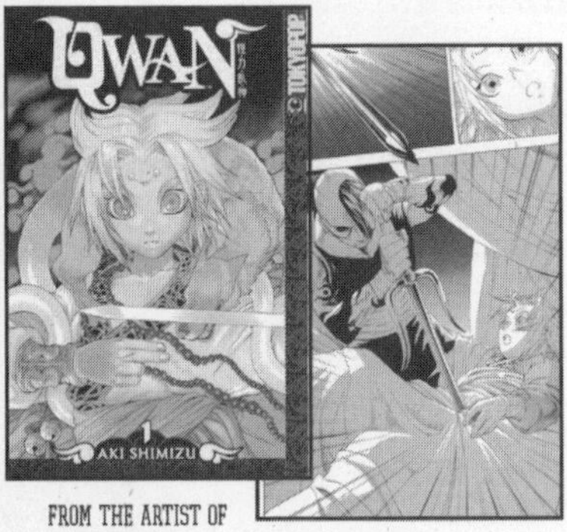
QWAN
1
AKI SHIMIZU
TOKYOPOP

FROM THE ARTIST OF SUIKODEN III

BY AKI SHIMIZU

Qwan is a series that refuses to be pigeonholed. Aki Shimizu combines Chinese history, mythology, fantasy and humor to create a world that is familiar yet truly unique. Her creature designs are particularly brilliant—from mascots to monsters. And Qwan himself is great—fallen to Earth, he's like a little kid, complete with the loud questions, yet he eats demons for breakfast. In short, *Qwan* is a solid story with great character dynamics, amazing art and some kick-ass battle scenes. What's not to like?

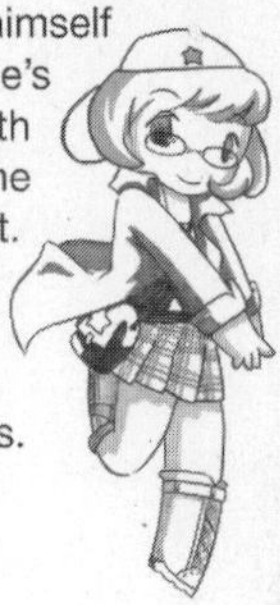

~Carol Fox, Editor

LAMENT OF THE LAMB

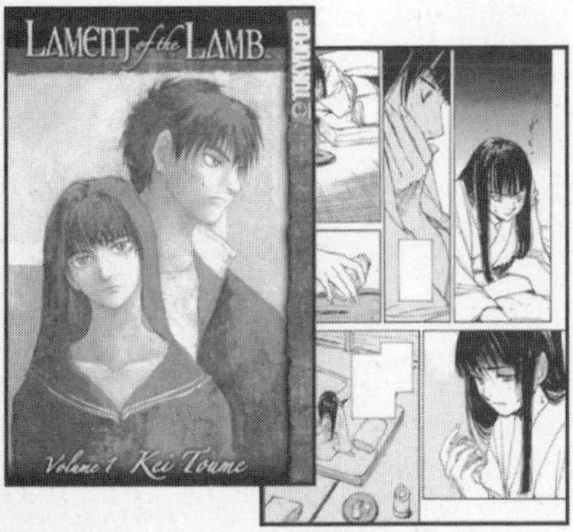
LAMENT of the LAMB
TOKYOPOP
Volume 1 Kei Toume

BY KEI TOUME

Kei Toume's *Lament of the Lamb* follows the physical and mental torment of Kazuna Takashiro, who discovers that he's cursed with a hereditary disease that makes him crave blood. *Lament* is psychological horror at its best—it's gloomy, foreboding and emotionally wrenching. Toume brilliantly treats the story's vampirism in a realistic, subdued way, and it becomes a metaphor for teenage alienation, twisted sexual desire and insanity. While reading each volume, I get goose bumps, I feel uneasy, and I become increasingly depressed. Quite a compliment for a horror series!

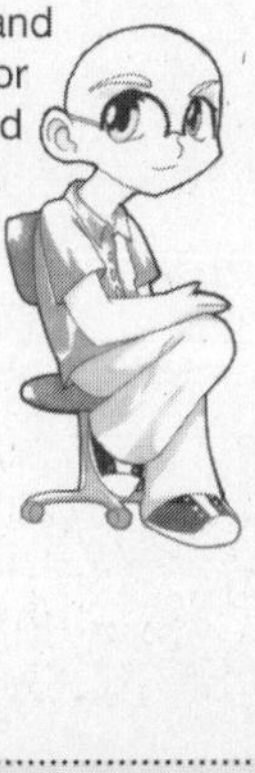

~Paul Morrissey, Editor

THE SEIKAI TRILOGY

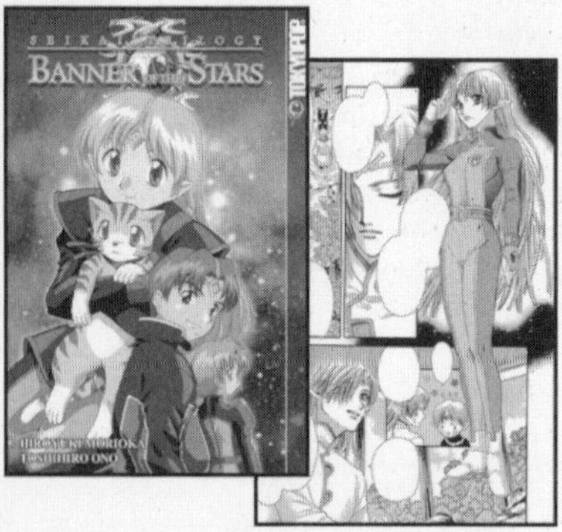
BANNER of the STARS

BY AYA YOSHINAGA, HIROYUKI MORIOKA, TOSHIHIRO ONO, AND WASOH MIYAKOSHI

The Seikai Trilogy is one of TOKYOPOP's most underrated series. Although the trilogy gained popularity through the release of the anime, the manga brings a vitality to the characters that I feel the anime never did. The story is a heart-warming, exciting sci-fi adventure epic, the likes of which we haven't seen since *Star Wars*. *Banner of the Stars II*, the series' finale, is a real page-turner—a prison colony's security is compromised due to violent intergalactic politics. Each manga corresponds to the story from the novel...however, unless you read Japanese, the only way to enjoy the story thus far is through these faithful comic adaptations.

~Luis Reyes, Editor

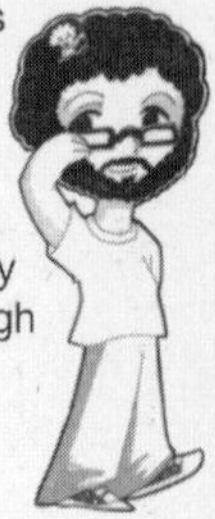

REMOTE

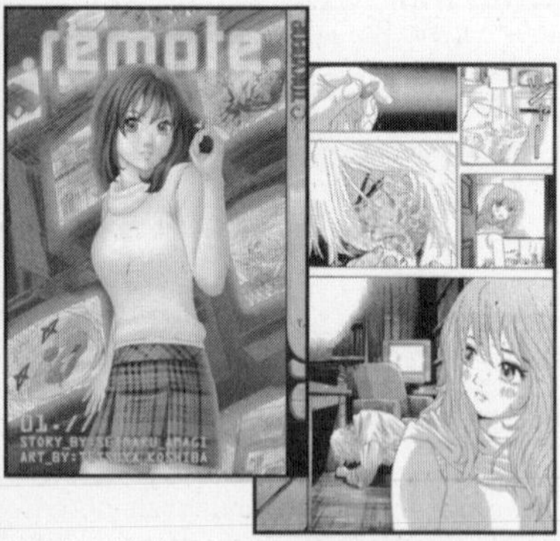
remote.

BY SEIMARU AMAGI AND TETSUYA KOSHIBA

Imagine Pam Anderson starring in *The Silence of the Lambs* and you've got a hint of what to expect from Seimaru Amagi and Tetsuya Koshiba's *Remote*. Completely out of her element, Officer Kurumi Ayaki brings down murderers, mad bombers and would-be assassins, all under the guidance of the reclusive Inspector Himuro. There's no shortage of fan-service and ultraviolence as Kurumi stumbles through her cases, but it's nicely balanced by the forensic police work of the brilliant Himuro, a man haunted by his past and struggling with suppressed emotions awakened by the adorable Kurumi.

~Bryce P. Coleman, Editor

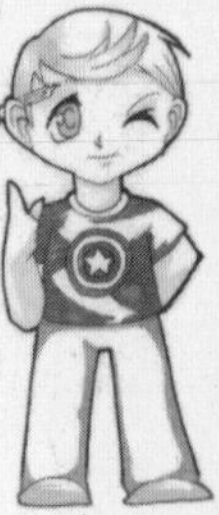

SHOWCASE

TOKYOPOP MANGA SUPPLEMENT

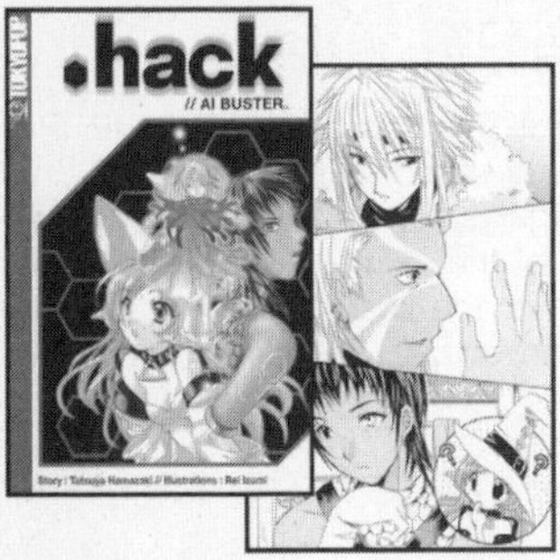
.hack
// AI BUSTER
Story : Tatsuya Hamazaki // Illustrations : Rei Izumi

.HACK//AI BUSTER - NOVEL

BY TATSUYA HAMAZAKI

In the epic prequel to *.hack*, the avatar Albireo is a solo adventurer in The World, the most advanced online fantasy game ever created. When he comes across Lycoris, a strange little girl in a dungeon, he soon comes to realize that she may hold a very deadly secret—a secret that could unhinge everything in cyberspace... and beyond!

Discover the untold origins of the phenomenon known as *.hack*!

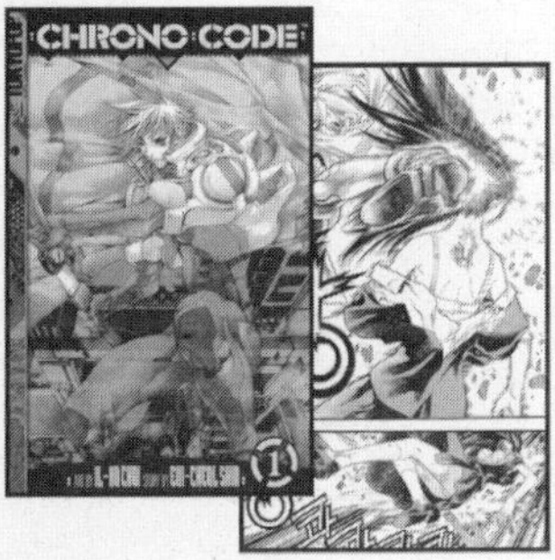
CHRONO CODE

CHRONO CODE

BY EUI-CHEOL SHIN & IL-HO CHOI

Time flows like a river, without changing its course. This is an escape from the river's flow...

Three people must cross time and space to find each other and change their destinies. However, a powerful satellite, a secret code and the future police impede their progress, and their success hinges on an amnesiac who must first uncover the true nature of her past in order to discover who her friends are in the future.

T
TEEN
AGE 13+

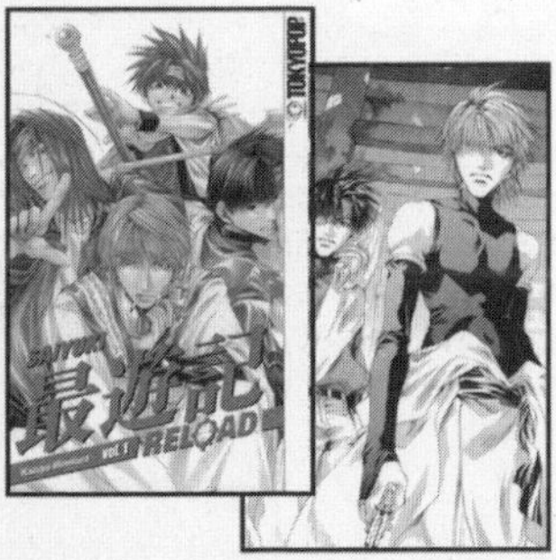
TOKYOPOP
最遊記
RELOAD

SAIYUKI RELOAD

BY KAZUYA MINEKURA

Join Sanzo, Gojyo, Hakkai, Goku and their updated wardrobe as they continue their journey west toward Shangri-La, encountering new challenges and new adventures along the way. But don't be fooled by their change in costume: The fearsome foursome is just as ferocious and focused as before…if not more so.

The hit manga that inspired the anime, and the sequel to TOKYOPOP's hugely popular *Saiyuki*!

OT
OLDER TEEN
AGE 16+

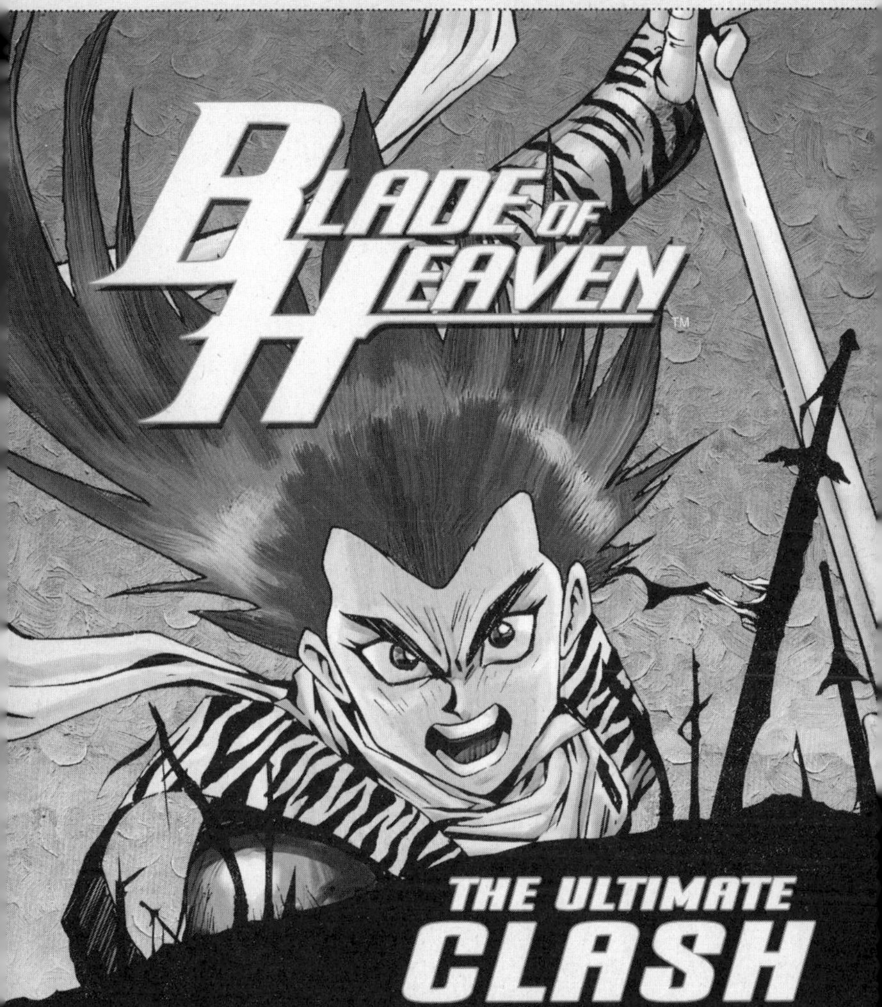

BLADE OF HEAVEN™

THE ULTIMATE CLASH IS ABOUT TO BEGIN!

When Soma, a human, is accused of stealing the Heaven King's Sword, the otherwordly order is knocked out of balance. Heavenly beings and demons clash for ultimate supremacy. The hope for salvation rests with Soma, the heavenly princess, and the Blade of Heaven—each holds the key to preventing all Hell from breaking loose!

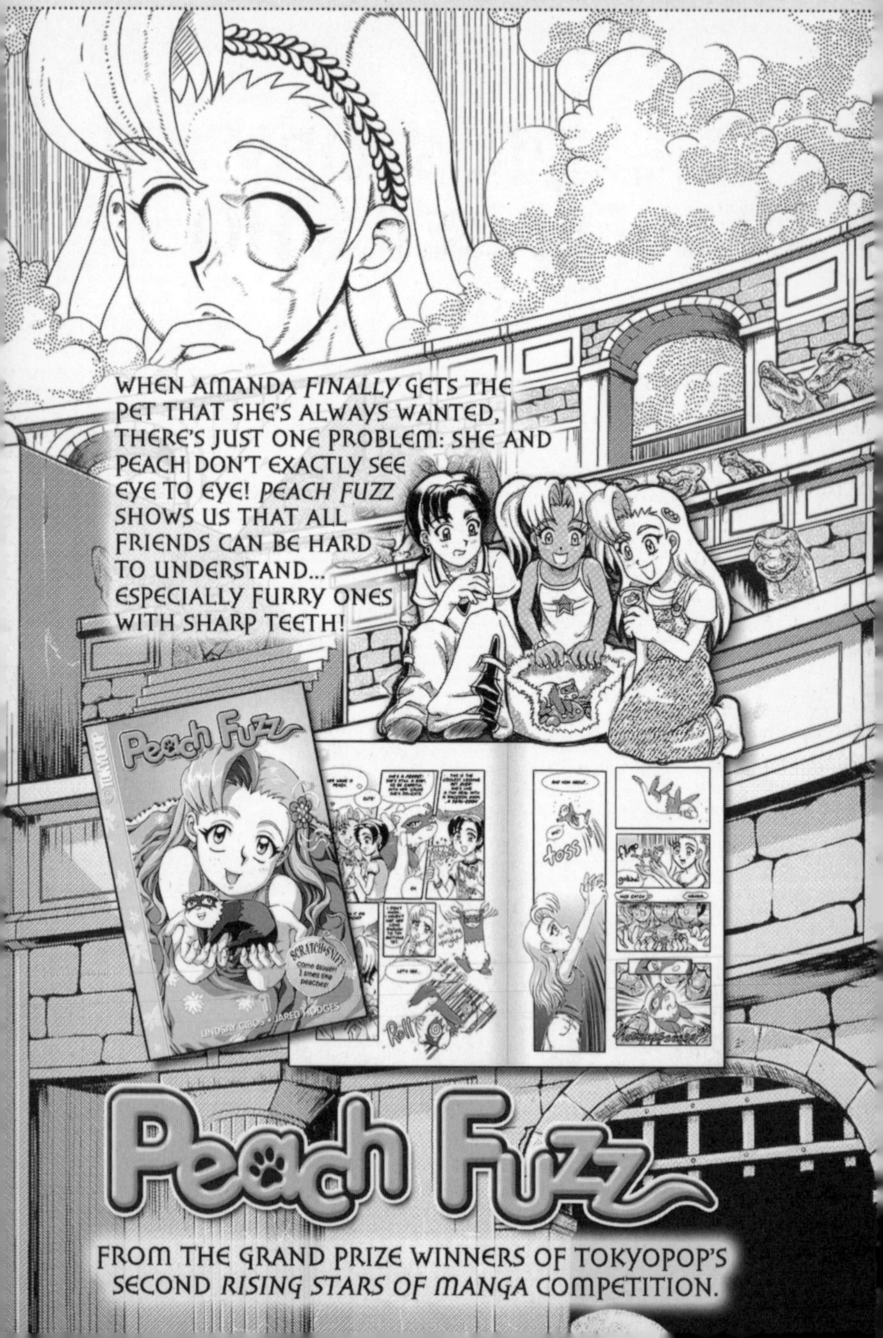
WHEN AMANDA *FINALLY* GETS THE PET THAT SHE'S ALWAYS WANTED, THERE'S JUST ONE PROBLEM: SHE AND PEACH DON'T EXACTLY SEE EYE TO EYE! *PEACH FUZZ* SHOWS US THAT ALL FRIENDS CAN BE HARD TO UNDERSTAND... ESPECIALLY FURRY ONES WITH SHARP TEETH!
Peach Fuzz
SCRATCH+SNIFF
LINDSAY CIBOS • JARED HODGES
toss
Roll
Peach Fuzz
FROM THE GRAND PRIZE WINNERS OF TOKYOPOP'S SECOND *RISING STARS OF MANGA* COMPETITION.

WARCRAFT

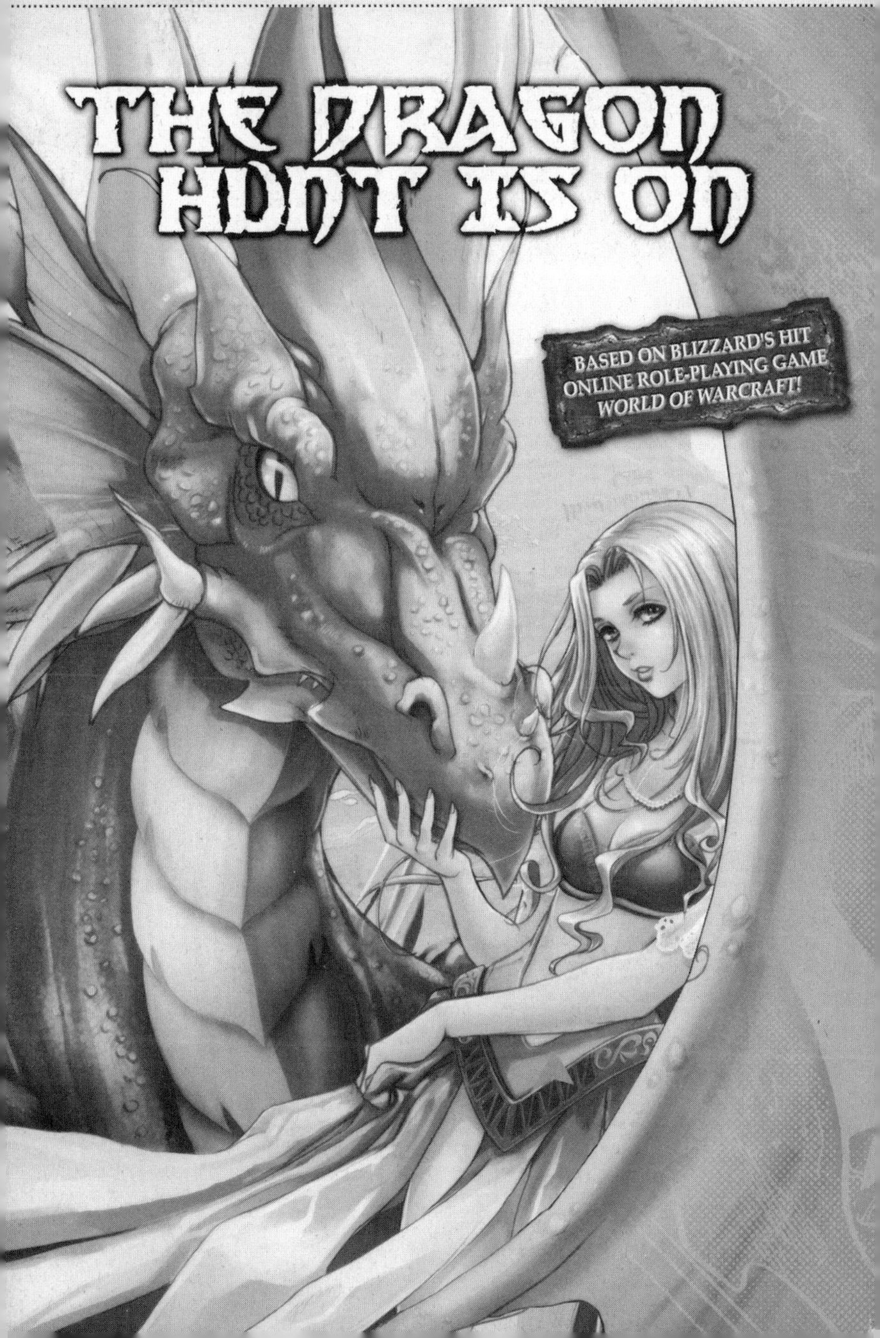
THE DRAGON HUNT IS ON
BASED ON BLIZZARD'S HIT ONLINE ROLE-PLAYING GAME *WORLD OF WARCRAFT!*

STOP!

This is the back of the book.
You wouldn't want to spoil a great ending!

This book is printed "manga-style," in the authentic Japanese right-to-left format. Since none of the artwork has been flipped or altered, readers get to experience the story just as the creator intended. You've been asking for it, so TOKYOPOP® delivered: authentic, hot-off-the-press, and far more fun!

DIRECTIONS

If this is your first time reading manga-style, here's a quick guide to help you understand how it works.

It's easy... just start in the top right panel and follow the numbers. Have fun, and look for more 100% authentic manga from TOKYOPOP®!